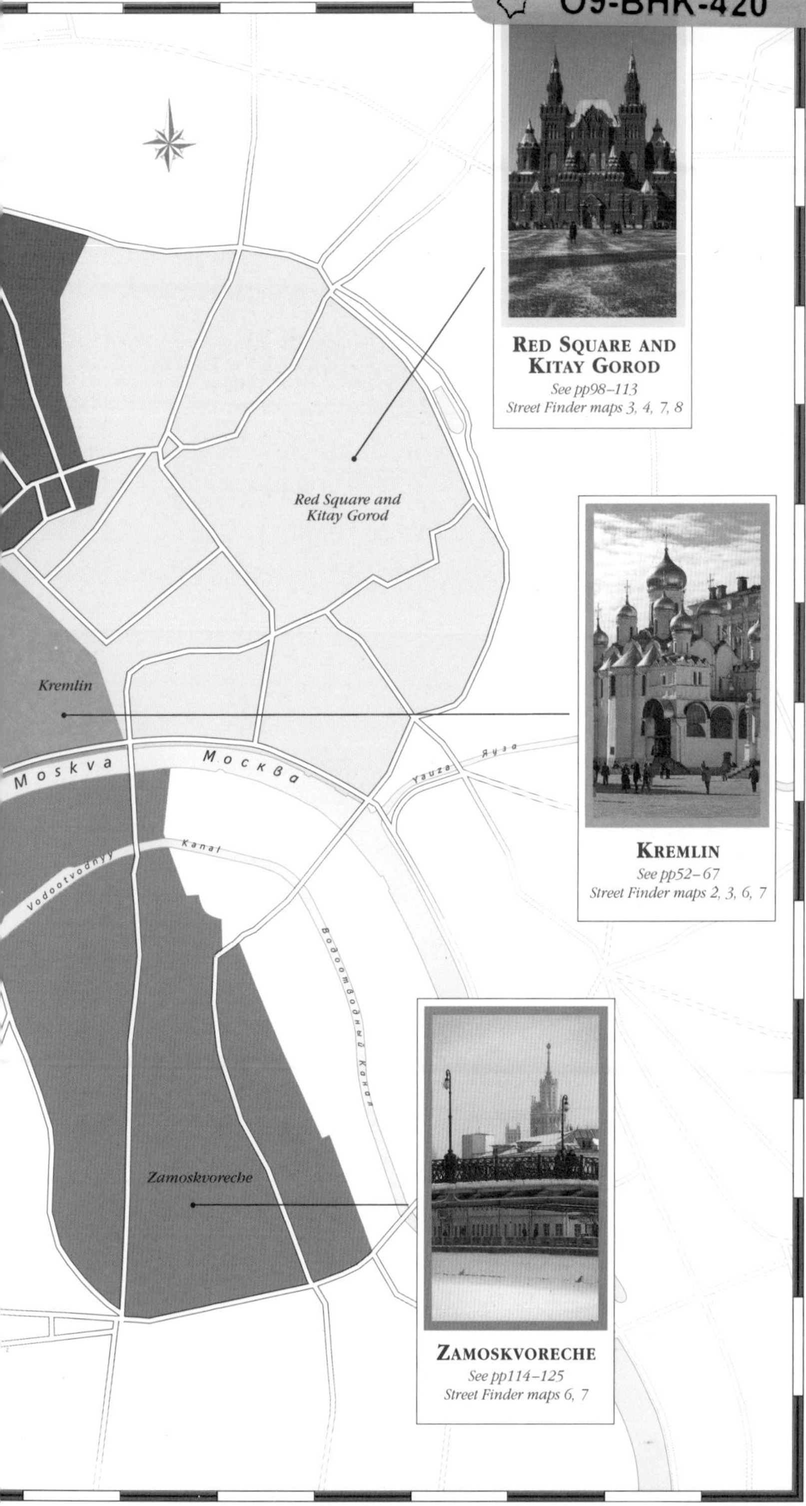

RED SQUARE AND KITAY GOROD
See pp98–113
Street Finder maps 3, 4, 7, 8

KREMLIN
See pp52–67
Street Finder maps 2, 3, 6, 7

ZAMOSKVORECHE
See pp114–125
Street Finder maps 6, 7

EYEWITNESS TRAVEL GUIDES

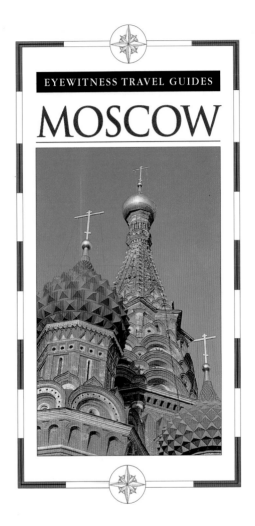

MOSCOW

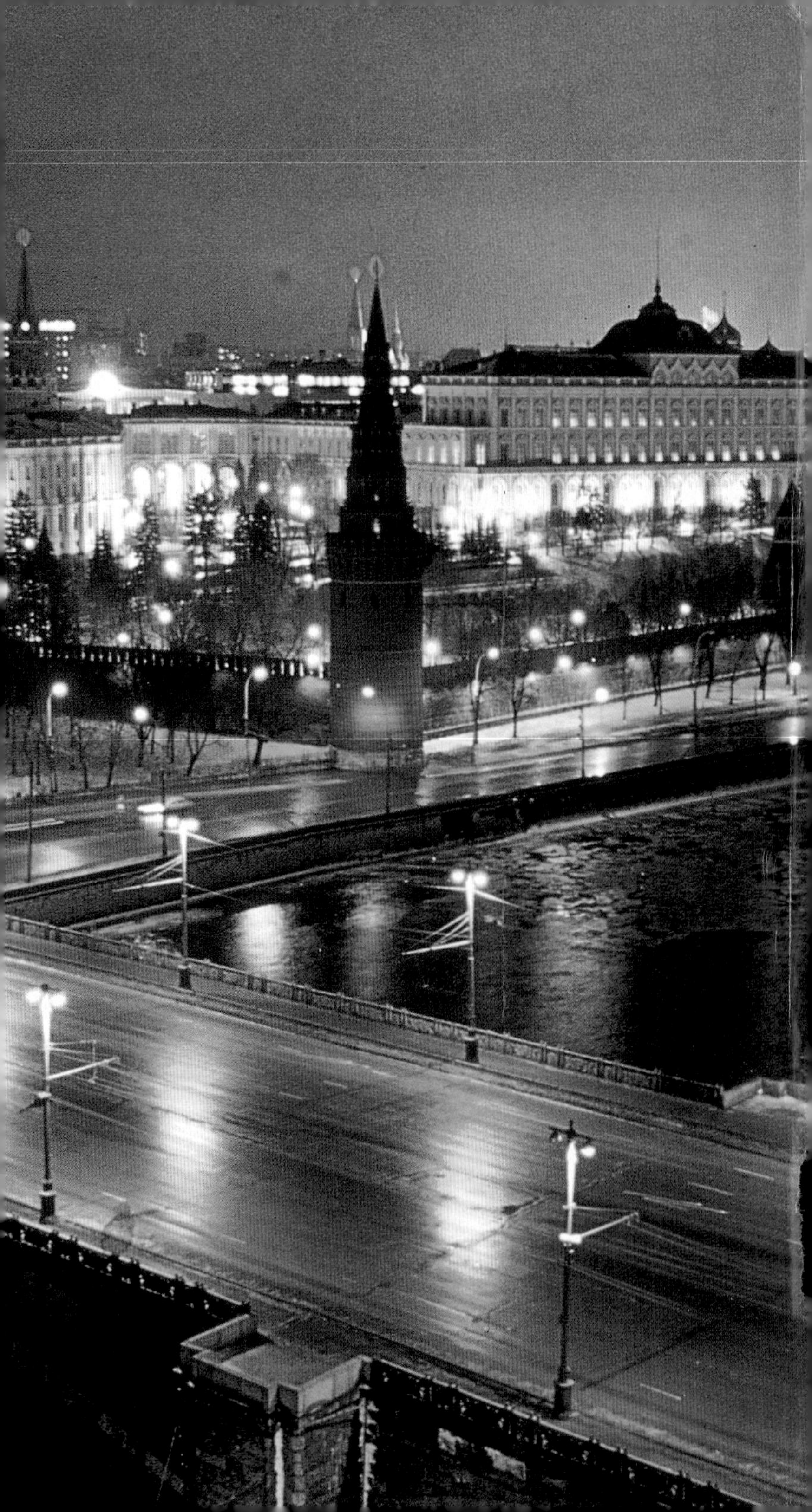

EYEWITNESS TRAVEL GUIDES

MOSCOW

Main contributors:

CHRISTOPHER AND MELANIE RICE

DK

DK PUBLISHING

LONDON, NEW YORK,
MELBOURNE, MUNICH AND DELHI
www.dk.com

PROJECT EDITOR Marcus Hardy
ART EDITOR Marisa Renzullo
EDITORS Catherine Day, Jane Oliver, Lynda Warrington
US EDITORS Michael Wise, Mary Sutherland
DESIGNERS Gillian Andrews, Carolyn Hewitson,
Paul Jackson, Elly King, Nicola Rodway
VISUALIZER Joy Fitzsimmons
MAP CO-ORDINATORS Emily Green, David Pugh
DTP DESIGNERS Samantha Borland, Pamela Shiels
PICTURE RESEARCHER Brigitte Aurora

MAIN CONTRIBUTORS
Christopher Rice, Melanie Rice

MAPS
Maria Donnelly (Colourmap Scanning Ltd)

PHOTOGRAPHER
Demetrio Carrasco

ILLUSTRATORS
Stephen Conlin, Richard Draper, Stephen Gyapay,
Claire Littlejohn, Chris Orr & Associates

•

Reproduced by Colourscan, Singapore
Printed and bound by South China Printing Co. Ltd., China

First American Edition, 1998
04 05 10 9 8 7 6 5 4

Published in the United States by
DK Publishing, Inc., 375 Hudson Street,
New York, New York 10014
Reprinted with revisions 2000, 2001, 2004

Published in Great Britain by Dorling Kindersley Limited.

ISSN 1542-1554

ISBN 0-7894-9726-3

THROUGHOUT THIS BOOK, FLOORS ARE REFERRED TO IN ACCORDANCE WITH EUROPEAN USAGE, I.E. THE "FIRST FLOOR" IS THE FLOOR ABOVE GROUND LEVEL.

The information in this Dorling Kindersley Travel Guide is checked regularly.

Every effort has been made to ensure that this book is as up-to-date as possible at the time of going to press. Some details, however, such as telephone numbers, opening hours, prices, gallery hanging arrangements and travel information are liable to change. The publishers cannot accept responsibility for any consequences arising from the use of this book, nor for any material on third party websites, and cannot guarantee that any website address in this book will be a suitable source of travel information. We value the views and suggestions of our readers very highly. Please write to: Publisher, DK Eyewitness Travel Guides, Dorling Kindersley, 80 Strand, London WC2R 0RL, Great Britain.

CONTENTS

Socialist-Realist sculpture of Soviet farm workers at the All-Russian Exhibition Center *(see p145)*

The Tretyakov Gallery *(see pp118–21)*, housing Russian fine art

Magnificent iconostasis at the Danilovskiy Monastery *(see pp136–7)*

The Tsar Bell *(see p57)*, created for Tsarina Anna, in the Kremlin

Travellers' Needs

Survival Guide

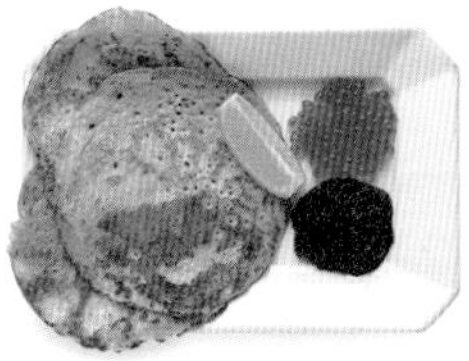

Blinis with black and red caviar *(see p176)*, a Russian specialty

St. Basil's Cathedral *(see pp108–9)*

How to Use this Guide

Neo-Classical statue, Kuskovo, (see pp142–3)

This guide will help you to get the most from your visit to Moscow. It provides expert recommendations together with detailed practical information. *Introducing Moscow* maps the city and sets it in its geographical, historical and cultural context, and the quick-reference timeline on the history pages gives the dates of Russia's rulers and significant events. *Moscow at a Glance* is an overview of the city's main attractions. *Moscow Area by Area* starts on page 50 and describes all the important sights, using maps, photographs and illustrations. The sights are arranged in three groups: those in Moscow's central districts, those a little further afield, and finally those beyond Moscow which require one- or two-day excursions. Hotel, restaurant and entertainment recommendations can be found in *Travellers' Needs*, while the *Survival Guide* includes tips on everything from transport and telephones to personal safety.

Finding Your Way around the Sightseeing Section

Each of the seven sightseeing areas is colour-coded for easy reference. Every chapter opens with an introduction to the area it covers, describing its history and character. For central districts, this is followed by a Street-by-Street map illustrating a particularly interesting part of the area; for sights further away, by a regional map. A simple numbering system relates sights to the maps. Important sights are covered by several pages.

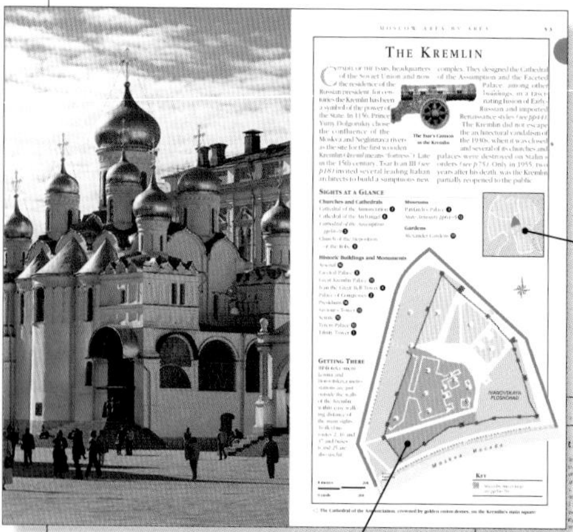

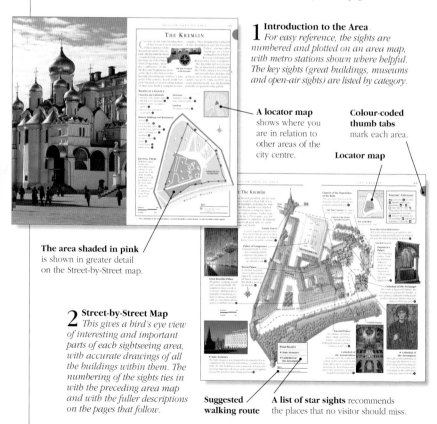

1 Introduction to the Area
For easy reference, the sights are numbered and plotted on an area map, with metro stations shown where helpful. The key sights (great buildings, museums and open-air sights) are listed by category.

A locator map shows where you are in relation to other areas of the city centre.

Colour-coded thumb tabs mark each area.

Locator map

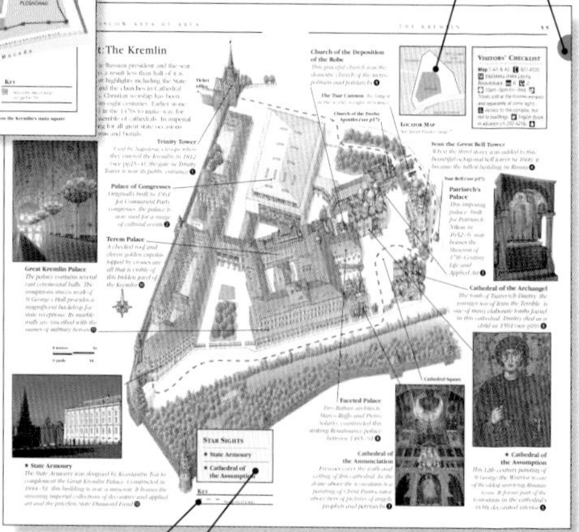

The area shaded in pink is shown in greater detail on the Street-by-Street map.

2 Street-by-Street Map
This gives a bird's eye view of interesting and important parts of each sightseeing area, with accurate drawings of all the buildings within them. The numbering of the sights ties in with the preceding area map and with the fuller descriptions on the pages that follow.

Suggested walking route

A list of star sights recommends the places that no visitor should miss.

Moscow Area Map

The coloured areas shown on this map *(see pp14–15)* are the five main sightseeing areas into which central Moscow has been divided for this guide. Each is covered in a full chapter in the *Moscow Area by Area* section *(pp50–125)*. The areas are also highlighted on other maps throughout the book. In *Moscow at a Glance (pp36–49)*, for example, they help you locate the most important sights that no visitor should miss. The maps' coloured borders match the coloured thumb tabs at the top corner of each page.

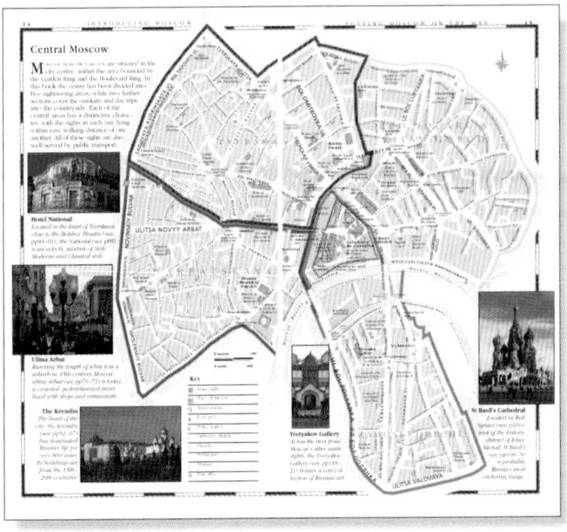

Numbers refer to each sight's position on the area map and its place in the chapter.

Practical information lists all the information you need to visit every sight, including a map reference to the *Street Finder* maps *(pp220–37)*.

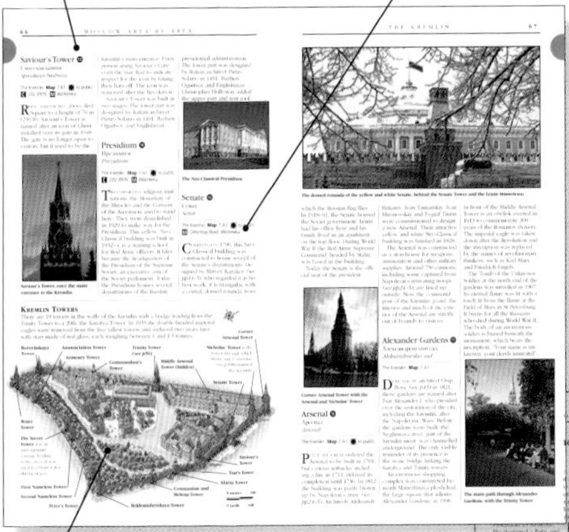

3 Detailed information on each sight

All the important sights are described individually. They are listed to follow the numbering on the area map at the start of the section. The key to the symbols summarizing practical information is on the back flap.

A visitors' checklist provides the practical information you will need to plan your visit.

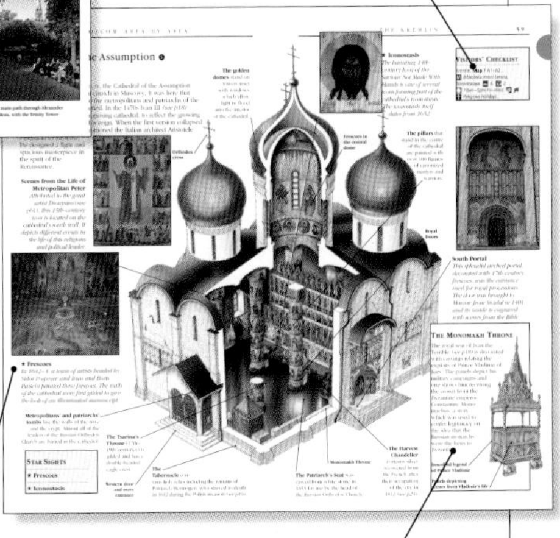

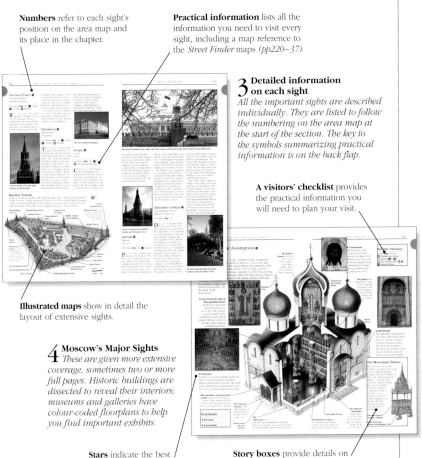

Illustrated maps show in detail the layout of extensive sights.

4 Moscow's Major Sights

These are given more extensive coverage, sometimes two or more full pages. Historic buildings are dissected to reveal their interiors; museums and galleries have colour-coded floorplans to help you find important exhibits.

Stars indicate the best features or works of art.

Story boxes provide details on famous people or historical events.

INTRODUCING MOSCOW

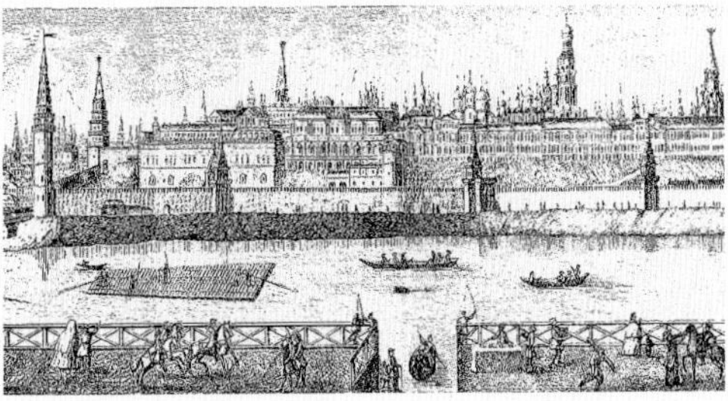

Putting Moscow on the Map

The Russian Federation (usually simply known as Russia) stretches from the Baltic to the Pacific. With an area of 17 million sq km (6.6 million sq miles), it was the largest of the USSR's 15 republics and is now the world's largest country, almost twice the size of the US. Moscow, the capital with 9 million inhabitants, lies at the heart of European Russia. St Petersburg is Russia's second largest city. Russia is a member of the CIS – a commonwealth of most of the former Soviet republics.

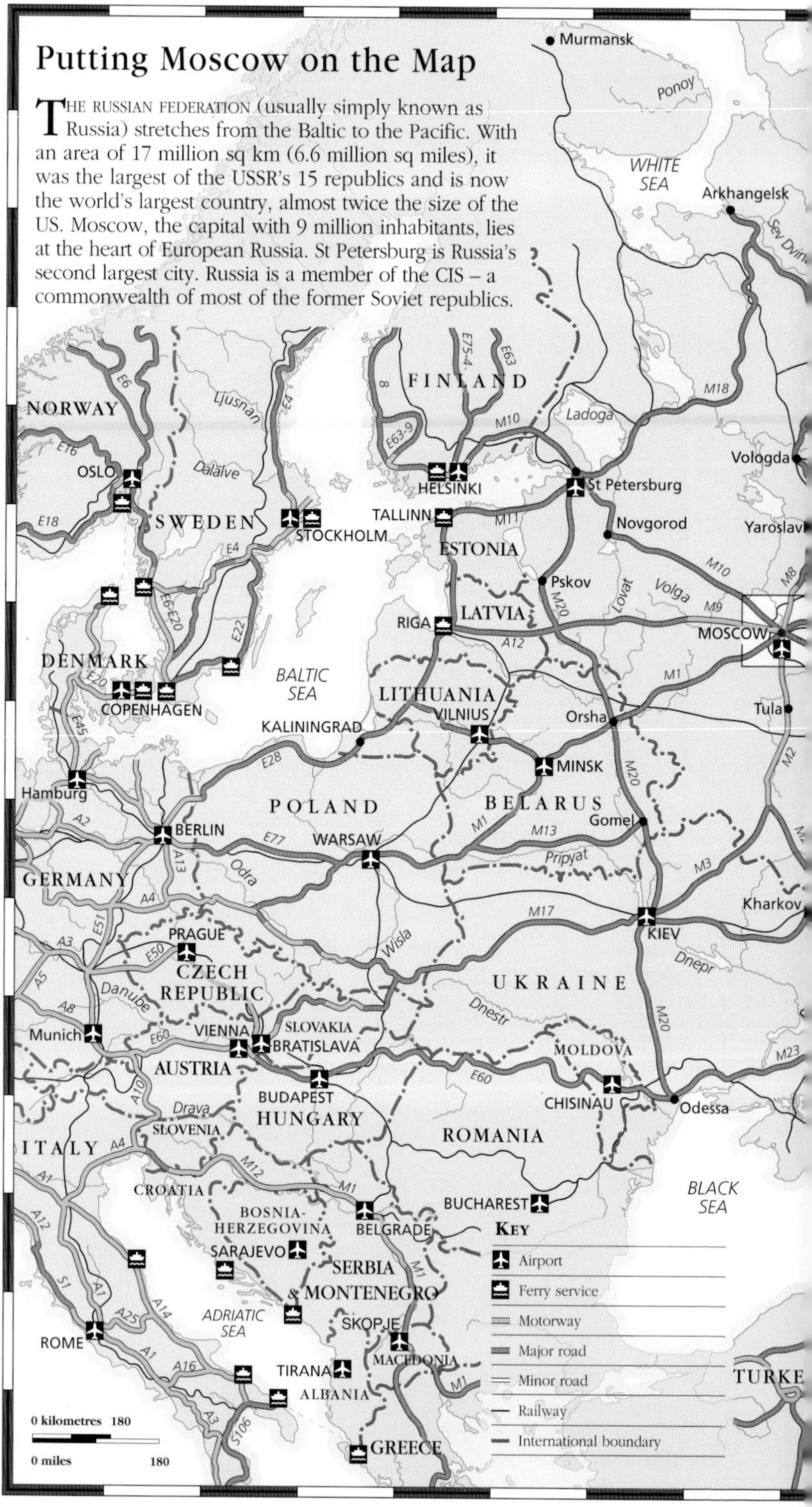

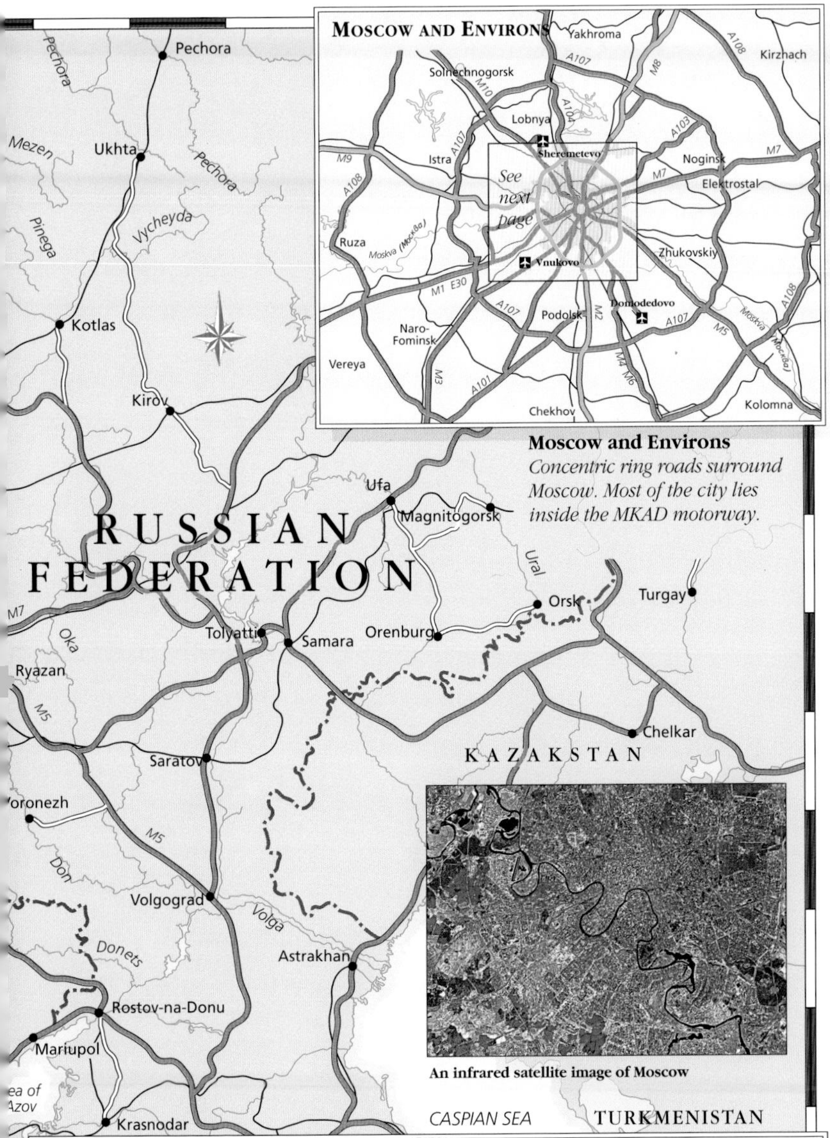

Moscow and Environs
Concentric ring roads surround Moscow. Most of the city lies inside the MKAD motorway.

An infrared satellite image of Moscow

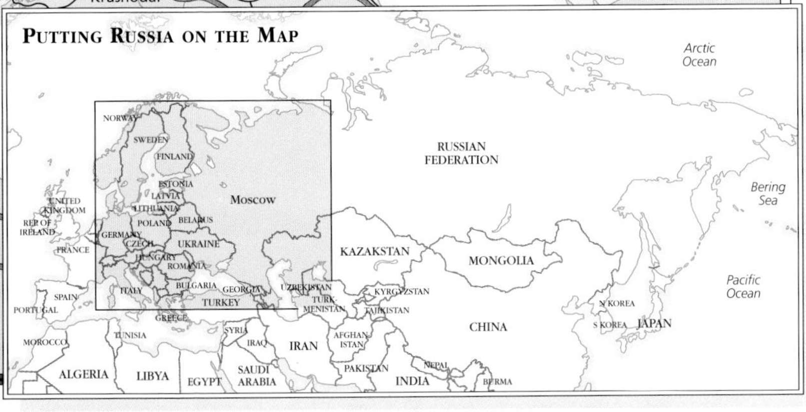

Greater Moscow

An enormous, sprawling city, Moscow has grown rapidly over the past decades and, as a result, mostly comprises high-rise suburbs surrounding a relatively compact historic centre. Most areas of the city are served by the famously efficient metro system as well as buses, trams and trolleybuses *(see pp214–17)*. Much, but not all, of the city lies within the MKAD orbital motorway, which is one of six concentric ring roads.

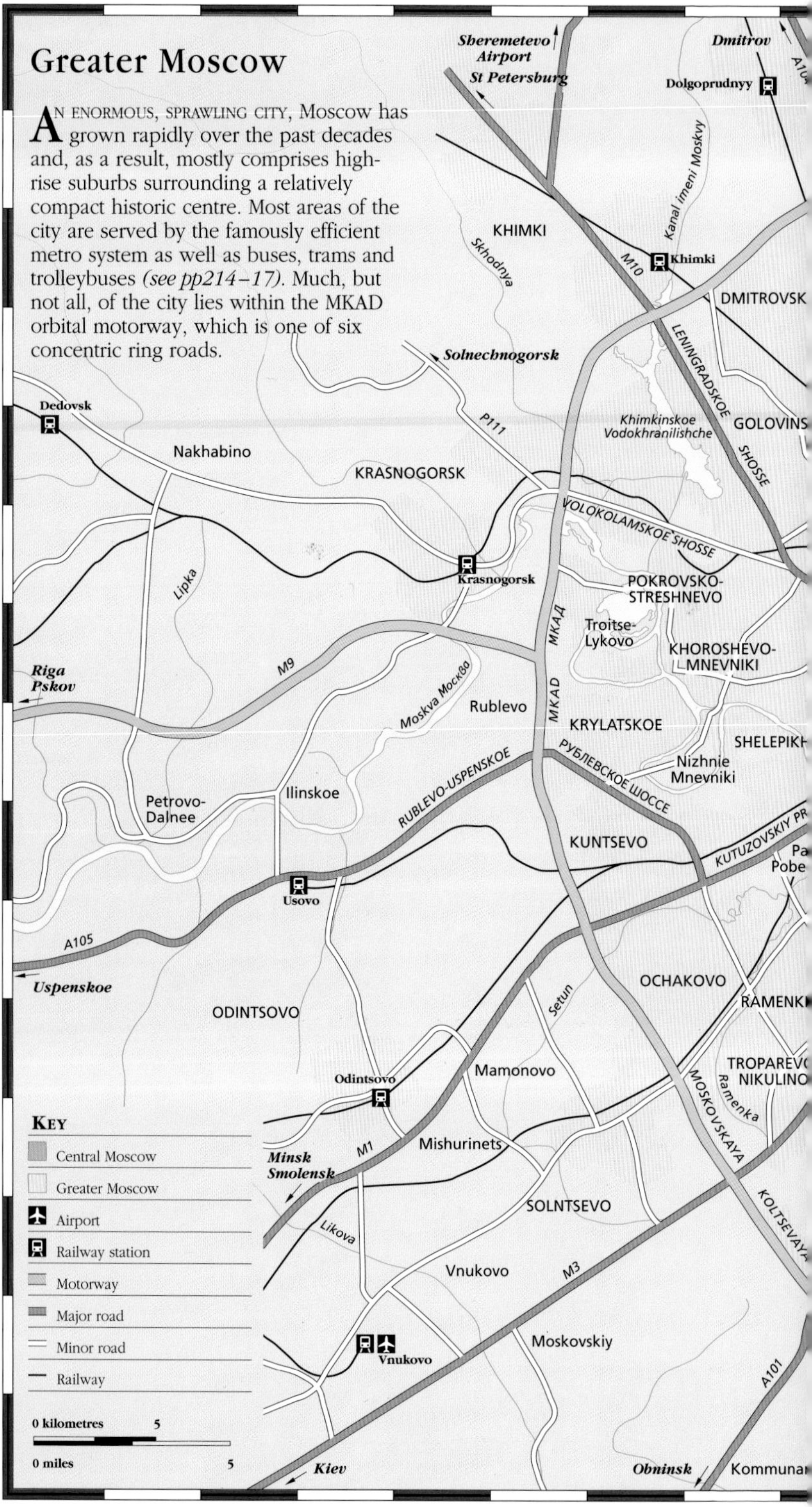

Yaroslavl
Sergiev Posad
Korolev
KOROLEV
OLGOPRUDNYY
MYTISHCHI
M8
MOSKOVSKAYA KOLTSEVAYA AVTOMOBILNAYA DOROGA
DMITROVSKOE SHOSSE
LIANOZOVO
BIBIREVO
BABUSHKINO
LOSINIY OSTROV
Yauza
ALTUFEVSKOE SHOSSE
MEDVEDKOVO
YAROSLAVSKOE SHOSSE
МОСКОВСКАЯ КОЛЬЦЕВАЯ АВТОМОБИЛЬНАЯ ДОРОГА
SVIBLOVO
ЩЕЛКОВСКОЕ ШОССЕ
GOLYANOVO
BALASHIKHA
SHCHELKOVSKOE SHOSSE
PROSPEKT MIRA
Yauza
Ostankino
Nizniy Novgorod
IZMAYLOVO
BOGORODSKOE
A103
M7
LENINGRADSKIY PR
Izmaylovo
Park
Rizhskiy
Yaroslavskiy
Leningradskiy
REUTOV
МКАД
Kazanskiy
Belorusskiy
SHOSSE ENTUZIASTOV
Reutovo
MOSCOW
See next page
Kurskiy
Pehorka
МКАД
Kuskovo
Kievskiy
VESHNYAKI
Paveletskiy
M5
RYAZANSKIY PROSPEKT
VOLGOGRADSKIY PROSPEKT
LYUBERTSY
Vorobevy
Gory
Lyubertsy
PROSPEKT ANDROPOVA
ВОЛГОГРАДСКИЙ ПРОСПЕКТ
Nizhnie
Kotly
NAGATINO
PROSPEKT
LYUBLINO
CHEREMUSHKI
INSKIY
ULITSA
KASHIRSKOE SHOSSE
MARINO
KAPOTNYA
Kolomenskoe
Moskva Москва
Ryazan
ZYUZINO
PROFSOYUZNAYA
TSARITSYNO
ZYABLIKOVO
DZERZHINSKIY
Tsaritsyno
OREKHOVO-
BORISOVO
VARSHAVSKOE SHOSSE
МОСКОВСКАЯ КОЛЬЦЕВАЯ АВТОМОБИЛЬНАЯ ДОРОГА
YASENEVO
LYTKARINO
Ostrov
AVTOMOBILNAYA DOROGA
BITTSA
Molokovo
VIDNOE
M4 M6
Domodedovo
Airport
Tula
Orel
M2
Vidnoe

Central Moscow

Most of Moscow's sights are situated in the city centre, within the area bounded by the Garden Ring and the Boulevard Ring. In this book the centre has been divided into five sightseeing areas, while two further sections cover the outskirts and day trips into the countryside. Each of the central areas has a distinctive character, with the sights in each one lying within easy walking distance of one another. All of these sights are also well served by public transport.

Hotel National
Located in the heart of Tverskaya, close to the Bolshoy Theatre (see pp90–91), *the National* (see p89) *is an eclectic mixture of Style Moderne and Classical style.*

Ulitsa Arbat
Running the length of what was a suburb in 15th-century Moscow, ulitsa Arbat (see pp70–71) *is today a crowded, pedestrianized street, lined with shops and restaurants.*

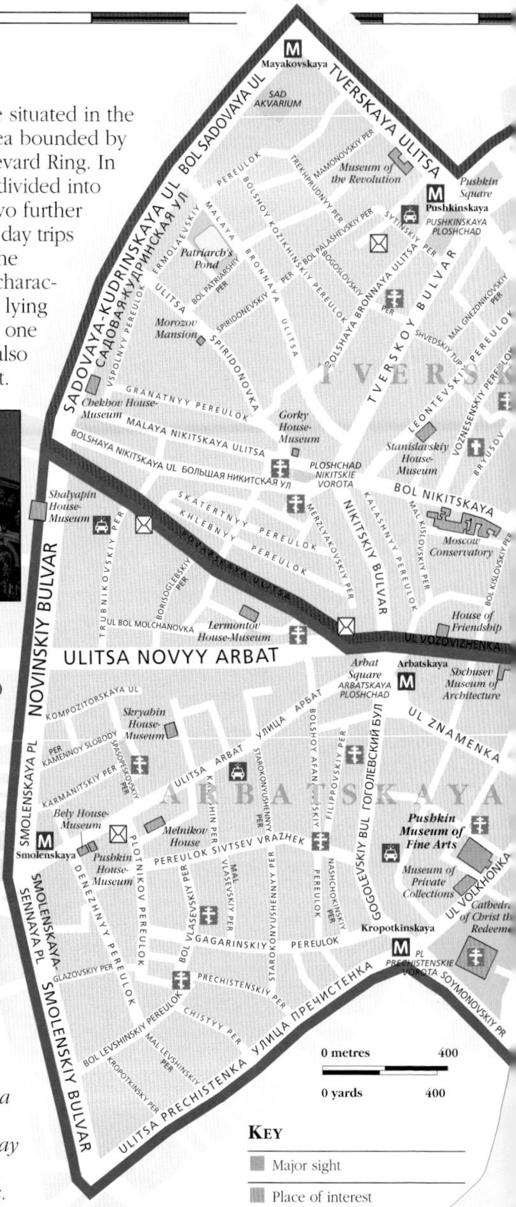

Key

- Major sight
- Place of interest
- Metro station
- River boat pier
- Police station
- Orthodox church
- Non-Orthodox church
- Synagogue
- Mosque
- Post office

The Kremlin
The heart of the city, the Kremlin (see pp52–67) *has dominated Russian life for over 800 years. Its buildings are from the 15th–20th centuries.*

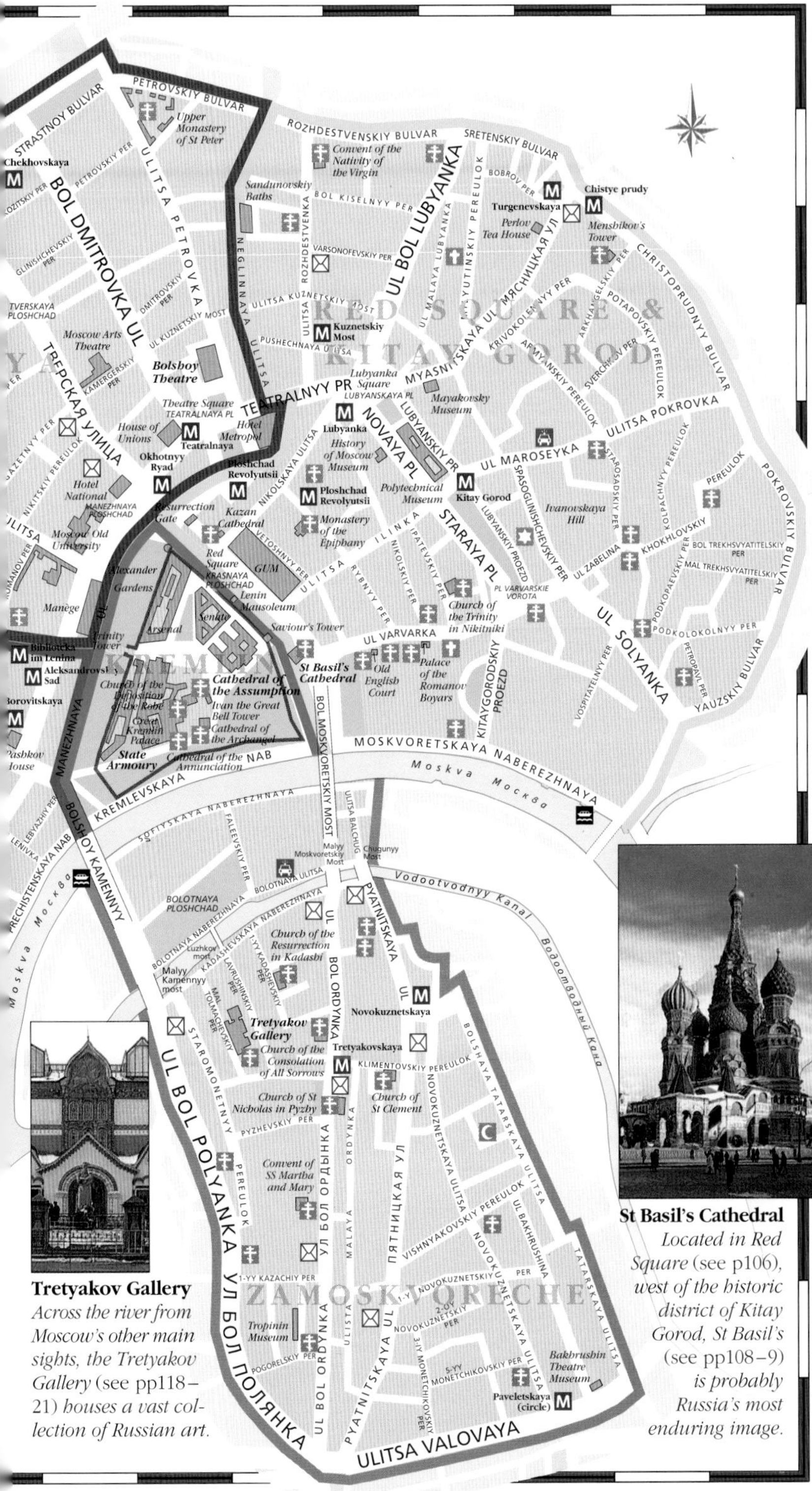

Tretyakov Gallery
Across the river from Moscow's other main sights, the Tretyakov Gallery (see pp118–21) *houses a vast collection of Russian art.*

St Basil's Cathedral
Located in Red Square (see p106)*, west of the historic district of Kitay Gorod, St Basil's* (see pp108–9) *is probably Russia's most enduring image.*

THE HISTORY OF MOSCOW

FROM HER 12TH-CENTURY ORIGINS *as an obscure defensive outpost, Moscow came to govern one sixth of the earth's surface and cast her shadow even further. The story of her rise is laced with glory and setbacks, including the two centuries when St Petersburg was the capital of Russia and Moscow lived the life of a dignified dowager.*

THE FIRST SETTLERS

The forested area around Moscow was sparsely populated, but the fertile lands of southern Russia and the Ukraine had long supported trade routes between the Orient and Europe. It was here that the Slavs, the ancestors of the Russian people, first settled. They came from Eastern Europe in the 6th century, and established isolated villages along the major rivers. In the 8th century they came into contact with the Varangians (Vikings), who navigated these waterways to trade amber, furs and fair-skinned slaves.

KIEVAN RUS

Endemic in-fighting between the Slavic tribes was quelled when Rurik, a Varangian chief, assumed power in the region. Rurik settled in Novgorod, but his successor Oleg took Kiev and made it his capital. In 988 Grand Prince Vladimir I, a descendant of Rurik, was baptised into Orthodox Christianity *(see p137)* and married the sister of the Byzantine emperor. Vladimir's conversion deeply affected the future of Russia, which remained an Orthodox country right into the 20th century.

Vladimir's conversion in the *Baptism of Russia* by Vasnetsov

Bloodthirsty and fearless, this lacquer box shows Mongol warriors riding into battle

THE MONGOL INVASION

By the 12th century, Kiev's supremacy had already been challenged by the powerful Russian principalities to the north, including Rostov-Suzdal *(see p155)*, of which the wooden kremlin at Moscow formed part. As a result, when the fierce horse-borne Mongols invaded in 1237, the disunited Russians fell easy victims to the well-organized troops of Batu Khan. For the next 240 years the Russian principalities paid an exorbitant yearly tribute to the khans, though they were left to govern themselves.

TIMELINE

c. 800 Varangians arrive in the region to trade and find local tribes in conflict

Rurik, Varangian chief

988 Grand Prince Vladimir I converts to Christianity

1147 Moscow first documented, as the site of a small fortress

1156 Prince Yuriy Dolgorukiy builds Moscow's first wooden kremlin

1240 Mongols control most of Rus after the sack of Kiev

800 | 900 | 1000 | 1100 | 1200

862 Rurik takes Novgorod and establishes a Varangian stronghold

882 Rurik's successor Oleg takes Kiev and makes it capital

863 Missionaries Cyril and Methodius invent the Cyrillic alphabet, based on the Greek one; literacy grows with the spread of Christianity

1108 The town of Vladimir *(see p155)* is founded

1223 First Mongol raid

1236–42 Prince Aleksandr Nevskiy of Novgorod defeats first the invading Swedes and then the Teutonic Knights

◁ **The symbol of Moscow, St George and the Dragon, on a 15th-century icon housed in the Tretyakov Gallery**

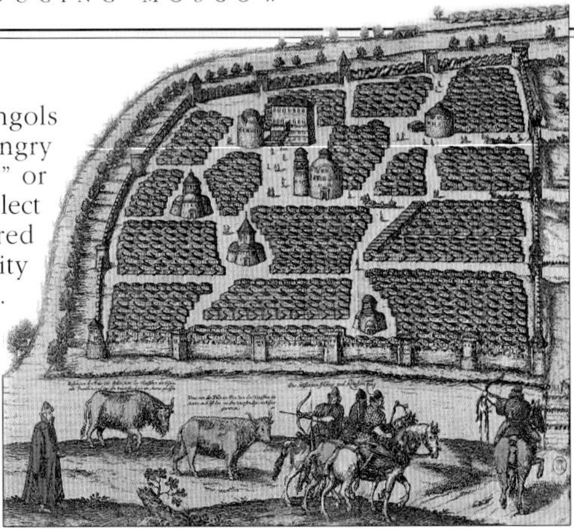

Map of 16th-century Moscow, showing neat rows of wooden houses and several churches behind the city's first stone walls

THE RISE OF MOSCOW

In the 14th century, the Mongols chose Moscow's power-hungry Grand Prince Ivan I, "Kalita" or "Moneybags" (1325–40), to collect tribute from all their conquered principalities, giving the city supremacy over its neighbours. Ivan had already shown his obsequiousness by crushing a revolt against the Mongols led by his neighbour, the Grand Prince of Tver. Yet the Mongols were sealing their own fate, for, as Moscow flourished under their benevolence, she ultimately became a real threat to their power. Within 50 years an army of soldiers from several Russian principalities, led by Moscow's Grand Prince Dmitriy Donskoy (1359–89), inflicted their first defeat on the Mongols, and the idea of a Russian nation was born.

It was not until the reign of Ivan III, "the Great" (1462–1505), when Moscow ruled a kingdom which stretched as far as the Arctic Ocean and the Urals, that the Mongols were finally vanquished. Ivan married the niece of the last emperor of Byzantium, who had fled Constantinople when it had fallen to the Ottomans in 1453. This increased Moscow's prestige further, and particularly her claim to being the last defender of true Orthodoxy. Ivan also sought to assert Moscow's status through a grand building programme. He started the tradition of importing foreign architects, including the Italians *(see p44)* who built the present Kremlin walls.

Ivan the Terrible (1533–84)

IVAN THE TERRIBLE

It was Ivan the Great's grandson, Ivan IV, "the Terrible" (1533–84), who transformed himself from Grand Prince of Moscow to "Tsar of All the Russias". During his reign Russia expanded beyond the Urals into Siberia and strong trading links were established with England. Moscow's walls were strengthened for, even as late as 1571, the Crimean Mongols continued to venture sporadic attacks on the Russian capital.

Yet, powerful though he was, Ivan suffered dreadful paranoia. After the death of his beloved wife Anastasia, he became convinced that she had been poisoned by the boyars *(see p20)* and set up Russia's first police state. A sinister force of black-hooded agents called the *oprichniki* murdered whole villages to stamp out the tsar's supposed enemies. Ivan also imposed restrictions on the aristocracy and peasantry alike, establishing those

TIMELINE

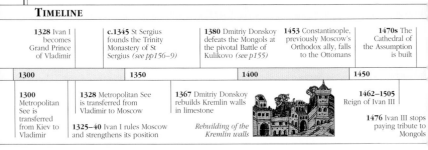

1328 Ivan I becomes Grand Prince of Vladimir

c.1345 St Sergius founds the Trinity Monastery of St Sergius *(see pp156–9)*

1380 Dmitriy Donskoy defeats the Mongols at the pivotal Battle of Kulikovo *(see p155)*

1453 Constantinople, previously Moscow's Orthodox ally, falls to the Ottomans

1470s The Cathedral of the Assumption is built

1300 | **1350** | **1400** | **1450**

1300 Metropolitan See is transferred from Kiev to Vladimir

1328 Metropolitan See is transferred from Vladimir to Moscow

1325–40 Ivan I rules Moscow and strengthens its position

1367 Dmitriy Donskoy rebuilds Kremlin walls in limestone

Rebuilding of the Kremlin walls

1462–1505 Reign of Ivan III

1476 Ivan III stops paying tribute to Mongols

autocratic traditions that were to prove the country's downfall. Ivan's more immediate legacy was his contribution to the end of the Varangian dynasty, the murder of his only competent son, also named Ivan, in a paranoid rage.

The Time of Troubles

This ushered in a period known as the Time of Troubles. For fourteen years, Ivan's retarded son Fyodor (1584–98) ruled under the guidance of Boris Godunov, a former and much-hated *oprichnik*. When Fyodor died childless, Godunov installed himself in the Kremlin, but he soon become target of a pretender to the throne. The pretender claimed to be Ivan the Terrible's dead youngest son Dimitry, sought support from Poland and marched on Moscow with an army of 4,000 in 1604. With the death of Boris Godunov in 1605 he was installed on the throne. The pretender was soon to enrage the Moscow boyars, who killed him, and replaced him with Vasiliy Shuiskiy, a boyar of some distinction. Faced with a second "False Dmitry" marching on Moscow in 1607, Shuiskiy appealed to Sweden for help only to provoke a new Polish intervention. The Poles reached Moscow in 1610 and Shuiskiy was then deposed by the boyars. In the north, the Swedes used the internal instability of Russia to capture Novgorod. Only in these desperate circumstances did the Russians finally unite to expel the occupying Poles, under the leadership of Minin and Prince Pozharskiy *(see p108)*. The siege of the Kremlin thus ended in 1612.

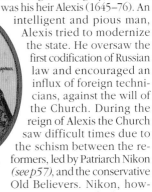

Boris Godunov (1598–1605)

The First Romanovs

Determined to put an end to this period of anarchy, Moscow's leading citizens came together to nominate the 16-year old Mikhail Romanov, great-nephew of Ivan's first wife Anastasia, as hereditary tsar, thus initiating the 300-year rule of the Romanovs. Under Mikhail (1613–45), who ruled with his father Filaret, the patriarch of Moscow, Russia recovered from her exhausting upheavals. His greatest legacy, however, was his heir Alexis (1645–76). An intelligent and pious man, Alexis tried to modernize the state. He oversaw the first codification of Russian law and encouraged an influx of foreign technicians, against the will of the Church. During the reign of Alexis the Church saw difficult times due to the schism between the reformers, led by Patriarch Nikon *(see p57)*, and the conservative Old Believers. Nikon, however, grew too important for his own good which resulted in Alexis asserting the power of the State over the Church.

Ambassadors of the Council of the Realm entreating young Mikhail Romanov to accept the tsar's crown in 1613

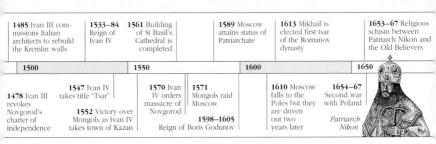

1485 Ivan III commissions Italian architects to rebuild the Kremlin walls

1533–84 Reign of Ivan IV

1561 Building of St Basil's Cathedral is completed

1589 Moscow attains status of Patriarchate

1613 Mikhail is elected first tsar of the Romanov dynasty

1653–67 Religious schism between Patriarch Nikon and the Old Believers

1500 | **1550** | **1600** | **1650**

1478 Ivan III revokes Novgorod's charter of independence

1547 Ivan IV takes title "Tsar"

1552 Victory over Mongols as Ivan IV takes town of Kazan

1570 Ivan IV orders massacre of Novgorod

1571 Mongols raid Moscow

1598–1605 Reign of Boris Godunov

1610 Moscow falls to the Poles but they are driven out two years later

1654–67 Second war with Poland

Patriarch Nikon

Medieval Moscow

Moscow developed in 400 years from an isolated wooden fortress (kremlin), built in 1156, into a thriving capital city, "shining like Jerusalem from without, but like Bethlehem inside". Its circle of outer walls enclosed a series of smaller districts centred on the Kremlin, whose wooden stockade was replaced with white limestone in 1367 to protect the city from Mongol raids, and by massive brick walls in 1495. It boasted a clutch of stone cathedrals, befitting its role as the "Third Rome" after the fall of Constantinople in 1453. Next to the Kremlin lay Red Square, where public spectacles ranged from executions to fairs. The rest of the city housed boyars, merchants, servants, hawkers and artisans.

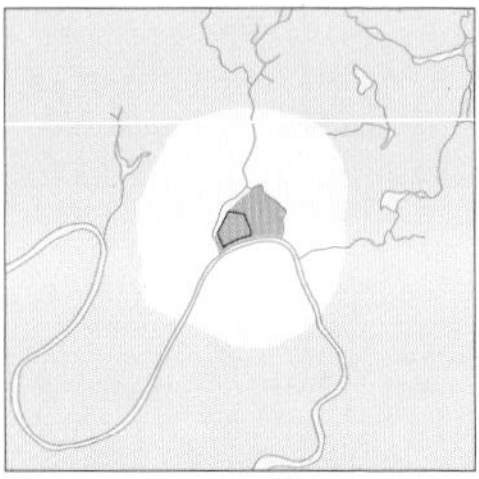

Extent of the City

13th century 1590

Andrey Rublev (c.1370–1430)
Moscow's finest icon painter, Andrey Rublev is seen here painting a fresco at the Monastery of the Saviour and Andronicus (see p140). *Icons* (see p61) *were used for the religious education of the people.*

The public sauna *(banya)* was always sited near water, isolated where possible from the dense crush of wooden housing.

The Walled City
Vasnetsov's *(see p144)* painting of the Kremlin in the 15th century shows the warren of wooden houses which surrounded the palaces and churches. Among them were the renowned Kremlin workshops.

A Silver Kovsh
Originally made in wood, this ceremonial drinking vessel, known as a kovsh, *began to be crafted in metal in the 14th century. Elaborately decorated* kovshi *were often given by the tsar to favoured subjects. These treasured artifacts would be displayed as a symbol of wealth when not in use.*

Boyars and Merchants
Though richly dressed, boyars (noblemen) in medieval Russia were largely illiterate and often crude in their habits. Their material needs were looked after by merchants who traded in furs from the north and silk from Turkey.

Foreigners in Moscow
From the 16th century, foreign diplomats and traders began to visit the isolated and xenophobic Russia. The adventurer Richard Chancellor, who attempted to find the northwest passage to the Orient but ended up in Russia, managed to negotiate a trading treaty with Ivan the Terrible.

Where to See Medieval Moscow

The Kremlin's medieval buildings include its Cathedrals of the Assumption *(see pp58–9)*, the Archangel *(p60)* and the Annunciation *(p60)*. The State Armoury *(pp64–5)*, also in the Kremlin, displays medieval artifacts and armour while the daily life of the nobility is recreated in the Palace of the Romanov Boyars *(pp102–3)*. St Basil's Cathedral *(pp108–9)* also dates from this time.

The dining room *in the Palace of the Romanov Boyars.*

Wooden houses could be bought pre-fabricated from a market outside the city walls. They quickly replaced houses that were lost in Moscow's frequent fires.

Limestone walls, erected by Dmitriy Donskoy *(see p155)*

Cathedral of the Assumption

Small trading vessels thronged the banks of the Moskva river, unloading goods for the growing city. Russia's rivers were her trading routes and were far more efficient than travel by land.

Building a Cathedral
During the reign of Ivan I (1325–40), when the first stone Cathedral of the Assumption was built, Metropolitan Peter moved to Moscow to be head of the Orthodox Church. This manuscript illustration shows him blessing the new cathedral.

Ivan the Terrible
Though Ivan IV's reign (1533–84) did much to benefit Russia, he certainly deserved his epithet. Among the many souls on his conscience was his only worthy son and heir, Ivan, killed in a fit of rage which the tsar regretted for the rest of his life.

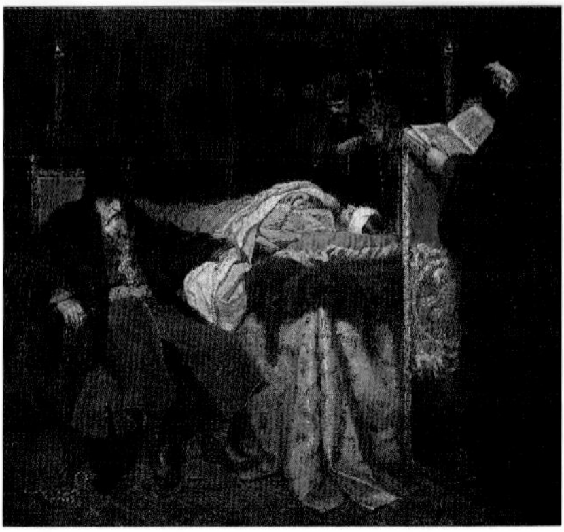

Peter the Great

The extraordinary reign of Alexis's son Peter I, "the Great", really put Russia back on her feet. Brought up in an atmosphere of reform, Peter was determined to make Russia a modern European state. In 1697, he became the first tsar ever to go abroad, with the particular aim of studying shipbuilding and other European technologies. On his return, he began immediately to build a Russian navy, reformed the army and insisted on Western-style clothing for his courtiers. At Poltava in 1709, Peter dramatically defeated the Swedes, who had been a threat to Russia for a century, and stunned Europe into taking note of an emerging power.

Vasiliy Surikov's portrayal of Peter the Great watching Streltsy Guards being led to their deaths in 1698, as punishment for their earlier rebellion

Peter's effect on Moscow was double-edged. At the age of ten he had seen relatives murdered in the Kremlin during the Streltsy Rebellion. This revolt had sprung from rivalry between his mother's family, the Naryshkins, and that of his father's first wife, the Miloslavskiys, over the succession. In the end Peter was made co-tsar with his half-brother Ivan, but developed a pathological distrust of Moscow. He took a long-awaited and grim revenge on the Streltsys 16 years later, when he executed over a thousand of them. He also began to build a new city on the boggy banks of the Neva to the north and ordered the imperial family and government to move. In 1712 he declared the cold, damp St Petersburg capital of Russia. For the next 200 years Moscow was Russia's second city.

Tsar Peter the Great (1682–1725)

Tsarina Elizabeth (1741–62)

The Petticoat Period

After Peter the Great's death in 1725, Russia was ruled by women for most of the 18th century: Catherine I, Anna, Elizabeth and Catherine II. Though they were all crowned in the Cathedral of the Assumption *(see pp58–9)*, most preferred to live in Europeanized St Petersburg. However, Elizabeth, Peter's boisterous, fun-loving daughter, insisted on living in [illegible] periodically. During Pete[illegible]structions in stone outsi[illegible]ng had been banned, but under Elizabeth a flurry of new buildings appeared in Moscow, especially since some of Russia's leading families preferred to live there.

Timeline

1682 The Streltsy Rebellion; Peter I is co-tsar with half-brother Ivan V and his half-sister Sophia as regent

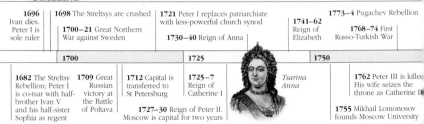

1696 Ivan dies. Peter I is sole ruler

1698 The Streltsys are crushed

1700

1700–21 Great Northern War against Sweden

1709 Great Russian victory at the Battle of Poltava

1712 Capital is transferred to St Petersburg

1721 Peter I replaces patriarchiate with less-powerful church synod

1725

1725–7 Reign of Catherine I

1727–30 Reign of Peter II. Moscow is capital for two years

1730–40 Reign of Anna

Tsarina Anna

1741–62 Reign of Elizabeth

1750

1755 Mikhail Lomonosov founds Moscow University

1762 Peter III is kille[d]. His wife seizes the throne as Catherine I[I]

1768–74 First Russo-Turkish War

1773–4 Pugachev Rebellion

Elizabeth founded Russia's first university in Moscow *(see p94)*, under the guidance of Russia's 18th-century Renaissance man, the poet, scientist and academic Mikhail Lomonosov. But Moscow was still protected from the Westernization affecting the capital and thus retained a more purely Russian soul and identity.

Catherine the Great (1762–96)

Catherine the Great

In 1762 Catherine II, "the Great", a German princess, usurped the throne of her feeble husband Peter III with the help of her lover Grigoriy Orlov, a guards officer. Under her energetic, intelligent leadership, the country saw another vast expansion in its prestige and made territorial gains at the expense of Turkey and its old adversary Poland. Catherine purchased great collections of European art and books (including Voltaire's library) and in 1767 published her *Nakaz* (Imperial Instruction) upon which a reform of Russia's legal system was to be based. Unsurprisingly, this modern European monarch regarded Moscow as inward-looking and backward and spent little time there.

19th-Century Moscow

Napoleon's invasion in 1812 and the heroic part played in his defeat by Moscow *(see pp24–5)* appeared to reinvigorate the city. Aleksandr Herzen *(see p71)* claimed that "Moscow was again made the 'capital' of the Russian people by Napoleon", and, indeed, the destruction of two thirds of the city by fire resulted in a bold new architectural plan. The Napoleonic Wars also marked a turning point in Russian political history, as soldiers returned from Europe bringing with them the seeds of liberal ideas. Far from the court of Nicholas I, the Iron Tsar, Moscow became a fertile environment for underground debate among early revolutionaries such as Herzen and the Decembrists. Yet most of Moscow society was trapped in a comfortable and conservative cocoon, financed by the system of serfdom. With the Emancipation of the Serfs in 1861, however, the economic strength of most nobles was radically curtailed. The freed serfs who were too poor to buy their own land, flocked to the factories of mercantile and industrial entrepreneurs. In Moscow, at the old heart of the empire, these entrepreneurs came to usurp the position of the aristocrats, making vast fortunes from trade, textiles, railways, banking and publishing, and financing a renaissance in the Russian arts on the proceeds.

The Bolshoy Theatre, favoured by Moscow's aristocracy, along with balls and lavish suppers, for an evening's entertainment

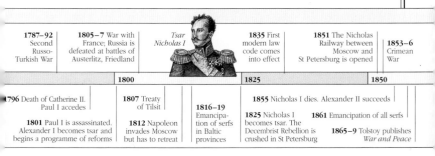

1787–92 Second Russo-Turkish War

1805–7 War with France; Russia is defeated at battles of Austerlitz, Friedland

Tsar Nicholas I

1835 First modern law code comes into effect

1851 The Nicholas Railway between Moscow and St Petersburg is opened

1853–6 Crimean War

1800 · 1825 · 1850

1796 Death of Catherine II. Paul I accedes

1801 Paul I is assassinated. Alexander I becomes tsar and begins a programme of reforms

1807 Treaty of Tilsit

1812 Napoleon invades Moscow but has to retreat

1816–19 Emancipation of serfs in Baltic provinces

1825 Nicholas I becomes tsar. The Decembrist Rebellion is crushed in St Petersburg

1855 Nicholas I dies. Alexander II succeeds

1861 Emancipation of all serfs

1865–9 Tolstoy publishes *War and Peace*

War and Peace

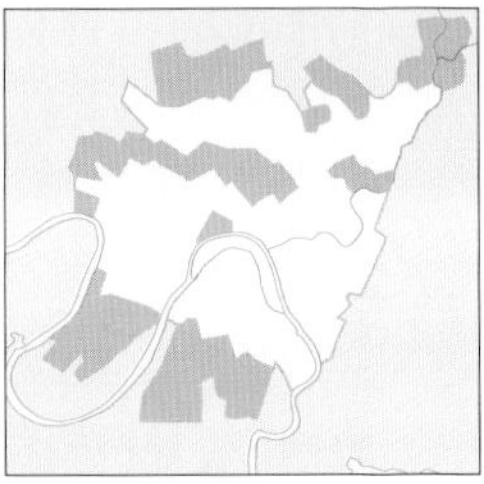

Extent of the City

1812, before the fire

Areas razed by the fire

RUSSIA'S GLORIOUS RISE to the ranks of a world power accelerated in the period between 1800 and 1830. Even though she suffered severe defeats against France, including the Battle of Austerlitz (1805), and signed the Treaty of Tilsit in 1807. The uneasy peace ended in 1812, with the invasion of Napoleon's Grande Armée. But Russia turned disaster into victory and in 1814–15, Tsar Alexander I sat down to decide Europe's future at the Congress of Vienna. The war marked an important cultural shift in Russia as liberal Western European political ideas first filtered into the country, although their time had not yet come.

Alexander I (1801–25)
The handsome young tsar was initially infected by the ideals of enlightened government, but became increasingly influenced by his reactionary advisers.

The Kremlin was damaged more by the looting of the French than by the fire outside.

Napoleon stayed in the tsar's apartments for a few days before retreating to safety outside the city.

The French soldiers soon fell to undisciplined drinking and looting.

Moscow Burning

After Field Marshal Mikhail Kutuzov's retreat at Borodino, the French army was able to enter Moscow. But Muscovites set light to their city and fled. In just four days, two thirds of the city burnt down, leaving the army without shelter or provisions. Combined with Alexander I's refusal to negotiate while Napoleon remained on Russian territory, this resulted in the French emperor's defeat.

Battle of Borodino, September 1812
The Battle of Borodino (see p152) *lasted 15 hours, causing the death of 70,000 men, half of them French. Yet Napoleon declared the battle a victory and advanced on Moscow.*

Retreat of Napoleon's Grande Armée
Facing the winter without supplies, the army began its retreat in October. Only 30,000 out of 600,000 men made it back.

Empire Style
Many things, from chairs to plates, were designed in the popular Empire style (see p45). *This cup and saucer with a Classical motif were made at the Popov factory near Moscow in 1810.*

Where to See Neo-Classical Moscow

Pediment, Kuskovo Palace

Early examples of Neo-Classicism can be seen at the palaces of Ostankino *(see p144)* and Kuskovo *(pp142–3)*, at Pashkov House *(p75)* and at Moscow Old University *(p94)*. The fire of 1812 allowed vast areas to be developed to an Empire-style city plan. Bolshaya Nikitskaya ulitsa *(p93)*, ulitsa Prechistenka *(p74)* and Theatre Square *(p88)* are lined with fine buildings from this time.

New fires were started deliberately throughout the city, on the orders of the tsarist governor.

The river proved no barrier to the fire, whipped up by a fierce wind.

Moscow University
It was after the Napoleonic Wars that the University of Moscow, founded in 1755, gained a reputation as a hotbed of liberalism. However, political discussions still had to be conducted at secret salons.

Alexander Pushkin
The great Romantic poet Alexander Pushkin (see p73) *captured the spirit of the time. Pushkin and his wife Natalya were often invited to court balls, such as the one shown here. This enabled Nicholas I to keep an eye on the liberal poet as well as on his enchanting wife.*

The Millstone of Serfdom
In the shadow of the nobility's easy life, and to a great extent enabling it, were millions of serfs toiling in slavery on large estates. This painting shows a serf owner settling his debts by selling a girl to a new master.

The End of an Empire

Though the 1890s saw rapid advances in industrialization, Russia experienced a disastrous slump at the turn of the 20th century. Nicholas II's diversionary war with Japan backfired, causing economic unrest, adding to the misery of the working classes and finally culminating in the 1905 Revolution. On 9th January 1905, a demonstration in St Petersburg carried a petition of grievances to the tsar and was met by bullets. News of this "Bloody Sunday" spread like wildfire and strikes broke out all over the country. To avert further disaster Nicholas had to promise basic civil rights, and an elected parliament which he, however, simply dissolved whenever it displeased him. This high-handed behaviour, along with the imperial family's friendship with the "holy man" Rasputin, further damaged the Romanovs' reputation.

The outbreak of World War I brought a surge of patriotism which the inexperienced Nicholas sought to ride by taking personal command of the troops. By late 1916, however, Russia had lost 3,500,000 men, morale at the front was very low and supplies of food at home had become increasingly scarce.

The Bolshevik **by Boris Kustodiev, painted in 1920**

Tsar Nicholas II surrounded by his wife Alexandra, their four daughters and Tsarevich Alexis in 1913

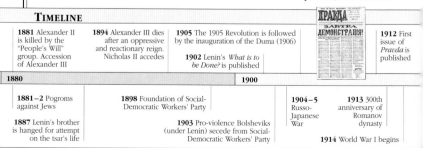

Revolution and Civil War

In early 1917 strikes broke out in St Petersburg. People took to the streets, jails were stormed and the February Revolution began. The tsar was forced to abdicate and his family was placed under house arrest. Exiled revolutionaries flooded back into the country to set up workers' and soldiers' soviets. Elected by the workers as an alternative to an unelected provisional government they formed a powerful anti-war lobby. In October the leadership of the Bolsheviks, urged on by Lenin, decided on an armed uprising, under the rallying cries of "All power to the soviets!" and "Peace, bread and land". In the early hours of 26th October, they arrested the provisional government in St Petersburg's Winter Palace.

Within months the Bolsheviks had shown themselves as careless of democracy as the tsar, dismissing the constituent assembly and setting up their own secret police, the Cheka.

Timeline

1881 Alexander II is killed by the "People's Will" group. Accession of Alexander III

1881–2 Pogroms against Jews

1887 Lenin's brother is hanged for attempt on the tsar's life

1894 Alexander III dies after an oppressive and reactionary reign. Nicholas II accedes

1898 Foundation of Social-Democratic Workers' Party

1880

1900

1902 Lenin's *What is to be Done?* is published

1903 Pro-violence Bolsheviks (under Lenin) secede from Social-Democratic Workers' Party

1904–5 Russo-Japanese War

1905 The 1905 Revolution is followed by the inauguration of the Duma (1906)

ПРАВДА
ЗАВТРА
ДЕМОНСТРАЦІЯ!

1912 First issue of *Pravda* is published

1913 300th anniversary of Romanov dynasty

1914 World War I begins

In March 1918, however, they stayed true to their promise and took Russia out of World War I, instead plunging the soldiers straight into a vicious civil war. The capital was moved back to Moscow, and from here Lenin and his government directed their "Red" army against the diverse coalition of anti-revolutionary groups known as the "Whites". When White soldiers got closer to the exiled Romanovs in Yekaterinburg in July 1918, the royal family was brutally butchered by its captors. But the Whites were a disparate force, and by November 1920 Soviet Russia was rid of them, only to face two years of appalling famine.

A 1937 propaganda poster showing Joseph Stalin

THE STALIN YEARS

In the five years after Lenin's death in 1924, Joseph Stalin used his position as General Secretary of the Communist Party to remove rivals such as Leon Trotsky and establish his dictatorship.

The terror began in the countryside, with the collectivization of agriculture which forced the peasantry to give up their land, machinery and livestock to collective farms in return for a salary. During this time, and in the ensuing famine of 1931–2, up to 10 million people are thought to have died.

The first major purge of intellectuals took place in urban areas in 1928–9. Then, in December 1934, Sergey Kirov, the local party leader in Leningrad, was

Cathedral of the Redeemer, torn down on the orders of Stalin as part of his new city plan ***(see pp74–5)***

assassinated on the secret orders of Stalin, although the murder was blamed on an underground anti-Stalinist cell. This was the catalyst for five years of purges, by the end of which over a million people had been executed and some 15 million arrested and sent to labour camps, where they often died.

In his purge of the Red Army in 1937–8, Stalin dismissed or executed three quarters of his officers. When the Germans invaded in 1941 they were able to advance rapidly, subjecting Leningrad to a horrendous siege of nearly 900 days. But Moscow was never taken since Hitler, like Napoleon before him, underestimated both the harshness of the Russian winter and his enemies' willingness to fight.

After the German defeat, the Russian people, who had lost over 20 million souls in the war, were subjected to a renewed internal terror by Stalin, which lasted until his death in 1953.

"Let us defend our beloved Moscow", 1941 propaganda poster

1917 The Russian revolution *(see pp28–9)*

1918 Civil War starts. Capital moves to Moscow

1920

1921 Lenin bans all opposition. NEP (New Economic Policy) is introduced

1922 Stalin becomes General Secretary

1924 Lenin dies

1932 Socialist Realism becomes the officially approved style in art

1934 Leningrad Party Secretary Sergey Kirov is murdered; purges begin

Sergey Kirov

1939 Nazi-Soviet pact

1940

1941 Hitler attacks Soviet Union, reaches outskirts of Moscow. Siege of Leningrad

1947 The term "Cold War" is coined

The Russian Revolution

THE RUSSIAN REVOLUTION, which began in St Petersburg and made Moscow once more a capital city, was pivotal to the history of the 20th century. By late 1916, with Russia facing defeat in World War I and starvation at home, even ministers and generals were doubting the tsar's ability to rule. In 1917 there were two uprisings, the February Revolution which began with massive strikes and led to the abdication of Nicholas II, and the October Revolution which overturned the provisional government and swept the Communists to power. They emerged victoriously from the Civil War that followed, to attempt to build a new society.

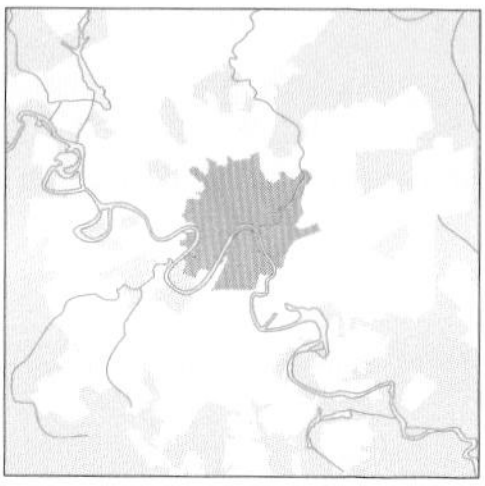

EXTENT OF THE CITY

1917 | Today

The Ex-Tsar
Nicholas II, seen here clearing snow during his house arrest outside St Petersburg, was later taken with his family to Yekaterinburg in the Urals. There, in 1918, they were shot and their bodies thrown down a mine shaft.

REDS OUTSIDE THE KREMLIN

In October, the fight for control of the Kremlin was intense in comparison to the one in St Petersburg. The Bolshevik seizure was reversed after three days, and it took the revolutionaries another six days to overcome loyalist troops in the fortress and elsewhere in the city.

Many soldiers deserting from the front were happy to put on the new Red Army uniform instead.

Middle class people as well as the poor took part in the Revolution.

Women took part in demonstrations and strikes.

Comrade Lenin
A charismatic speaker, depicted here by Viktor Ivanov, the exiled Lenin returned in April to lead the Revolution. By late 1917 his Bolshevik party had gained power.

Revolutionary Plate
Ceramics with revolutionary themes, mixed with touches of Russian folklore, were produced to commemorate special events. This plate marks the founding of the Third International Communist group in 1919.

Leon Trotsky
The intellectual Trotsky played a leading military role in the Revolution. In 1928, during the power struggle after Lenin's death, he was exiled by Stalin. He was murdered in Mexico, in 1940, by a Stalinist agent.

Propaganda
One hallmark of the Soviet regime was its powerful propaganda. Many talented artists were employed to design posters, which spread the Socialist message through striking graphics. During the Civil War (1918–20), posters such as this one extolled the "pacifist army of workers" to support War Communism.

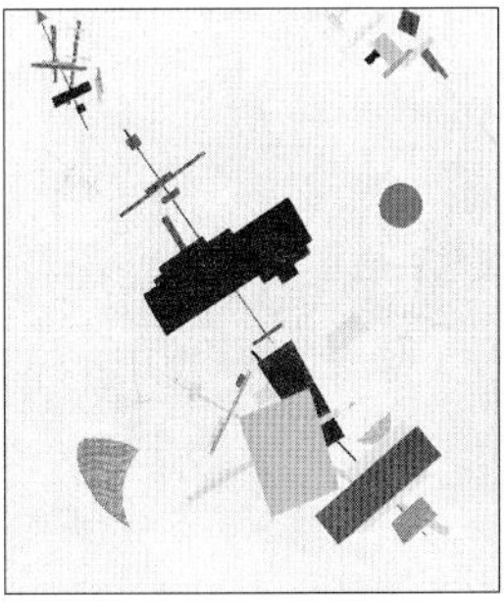

Avant-Garde Art
Even before 1917, Russia's artists had been in a state of revolution, producing the world's first truly abstract paintings. A fine example of avant-garde art is Supremus No. 56, *painted in 1916 by Kazimir Malevich.*

Banner proclaiming freedom to the world

Old and young were swept away by the revolutionary fervour.

New Values
Traditions were radically altered by the Revolution; instead of church weddings, couples exchanged vows under the red flag. Loudly trumpeted sexual equality meant that women had to work twice as hard – at home and in the factories.

TIMELINE

1917

February Revolution in St Petersburg

March The tsar is persuaded to abdicate. Provisional government is led by Prince Lvov

July Kerenskiy becomes prime minister of provisional government

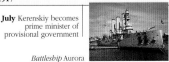

Battleship Aurora

October Bolsheviks storm Winter Palace in St Petersburg, after signal from *Aurora*, and oust provisional government

December Lenin forms the Cheka (secret police)

1918

1918 January Trotsky becomes Commissar of War

March Bolsheviks sign Brest-Litovsk peace treaty with Germany, taking Russia out of World War I. Capital is moved to Moscow

July Start of Civil War. Tsar and family murdered in prison at Yekaterinburg

The Washington Dove of Peace (1953), a Russian caricature from the days of the Cold War

Behind the Iron Curtain

Three years after Stalin's death his successor, Nikita Khrushchev, denounced his crimes at the 20th Party Congress and the period known as "The Thaw" began. Thousands of political prisoners were released and books critical of Stalin were published. In foreign affairs, things were not so liberal. Soviet tanks invaded Hungary in 1956 and in 1962 Khrushchev's decision to base nuclear missiles on Cuba brought the world to the brink of nuclear war.

First in Space

Under Khrushchev the Soviet Union achieved her greatest coup against the West, when she sent *Sputnik 1* into space in 1957. That same year the dog Laika was the first living creature in space, on *Sputnik 2*. She never came back but, four years later, Yuriy Gagarin made history as the first man in space, returning as a hero. The Soviets lost the race to put a man on the moon, but the space programme was a powerful propaganda tool, backing the claims of politicians that Russia would soon catch up with and overtake the West.

***Sputnik 2* and the space dog Laika, 1957**

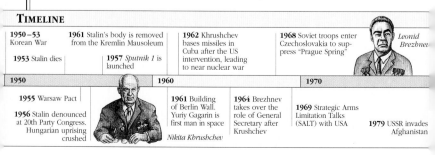

When Leonid Brezhnev took over in 1964, the intellectual climate froze once more. The first ten years of his office were a time of relative plenty, but beneath the surface there was a vast black market and growing corruption. The party apparatchiks, who benefitted from the corruption, had no interest in rocking the boat. When Brezhnev died in 1982, the Politburo was determined to prevent the accession of a younger generation. He was succeeded by the 68-year-old Andropov, followed by the 72-year-old Chernenko.

Glasnost and Perestroika

It was only in 1985, when the new leader, 53-year-old Mikhail Gorbachev, announced his policies of perestroika (restructuring) and *glasnost* (openness), that the true bankruptcy of the old system became apparent. Yet he had no idea of the immense changes that they would bring in their wake. For the first time since 1917 the elections to the Congress of People's Deputies in 1989 contained an element of true choice, with rebels such as human-rights campaigner Andrey Sakharov and Boris Yeltsin winning seats. In the autumn and winter of that year the Warsaw Pact disintegrated as country after country in Eastern Europe declared its independence from the Soviet Union. Local elections within the Union in 1990 brought nationalist candidates to power in the republics and democrats in the most important Russian local councils.

Mikhail Gorbachev with George Bush

Timeline

1950–53 Korean War

1953 Stalin dies

1961 Stalin's body is removed from the Kremlin Mausoleum

1957 *Sputnik 1* is launched

1962 Khrushchev bases missiles in Cuba after the US intervention, leading to near nuclear war

1968 Soviet troops enter Czechoslovakia to suppress "Prague Spring"

Leonid Brezhnev

1950 — 1960 — 1970

1955 Warsaw Pact

1956 Stalin denounced at 20th Party Congress. Hungarian uprising crushed

Nikita Khrushchev

1961 Building of Berlin Wall. Yuriy Gagarin is first man in space

1964 Brezhnev takes over the role of General Secretary after Krushchev

1969 Strategic Arms Limitation Talks (SALT) with USA

1979 USSR invades Afghanistan

Communist hero fallen from grace after the 1991 coup

In 1991 the Baltic Republics and Russia herself seceded from the Soviet Union. With his massive victory in the election for President of the Russian Republic, Yeltsin gained the mandate he needed to deal the death blow to the Soviet Union. It came after the military coup against Gorbachev in August 1991, when Yeltsin's stand against the tanks in Moscow made him a hero. After Gorbachev's return from house arrest in the Crimea, Yeltsin forced him to outlaw the Communist Party. By the end of the year the Soviet Union was no more as all the republics declared their independence.

Moscow 850-years poster

Moscow Today

The 1990s have had a profound effect on the drab old Moscow of Soviet times. With Russia's vast natural resources attracting a rush of inward investment, Moscow saw the lion's share of that money passing through its hands. A wealthy elite, the "New Russians", suddenly had a vastly improved standard of living and, for instance, car ownership in the city quadrupled in 1991–7. No amount of nightclubs seemed able to soak up their desire to party. Much of the city was renovated in 1997 in honour of Moscow's 850th anniversary. The Cathedral of Christ the Redeemer *(see p74)*, demolished by Stalin in 1931, was rebuilt as part of the restoration programme. This was also a sign of the renewed importance of the Orthodox Church, which was forced underground during the Soviet era. Churches are now filled once again for weddings, baptisms and religious holidays. The crime rate has fallen from its dizzying high in 1995, as the city's criminal groups, or *mafiya,* have resolved their territorial battles. Moscow's mayor in the mid-1990s, Yuriy Luzhkov, has used the city's affluence to cosmetic aplomb and yet, for most citizens, in contrast to the New Russians, the riches are just a mirage. Moscow is now among the most expensive cities in the world, yet plenty of workers take home pay packets that would seem more typical of the Third World.

A church wedding, popular once more since religion has gained new importance among the young

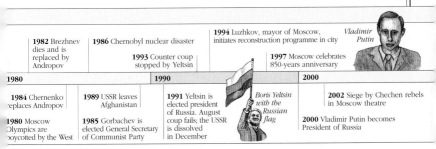

1982 Brezhnev dies and is replaced by Andropov

1986 Chernobyl nuclear disaster

1993 Counter coup stopped by Yeltsin

1994 Luzhkov, mayor of Moscow, initiates reconstruction programme in city

1997 Moscow celebrates 850-years anniversary

Vladimir Putin

1980 | **1990** | **2000**

1984 Chernenko eplaces Andropov

1980 Moscow lympics are oycotted by the West

1989 USSR leaves Afghanistan

1985 Gorbachev is elected General Secretary of Communist Party

1991 Yeltsin is elected president of Russia. August coup fails; the USSR is dissolved in December

Boris Yeltsin with the Russian flag

2002 Siege by Chechen rebels in Moscow theatre

2000 Vladimir Putin becomes President of Russia

Moscow Through the Year

Muscovites are ready to celebrate at any time and take their public holidays seriously. Flowers play a particularly important role, from mimosa for International Women's Day to lilac as a symbol that summer is on its way. All the official holidays, as well as some local festivals such as City Day, are marked with concerts and night-time fireworks all over the city. Music, whether classical, folk or contemporary, is the central theme of a large number of festivals, bringing in talent from all over the world. For really big celebrations top Russian and international singers perform for crowds of thousands in Red Square. Even without an official holiday, people love to get out and about, whether skiing in winter, picnicking in spring or summer, or gathering mushrooms in autumn.

Lilac, a sign that summer is coming

Performers wearing papier-mâché costumes at The Rite of Spring

Spring

When flocks of rooks appear in the city, usually in late March, and the violets and snowdrops bloom, spring is reckoned to have arrived.

To warm themselves up after the months of cold, locals celebrate *maslennitsa*, the feast of blini-making before Lent. Willow branches with catkins are gathered as a symbol of the approaching Palm Sunday and on Forgiveness Sunday, just before Lent, people ask forgiveness of those they may have offended in the past year.

Easter service, Trinity Monastery of St Sergius *(see pp156–9)*

Wealthy Muscovites usually make a first visit to their *dacha* at this time to put the garden in order and to plant their own fruits and vegetables.

March

Maslenitsa end Feb–early Mar. A festival involving events such as concerts and carnivals held at venues throughout the city.
International Women's Day *(Mezhdunarodnyy den zhenshchin)*, 8 Mar. Men buy flowers for their womenfolk and congratulate them on the holiday with the words *"s prazdnikom"*. Theatres hold special performances.
St Patrick's Day, first Sunday after 16 March. Moscow's Irish community organize a few local marches and concerts.
Easter Sunday *(Paskha)*, March–early May, following the Orthodox calendar. Churches are filled with chanting and candles. After the greeting *Khristos voskres* (Christ is risen) and the reply *Voistine voskres* (He is truly risen), people kiss one another three times.

April

April Fool's Day *(Den durakov)*, 1 Apr. Russians play tricks with particular glee.
Cosmonauts' Day *(Den kosmonavtiki)*, 12 Apr. Space exploration was one of the glories of the Soviet Union and is celebrated with fireworks.
Alternative Festival, end Apr–May. Annual modern music festival in Gorky Park.
Moscow Forum, end Apr–May. Annual festival of classical and modern music held at various city venues.

War veterans on parade in Red Square on Victory Day

May

Labour Day *(Den truda)*, 1 May. In the Soviet era, huge military parades filled Red Square. Now much more low-key, with impromptu concerts.
Victory Day *(Den pobedy)*, 9 May. War veterans fill Red Square and Tverskaya ulitsa in memory of the 1945 Nazi surrender. A military parade is held in Red Square.
Border Troopers' Day *(Den pogranichnika)*, 28 May. Retired Border Troopers gather at the Bolshoy Theatre and in Gorky Park to get drunk, sing and watch fireworks.

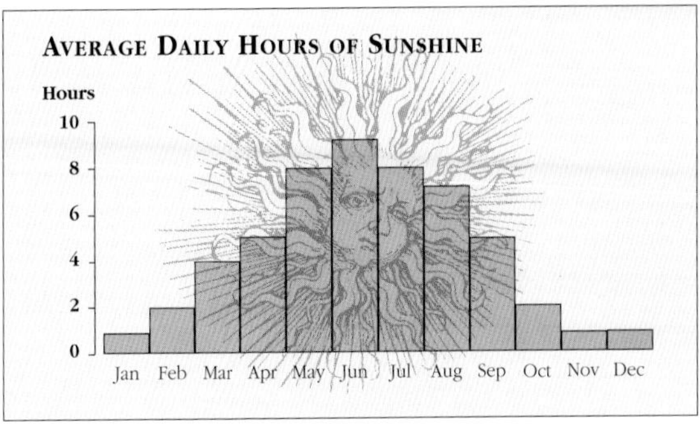

Sunshine Chart
Moscow is often thought of as a cold and snowy city. However, it has more hours of sunshine in the summer months than many cities in northern Europe. May, June and July are the sunniest months. The short, cold days of winter provide a stark contrast, with an average of only around one hour of sunshine a day.

SUMMER

LIFE IN MOSCOW is much less hectic in July and August as most enterprises close down for their summer breaks and many Muscovites move out of the city, either to their *dacha* or to spend holidays abroad. Although most of the theatres also close or go on tour for these two months, there is still plenty going on in and around the city for the visitor to enjoy. Some of the large estates and stately homes outside Moscow, such as Kuskovo *(see pp142–3)* and Ostankino Palace *(see pp144–5)*, hold outdoor concerts at this time of year. Gorky Park offers a number of options on a fine summer day – from bungee jumping or hiring a rowing boat or pedalo to enjoying a picnic. Outdoor cafés and bars are a favourite with Muscovites remaining in the city and there is even an outdoor casino at the Marilyn Entertainment Complex, at Krasina ulitsa 14.

Women in national costume for Peter the Great's birthday

JUNE

Trinity Sunday *(Troitsa)*, late May–late June. Believers and atheists alike go to tidy the graves of their loved ones and drink a toast to their souls.
Tchaikovsky International Competition, June, held every four years (next in 2006). One of the world's most prestigious musical awards *(see p192)*. Concerts are held throughout the city.
Independence Day *(Den nezavisimosti)*, 12 Jun. The day Russia became independent of the Soviet Union is marked with firework displays.
Peter the Great's Birthday *(Den rozhdeniya Petra Pervovo)*, first Sunday after 9 Jun. Costumed celebrations at Kuskovo *(see pp142–3)*.
International Music Assemblies Festival, mid-June. Russian music through eight centuries performed at concert halls and art galleries.

Relaxing on a summer's day at an outdoor café in Arbat

JULY

US Independence Day, 4 July. A big celebration takes place, enjoyed by Moscow's huge American community and pro-Western Muscovites at the Kuskovo estate.
Navy Day *(Den voenno-morskovo flota)*, first Sunday after 22 July. Spectacular fireworks are accompanied by costumed celebrations across the city. Since Moscow is not a port city, celebrations are not on as lavish a scale as those held in St Petersburg.
Moscow International Film Festival, held every two years (in odd-numbered years) in July or August *(see p193)*. A glamorous event attended by both celebrities and the general public, and featuring the latest releases from all over the world.

AUGUST

Summer Music Festival, throughout Aug. Evening recitals of classical music featuring distinguished graduates of the Moscow Conservatory.
Moscow Annual Airshow, end of Aug, in the town of Zhukovskiy, south-east of Moscow. A chance to see famous Russian aeroplanes.
Russian Cinema Day, 27 Aug. Showings of favourite, mostly Russian, films on television and in cinemas all over the city.

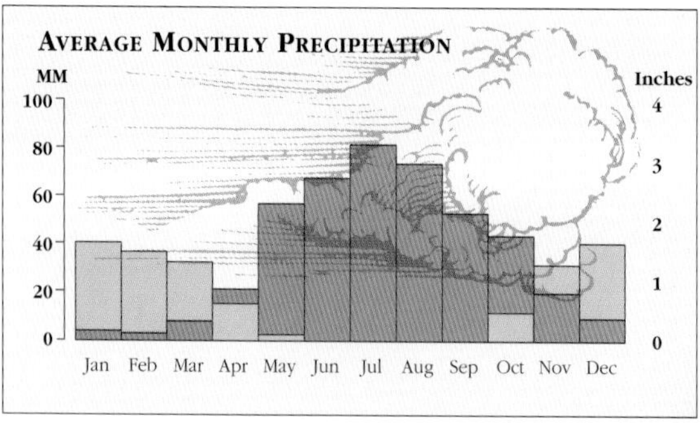

Precipitation Chart
In the winter months, precipitation falls mainly as snow, most of which settles until the spring, reaching a depth of 35 cm (14 in). In summer, even hot days are often interrupted by brief, but heavy, rain showers.

AUTUMN

CITY LIFE begins to pick up as people return from the country and prepare their children for school. In the last weeks of August, Moscow is filled with posters noting the advent of the school year and shops are packed with parents buying new school clothes and books. Theatres open again in September, with premieres of plays and operas.

The crisp autumn weather is perfect for mushroom gathering. Muscovites often head out early in the morning to the forests around the city to hunt for white (the favourite) and brown mushrooms, orange-cap bolens, chanterelles and oyster mushrooms. However, dangerously poisonous as well as edible mushrooms abound and gathering them is best left to the experts.

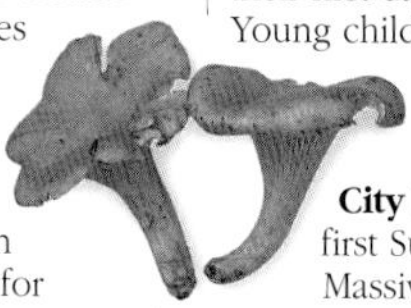

Chanterelle mushrooms

Other popular autumnal pastimes include horse riding at the Hippodrome *(see p194)* and taking a boat trip along the Moskva river.

SEPTEMBER

New Academic Year *(Novyy uchebnyy god)*, 1 Sep. Moscow is full of children heading for their first day back at school. Young children, especially those going for the first time, take flowers with them.

City Day *(Den goroda)*, first Sunday in Sep. Massive costumed celebrations, concerts and theatrical performances are held all over the city to celebrate the founding of Moscow in 1147 *(see p17)*.

OCTOBER

Talents of Russia *(Talanty Rossii)*, 1–10 Oct. Festival of classical music, with musicians from all over the country.

Children with flowers for teachers at the start of the new school year

Punk Festival, early Oct. Russian bands play in Gorky Park and at other venues.

NOVEMBER

Students of the Moscow ballet schools give the first of their annual winter performances at various venues. This is the worst month to visit as Moscow is dirty and slushy.

Day of Reconciliation *(Den primireniya)*, 7 Nov. Previously called the Day of the Great October Socialist Revolution. Now celebrated mainly by the Communist Party.

Open-air folk dancing at Moscow's City Day celebrations

PUBLIC HOLIDAYS

New Year's Day (1 Jan)
Russian Orthodox Christmas (7 Jan)
International Women's Day (8 Mar)
Easter Sunday (Mar/Apr/May)
Labour Day (1 May)
Victory Day (9 May)
Independence Day (12 Jun)
Day of Reconciliation (7 Nov)
Constitution Day (12 Dec)

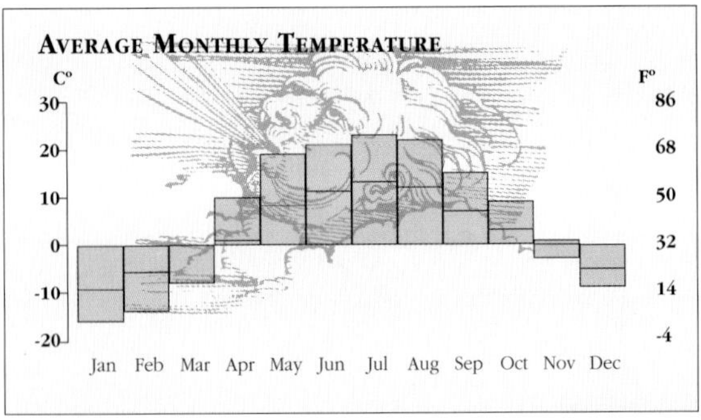

Temperature Chart
The chart shows the average minimum and maximum temperatures for each month. Winter temperatures well below freezing may seem daunting, and do limit the length of time it is possible to stay out, but the cold is dry and can be exhilarating and there is very little wind.

WINTER

As the ice thickens and the snow deepens, people head outdoors. Gorky *(see p129)*, Sokolniki and Luzhniki parks become the venues for ice-skating and skiing. The hardened locals, the so-called "walruses", break the ice at Serebryaniy Bor on the western outskirts of Moscow to take a dip early every morning.

In the midst of winter sports come New Year and Christmas. New Year is the big holiday, while Christmas is celebrated on 7 January, in accordance with the Orthodox calendar. Many people also still celebrate Old New Year which falls a week later on 14 January.

One great pleasure of this season is the Christmas ballet, *The Nutcracker*, performed at the Bolshoy Theatre *(see pp90–91)* largely by children.

DECEMBER

Constitution Day *(Den konstitutsii)*, 12 Dec. Fireworks are set off at 10pm to mark President Yeltsin's constitution.
New Year's Eve *(Novyy god)*, 31 Dec. Still the biggest holiday of the year, New Year's Eve is celebrated with the local *shampanskoe (see p179)*. This is a family celebration: at circuses and balls, actors dress up as the traditional bringers of presents, the Snow Maiden and Grandfather Frost.
Svyatoslav Richter December Nights *(Dekabrskie vechera imeni Svyatoslava Rikhtera)*, throughout Dec. Classical music dedicated to the Russian pianist at the Pushkin Museum of Fine Arts *(see pp78–81)*.
Russian Winter *(Russkaya zima)*, end Dec–mid Jan. Classical music festival.

An ice sculpture of an octopus, part of the festival in Gorky Park

JANUARY

Russian Orthodox Christmas *(Rozhdestvo)*, 7 Jan. Christmas is celebrated in a quieter fashion than Easter, with a traditional visit to an evening service on Christmas eve, when bells ring out through the frosty air from all over Moscow. Children's celebrations are held at various venues, including the Great Kremlin Palace *(see p63)*. The parties are called *Yolka* (Christmas tree).
Christmas Premier Festival, end Dec–mid Jan. Annual classical music festival.
Christmas in Moscow, first two weeks in Jan. Festival of medieval and classical music.
Ice Sculpture Festival in Gorky Park. This festival lasts for several months, but it is never possible to tell exactly when it will start. It depends entirely on the weather and some years can start as early as December. During the festival Gorky Park is taken over by numerous ice sculptures, usually of fairy-tale characters, which remain in the park until the thaw.
Tatyana's Day *(Tatyanin den)*, 25 Jan. St Tatyana's feast day is largely a holiday for students rather than a religious holiday, since the decree founding Moscow University *(see p94)* was signed on this day in 1755

Fisherman fishing through a hole in the ice

Street entertainer

FEBRUARY

International Festival of the Orthodox Church, throughout Feb. The music and cultural heritage of the Orthodox Church is celebrated in various city venues.
Valentine's Day *(Den svyatovo Valentina)*, 14 Feb. A recent addition to Moscow's calendar, although it is not as popular as it is in the West.
Defenders of the Motherland Day *(Den zashchitnikov rodiny)*, 23 Feb. Low-key male version of Women's Day. Elderly veterans, and men generally, receive presents.

Moscow at a Glance

More than 100 places of interest are described in the *Area by Area* section of this book. These range from the historic treasures of State and Church, enclosed within the Kremlin walls, to galleries housing incomparable religious icons among spectacular collections of Russian and Western art. The city's liveliest streets and most beautiful parks, which offer different attractions in winter and summer, are also included. To help make the most of a visit, the next 12 pages offer a guide to the very best that Moscow has to offer. Museums and architecture each have their own section, and there is a special feature on Moscow's grandiose metro stations. The sights mentioned here are cross-referenced to their own full entries for ease of use. Below is a selection of the top sights that no visitor should miss.

Moscow Top Ten Attractions

Bolshoy Theatre
See pp90–91.

St Basil's Cathedral
See pp108–9.

Tretyakov Gallery
See pp118–21.

Kolomenskoe
See pp138–9.

Red Square
See p106.

Lenin Mausoleum
See p107.

Kremlin Sights

State Armoury
See pp64–5.

Cathedral of the Assumption
See pp58–9.

Pushkin Museum of Fine Arts
See pp78–81.

Kuskovo
See pp142–3.

◁ **The Ivan the Great Bell Tower, with the huge Tsar Bell in front of it and the Assumption Belfry to the right**

Moscow's Best: Metro Stations

NOT MANY OF THE WORLD'S underground railways can claim to be tourist attractions and artistic monuments in their own right. The Moscow metro is an exception. Its station platforms and concourses resemble miniature palaces with chandeliers, sculptures and lavish mosaics. Moreover, this is one of the busiest and most efficient metro networks in the world. Some of the finest stations are shown here and further information can be found on pp40–41. Practical details about using the metro are given on pp214–16.

Belorusskaya
Named after the nearby Belorusskiy railway station, Belorusskaya has a central hall with mosaics of rural scenes and a tiled floor based on a traditional pattern from a Belorussian rug.

Mayakovskaya
A bust of poet Vladimir Mayakovsky stands in this station, which is named in his honour. Recesses in the ceiling contain a series of mosaics depicting planes and sporting scenes.

Kievskaya
Large, ostentatious mosaics decorate the walls of this station. They include idealized scenes representing Russia's friendship with the Ukraine and pictures of Soviet agriculture.

Kropotkinskaya
Clean lines and simple colours distinguish this elegant station, designed by Aleksey Dushkin in the 1930s. It is named after the anarchist, Prince Pyotr Kropotkin.

Park Kultury
Niches in the walls of this station's central hall hold white, marble bas-relief medallions. These show people involved in various recreational activities such as ice-skating, reading, playing chess and dancing.

Teatralnaya
The differing cultures of the republics of the former Soviet Union provide the theme for this station. The ceiling panels depict some of their national costumes.

Komsomolskaya
This is the main entrance to Komsomolskaya station, named in honour of the Communist Youth League (Komsomol) which helped to construct the metro.

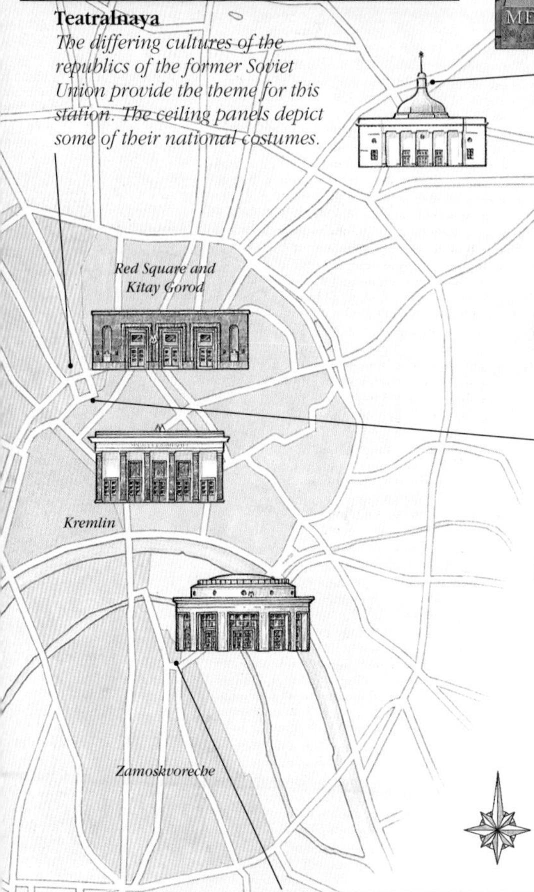

Ploshchad Revolyutsii
The main hall of this station contains lifesize bronze statues of ordinary citizens, such as a farmer, who helped to build the Soviet State.

Novokuznetskaya
A bas-relief frieze runs along the central hall of this station, which was constructed in 1943. The frieze shows a variety of Russian military heroes, such as World War II soldiers.

Exploring the Moscow Metro

Bas-relief at Park Kultury

When the idea of an underground railway was first proposed for Moscow in 1902 the idea was rejected by one local newspaper as "a staggeringly impudent encroachment on everything Russian people hold dear in the city of Moscow". By the 1930s, however, the need for better transportation had become urgent as the population of the city more than doubled to meet the demands of rapid industrialization. Two prominent young Communists, Nikita Khrushchev and Lazar Kaganovich, were entrusted with building a metro that would serve as a showcase for socialism and the achievements of workers and peasants.

Members of the Communist Youth League helping to build the metro

Building the Metro

Construction work on the metro began in December 1931, during the period of Stalin's first Five Year Plan of 1928–33. The Communist Party decreed that "the whole country will build the metro", so workers – both men and women – were drafted in from all over the Soviet Union. They were assisted by soldiers of the Red Army and by over 13,000 members of the Communist Youth League (Komsomol).

The latter worked as volunteers in their free time and their massive contribution was commemorated by naming **Komsomolskaya** after them. The materials, too, came from different parts of the country: rails from the steelworks of Kuznetsk, marble from the Urals and Caucasus and granite from Karelia and the Ukraine.

Work was completed on the first 11.6-km (7.2-mile) section of track, linking Sokolniki with **Park Kultury**, in February 1935 and the first 13 stations were opened in May. Many of those who had worked on the project were subsequently rewarded with medals, including the much-coveted Order of Lenin. Construction work continued rapidly and by 1939 there were 22 stations serving over one million passengers.

Metro Decoration

Some of the Soviet Union's finest artists were employed to decorate the metro. Working within the confines of Socialist Realism *(see p135)*, many dealt with themes such as the Revolution, national defence and the Soviet way of life.

The earliest metro stations are generally regarded as the most architecturally successful. **Mayakovskaya**, designed by Aleksey Dushkin in 1938, won the Grand Prix at the New York World's Fair. Its spacious halls are supported by columns of stainless steel and marble. **Kropotkinskaya** (1935) and **Ploshchad Revolyutsii** (1938) are also by Dushkin. The main hall of the latter has a series of marble-lined arches. On either side of each stands a life-sized bronze figure cast by sculptor Matvey Manizer. Red Guards, workers, sailors, sportsmen and women, a Young Pioneer and a mother and child are among the "everyday heroes" who made the Revolution possible or helped to build the subsequent Soviet State.

Several stations, including **Komsomolskaya**, consist of two or more linked sections on different metro lines. One of Komsomolskaya's two sections, on the Kirovo-Frunzenskaya line, was built in 1935. Its decor is relatively restrained, with rose-coloured marble pillars and majolica panels by Yevgeniy Lanseray showing heroic metro workers. The other station, on the circle line, was completed 17 years later and is much more ostentatious, with florid stucco mouldings and glittering chandeliers. Designed by leading architect Aleksey Shchusev it was also a prizewinner at the New York

The simple, yet stylish, Mayakovskaya, designed by Aleksey Dushkin

Metro Statistics

The Moscow metro is still expanding, but there are already 165 stations and approximately 265 km (155 miles) of track. Over 9,300 trains operate every day, travelling at speeds of up to 90 km/h (56 mph). The Moscow metro carries 8–9 million passengers per day, more than the London and New York systems combined. During peak periods trains arrive at stations every 1–2 minutes.

World's Fair. The gold mosaics showing military parades and figures from Russian history are the work of artist Pavel Korin.

Martial themes predominated during and after World War II. At **Novokuznetskaya** (1943), for example, architects Vladimir Gelfreikh and Igor Rozhin commissioned a bas-relief frieze from Nikolay Tomskiy showing Russian military heroes as diverse as Minin and Pozharskiy *(see p108)* and Field Marshal Kutuzov *(see p152)*.

The decor of the metro was intended to inspire people, and many of the stations built in the 1940s and 1950s extol the virtues of the Soviet regime. Ceramic panels at **Teatralnaya** (1940) celebrate the arts of the former Soviet Republics, while mosaics at **Belorusskaya** (1952) and **Kievskaya** (1937 and 1954) show healthy, contented peasants celebrating agricultural abundance. These ignore the terrible famine resulting from Stalin's forced collectivization policy of the early 1930s.

In the Soviet mind, athletic prowess was the natural preparation for heroic achievement. Sport and recreation are the twin themes of the bas-reliefs by artist Sergey Rabinovich at **Park Kultury** (1935 and 1949).

Even the station exteriors above ground were designed to work as propaganda. Seen from above, the entrance to **Arbatskaya** (1935) is in the shape of the Soviet red star.

Although financial constraints now impose limits on artists and architects working on the metro, artistic leeway has still been possible in the design of some of the newer stations such as **Chekhovskaya**, built in 1987.

Part of Komsomolskaya, designed by architect Aleksey Shchusev

Revolutionary figures at Belorusskaya

The Metro and War

THE EARLY METRO lines were laid deep underground so that they could be used as bomb shelters in times of war. By November 1941 German troops had reached the outskirts of Moscow and the Soviet Union was fighting for survival. **Mayakovskaya**, completed just three years earlier, became the headquarters of the Anti-Aircraft Defence Forces. It was in the station's spacious central hall that Stalin addressed generals and party activists the evening before the Red Army marched off to the front.

Kirovskaya (now known as **Chistye Prudy**) was the headquarters of the General Staff throughout World War II. It was here that Stalin and his advisors planned the first offensives against the Nazis.

Consequently, the metro system became an important symbol of resistance to the Nazi invasion. In fact, its propaganda value was deemed so great that the designs for the mosaics at **Novokuznetskaya** were evacuated from St Petersburg when their creator, Viktor Frolov, died there during the prolonged siege of 1941–4.

The entrance to Arbatskaya, in the shape of the Soviet red star

Metro Museum

THE HISTORY and workings of the Moscow metro are fully explained in this interesting museum, located above the main hall of Sportivnaya in Sparrow Hills *(see p129)*. Some rather dated photomontages show the construction of the track and stations. There are displays of equipment, including signalling points and ticket barriers, models of trains and escalators, a reconstruction of a driver's cabin and the first ticket, sold in 1935.

Moscow Metro Museum
Sportivnaya metro. Tel. *222 7309.*
Open *9am–3:30pm Tue–Fri, 11am–5:30pm Mon.* Guided tours *(book in advance).*

Where to See the Metro

Arbatskaya **Map** 6 E1
Belorusskaya **Map** 1 C2
Chekhovskaya **Map** 2 F4
Chistye Prudy **Map** 3 C4
Kievskaya **Map** 5 B2
Komsomolskaya **Map** 4 D2
Kropotkinskaya **Map** 6 E2
Mayakovskaya **Map** 2 E3
Novokuznetskaya **Map** 7 B3
Park Kultury **Map** 6 D4 & 6 E3
Ploshchad Revolyutsii **Map** 3 A5
Teatralnaya **Map** 3 A5

Moscow's Best: Architecture

Visitors to Moscow are often pleasantly surprised by the wealth and variety of architecture the city has to offer. As well as magnificent palaces and cathedrals, such as those in the Kremlin, there are also smaller churches and chapels, homely boyars' residences, imposing Neo-Classical mansions and some beautiful municipal buildings. A stark contrast to this older architecture is provided by early 20th-century Constructivist buildings and Communist landmarks such as Stalinist-Gothic skyscrapers. For further information about architecture see pp44–5.

Moscow Old University
The colonnade of pillars along the front of this building and its ochre and white colouring are typical Neo-Classical features.

Gorky House-Museum
Stunning stained-glass windows grace the Gorky House-Museum, a Style-Moderne masterpiece built by Fyodor Shekhtel in 1900.

Cathedral of the Assumption
A miraculous fusion of Renaissance and Early-Russian styles, this superb cathedral was built in 1475–9 to a design by Italian architect Aristotele Fioravanti.

Foreign Ministry
This is one of seven skyscrapers designed in a hybrid style often referred to as Stalinist Gothic. The Foreign Ministry building was finished in 1952 shortly before Stalin's death.

Pashkov House
The colonnaded porch of the Neo-Classical Pashkov House has a low, wide pediment with relief sculptures.

Polytechnical Museum
The central part of the Polytechnical Museum, built in 1877, is the work of Ippolit Monighetti. It is an outstanding example of Russian Revival, a style that draws heavily on the architecture of Russia's past.

St Basil's Cathedral
Pointed roofs over the entrance steps and tiers of arched gables typify the stunning architectural diversity of this cathedral, built in 1555–61 for Ivan the Terrible.

Old English Court
Presented to an English trade delegation in 1556, this 16th-century, whitewashed, stone house has a wooden roof and few windows.

0 metres 600

0 yards 600

Church of the Resurrection in Kadashi
This Moscow-Baroque church has tiers of ornate limestone carvings in place of the kokoshniki *gables normally seen on Early-Russian churches. The church's onion domes are a traditional feature, but they are an unusual jade green colour.*

Exploring Moscow Architecture

Part of a floral fresco in St Basil's Cathedral

RUSSIAN ARCHITECTURE has always been innovative. The medieval Novgorod, Yaroslavl and Pskov schools of architecture developed several of the distinctive features found on Moscow's churches. These included the onion dome, rounded *zakomary* gables and *kokoshniki* gables, which are semi-circular or shaped like the cross-section of an onion. In later centuries Moscow's architects became increasingly influential, developing new styles, such as Constructivism, and giving a Russian flavour to others.

Study in the Palace of the Romanov Boyars

EARLY RUSSIAN

MOSCOW'S EARLIEST buildings were constructed entirely from wood. From around the 14th century, stone and brick began to be used for important buildings, but wood continued to be the main building material until the great fire of 1812 *(see p24)* when much of the city was burnt to the ground.

The majority of Moscow's oldest surviving buildings are churches. One of the earliest is the Cathedral of the Saviour in the **Monastery of the Saviour and Andronicus** *(see p140)*.

In the 15th and 16th centuries the tsars employed a succession of Italian architects to construct prestigious buildings in the Kremlin. They combined the Early-Russian style with Italian Renaissance features to create magnificent buildings such as the **Cathedral of the Assumption** *(see pp58–9)*.

Another 16th-century innovation was the spire-like tent roof, used, for example, on **St Basil's Cathedral** *(see pp108–9)*. In the mid-17th century Patriarch Nikon banned its use, insisting that plans for new churches must be based on ancient Byzantine designs.

The majority of Moscow's early secular buildings have not survived. The few exceptions include the ornate 16th-century **Palace of the Romanov Boyars** *(see pp102–3)* and the charming early 16th-century **Old English Court** *(see p102)*.

THE NEW PATRIOTISM

The reconstruction of the city's pre-Revolutionary buildings, including the **Kazan Cathedral** *(see p105)* and the **Cathedral of Christ the Redeemer** *(see p74)*, is evidence of a growing nostalgia for Russia's past, and a renewed interest in the nation's architectural heritage. The revival of the Orthodox Church, in particular, has led to the restoration of hundreds of churches across Moscow.

The Cathedral of Christ the Redeemer, rebuilt in 1994–7

The Baroque Gate Church of the Intercession at Novodevichiy

BAROQUE

THE BRIDGE TOWER (1670s) at **Izmaylovo Park** *(see p141)* is an early example of Moscow Baroque. Its filigree limestone trimmings and pilaster decoration, set against a background of red brick, are typical of the style. The gate churches in the **Novodevichiy Convent** *(see pp130–31)*, the buildings of the **Krutitskoe Mission** *(see p140)* and the spectacular **Church of the Resurrection in Kadashi** *(see p122)*, with its limestone ornamentation carved to resemble lace, are also fine examples of this style of architecture.

A number of Baroque buildings, including the **Church of the Intercession in Fili** *(see p128)*, were built with money from the wealthy and powerful Naryshkin family. This has led to Moscow Baroque also being known as Naryshkin Baroque.

NEO-CLASSICAL

THE ACCESSION of Catherine the Great in 1762 heralded a new direction for Russian architecture. She favoured the Neo-Classical style, which drew on simple geometric shapes from the architecture of ancient Greece and Rome. This style has been used to great effect in the remarkable **Pashkov House** *(see p75)*, thought to have been designed by Vasiliy Bazhenov in 1784.

Bazhenov's assistant, the prolific Matvey Kazakov, demonstrated the flexibility of Neo-Classicism in his designs for a wide range of buildings, including churches, hospitals, the **Moscow Old University** *(see p94)* and the **House of Unions** *(see pp88–9)*. He is best known for the **Senate** *(see pp66–7)* in the Kremlin.

The huge fire that followed Napoleon's brief occupation of the city in 1812 led to a wholesale reconstruction. Moscow's nobility built new homes along **ulitsa Prechistenka** *(see p74)* in the newly fashionable Empire style. Leading architects of this more decorative style included Afanasiy Grigorev and Osip Bove, who designed **Theatre Square** *(see p88)*.

A Neo-Classical bas-relief in the House of Unions, built in the 1780s

Historicism and Style Moderne

Historicism replaced Neo-Classicism in the mid-19th century. It arose from a desire to create a national style by reviving architectural styles from the past. The **Great Kremlin Palace** *(see p63)* and **State Armoury** *(see pp64–5)*, both designed by Konstantin Ton around 1840, are typical. They combine various styles including Renaissance, Classical and Baroque. Ton also designed the extravagant Byzantine-style

The House of Friendship, a wonderful example of Eclecticism

Cathedral of Christ the Redeemer *(see p74)*, finished in 1883 and rebuilt in 1994–7.

Eclecticism combined past and present architectural styles from all over the world to create fantastical buildings such as the **House of Friendship** *(see p95)*, which was designed by Vladimir Mazyrin in 1898.

Traditional wooden architecture and folk art were rich sources of inspiration for the architects that formulated the Russian-Revival style. The flamboyant **Historical Museum** *(see p106)* and **Polytechnical Museum** *(see p110)* are fine examples of the genre. However, the finest, and most functional, is **GUM** *(see p107)* designed by Aleksandr Pomerantsev.

Mosaic of irises from the frieze around the Gorky House-Museum

Style Moderne was a radical new architectural style akin to Art Nouveau. One of the earliest examples is the **Hotel Metropol** *(see p88)*, designed in 1899 by Englishman William Walcot. The greatest advocate of Style Moderne was Fyodor Shekhtel. The mansion he built for Stepan Ryabushinskiy is now the **Gorky House-Museum** *(see p95)*. It is highly unconventional and uses mosaic friezes, glazed brick and stained glass to stunning effect.

The Style-Moderne Gorky House-Museum

Architecture after the Revolution

Constructivism was a novel attempt to combine form and function, and was the most popular style to emerge in the decade after the Revolution. The offices of the newspaper **Izvestiya**, on Pushkin Square *(see p97)*, were designed by Grigoriy Barkhin in 1927. His use of glass and reinforced concrete to create geometrical designs is typical of the Constructivist style. Another leading Constructivist was Konstantin Melnikov. The unique **Melnikov House** *(see p72)*, which consists of two interlocking cylinders, is the home that he built for himself in 1927.

In the 1930s Stalin formulated a grand plan to rebuild large areas of the city. He favoured a new monumental style and Constructivism went out of vogue. The monumental style is exemplified by Aleksey Shchusev's grandiose "proletarian" apartments at the lower end of Tverskaya ulitsa and culminates in Stalinist Gothic. This term is used to describe the seven matching skyscrapers erected at key points in the city in the 1940s and 1950s. The **Foreign Ministry** building *(see p70)*, designed by architects Mikhail Minkus and Vladimir Gelfreikh, is typical of this style, which is often called "wedding-cake" architecture.

Moscow's Best: Museums

Moscow has more than 80 museums offering a fascinating insight into the history and culture of the people of Russia. Some, such as the Tretyakov Gallery and State Armoury, have collections including works by world-famous artists and craftsmen, while others house exhibits of local or specialist interest. Among the most evocative are those commemorating the lives of artists, writers and musicians. The rooms where they lived and worked have been lovingly preserved. For further information on museums see pp48–9.

State Armoury
This elaborate 17th-century enamel work is exhibited in the State Armoury, along with a dazzling array of gold and silverware, jewellery and royal regalia. The current Armoury building was constructed in 1844 on the orders of Tsar Nicholas I.

Shalyapin House-Museum
Portraits of the opera star Fyodor Shalyapin on display in his former home include formal paintings, images of him on stage and drawings by his children.

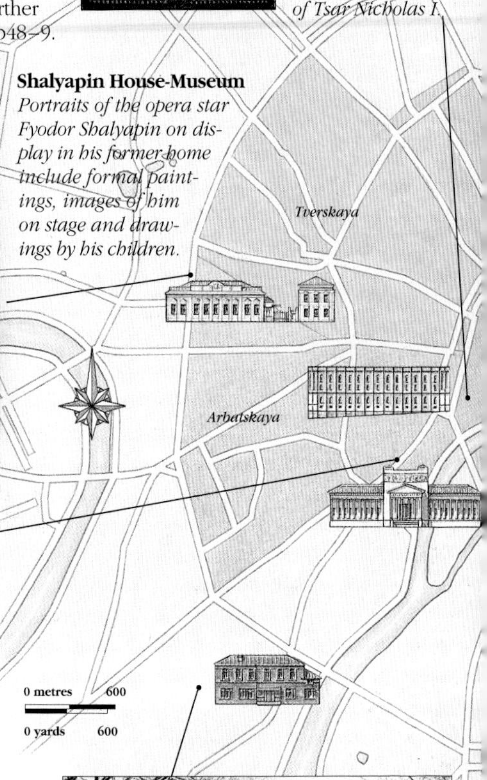

Pushkin Museum of Fine Arts
In addition to a magnificent collection of European art, this gallery houses artifacts from ancient Egypt, Greece and Rome, including this Egyptian funeral mask.

Tolstoy House-Museum
For over 20 years this traditional house was the winter home of Leo Tolstoy, author of the epic novel War and Peace. *It is now an evocative museum which recaptures the daily lives of the writer and his family.*

Lenin Mausoleum
The red and black pyramid of the Lenin Mausoleum was erected in 1930 to a design by architect Aleksey Shchusev. It contains the embalmed body of Vladimir Lenin, the first Soviet leader.

Mayakovsky Museum
This thought-provoking museum commemorates the revolutionary poet, playwright and artist Vladimir Mayakovsky. The abstract exhibits in this room symbolize his childhood in Georgia.

Palace of the Romanov Boyars
The restored interiors and luxurious clothes and possessions in this house effectively evoke the daily lives of the Moscow aristocracy in the 16th and 17th centuries. The house was constructed for boyar Nikita Romanov.

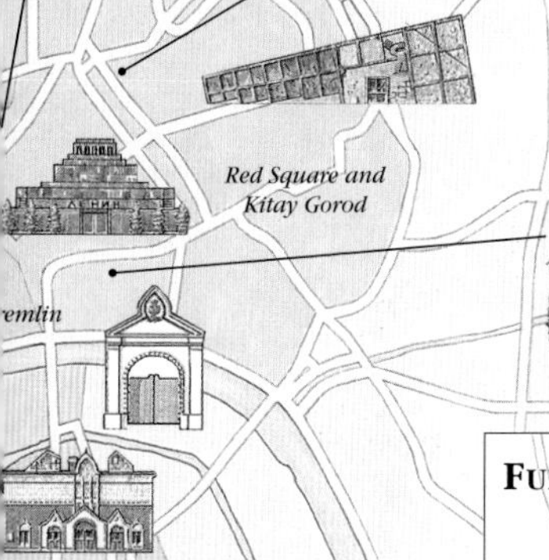

Tretyakov Gallery
Valentin Serov's Girl with Peaches *(1887) in the Tretyakov Gallery is part of the largest collection of Russian art in the world.*

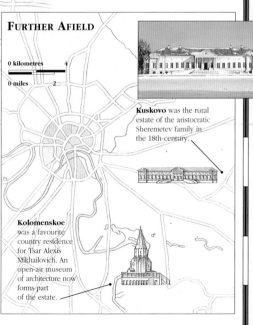

Further Afield

Kuskovo was the rural estate of the aristocratic Sheremetev family in the 18th-century.

Kolomenskoe was a favourite country residence for Tsar Alexis Mikhailovich. An open-air museum of architecture now forms part of the estate.

Exploring Moscow's Museums

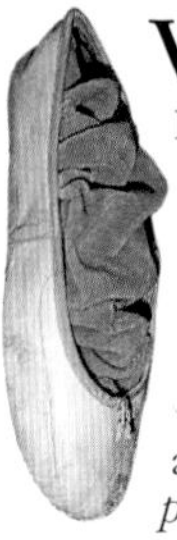

Nijinsky's ballet shoe, Bakhrushin Theatre Museum

WHEREVER VISITORS' INTERESTS LIE, whether it be in painting and the fine arts, science, the Revolution, the history of the Russian theatre or the lives of the nobility, there will be something in Moscow's museums to appeal to them. As well as the many museums in the city, there are a number of country estates in the area around Moscow. Several of these, including Kuskovo and Kolomenskoe, are easily accessible by metro and make good half-day or day excursions *(see p219)*. However, it is worth bearing in mind that a number of museums are currently undergoing much-needed renovation and, in some cases, ideological reassessment.

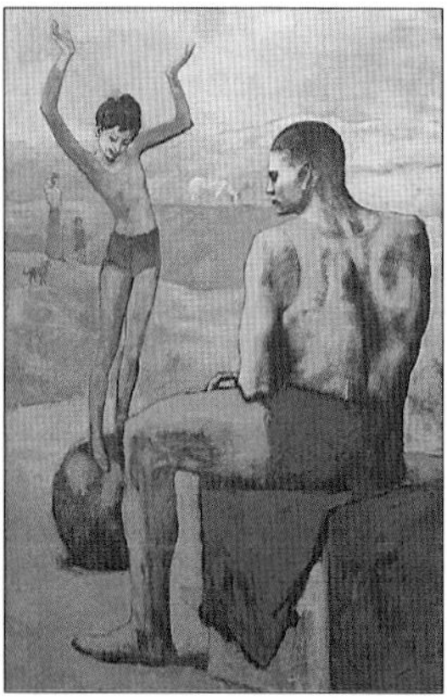

***Young Acrobat on a Ball* by Picasso, in the Pushkin Museum of Fine Arts**

PAINTING AND DECORATIVE ARTS

THE WORLD'S most important collection of Russian art is on display in the recently renovated **Tretyakov Gallery** *(see pp118–21)*. The gallery owns over 100,000 works, but only a fraction of them are on show at any one time. They include amongst others, paintings by most of the group of artists called the Wanderers *(peredvizhniki)*. The gallery's extensive collection of post-Revolution (20th-Century) art is now housed in the **New Tretyakov Gallery** *(see p135)*. The **Tropinin Museum** *(see pp124–5)* has a fine collection of works by the 19th-century portrait artist Vasiliy Tropinin and his contemporaries.

The **Museum of Private Collections** *(see p75)* is a new gallery, housed in a 19th-century building. It exhibits previously unseen drawings, watercolours, sketches and paintings, mainly by Russian artists of the 19th and 20th centuries.

Next door is the **Pushkin Museum of Fine Arts** *(see pp78–81)*, which is particularly known for its collection of works by Impressionist, Post-Impressionist and 20th-century artists. Visitors can also see earlier paintings by artists such as Botticelli, Rembrandt and Rubens, and outstanding artifacts from ancient Egypt donated by the Russian egyptologist Vladimir Golenishchev.

A superb collection of decorative and applied art spanning the last seven centuries or so is housed in the **State Armoury** *(see pp64–5)* in the Kremlin. There are rooms devoted to arms and armour, jewellery, gold and silverware, religious vestments and imperial regalia.

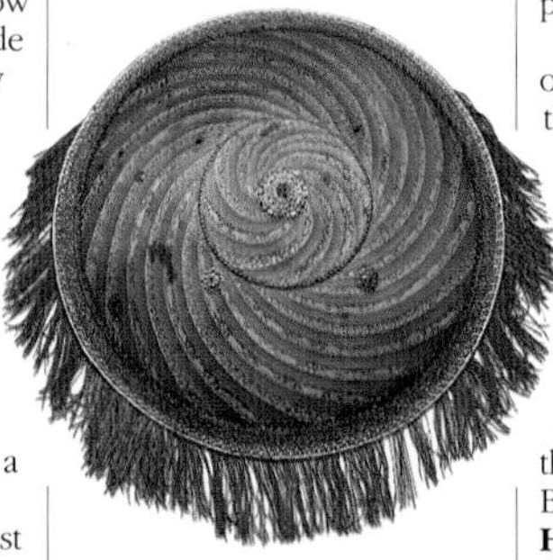

A 16th-century Persian shield on display in the State Armoury

The elegant drawing room of the Lermontov House-Museum

HOUSE-MUSEUMS

THE HOUSES and flats where many important Russian cultural figures lived have been preserved as museums. The sturdy, timber-framed **Tolstoy House-Museum** *(see p134)* contains many personal possessions that belonged to Leo Tolstoy. The novelist and his family spent many winters in the house. Among their regular visitors was the playwright Anton Chekhov. The house where this writer began his career in the 1880s is also open to the public as the **Chekhov House-Museum** *(see p96)*. Across the road from Chekhov's house is the **Shalyapin House-Museum** *(see p83)* where the great opera singer, Fyodor Shalyapin, lived. Visitors can enjoy the beautifully furnished rooms while listening to old recordings of his singing.

The **Stanislavskiy House-Museum** *(see p93)* is the former home of Konstantin Stanislavskiy, theatrical director and the co-founder of the Moscow Arts Theatre *(see p92)*. It contains costumes, props and other memorabilia.

Along with a few items once owned by Alexander Pushkin, the **Pushkin House-Museum** *(see p73)* contains an interesting display of pictures that show what Moscow was like in 1831, when the poet lived here. The **Bely House-Museum** *(see p73)*, in the building next door, was once the home of the Symbolist poet, Andrei Bely. Nearby is the **Skryabin House-Museum** *(see p72)*, the last home of composer Aleksandr Skryabin.

The tower blocks of Novyy Arbat dwarf the **Lermontov House-Museum** *(see pp82–3)*, the simple timber house where Pushkin's contemporary, the poet Mikhail Lermontov, was brought up by his grandmother in the early 1830s.

The extraordinary life of Vladimir Mayakovsky is brilliantly realized in the displays in the **Mayakovsky Museum** *(see p111)*. This flat, near the former KGB building *(see p112)*, is where the Futurist poet lived from 1919–30.

The artist Viktor Vasnetsov designed his own home. In his studio, now the **Vasnetsov House-Museum** *(see p144)*, visitors can see his enormous canvases based on folk tales.

The **Tchaikovsky House-Museum** *(see p153)* at Klin still contains furnishings used by composer Pyotr Tchaikovsky, including the desk where he finished his *Sixth Symphony*.

Country Estates

Several palaces and estates on the outskirts of Moscow are open to the public. **Ostankino Palace** *(see pp144–5)*, built in the 18th century for the fabulously wealthy Sheremetev family, is famous for its exquisite theatre, where serf actors and musicians once took the stage. **Kuskovo** *(see pp142–3)* was also built for the Sheremetevs. In the palace's beautiful gardens is a ceramics museum.

A number of superb 16th- and 17th-century buildings still stand at the former royal estate of **Kolomenskoe** *(see pp138–9)*. Also on the estate is a fascinating museum of wooden architecture.

Picturesque, Gothic-style ruins are all that remain of the palace at **Tsaritsyno** *(see p137)*. This ambitious project, commissioned by Catherine the Great, was never finished.

Works of art by 19th- and 20th-century Russian artists are on show at the **Abramtsevo Estate-Museum** *(see p154)*, formerly an artists' colony.

Sweet wrappers, boxes and scales in the Museum of Modern History

History Museums

A number of museums and other sites in and around the city provide fascinating glimpses into Moscow's past.

The **History of Moscow Museum** *(see p111)* traces the city's history, with earliest exhibits including archaeological finds from around the Kremlin. There is speculation that the museum may be moved.

The life of the boyars *(see p20)* in Moscow in the early 17th century is recreated in the **Palace of the Romanov Boyars** *(see pp102–3)*.

Clay sledge in the History of Moscow Museum

Visitors interested in Napoleon's winter invasion of Russia in 1812 *(see pp23–4)* will want to make the day trip to **Borodino** *(see p152)*. This was the scene of one of the bloodiest encounters of the campaign. There are over 30 monuments around the battlefield and a museum nearby tells the story of the battle. They may also like to visit the **Borodino Panorama Museum** *(see p129)* on Kutuzovskiy prospekt. This circular pavilion contains an enormous painting of the famous battle.

The monumental scale of the **Lenin Mausoleum** *(see p107)*, containing Lenin's embalmed body, gives an insight into the importance of the role played by Lenin *(see pp27–8)* in 20th-century Russian history.

Displays at the **Museum of Modern History** *(see p97)* cover Russian history from 1900 until the collapse of the Soviet Union in 1991. Sweet wrappers depicting Marx and Lenin and home-made grenades are among the exhibits.

The **Museum of the Great Patriotic War** *(see p129)* has dioramas of major battles from World War II, shown largely from a Soviet viewpoint.

Specialist Museums

Among the city's handful of specialist museums is the **Polytechnical Museum** *(see p110)*, which charts important developments in science and technology in Russia.

The **Bakhrushin Theatre Museum** *(see p125)* houses an exciting collection of theatre memorabilia, including ballet shoes worn by Nijinsky, while the **Shchusev Museum of Architecture** *(see p82)* gives a history of Russian architecture.

A model of a reactor from a nuclear power station, one of the displays at the Polytechnical Museum

ТУАЛЕ
100 М

MOSCOW AREA BY AREA

The Kremlin

Citadel of the tsars, headquarters of the Soviet Union and now the residence of the Russian president, for centuries the Kremlin has been a symbol of the power of the State. In 1156, Prince Yuriy Dolgorukiy chose the confluence of the Moskva and Neglinnaya rivers as the site for the first wooden Kremlin (*kreml* means "fortress"). Late in the 15th century, Tsar Ivan III *(see p18)* invited several leading Italian architects to build a sumptuous new complex. They designed the Cathedral of the Assumption and the Faceted Palace, among other buildings, in a fascinating fusion of Early-Russian and imported Renaissance styles *(see pp44)*. The Kremlin did not escape the architectural vandalism of the 1930s, when it was closed and several of its churches and palaces were destroyed on Stalin's orders *(see p75)*. Only in 1955, two years after his death, was the Kremlin partially reopened to the public.

The Tsar's Cannon in the Kremlin

Sights at a Glance

Churches and Cathedrals
Cathedral of the Annunciation 7
Cathedral of the Archangel 6
Cathedral of the Assumption pp58–9 5
Church of the Deposition of the Robe 9

Museums
Patriarch's Palace 3
State Armoury pp64–5 12

Gardens
Alexander Gardens 17

Historic Buildings and Monuments
Arsenal 16
Faceted Palace 8
Great Kremlin Palace 11
Ivan the Great Bell Tower 4
State Kremlin Palace 2
Presidential Administration 14
Saviour's Tower 13
Senate 15
Terem Palace 10
Trinity Tower 1

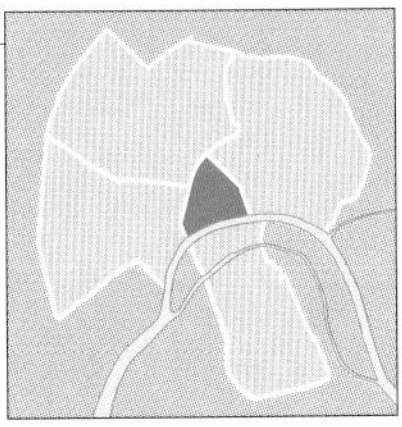

Getting There

Biblioteka imeni Lenina and Borovitskaya metro stations are just outside the walls of the Kremlin, within easy walking distance of the main sights. Trolleybus routes 1, 2, 12, and 33 and buses 6 and K are also useful.

0 metres 200
0 yards 200

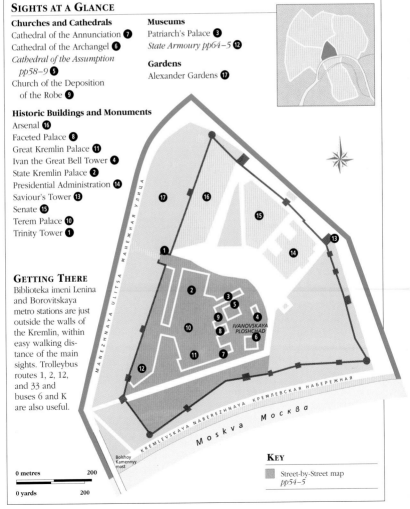

Key
Street-by-Street map *pp54–5*

◁ **The Cathedral of the Annunciation, crowned by golden onion domes, on the Kremlin's main square**

Street by Street: The Kremlin

The Kremlin is home to the Russian president and the seat of his administration. As a result less than half of it is accessible to the public, but highlights including the State Armoury, the Patriarch's Palace and the churches in Cathedral Square are open to visitors. Christians have worshipped on this site for more than eight centuries, but their early stone churches were demolished in the 1470s to make way for the present magnificent ensemble of cathedrals. In imperial times, these were the setting for great state occasions such as coronations, baptisms and burials.

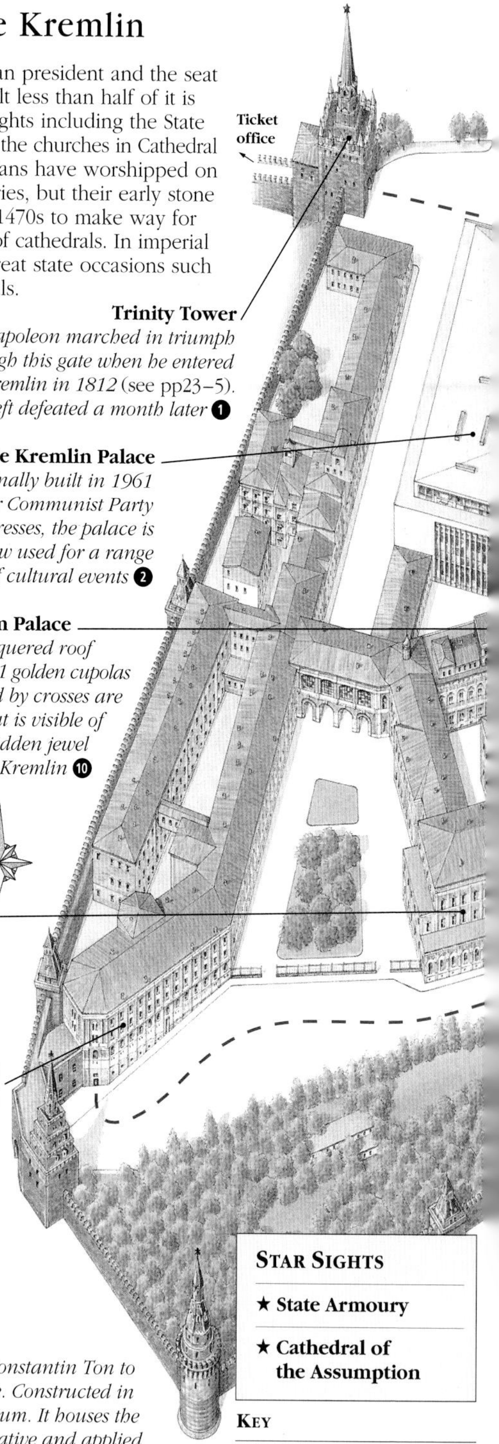

Trinity Tower
Napoleon marched in triumph through this gate when he entered the Kremlin in 1812 (see pp23–5). *He left defeated a month later* ❶

State Kremlin Palace
Originally built in 1961 for Communist Party congresses, the palace is now used for a range of cultural events ❷

Terem Palace
A chequered roof and 11 golden cupolas topped by crosses are all that is visible of this hidden jewel of the Kremlin ❿

Great Kremlin Palace
The palace contains several vast ceremonial halls. The sumptuous stucco work of St George's Hall provides a magnificent backdrop for state receptions. Its marble walls are inscribed with the names of military heroes ⓫

0 metres 50

0 yards 50

★ **State Armoury**
The State Armoury was designed by Konstantin Ton to complement the Great Kremlin Palace. Constructed in 1844–51, this building is now a museum. It houses the stunning imperial collections of decorative and applied art and the priceless State Diamond Fund ⓬

Star Sights

★ **State Armoury**

★ **Cathedral of the Assumption**

Key

— — — Suggested route

Locator Map
See Street Finder, maps 6 & 7

Visitors' Checklist

Map 7 A1 & A2. 921 4720. Biblioteka imeni Lenina, Borovitskaya. 6, K. 1, 2, 12, 33. 10am–5pm Fri–Wed. Tickets sold at the Kremlin entrance and separately at some sights. complex, but not buildings. English (book in advance on 202 4256). www.kremlin.museum.ru

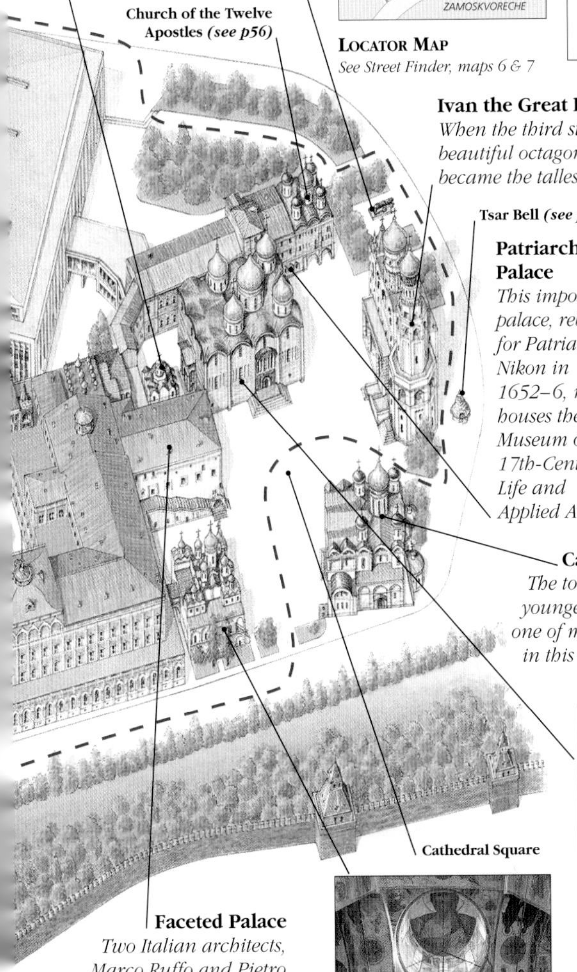

Church of the Deposition of the Robe
This graceful church was the domestic church of the metropolitans and patriarchs ❾

The Tsar Cannon, cast in 1586, weighs a massive 40 tonnes.

Church of the Twelve Apostles ***(see p56)***

Ivan the Great Bell Tower
When the third storey was added to this beautiful octagonal bell tower in 1600, it became the tallest building in Russia ❹

Tsar Bell ***(see p57)***

Patriarch's Palace
This imposing palace, rebuilt for Patriarch Nikon in 1652–6, now houses the Museum of 17th-Century Life and Applied Art ❸

Cathedral of the Archangel
The tomb of Tsarevich Dmitry, the younger son of Ivan the Terrible, is one of many elaborate tombs found in this cathedral. Dmitry died as a child in 1591 (see p19) ❻

Cathedral Square

Faceted Palace
Two Italian architects, Marco Ruffo and Pietro Solario, constructed this striking Renaissance palace between 1485 and 1491 ❽

Cathedral of the Annunciation
Frescoes cover the walls and ceiling of this cathedral. In the dome above the iconostasis is a painting of Christ Pantocrator, above tiers of pictures of angels, prophets and patriarchs ❼

★ Cathedral of the Assumption
This 12th-century painting of St George the Warrior is one of the oldest surviving Russian icons. It forms part of the iconostasis in the cathedral's richly decorated interior ❺

Trinity Tower, with the modern Palace of Congresses on the right

Trinity Tower ❶

Троицкая башня

Troitskaya bashnya

The Kremlin. **Map** 7 A1.

THIS TOWER takes its name from the Trinity Monastery of St Sergius *(see pp156–9)*, which once had a mission nearby. The tower's Trinity Gate used to be the entrance for patriarchs and the tsars' wives and daughters. Today it is one of only two that admit visitors. The other is in the Borovitskaya Tower *(see p66)* to the southwest.

At 76 m (249 ft) high, the seven-storey Trinity Tower is the Kremlin's tallest. It was built in 1495–9 and in 1516 was linked by a bridge over the Neglinnaya river to the Kutafya Tower. The river now runs underground and the Kutafya Tower is the sole survivor of the circle of towers that were originally built to defend the Kremlin walls.

In September 1812 Napoleon triumphantly marched his army into the Kremlin through the Trinity Gate – they left only a month later when the Russians set fire to the city *(see pp24–5)*.

State Kremlin Palace ❷

Ґосуддрственныи Кремлёвский дворєц

Gosudarstvennyy Kremlevskiy dvorets

The Kremlin. **Map** 7 A1. ☐ *for performances only.*

COMMISSIONED BY Russian premier Nikita Khrushchev in 1959 to host Communist Party conferences, the Palace of Congresses is the Kremlin's only modern building. It was completed in 1961 by a team of architects led by Mikhail Posokhin. Roughly 120 m (395 ft) long, the palace was sunk 15 m (49 ft) into the ground so as not to dwarf the surrounding buildings.

Tsarevich Alexis' school book

Until 1991 the 6,000-seat auditorium was the venue for political meetings. Now it is used by the Kremlin Ballet Company *(see p192)* and for staging operas and rock concerts.

Refurbished residence of a boyar in the Patriarch's Palace

Patriarch's Palace ❸

Патриарший дворец

Patriarshiy dvorets

The Kremlin. **Map** 7 A1.
☐ *10am–5pm Fri–Wed.*

THE METROPOLITANS of the Russian Orthodox Church lived on the site of the current Patriarch's Palace for many years. In the 16th century, the patriarchate was created, and the patriarch took over from the metropolitans as the most senior figure in the Russian Church. As a result the bishops of Krutitsy became metropolitans *(see p140)* while the patriarch lived in the Kremlin.

When Nikon became the patriarch in 1652, he felt that the existing residence and the small Church of the Deposition of the Robe *(see pp62–3)* were not grand enough for him. He had the residence extended and renovated to create the Patriarch's Palace, with its integral Church of the Twelve Apostles. Completed in 1656, the work was carried out by a team of master builders led by Ivan Semenov and Aleksey Korolkov.

The palace is now the Museum of 17th-Century Life and Applied Art, which comprises more than 1,000 exhibits drawn from the State Armoury collection *(see pp64–5)* and from churches and monasteries that were destroyed by Stalin in the 1930s *(see p75)*.

Entry to the museum is up a short flight of stairs. The first room houses an exhibition on the history of the palace. In the Gala Antechamber is a dazzling array of 17th-century patriarchs' robes. Some of Nikon's own vestments are on display, including a chasuble *(sakkos)*, a set of beautifully carved staffs and a cowl made from damask and satin, and embroidered with gold thread, gemstones and pearls.

Two rooms in the museum have been refurbished in the style of a 17th-century boyar's apartment. In one of them is a display of old, hand-written books, including Tsarevich Alexis' primer. Each page features one letter of the alphabet and a selection of objects beginning with that letter.

The impressive Chamber of the Cross, to the left of the stairs, has an area of 280 sq m (3,013 sq ft). When this ceremonial hall was built, it was the largest room in Russia without columns supporting its roof. Its ceiling is painted with a delicate tracery of flowers. The room was later used for producing consecrated oil called *miro* for all the churches in Russia, and the silver vats and ornate stove used still stand in the room.

Nikon's rejection of new architectural forms, such as tent roofs, dictated a traditional design for the Church of the Twelve Apostles. Located to the right of the stairs, it houses some brilliant icons, including works by master iconographers such as Semen Ushakov. The iconostasis dates from around 1700. It was brought to the church from the Kremlin Convent of the Ascension prior to its demolition in 1929.

PATRIARCH NIKON

A zealous reformer of the Russian Orthodox Church, Patriarch Nikon was so intent on returning it to its Byzantine roots that he caused his adversaries, the Old Believers, to split from the rest of the Church. Nikon also advocated the supremacy of Church over State, angering Tsar Alexis *(see p19)*. His autocratic style made him unpopular and he retreated to a monastery outside the city. He was deposed in 1667.

Ivan the Great Bell Tower, with the Assumption Belfry and annexe

Ivan the Great Bell Tower ❹

Колокольня Ивана Великого
Kolokolnya Ivana Velikovo

The Kremlin. **Map** 7 A1.

THIS ELEGANT OCTAGONAL bell tower was built in 1505–8 to a design by Marco Bon Friazin. It takes its name from the Church of St Ivan Climacus, which stood on the site in the 14th century. The bell tower is called "the Great" because of its height. In 1600 it became the tallest building in Moscow when Tsar Boris Godunov had a third storey added to extend it to 81 m (266 ft).

The four-storey Assumption Belfry, with its single gilded dome, was built beside the bell tower by Petrok Maliy in 1532–43. It holds 21 bells, the largest of which, the 64-tonne Assumption Bell, traditionally tolled three times when the tsar died. A small museum on the first floor houses changing displays about the Kremlin. The tent-roofed annexe next to the belfry was commissioned by Patriarch Filaret in 1642.

Outside the bell tower is the enormous Tsar Bell. The largest in the world, it weighs over 200 tonnes. Tsar Alexis commissioned the original, which fell from the bell tower and shattered in a fire in 1701. The fragments were used in a second bell ordered by Tsarina Anna. This still lay in its casting pit when the Kremlin caught fire again in 1737. Cold water was poured over the hot bell and a large piece (displayed beside the bell) broke off.

The Tsar Bell, the largest in the world, with the 11-tonne section that broke off

Cathedral of the Assumption ❺

Успенский собор
Uspenskiy sobor

FROM THE EARLY 14TH CENTURY, the Cathedral of the Assumption was the most important church in Moscow. It was here that princes were crowned and the metropolitans and patriarchs of the Orthodox Church were buried. In the 1470s Ivan the Great *(see p18)* decided to build a more imposing cathedral, to reflect the growing might of the nation during his reign. When the first version collapsed possibly in an earthquake, Ivan summoned the Italian architect Aristotele Fioravanti to Moscow. He designed a light and spacious masterpiece in the spirit of the Renaissance.

Scenes from the Life of Metropolitan Peter
Attributed to the great artist Dionysius (see p61)*, this 15th-century icon is located on the cathedral's south wall. It depicts different events in the life of this religious and political leader.*

★ Frescoes
In 1642–4, a team of artists headed by Sidor Pospeev and Ivan and Boris Paisein painted these frescoes. The walls of the cathedral were first gilded to give the look of an illuminated manuscript.

The golden domes stand on towers inset with windows which allow light to flood into the interior of the cathedral.

Orthodox cross

Metropolitans' and patriarchs' tombs line the walls of the nave and the crypt. Almost all of the leaders of the Russian Orthodox Church are buried in the cathedral.

The Tsarina's Throne (17th–19th centuries) is gilded and has a double-headed eagle crest.

Western door and main entrance

The Tabernacle contains holy relics including the remains of Patriarch Hermogen, who starved to death in 1612 during the Polish invasion *(see p19)*.

STAR FEATURES

- ★ **Frescoes**
- ★ **Iconostasis**

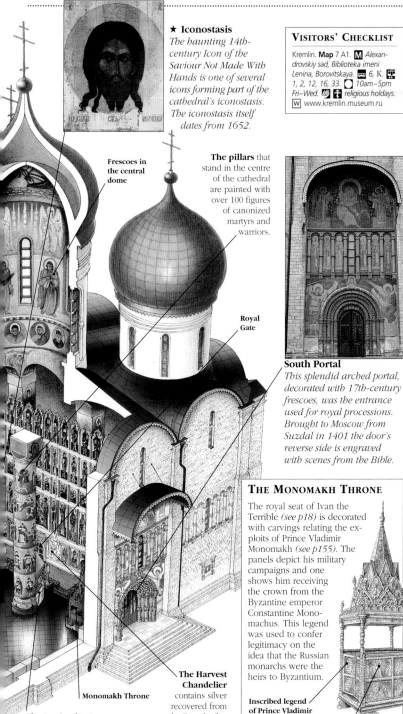

★ Iconostasis
The haunting 14th-century Icon of the Saviour Not Made With Hands is one of several icons forming part of the cathedral's iconostasis. The iconostasis itself dates from 1652.

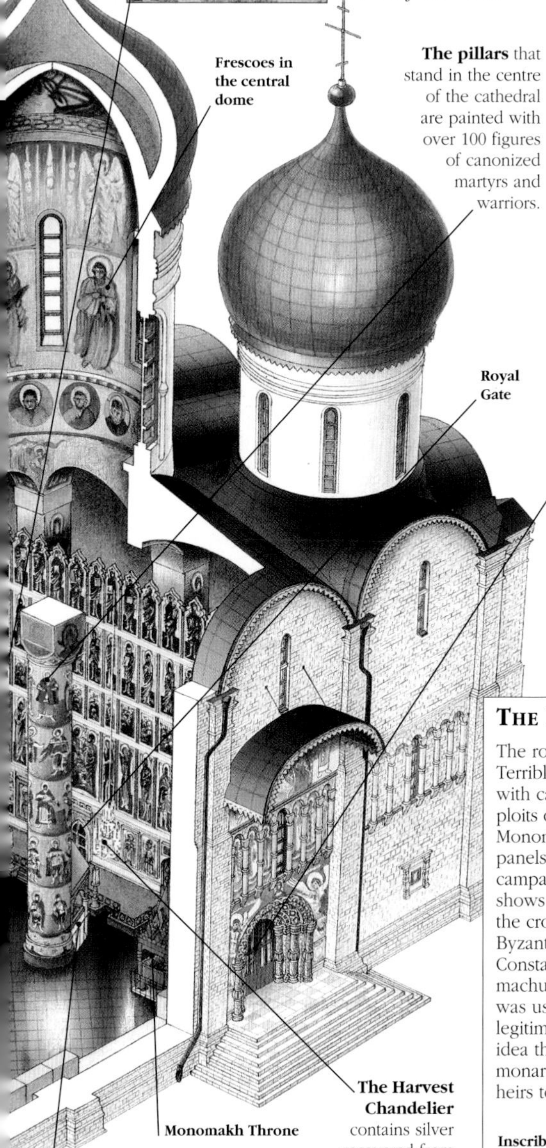

Frescoes in the central dome

The pillars that stand in the centre of the cathedral are painted with over 100 figures of canonized martyrs and warriors.

Royal Gate

Monomakh Throne

The Patriarch's Seat was carved from white stone in 1653 for use by the head of the Russian Orthodox Church.

The Harvest Chandelier contains silver recovered from the French after their occupation of the city in 1812 *(see pp23–5)*.

Visitors' Checklist

Kremlin. **Map** 7 A1. M *Alexandrovskiy sad, Biblioteka imeni Lenina, Borovitskaya.* 6, K. 1, 2, 12, 16, 33. 10am–5pm Fri–Wed. *religious holdays.* W www.kremlin.museum.ru

South Portal
This splendid arched portal, decorated with 17th-century frescoes, was the entrance used for royal processions. Brought to Moscow from Suzdal in 1401 the door's reverse side is engraved with scenes from the Bible.

The Monomakh Throne

The royal seat of Ivan the Terrible *(see p18)* is decorated with carvings relating the exploits of Prince Vladimir Monomakh *(see p155)*. The panels depict his military campaigns and one shows him receiving the crown from the Byzantine emperor Constantine Monomachus. This legend was used to confer legitimacy on the idea that the Russian monarchs were the heirs to Byzantium.

Inscribed legend of Prince Vladimir

Panels depicting scenes from Vladimir's life

Cathedral of the Archangel ❻

Архангельский собор

Arkhangelskiy sobor

The Kremlin. **Map** 7 A2.

THIS WAS the last of the great cathedrals in the Kremlin to be built. It was commissioned by Ivan III in 1505, shortly before his death. Designed by a Venetian architect, Aleviz Novyy, it is a skilful combination of Early-Russian and Italian Renaissance architecture. The most striking of the Italian features is the scallop shell motif underneath the *zakomary* gables *(see p44)*.

This site was the burial place for Moscow's princes and tsars from 1340, first in an earlier cathedral and then in the current building. The tombs of the tsars, white stone sarcophagi with bronze covers inscribed in Old Slavonic, are in the nave. The tomb of Tsarevich Dmitry, the youngest son of Ivan the Terrible *(see p18)*, has a carved, painted canopy above it. The tsars were no longer buried here after the capital city was moved to St Petersburg in 1712. Peter II, who died of smallpox in Moscow in 1730, was the only later ruler to be buried here.

The walls, pillars and domes of the cathedral are covered with superb frescoes painted in 1652–66 by a team of artists led by Semen Ushakov, the head of the icon workshop in the State Armoury *(see pp64–5)*. There are over 60 full-length idealized portraits of Russian rulers, as well as some striking images of the Archangel Michael, traditionally the protector of the rulers of early Moscow.

The fresco in the cathedral's central cupola depicts the threefold nature of God. The Father holds the Son on his lap and the Holy Spirit, in the form of a white dove, hovers between them.

The four-tiered iconostasis was constructed in 1680–81. However, the Icon of the Archangel Michael on the lowest tier dates from the 14th century.

The glorious Cathedral of the Annunciation

Cathedral of the Annunciation ❼

Благовещенский собор

Blagoveshchenskiy sobor

The Kremlin. **Map** 7 A2.

UNLIKE THE OTHER Kremlin cathedrals, which were created by Italians, the ornate Cathedral of the Annunciation is a wholly Russian affair. Commissioned by Ivan III in 1484 as a royal chapel, it stands beside the Faceted Palace *(see p62)*, which is all that remains of a large palace built for Ivan III around the same time. The cathedral, built by architects from Pskov *(see p44)*, originally had three domes and open galleries on all sides but, after a fire in 1547, the corner chapels were added and the galleries were enclosed. On the south façade is the Groznenskiy Porch, added by Ivan the Terrible when he contravened church law by marrying for the fourth time in 1572. Barred from attending religious services, he could only watch through a grille in the porch.

The whole of the interior of the cathedral, including the galleries, is painted with frescoes. The artwork around the iconostasis was painted in 1508 by the monk Feodosius, the son of the icon painter Dionysius who worked on the Cathedral of the Assumption *(see pp58–9)*. The warm colours of the frescoes create an atmosphere of intimacy (this was the tsars' family church). At the same time the vertical thrust of the pillars draws the eye upwards to the cupola and its awe-inspiring painting of Christ Pantocrator (Christ as ruler of the universe).

Three of the greatest masters of icon painting in Russia contributed to the iconostasis, widely considered the finest in Russia. Theophanes the Greek painted the images of Christ, the Virgin and the Archangel Gabriel in the Deesis Tier, while the Icon of the Archangel Michael on this tier is attributed to Andrey Rublev. Several of the icons in the Festival Tier, including *The Annunciation* and *The Nativity* were also painted by Rublev. Most of the other icons in this tier, including the *The Last Supper* and *The Crucifixion* are the work of Prokhor Gorodetskiy.

The fresco in the central cupola of the Cathedral of the Archangel

The Art of Icon Painting in Russia

THE RUSSIAN ORTHODOX church uses icons for both worship and teaching and there are strict rules for creating each image. Icons were thought to be imbued with power from the saint they depicted and were invoked for protection during wars. Because content was more important than style, old revered icons were often repainted. The first icons were brought to Russia from Byzantium. Kiev was Russia's main icon painting centre until the Mongols conquered it in 1240. Influential schools then sprang up in Novgorod and the Vladimir-Suzdal area. The Moscow school was founded in the late 14th century and its greatest period was during the 15th century, when renowned icon-painters such as Andrey Rublev and Dionysius were at work.

Festival Tier icon

The Virgin of Vladimir, *from 12th-century Byzantium, is highly venerated and has had a profound influence on Russian iconography.*

Theophanes the Greek *(c.1340–1405) is thought to have painted this icon of the Assumption (ascent into heaven) of the Virgin Mary. Originally from Byzantium, Theophanes became famous first in Novgorod and then in Moscow. The figures in his icons are renowned for their delicate features and individual expressions.*

Andrey Rublev *became a monk at the Trinity Monastery of St Sergius* (see pp156–9). *Later he moved to a monastery in Moscow. Rublev painted this icon of the Archangel Michael in about 1410. The benevolent appearance of the archangel is typical of Rublev's figures.*

ICONOSTASIS

Separating the sanctuary from the main part of the church, the iconostasis also symbolizes the boundary between the spiritual and temporal worlds. The icons are arranged in tiers (usually four, five or six), each with its own subject matter and significance.

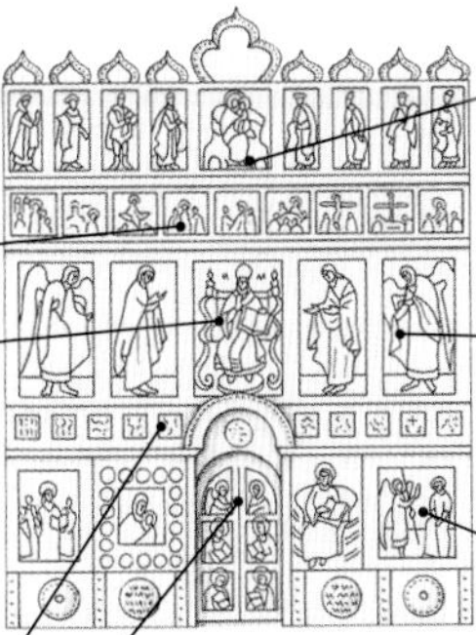

The Festival Tier depicts important feast days and holidays in the Russian Orthodox calendar.

The top tier of the iconostasis depicts patriarchs and prophets of the Old Testament.

Christ Enthroned is always shown at the centre of the Deesis Tier, and is normally flanked by the Virgin Mary and John the Baptist.

The Deesis Tier is the most important in the iconostasis and depicts saints, apostles and archangels.

An additional tier between the Local and Deesis Tiers often depicts the months of the year.

The Royal Gate, at the centre of the Local Tier, is usually decorated with panels showing the four apostles and the Annunciation – when Mary learns she is to bear the Son of God. The gate represents the entrance from the temporal to the spiritual world.

The Local Tier contains icons of saints with a strong link to the church, such as the church's namesake or saints after whom patrons of the church were named.

The enormous vaulted main hall of the Faceted Palace, which was lavishly repainted in the 1880s

Faceted Palace ❽

Грановитая палата

Granovitaya palata

The Kremlin. **Map** 7 A2. ● *to public.*

In the 19th century, the Faceted Palace, along with the Terem Palace, was incorporated into the Great Kremlin Palace. Named after its distinctive stonework façade, the Faceted Palace is all that is left of a larger 15th-century royal palace. It was commissioned by Ivan III *(see p18)* in 1485 and finished six years later. The Faceted Palace is the work of two Italian architects, Marco Ruffo and Pietro Solario.

The first floor of the Faceted Palace consists of the main hall and adjoining Sacred Vestibule. Both are decorated with rich frescoes and gilded carvings. The splendid vaulted main hall has an area of about 500 sq m (5,380 sq ft). It was the throne room and banqueting hall of the tsars and is now used for holding receptions.

On the palace's southern façade is the Red Staircase. The tsars passed down this staircase on their way to the Cathedral of the Assumption for their coronations. The last such procession was at the coronation of Nicholas II in 1896.

In the Streltsy Rebellion of 1682 *(see p22)* several of Peter the Great's relatives were hurled down the Red Staircase onto the pikes of the Streltsy guard.

Demolished by Stalin in the 1930s, the staircase was rebuilt in 1994 at great expense.

The southern façade of the Faceted Palace, with the Red Staircase

Church of the Deposition of the Robe ❾

Церковь Ризположения

Tserkov Rizpolozheniya

The Kremlin. **Map** 7 A1.

Crowned by a single golden dome, this beautiful, but simply designed, church was built as the domestic church of the metropolitans in 1484–6. It was designed by architects from Pskov *(see p44)*.

The church is named after a Byzantine feast day, which celebrates the arrival, in the city of Constantinople, of a robe supposed to have belonged to the Virgin Mary. The robe is believed to have saved the city from invasion several times.

The exterior of the church has distinctive *ogee* arches, which are shaped like the cross-section of an onion and feature on many Russian churches from this period. They are a favourite device of the Pskov school of architecture. Inside the church, the walls and slender columns are covered with 17th-century frescoes by artists including Ivan Borisov, Sidor Pospeev and Semen Abramov. Many depict scenes from the life of the Virgin. Others depict Christ, the prophets, royalty and the Moscow metropolitans.

The impressive iconostasis was created by Nazariy Istomin in 1627. To the left of the royal gate is a splendid image of the Trinity and to its right is the patronal Icon of the Deposition of the Virgin's Robe.

The small, single-domed Church of the Deposition of the Robe

Terem Palace ⓾

Теремной дворец

Teremnoy dvorets

The Kremlin. **Map** 7 A2. ● *to public.*

COMMISSIONED BY Tsar Mikhail Romanov *(see p19)*, the Terem Palace was built next to the Faceted Palace in 1635–7. It was constructed by a team of stonemasons led by Bazhen Ogurtsov. The palace takes its name from the *terem*, a pavilion-like structure with a red and white chequered roof on top of the main building. The interior has small, low-vaulted, simply furnished rooms.

The tsar had five sumptuous rooms situated on the third floor of the palace. The anteroom, where boyars *(see p20)* and foreign dignitaries waited to be received, leads into the council chamber, where the tsar held meetings with boyars.

The ornately decorated anteroom in the Terem Palace

Beyond this are the throne room, the tsar's bedchamber and a small prayer room.

Most of the splendid Terem Palace is not visible from the areas of the Kremlin to which the public have access. The eleven richly decorated onion domes of the four palace churches, at one end of the palace, are all that can be seen.

Great Kremlin Palace ⓫

Большой Кремлёвский дворец

Bolshoy Kremlevskiy dvorets

The Kremlin. **Map** 7 A2. ● *to public.*

THE IMPRESSIVE 125-m (410-ft) façade of this yellow and white palace is best admired from the Kremlin embankment, outside the Kremlin walls. The Great Kremlin Palace was built to replace the 18th-century Kremlin Palace that previously stood on the site but had become dilapidated. In 1837 Tsar Nicholas I commissioned the Great Kremlin Palace as the Moscow residence of the royal family, where they stayed when visiting from St Petersburg, then the capital. Designed by a team of architects led by Konstantin Ton *(see p45)*, it took 12 years to build. Ton's design integrated the Terem and Faceted Palaces with the new palace, creating a single complex. He also rebuilt the State Armoury *(see pp64–5)*.

On the palace's ground floor are the luxurious private rooms of the royal family. The state chambers, on the first floor, include several vast ceremonial halls. The imposing St George's Hall has white walls engraved in gold with the names of those awarded the Order of St George, one of Russia's highest military decorations.

Despite spending massive amounts on the interior, the tsar rarely used the palace. In the 1930s two of the halls were joined to form a huge meeting room for the Supreme Soviet. Now the palace's halls are used to receive foreign dignitaries.

The Great Kremlin Palace viewed from the Kremlin embankment

State Armoury ⓬

Оружейная палата

Oruzheynaya palata

THE COLLECTION OF THE STATE ARMOURY represents the wealth accumulated by Russian princes and tsars over many centuries. The first written mention of a state armoury occurs in 1508, but there were forges in the Kremlin producing weapons and armour as early as the 13th century. Later, gold- and silversmiths, workshops producing icons and embroidery, and the Office of the Royal Stables all moved into the Kremlin. The original armoury was demolished in 1960 to make way for the State Kremlin Palace *(see p56)*. The current State Armoury was built as a museum on the orders of Nicholas I. It was designed by Konstantin Ton *(see p45)* in 1844 and was completed in 1851.

★ Fabergé Eggs

This egg, also a musical box, was made in 1904 in the St Petersburg workshops of the famous House of Fabergé. The egg forms part of a stylized model of the Kremlin.

Carriages and Sledges

This magnificent collection includes the beautiful gilded summer carriage shown here. It was presented to Catherine the Great (see p23) *by Count Orlov. The oldest carriage displayed was a gift from King James I of England to Boris Godunov.*

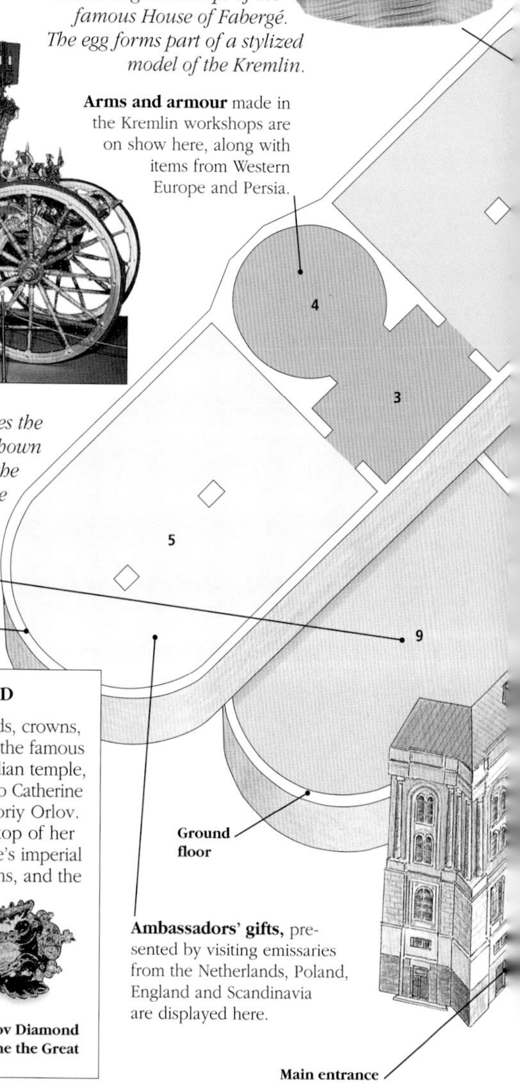

Arms and armour made in the Kremlin workshops are on show here, along with items from Western Europe and Persia.

Ambassadors' gifts, presented by visiting emissaries from the Netherlands, Poland, England and Scandinavia are displayed here.

THE STATE DIAMOND FUND

This dazzling exhibition of diamonds, crowns, jewellery and state regalia includes the famous Orlov Diamond. Taken from an Indian temple, it was one of many presents given to Catherine the Great by her lover Count Grigoriy Orlov. The tsarina had it mounted at the top of her sceptre. Also on show are Catherine's imperial crown, inset with almost 5,000 gems, and the Shah Diamond, which was given to Tsar Nicholas I by Shah Mirza.

The Orlov Diamond on the sceptre of Catherine the Great

★ Crown of Monomakh
Emperor Constantine Monomachus was said to have given this 13th- or 14th-century gold crown to Vladimir Monomakh (see p59). *Decorated with sable and gems, it was used at royal coronations until 1682.*

Visitors' Checklist

The Kremlin. **Map** 7 A2. 921 4720. *Alexandrovskiy sad, Biblioteka imeni Lenina, Borovitskaya.* *admittance at 10am, 12pm, 2:30pm and 4:30pm Fri–Wed.* *English (book in advance: 202 4256).* **State Diamond Fund** *229 2036.* *10am–1pm, 2pm–5pm Fri–Wed.* *English (book in advance).*

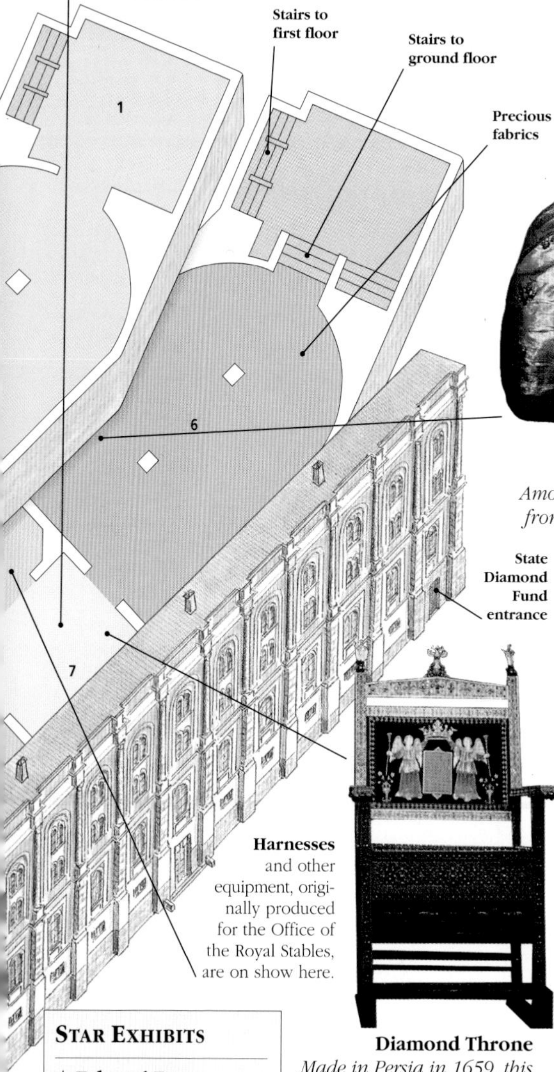

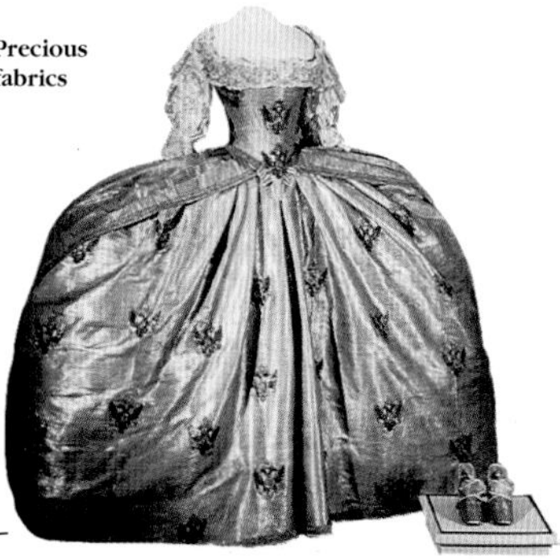

★ Catherine the Great's Coronation Dress
Among the richly decorated clothes from the royal court is an ornate brocade gown embroidered with double-headed eagles in gold thread. It was made in 1762 for Catherine the Great's coronation.

Gallery Guide

The State Armoury's main entrance leads to the ticket office in the basement. Stairs at the far end of the basement lead up to the exhibits. Rooms 1–5 on the first floor contain gold and silverware and arms and armour. Rooms 6–9 downstairs house royal regalia. The State Diamond Fund, a separate museum, is also housed in the State Armoury building.

Harnesses and other equipment, originally produced for the Office of the Royal Stables, are on show here.

Diamond Throne
Made in Persia in 1659, this throne was presented to Tsar Alexis (see p19) *by an Armenian trading company. It is encrusted with 900 diamonds and turquoises and is the most valuable throne in the collection.*

Star Exhibits

- ★ **Fabergé Eggs**
- ★ **Crown of Monomakh**
- ★ **Catherine the Great's Coronation Dress**

Key

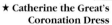

- Russian gold and silver
- Arms and armour
- Works by European craftsmen
- Russian dress and fabrics
- Carriages and harnesses
- State regalia
- Non-exhibition space

Saviour's Tower ⓭

Спасская башня

Spasskaya bashnya

The Kremlin. **Map** 7 B1.

Rising majestically above Red Square to a height of 70 m (230 ft), Saviour's Tower is named after an icon of Christ installed over its gate in 1648. The gate is no longer open to the public, but it used to be the Kremlin's main entrance.

Saviour's Tower, once the main entrance to the Kremlin

Every person using Saviour's Gate, even the tsar, had to indicate respect for the icon by taking his hat off. The icon was removed after the Revolution.

Saviour's Tower was built in two stages. The lower part was designed by Italian architect Pietro Solario in 1491. Bazhen Ogurtsov and Englishman Christopher Galloway added the upper part and tent roof in 1625. Originally the chimes of the clock played the *Preobrazhenskyy March* and *Kol' Slaven Nash Gospod' v Sione*. Now they play the Russian National Anthem.

Presidential Administration ⓮

Администрация Президента

Administraya Presidenta

The Kremlin. **Map** 7 A1. ● *to public.*

Two important religious institutions, the Monastery of the Miracles and the Convent of the Ascension, used to stand here. They were demolished in 1929 to make way for the Presidential Administration. The building was originally used as a training school for Red Army officers, and later as the headquarters of the Presidium of the Supreme Soviet, an executive arm of the Soviet parliament. Today it is home to part of the Russian presidential administration.

The Presidential Administration

Senate ⓯

Сенат

Senat

The Kremlin. **Map** 7 A1. ● *to public.*

Completed in 1790, this Neo-Classical building was constructed to house several of the Senate's departments. Designed by Matvey Kazakov *(see pp44–5)*, who regarded it as his best work, it is triangular, with a central, domed rotunda, from which the Russian flag flies.

Kremlin Towers

There are 19 towers in the walls of the Kremlin, with a bridge leading from the Trinity Tower to a 20th, the Kutafya Tower. In 1935 the double-headed imperial eagles were removed from the five tallest towers and replaced two years later with stars made of red glass, each weighing between 1 and 1.5 tonnes.

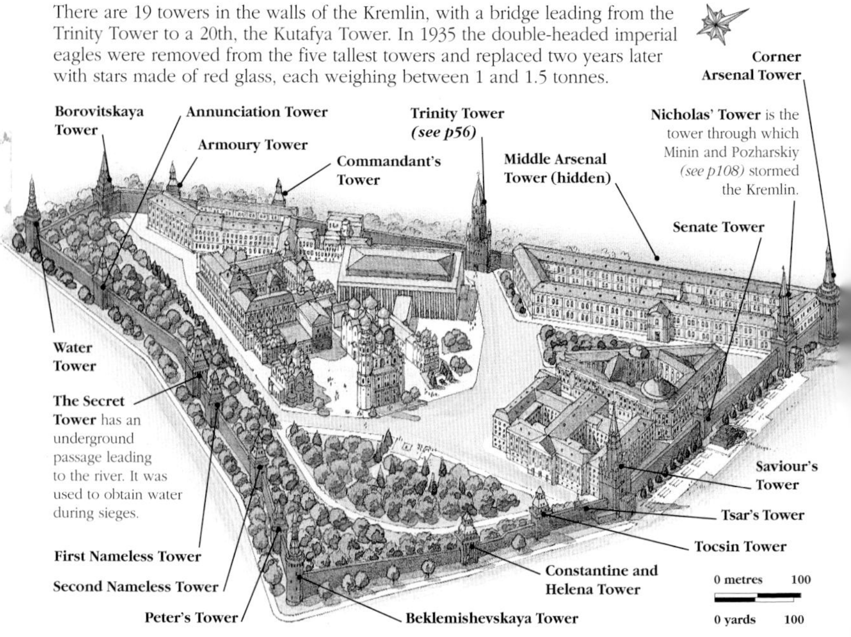

The domed rotunda of the yellow and white Senate, behind the Senate Tower and the Lenin Mausoleum

From 1918 to 1991, the Senate housed the Soviet government. Lenin had his office here and his family lived in a flat on the top floor. During World War II the Red Army Supreme Command, headed by Stalin, was based in the building.

Today the Senate is the official seat of the president of the Russian Federation.

Corner Arsenal Tower with the Arsenal and Nicholas' Tower

Arsenal ⓰

Арсенал

Arsenal

The Kremlin. **Map** 7 A1. ● *to public.*

PETER THE GREAT ordered the Arsenal to be built in 1701, but various setbacks, including a fire in 1711, delayed its completion until 1736. In 1812 the building was partly blown up by Napoleon's army *(see pp23–5)*. Architects Aleksandr Bakarev, Ivan Tamanskiy, Ivan Mironovskiy and Evgraf Tyurin were commissioned to design a new Arsenal. Their attractive yellow and white Neo-Classical building was finished in 1828.

The Arsenal was constructed as a storehouse for weapons, ammunition and other military supplies. Around 750 cannons, including some that were captured from Napoleon's retreating troops, are lined up outside. Now the command post of the Kremlin guard, the interior and much of the exterior of the Arsenal are strictly out of bounds to visitors.

Alexander Gardens ⓱

Александровский сад

Aleksandrovskiy sad

The Kremlin. **Map** 7 A1.

DESIGNED BY architect Osip Bove *(see p45)* in 1821, these gardens are named after Tsar Alexander I, who presided over the restoration of the city, including the Kremlin, after the Napoleonic Wars. Before the gardens were built, the Neglinnaya river, part of the Kremlin moat, was channelled underground. The only visible reminder of its presence is the stone bridge linking the Kutafya and Trinity towers.

In front of the Middle Arsenal Tower in the northern half of the gardens is an obelisk erected in 1913 to mark 300 years of the Romanov dynasty. The imperial eagle was taken down after the Revolution and the inscription was replaced by the names of revolutionary thinkers, such as Karl Marx and Friedrich Engels.

The Tomb of the Unknown Soldier, a short distance away, was unveiled in 1967. Its eternal flame was lit with a torch lit from the flame at the Field of Mars in St Petersburg. It burns for all the Russians who died in World War II. The body of a soldier is buried beneath the monument, which bears an inscription, "Your name is unknown, your deeds immortal".

In 1996, an huge shopping complex was constructed beneath Manezhnaya ploshchad, the large square to the north of Alexander Gardens.

Path through Alexander Gardens, with the Trinity Tower behind

LUCKY STRIKE

Arbatskaya

The name "Arbat" is thought to derive from a Mongol word meaning suburb, and was first applied in the 15th century to the entire area west of the Kremlin, then inhabited by the tsar's artisans and equerries. Though still commemorated in street names, the artisans moved elsewhere in the late 18th century. The aristocracy moved in and were followed by Moscow's professionals, intellectuals and artists, attracted by the area's rambling backstreets, dilapidated cottages and overgrown courtyards. In the Old Arbat, with its pedestrianized main street, there are historic churches, timber houses and early 19th-century mansions around pereulok Sivtsev Vrazhek. Yet, not far away are the kiosks, cafés and huge Soviet-era apartment blocks and shops of the New Arbat.

Fayoum portrait, Pushkin Museum

Sights at a Glance

Museums and Galleries
Bely House-Museum ❺
Lermontov House-Museum ⓭
Museum of Private Collections ❽
Pushkin House-Museum ❹
Pushkin Museum of Fine Arts pp78–81 ❾
Shalyapin House-Museum ⓮
Shchusev Museum of Architecture ⓫
Skryabin House-Museum ❶

Cathedrals
Cathedral of Christ the Redeemer ❼

Historic Buildings
Melnikov House ❸
Pashkov House ❿

Streets and Squares
Arbat Square ⓬
Spasopeskovskiy Pereulok ❷
Ulitsa Prechistenka ❻

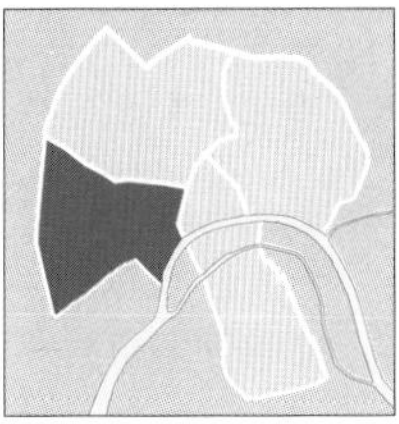

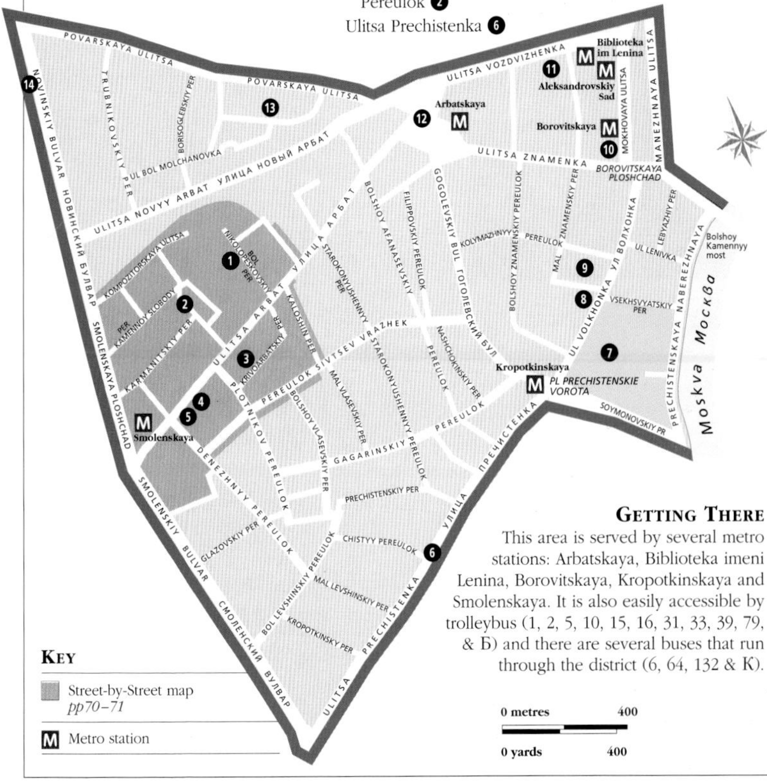

Getting There

This area is served by several metro stations: Arbatskaya, Biblioteka imeni Lenina, Borovitskaya, Kropotkinskaya and Smolenskaya. It is also easily accessible by trolleybus (1, 2, 5, 10, 15, 16, 31, 33, 39, 79, & Б) and there are several buses that run through the district (6, 64, 132 & К).

Key

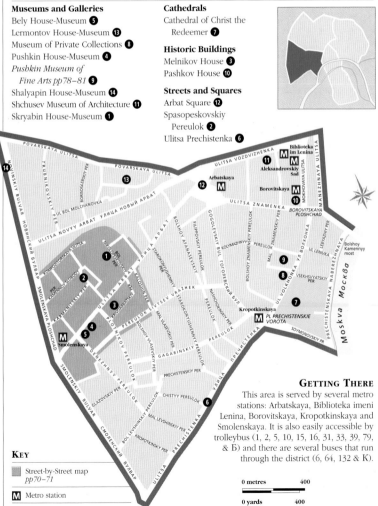

Street-by-Street map *pp70–71*

Metro station

◁ **Busy ulitsa Arbat, the heart of the Old Arbat, overlooked by the monumental Stalinist Foreign Affairs Ministry**

Street-by-Street: Old Arbat

At the heart of the old Arbat is the pedestrianized ulitsa Arbat. It is lined with antique shops, boutiques, souvenir stalls, pavement cafés and a variety of restaurants, from pizzerias and hamburger joints to lively examples of the traditional Russian pub (*traktir*). In the 19th century, the Old Arbat was the haunt of artists, musicians, poets, writers and intellectuals. Some of their homes have been preserved and opened as museums, and are among the district's many houses of that era that have been lovingly restored and painted in pastel shades of blue, green and ochre. Today, pavement artists, buskers and street poets give it a renewed bohemian atmosphere.

Spaso House is a grand Neo-Classical mansion. It has been the residence of the US ambassador since 1933.

This small garden contains a statue of the poet Alexander Pushkin.

Novyy Arbat ↑

★ Pushkin House-Museum
The poet Alexander Pushkin lived here just after his marriage in 1831. The interior of the house has been carefully renovated ❹

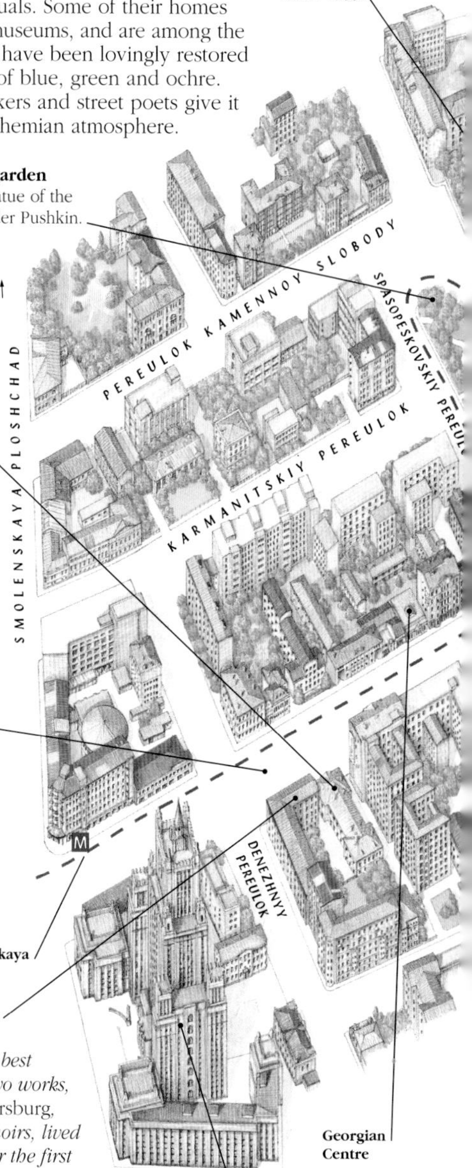

Ulitsa Arbat
By the time of the Soviet era, ulitsa Arbat had lost most of its 19th-century character. It was pedestrianized in 1985, however, and its lively shops, restaurants and cafés are now popular with Muscovites and visitors to the city alike.

Smolenskaya

Bely House-Museum
Andrei Bely, best known for two works, a novel, Petersburg, *and his memoirs, lived in this flat for the first 26 years of his life. It is now a museum and the exhibits on display include this photo of Bely with his wife and the fascinating illustration,* Line of Life (see p73) ❺

Georgian Centre

The Foreign Ministry is one of Moscow's seven Stalinist-Gothic skyscrapers *(see p45)*.

Spasopeskovskiy Pereulok
On one side of this peaceful lane is the 18th-century Church of the Saviour on the Sands, with its white bell tower. It overlooks a secluded square and garden, a reminder that the Arbat was at that time a genteel suburb ❷

Locator Map
See Street Finder, map 6

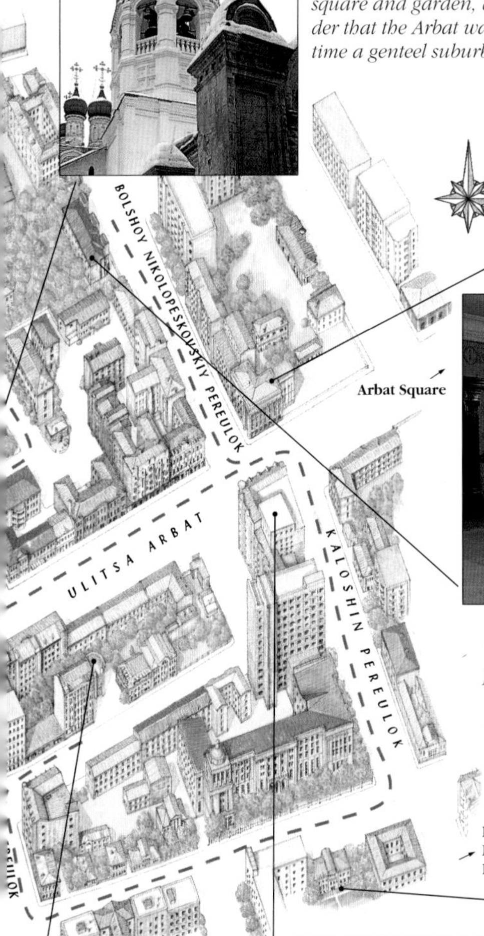

The Vakhtangova Theatre was established here in 1921 by Yevgeniy Vakhtangov, one of Moscow's leading theatre directors. The current theatre building dates from 1947.

★ Skryabin House-Museum
This comfortable apartment has been preserved as it was in 1912–15 when experimental composer Aleksandr Skryabin lived here. The furniture in the rooms is Style Moderne and the lighting is dim, since Skryabin disliked direct light ❶

The Herzen House-Museum was the home of the radical writer Aleksandr Herzen for three years from 1843.

0 metres 100

0 yards 100

These pre-Revolution apartments, designed for wealthy Muscovites, are decorated with fanciful turrets and sculptures of knights.

Melnikov House
This unusual cylindrical house is now dwarfed by the apartments on ulitsa Arbat. It was built in the 1920s by Constructivist architect Konstantin Melnikov, who lived here until his death in 1974 ❸

Star Sights

- ★ **Pushkin House-Museum**
- ★ **Skryabin House-Museum**

Key

– – – Suggested route

Skryabin House-Museum ❶
Дом-музей АН Скрябина
Dom-muzey AN Skryabina

Bolshoy Nikolopeskovskiy pereulok 11. **Map** 6 D1. *241 1901.* *Smolenskaya, Arbatskaya.* *Noon–6pm Wed, Fri, 10am–4pm Thu, Sat–Sun.* *English (book in advance).*

THE FLAT WHERE the pianist and composer Aleksandr Skryabin (1872–1915) died, at the age of 43, has been preserved as it was when he lived there. Skryabin studied at the Moscow Conservatory *(see p94)*, where he established an international reputation as a concert pianist. He was also a highly original composer and musical theorist, best known for his orchestral works such as *Prometheus* and *A Poem of Ecstasy*. Skryabin's music had a great influence on the young Igor Stravinsky (1882–1971), and leading composer Sergei Rachmaninov (1873–1943) was a regular visitor to his flat.

Although Skryabin spent much of his time abroad giving concerts, he was an aesthete and paid considerable attention to furnishing and decorating his fashionable apartment. The lofty rooms house his pianos, autographed manuscripts and Style-Moderne furniture. However, the most original item on show is a device for projecting flickering light. Regular concerts are held in the rooms on the ground floor.

A room in Aleksandr Skryabin's apartment, with one of his pianos

The Classical-style Spaso House on Spasopeskovskaya ploshchad

Spasopeskovskiy Pereulok ❷
Спасопесковский переулок
Spasopeskovskiy pereulok

Map 6 D1. *Smolenskaya.*

THE CHARMS of the Old Arbat have been preserved in this secluded lane and the peaceful adjoining square, Spasopeskovskaya ploshchad. In 1878, Vasiliy Polenov painted *A Moscow Courtyard*, depicting Spasopeskovskaya ploshchad as a bucolic haven in the midst of the city. Today the square still provides a respite from the hustle and bustle prevailing elsewhere.

At the centre of Polenov's picture, now in the Tretyakov Gallery *(see pp118–21)*, is the white bell tower of the Church of the Saviour on the Sands (Tserkov Spas na Peskakh) from which the lane gets its name. This 18th-century church still dominates the square. In front of it is a small garden dedicated to the poet Alexander Pushkin.

The handsome Classical-style mansion standing on the far side of the square was built in 1913 as a private residence. Known as Spaso House, it has been the home of the US ambassador since 1933.

Melnikov House ❸
Дом Мельникова
Dom Melnikova

Krivoarbatskiy pereulok 10. **Map** 6 D1. *Smolenskaya.* *to public.*

THIS UNIQUE HOUSE, almost hidden by office blocks, was designed by Konstantin Melnikov (1890–1974), one of Russia's greatest Constructivist architects *(see p45)*, in 1927.

Made from brick overlaid with white stucco, the house consists of two interlocking cylinders. These are studded with rows of hexagonal windows, creating a curious honeycomb effect. A spiral staircase rises through the space where the cylinders overlap, linking the light, airy living spaces.

Viktor Melnikov's studio in the Melnikov House

Melnikov's house was built for his family, but it was also to have been a prototype for future housing developments. However, his career was blighted when Stalin encouraged architects to adopt a new monumental style *(see p45)*. Although he had won the Gold Medal at the Paris World's Fair in 1925, Melnikov's work was ridiculed or ignored. However, he did remain in his house for the rest of his life, one of the very few residents of central Moscow allowed to live in a privately built dwelling.

Melnikov's son, artist Viktor Melnikov, now has a studio on the top floor of the house.

Alexander Pushkin

Born in 1799 into Russia's aristocracy, Alexander Pushkin is Russia's most famous poet. He had established a reputation as both a poet and a rebel by the time he was 20. In 1820, he was sent into exile because the Tsarist government did not approve of his liberal verse, but eventually was set free.

Pushkin's early work consisted of narrative poems such as *The Robber Brothers* (1821), and his most famous work is *Eugene Onegin* (1823–30), a novel in verse. From 1830 Pushkin wrote mostly prose. He developed a unique style in pieces such as *The Queen of Spades* (1834) and is credited with giving Russian literature its own identity.

Pushkin House-Museum ❹

Музей-квартира АС Пушкина

Muzey-kvartira AS Pushkina

Ulitsa Arbat 55. **Map** 6 D2.
241 4212. *Smolenskaya.*
11am–6pm Wed–Sun.
English (book in advance).

Alexander Pushkin rented this elegant, blue and white Empire-style flat for the first three months of his marriage to society beauty Natalya Goncharova. They were married in the Church of the Great Ascension on Bolshaya Nikitskaya ulitsa *(see p93)* in February 1831, when she was 18 years old. Pushkin wrote to his friend Pyotr Pletnev: "I am married – and happy. My only wish is that nothing in my life should change; I couldn't possibly expect anything better."

However, by May 1831 Pushkin had tired of life in Moscow, and the couple moved to St Petersburg, where sadly a tragic fate awaited him. Gossip began to circulate there that Pushkin's brother-in-law, a French officer called d'Anthès, was making advances to Natalya. Upon receiving letters informing him that he was now the "Grand Master to the Order of Cuckolds", Pushkin challenged d'Anthès to a duel. Mortally wounded in the contest, Pushkin died two days later.

The fascinating exhibition located in the museum's ground floor rooms gives an idea of what the city would have been like in the period when Pushkin was growing up, before the great fire of 1812. Among the prints, lithographs and watercolours are some unusual wax figures of a serf orchestra that belonged to the Goncharova family.

A portrait of Pushkin's wife, Natalya Goncharova

Pushkin and Natalya lived on the first floor. There are disappointingly few personal possessions here, although the poet's writing bureau and some family portraits are displayed. The atmosphere resembles a shrine more than a museum. Pushkin holds a special place in Russians' hearts and they treat his work and memory with reverence.

Bely House-Museum ❺

Музей-квартира Андрея Белого

Muzey-kvartira Andreya Belovo

Ulitsa Arbat 55. **Map** 6 D2.
241 7702. *Smolenskaya.*
11am–6pm Wed–Sun.

In the adjoining building to the Pushkin House-Museum is the childhood home of the symbolist writer Andrei Bely. Bely was born Boris Bugaev in 1880, but later adopted the name by which he is known as a writer. He grew up here before becoming a student at Moscow University *(see p94)*, where he began to write verse. He is best known, however, for *Petersburg*, a novel completed in 1916, and for his memoirs.

Only two rooms of the Bugaev family apartment have been preserved. A photographic exhibition on the writer's life and work is housed in one room. The most interesting item in the museum is the *Line of Life*, an illustration by Bely to show how his mood swings combined with cultural influences to direct his work.

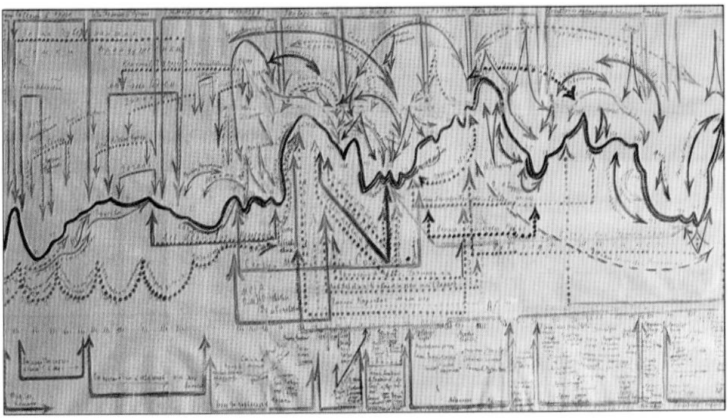

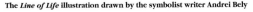

The *Line of Life* illustration drawn by the symbolist writer Andrei Bely

Stone eagles among the ornate decoration on No. 20 ulitsa Prechistenka

Ulitsa Prechistenka ❻

Улица Пречистенка

Ulitsa Prechistenka

Map 6 D3–E2. **M** *Kropotkinskaya.*

MOSCOW'S ARISTOCRACY first settled in this street in the late 18th century and their elegant mansions still line it today. In Soviet times it was known as Kropotkinskaya ulitsa, after Prince Pyotr Kropotkin, a famous anarchist *(see p23).*

The Empire-style house at No. 12 ulitsa Prechistenka is now the Pushkin Literary Museum (not to be confused with the Pushkin House-Museum, *see p73).* The house was originally designed for the Krushchev family (no connection with Nikita Krushchev) by Afanasiy Grigorev *(see p45)*, one of the leading exponents of this style in Moscow. The building has a wooden frame, skilfully hidden by Classical columns and ornate stucco decoration.

Across the street another great writer is honoured at No. 11 in the Tolstoy Literary Museum. In contrast to the Tolstoy House-Museum *(see p134)*, it concentrates on the man's work rather than his life. The building however, has no connection with Tolstoy; it was built in 1822, also to a design by Afanasiy Grigorev, for the noble Lopukhin family. On display are many letters, manuscripts and family portraits.

At No. 20 is an elegant two-storey mansion decorated with eagles, urns, heraldic symbols and scallop shells. Until 1861 it was home to General Aleksey Yermolov, a commander-in-chief in the Russian army. After the Revolution, the American dancer Isadora Duncan and the poet Sergey Yesenin lived here during their brief, tempestuous marriage. The two spoke no common language, and Yesenin stated his feelings by writing the Russian for "I love you" in lipstick on the bedroom mirror.

Lion at No. 16 ulitsa Prechistenka

The most distinguished house is at No. 19. Rebuilt after the 1812 fire *(see p24)* for the Dolgorukov family, it has an ochre and white façade. Adjoining it, at No. 21, is another early 19th-century mansion, now the Academy of Arts, where exhibitions are sometimes put on.

Cathedral of Christ the Redeemer ❼

Храм Христа Спасителя

Khram Khrista Spasitelya

Ulitsa Volkhonka 15. **Map** 6 F2. **M** *Kropotkinskaya.*

REBUILDING this cathedral, blown up on Stalin's orders in 1931, was the most ambitious of the construction projects undertaken by the enterprising mayor of Moscow, Yuriy Luzhkov. The basic structure of the new cathedral was built between 1994–97. For much of the intervening time, the site was occupied by an outdoor swimming pool, but this was eventually filled in.

The project courted controversy from the start, both on grounds of taste and cost. In 1995 a presidential decree declared that not a kopek of public money should be spent on it – funds were to be raised through donations from the public, the Russian Church and foreign donors among the big multinational companies operating in Russia. However, in practice, the better part of the total bill of over US$200 million came from the state budget, which raised objections at a time when Muscovites were suffering extreme poverty.

The original cathedral was built to commemorate the miraculous deliverance of Moscow from Napoleon's Grande Armée *(see pp23–4).* Begun in 1839, but not completed until 1883, it was designed by Konstantin Ton *(see p45).* The cathedral was the tallest building in Moscow at that time, the gilded dome rising to a height of 103 m (338 ft) and dominating the skyline for miles around. With a floor area of 9,000 sq m (97,000 sq ft), it could accommodate more than 10,000 worshippers.

In 1998, a small museum and a church on the ground floor opened to the public. There are spectacular views of the city from the dome.

Cathedral of Christ the Redeemer, rebuilt in the 1990s at huge cost

Stalin's Plan for a Palace of Soviets

The original Cathedral of Christ the Redeemer was to have been replaced by a Palace of Soviets – a soaring tower, 315 m (1,034 ft) high, topped by a 100-m (328-ft) statue of Lenin. It was designed as the highlight of Stalin's reconstruction of Moscow, much of the rest of which was realized: broad boulevards, skyscrapers and the metro system *(see pp38–41)* are now familiar features of the city. The result was also, however, the destruction of many supposedly unnecessary buildings, especially churches and monasteries, even inside the Kremlin. The scheme for the Palace of Soviets was eventually abandoned and the cathedral was rebuilt in the 1990s.

Artist's impression of Stalin's proposed awe-inspiring Palace of Soviets

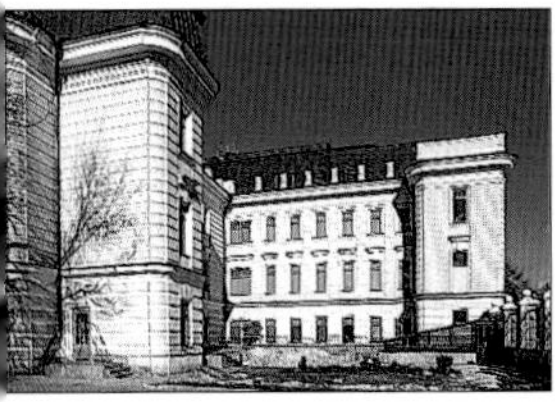

The Museum of Private Collections, housed in a former hotel

Museum of Private Collections ❽

Музей личных коллекций
Muzey lichnykh kollektsiy

Ulitsa Volkhonka 14. **Map** 6 F2. *203 1546. noon–6pm Wed–Sun. Kropotkinskaya.*

Before the revolution the Knyazhiy Dvor hotel, whose guests included Maxim Gorky and artist Ilya Repin, occupied this building.

The museum opened in 1994 and is based on private collections. The largest is that of Ilya Zilberstein, which includes a vast range of work by prominent Russian artists such as Ivan Shishkin, Ilya Repin and Konstantin Somov. There are also works by Aleksandr Rodchenko, and rooms devoted to periodic specialist exhibitions.

Pushkin Museum of Fine Arts ❾

See pp78–81.

Pashkov House ❿

Дом Пашкова
Dom Pashkova

Ulitsa Znamenka 6. **Map** 6 F1. *to public. Borovitskaya, Biblioteka imeni Lenina.*

This magnificent mansion was once the finest private house in Moscow and enjoys a wonderful hilltop location overlooking the Kremlin. It was built in the Neo-Classical style in 1784–8 for the fabulously wealthy Captain Pyotr Pashkov. Pashkov encouraged his architect, who is thought probably to have been Vasiliy Bazhenov *(see p44)*, to surpass himself – and every other residence in Moscow – with the grandeur of the design. The mansion's height was achieved by placing it on an enormous stone base and the building is surmounted by a beautifully proportioned rotunda. Surprisingly the most impressive façade is to the rear of the building, which originally led to a garden. The original main entrance is through an ornate stone gateway located on Starovagankovskiy pereulok.

In 1839, a relative of Captain Pashkov sold the house to the Moscow Institute for Nobles, which occupied the premises until 1861. It was then taken over by the Rumyantsev Museum, which moved to the capital from St Petersburg at that time. The museum brought with it an art collection and a library of more than one million volumes.

After the Revolution, the library was nationalized and renamed the Lenin Library. A new, and infinitely less attractive, extension for the rapidly expanding book collection was begun next door in 1928 and completed during the 1950s. Now known as the Russian State Library, it contains some 40 million items including books, periodicals, manuscripts, recordings, microfilms and pictures.

The imposing Pashkov House overlooking the Kremlin

Pushkin Museum of Fine Arts ❾

Музей изобразительных искусств имени АС Пушкина
Muzey izobrazitelnykh iskusstv imeni AS Pushkina

FOUNDED IN 1898, the Pushkin Museum houses an excellent collection of French Impressionist and Post-Impressionist paintings. It also has an enviable collection of old masters. Following the collapse of the Soviet Union *(see pp30–31)*, the curators admitted that they had countless works of art hidden away for ideological reasons. Some of these are now on show, including paintings by Russian-born artists Vasily Kandinsky and Marc Chagall. The museum building was designed by Roman Klein. It was originally built to house plaster casts of classical sculptures for Moscow University art students to use for research.

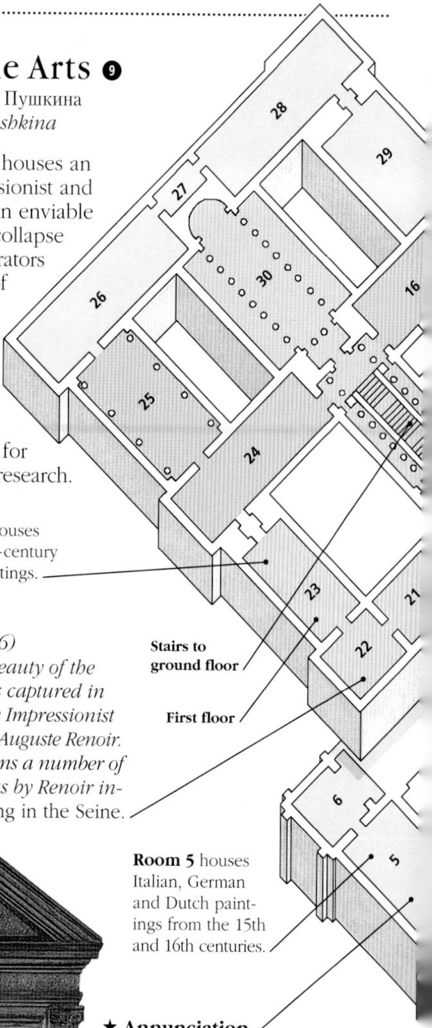

Room 23 houses mostly 19th-century French paintings.

Stairs to ground floor

First floor

★ Nude *(1876)*
The natural beauty of the female body is captured in this picture by Impressionist painter Pierre Auguste Renoir. The gallery owns a number of other paintings by Renoir including Bathing in the Seine.

Room 5 houses Italian, German and Dutch paintings from the 15th and 16th centuries.

Gallery Guide

The ticket office is in the entrance hall. The displays are spread over two floors, but although the museum halls are numbered, the layout is not strictly chronological. Paintings from the 17th and 18th centuries are on the ground floor while works from the 19th and 20th centuries are upstairs. Collections of art that date from before the 17th century can be found on both floors. The cloakroom and toilets are in the basement.

★ Annunciation
Painted around 1490 by Italian artist Sandro Botticelli, this work was originally part of a large altar-piece. It shows the angel Gabriel telling the Virgin Mary she is to bear the Son of God.

Star Exhibits

- ★ **Annunciation by Botticelli**
- ★ **Nude by Renoir**
- ★ **Montagne Ste-Victoire by Cézanne**

Altar Triptych
The panels of this altar-piece were painted by Pietro di Giovanni Lianori in the 14th century. Above the central image of the Virgin and Child is a picture of the crucifixion. Figures of the saints are painted on the triptych's wings.

★ Mont Ste-Victoire *(1905)*
This work by Paul Cézanne is one of the many views he painted of this mountain, east of Aix-en-Provence, after he settled in the region in 1886.

Visitors' Checklist

Ulitsa Volkhonka 12. **Map** 6 F2. ☎ *203 9578.* Ⓜ *Kropotkinskaya.* 🚌 *1, 2, 16, 33.* 🕐 *10am–6pm Tue–Sun.* English. Ⓦ www.museum.ru/gmii

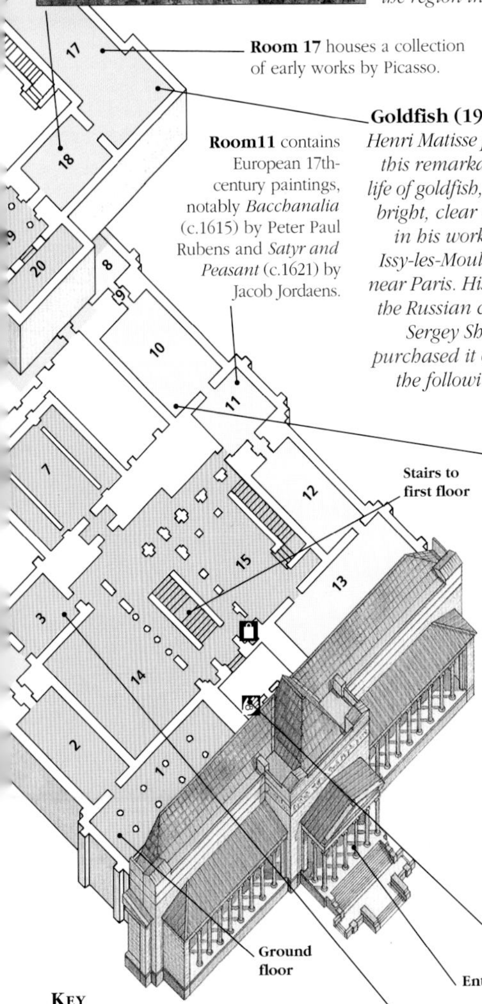

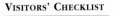

Room 17 houses a collection of early works by Picasso.

Room11 contains European 17th-century paintings, notably *Bacchanalia* (c.1615) by Peter Paul Rubens and *Satyr and Peasant* (c.1621) by Jacob Jordaens.

Goldfish (1911–12)
Henri Matisse painted this remarkable still life of goldfish, with its bright, clear colours, in his workshop at Issy-les-Moulineaux, near Paris. His friend, the Russian collector Sergey Shchukin, purchased it on sight the following year.

Ahasuerus, Haman and Esther
In this biblical scene by Rembrandt (1660), the Persian king, Ahasuerus, is flanked by his Jewish wife and his minister, Haman. Esther, lit by a single ray of light, accuses Haman of plotting to destroy the Jews.

Fayoum Portrait
Painted in the 1st century AD, this is one of a collection of portraits discovered at a burial ground at the Fayoum oasis in Egypt in the 1870s. They were painted while the subjects were still alive to be used as death masks on their mummies when they died.

Key

- Art of ancient civilizations
- European art 13th–16th centuries
- European art 17th–18th centuries
- European art 19th century
- Post-Impressionist and 20th-century European art
- Temporary exhibition space

Exploring the Pushkin Museum of Fine Arts

Religious icon (c.14th–15th century)

THE ACCUMULATED TREASURES of the Pushkin Museum of Fine Arts reflect the tastes of many private collectors, whose holdings were nationalized by the Soviet government after the Revolution. The most important of these belonged to two outstanding connoisseurs, Sergey Shchukin and Ivan Morozov. By 1914, Shchukin had acquired more than 220 paintings by French artists, including many by Cézanne. Even more importantly, Shchukin championed Matisse and Picasso when they were still relatively unknown. Morozov also collected canvases by these two painters along with pictures by Renoir, Van Gogh and Gauguin.

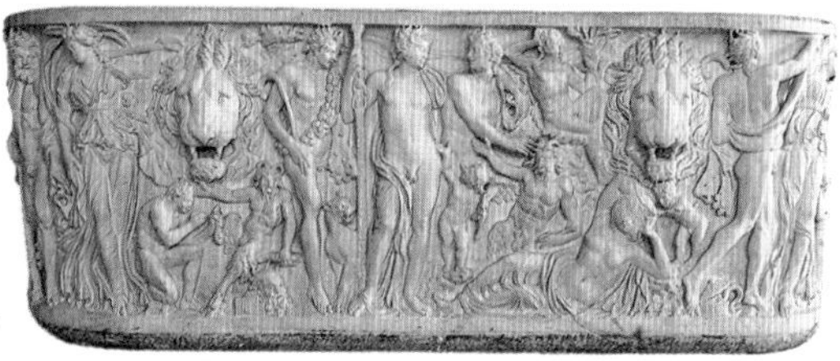

Greek marble sarcophagus, dating from around AD 210

Art of Ancient Civilizations

THE MUSEUM'S archaeological exhibits come from as far afield as ancient Mesopotamia and the Mayan Empire. Among them is a fascinating collection donated by the Egyptologist Vladimir Golenishchev in 1913. The display includes the renowned tomb portraits from Fayoum and two exquisite ebony figurines of the high priest Amen-Hotep and his wife, the priestess Re-nai.

There is also an assortment of items from ancient Greece and Rome including a fine collection of black-figure and red-figure style Greek vases.

The fabulous Treasure of Troy display, with gold artifacts excavated from the legendary city in the 1870s is now open to the public again.

European Art 13th–16th Centuries

THE PUSHKIN MUSEUM contains a small, but memorable, collection of Medieval and Renaissance art. It includes a series of altar panels painted in the Byzantine tradition by Italian artists. Siena was a major artistic centre in the 14th century and Simone Martini was a leading master of the Sienese school. His naturalistic images of St Augustine and Mary Magdalene, painted in the 1320s, are among the exhibits.

There are also a number of later religious pieces on show, including a triptych by Pietro di Giovanni Lianori. Two outstanding old masters painted in the 1490s are also displayed here: the superb *Annunciation*, painted by Sandro Botticelli, and the *Madonna and Child* by Pietro Perugino.

The museum is not so well endowed with German and Flemish art of the period. However, two notable exceptions are Pieter Breughel the Younger's *Winter Landscape with Bird Trap* and Lucas Cranach the Elder's *Virgin and Child*. Painted on wood, the latter places the Virgin and Child in the context of a typical German landscape.

European Art 17th–18th Centuries

THE PUSHKIN MUSEUM has an enviable collection of 17th-century Dutch and Flemish masters. It includes Anthony Van Dyck's accomplished portraits of the wealthy burgher, Adriaen Stevens, and his wife, Maria Boschaert, both painted in 1629, and some evocative landscapes by Jan Van Goyen and Jacob van Ruysdael. Also on show are still lifes by Frans Snyders, some delightful genre scenes by Jan Steen, Pieter de Hooch and Gabriel Metsu and several works by Peter Paul Rubens, including the characteristically flamboyant and sensual *Bacchanalia* (c.1615).

Six of Rembrandt's masterly canvases, along with some of his drawings and etchings, are displayed in the gallery. The paintings include the biblical *Ahasuerus, Haman and Esther* (1660), *Christ Driving the Money-Changers from the Temple* (1626) and *An Old Woman*, a sensitive portrait of the artist's mother (1654).

The gallery has a modest collection of Spanish and Italian paintings from the 17th and 18th centuries. Of the Spanish artists, Bartholomé Esteban Murillo, known for his religious scenes and portraits, is probably the best known. The works on show by Italian artists include *Betrothal of the Doge and the Sea* (1729–30) by

A section of the *Virgin and Child*, painted by Lucas Cranach the Elder in about 1525

Canaletto, widely considered the master of the style of urban landscape known as *veduta*.

The Pushkin Museum is justly famous for its collection of French art, which includes paintings of classical and epic subjects by a variety of artists. Among the paintings on show are Nicolas Poussin's dramatic work, *The Battle of the Israelites with the Amorri* (c.1625) and François Boucher's painting, *Hercules and Omphale* (1730s). The latter depicts the myth of Hercules, who was sold as a slave to Queen Omphale.

***Hercules and Omphale*, painted in the 1730s by François Boucher**

European Art 19th Century

In the early 19th century Classicism in art gradually yielded to Romanticism. Works such as *After the Shipwreck* (1847) by Eugène Delacroix, which portrays the sea as a force of nature, unpredictable and hostile to man, were the result of this shift. Works by other artists of the period, such as the landscape painters John Constable and Caspar David Friedrich, are also on show.

The Pushkin Museum has a fine collection of paintings by artists of the French Barbizon school, who were the predecessors of the Impressionists. These include landscapes by Camille Corot, François Millet and Gustave Courbet.

Paintings from the enormous collection of works by the Impressionists themselves are displayed in rotation. Visitors can look forward to a selection of canvases by artists such as Edouard Manet, Edgar Degas, Pierre Auguste Renoir and Claude Monet. The museum owns eleven paintings by Monet, including *Lilac in the Sun* (1873) and two from a series of 20 paintings of the cathedral at Rouen. There are also some excellent paintings by Renoir including *Nude* and the radiant *Portrait of the Actress Jeanne Samary* (1877). Alongside landscapes and street scenes by Alfred Sisley and Camille Pisarro are *Blue Dancers* (c.1899) and *Dancers at a Rehearsal* (1875–77), two of Degas' many ballet scenes.

***Improvisation No 20* by Vasily Kandinsky**

Sculptures by Auguste Rodin are also part of the collection. They include a bust of Victor Hugo and preparatory studies for the famous *Kiss* (1886) and *Burghers of Calais* (1884–6).

Claude Monet's *Rouen Cathedral at Sunset*, painted in 1894

Post-Impressionist and 20th-Century European Art

Post-impressionism is the term generally used to describe the various styles of painting developed by the generation of artists that came after the Impressionists. This school includes Vincent Van Gogh, Paul Cézanne and Paul Gauguin. A marvellous array of paintings by Paul Cézanne is on show in the gallery, including his *Self-portrait* (early 1880s), *Pierrot and Harlequin* (1888) and a late version of *Mont Ste-Victoire* (1905). His *Pierrot and Harlequin* (1888) depicts characters from the Mardi-Gras Carnivals.

In 1888, Paul Gauguin stayed with Van Gogh for two months in Arles. Gauguin's *Café in Arles* and Van Gogh's intense *Red Vineyards in Arles*, both painted during the visit, hang in the Pushkin Museum.

The gallery also has several later works by Van Gogh, including *The Prison Courtyard* (1890) and *Wheatfields in Auvers, After the Rain* (1890). His *Portrait of Dr Rey* (1889) emphasizes the sympathetic nature of the doctor who showed so much kindness to the sick artist.

In 1891 Gauguin moved to Tahiti and a number of works from this period, including *Are You Jealous?* (1892) and *The Great Buddha* (1899), are also displayed here.

Some of Henri Matisse's greatest masterpieces are in the Pushkin Museum, including *The Painter's Studio* (1911) and *Goldfish* (1911). There are also over 50 paintings by Matisse's friend, Pablo Picasso, including *Young Acrobat on a Ball*, painted in 1905, *(see p48)* and *Harlequin and His Companion*, dating from 1901.

A number of other 20th-century artists are also represented in the collection. Highlights include *The Artist and his Bride* (1980) by Marc Chagall and the abstract *Improvisation No. 20* by Vasily Kandinsky.

The wide expanse of Arbat Square, located between the Old and New Arbat

Shchusev Museum of Architecture ⓫

Музей архитектуры имени АВ Щусева

Muzey arkhitektury imeni AV Shchuseva

Ulitsa Vozdvizhenka 5. **Map** 6 F1. *290 4855.* *Alexandrovskiy sad, Biblioteka imeni Lenina, Borovitskaya, Arbatskaya.* **Main building** *11am–5:45pm Tue–Fri, 11am–4pm Sat & Sun.* **Apothecary's Office** *same as Main building.* *English.*

An enormous 18th-century mansion houses this museum dedicated to Russian architecture. It is named after the Soviet architect Aleksey Shchusev *(see p45)*, who carried out parts of Stalin's reconstruction of Moscow during the 1930s and also designed the monumental Lenin Mausoleum *(see p107)*.

The Museum once occupied the whole building, with beautiful displays covering the development of architecture from medieval times to the present day. Sadly it is now confined to two rather less ambitious exhibitions in the main building, and another display in the 17th-century former Apothecary's Office.

Various temporary exhibitions are on show throughout the year displaying different aspects of Russian architecture and architects.

A model of the Lenin Mausoleum in Red Square, in the Shchusev Museum of Architecture

Arbat Square ⓬

Арбатская площадь

Arbatskaya ploshchad

Map 6 E1. *Arbatskaya.*

A chaotic mass of kiosks, traffic and underpasses, Arbat Square is the link between the vividly contrasting areas of Old and New Arbat. Beneath the square, the underpasses contain a society of their own. Expect to come across an impromptu rock concert, kittens and puppies for sale and, in late summer, children selling bulbous, hand-picked mushrooms (though buying these may not be advisable).

On the corner of ulitsa Arbat is the yellow wedge-shaped Praga restaurant *(see p181)*, dating from before the Revolution, but reconstructed in 1954. Despite still retaining the elegance of its dining halls, it became a fairly uninspiring snack-bar during the later Soviet era. However, it has now been entirely refurbished to re-emerge as a very elegant establishment serving high-quality cuisine in a variety of national styles.

The small white building at the other end of the underpass dates from 1909, but it was redesigned three years later by Fyodor Shekhtel *(see p45)* for the pioneering Russian film studio boss, Aleksandr Khanzhonkov. Now known as the Arts Cinema *(see p193)*, it was one of the first cinemas to open in Moscow.

Lermontov House-Museum ⓭

Дом-музей МЮ Лермонтова

Dom-muzey MYu Lermontova

Ulitsa Malaya Molchanovka 2. **Map** 6 D1. *291 5298.* *Arbatskaya.* *2pm–4pm Wed, Fri, 11am–4pm Thu & Sat.*

A portrait of the poet and novelist Lermontov (1814–41) as a child

Tucked away behind the tower blocks of the New Arbat is the modest timber house that was once home to Mikhail Lermontov. The great Romantic poet and novelist lived here with his grandmother, Yelizaveta Arseneva, from 1829–32 while he was a student at Moscow University. While here, he wrote an early draft of his narrative poem *The Demon* (1839).

Lermontov was more interested in writing poetry than in his studies and left university without graduating. He then became a guardsman. However, he was exiled to the Caucasus for a year because of the bitter criticisms of the authorities expressed in his

Lermontov's tranquil study in the Lermontov House-Museum

poem *Death of a Poet* (1837). This poem about the death of Pushkin *(see p73)* marked a turning point in Lermontov's writing and is generally agreed to be the first of his mature works. His most famous composition, the novel *A Hero of our Time*, was written in 1840. Lermontov died the next year, aged only 26. Like Pushkin, he was killed in a duel.

There are only five rooms in the museum, but each bears testament both to Lermontov's dazzling intellectual gifts and also to his zest for life. The study on the mezzanine was his favourite room. Here he would play the guitar, piano and violin, and even compose music.

The drawing room, which still contains many of its original furnishings, was often the site of lively dancing, singing and masquerades.

Many of Lermontov's manuscripts are on display downstairs, together with drawings and watercolours, some by Lermontov himself.

Shalyapin House-Museum ⓮

Дом-музей Ф.И. Шаляпина

Dom-muzey FI Shalyapina

Novinskiy bulvar 25. **Map** 1 C5. *205 6236.* *Smolenskaya, Barrikadnaya.* *10am–5pm Tue & Sat, 11:30am–7pm Wed & Thu, 10am–3pm Sun.*

A STONE BUST and inscription outside a yellow Empire-style mansion record that one of the greatest opera singers of the 20th century once lived here. The renowned Russian bass, Fyodor Shalyapin, occupied this large house from 1910 until he emigrated from Soviet Russia in 1922.

Born in Kazan in 1873, Shalyapin began his career in great poverty, working as a stevedore on the Volga before his unique vocal talent was discovered. He made his international debut at La Scala, Milan, in 1901, and went on to sing a variety of the great operatic bass roles, including *Don Quixote*, *Ivan the Terrible* and *Boris Godunov*.

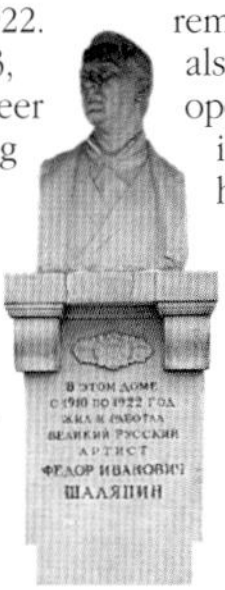

Stone bust of opera singer Shalyapin

Shalyapin died in Paris in 1938, but his remains have since been returned to Russia and were reburied in the Novodevichiy Cemetery *(see p131)* alongside other famous Russians.

This is one of Moscow's newer house-museums and one of the best. Amusing drawings of Shalyapin by his children and a china doll bought in France decorate the green-upholstered sitting room. The mementos in the blue study, meanwhile, include portraits of the singer in his various operatic roles.

The carved chair in front of the dining room stove was a gift from writer Maxim Gorky *(see p95)*, while the paintings on the walls are by the artist Konstantin Korovin.

The heavily labelled trunks stored in the box room are a reminder that Shalyapin was also in great demand at opera houses abroad. Other items on display in the house include the singer's make-up table and one of his wigs. In the concert room visitors can listen to recordings of Shalyapin at work. After singing for his guests, Shalyapin would often take them next door for a game of billiards. Shalyapin was not a very good loser and, depending on his mood, his wife would only invite friends with grace enough to let him win.

Pictures drawn by Shalyapin's children, on display in the sitting room

TVERSKAYA

AT HEART A COMMERCIAL district, Tverskaya centres on the road of the same name, which originally led to St Petersburg and was the processional route used by the tsars. Now Moscow's premier shopping street, Tverskaya ulitsa underwent a major redevelopment in the 1930s during the huge reconstruction of Moscow ordered by Stalin *(see p75)*. At that time many buildings were torn down so that the street could be widened and massive new apartment blocks were erected for workers. These looming grey buildings make the street a showcase of the monumental style of architecture *(see p45)* favoured by Stalin. The area's surprisingly tranquil backstreets have been home to many famous artists, writers and actors, and, despite Stalin's best efforts, still have some interesting pre-Revolutionary houses.

Shell detail on the House of Friendship

SIGHTS AT A GLANCE

Museums
Chekhov House-Museum 16
Gorky House-Museum 15
Museum of Modern History 19
Stanislavskiy House-Museum 9

Historic Buildings
Hotel Metropol 1
Hotel National 5
House of Friendship 14
House of Unions 4
Manège 13
Morozov Mansion 17
Moscow Conservatory 11
Moscow Old University 12

Monasteries
Upper Monastery of St Peter 21

Streets and Squares
Bolshaya Nikitskaya Ulitsa 10
Bryusov Pereulok 8
Patriarch's Pond 18
Pushkin Square 20
Theatre Square 2
Tverskaya Ulitsa 6

Theatres
Bolshoy Theatre pp90–91 3
Moscow Arts Theatre 7

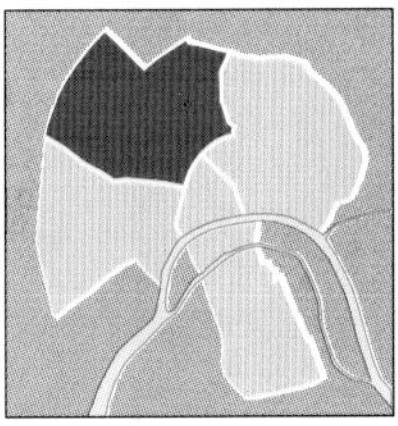

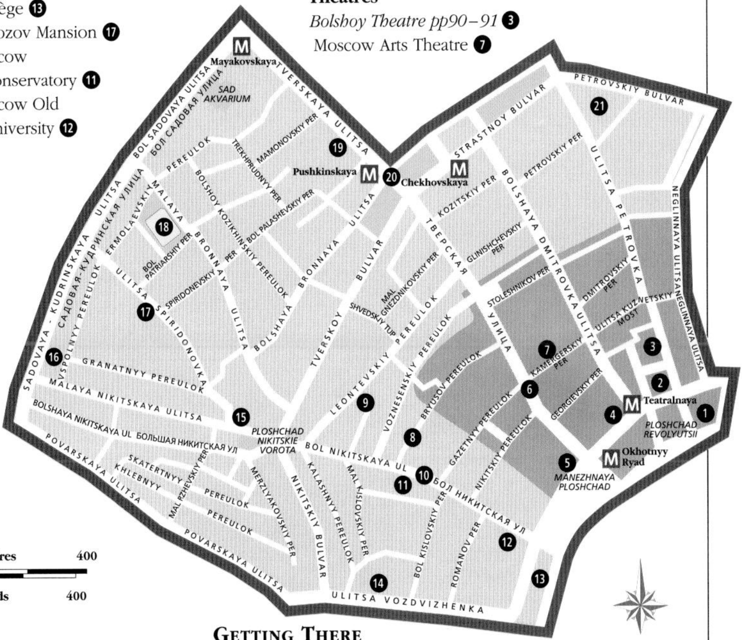

0 metres 400
0 yards 400

KEY

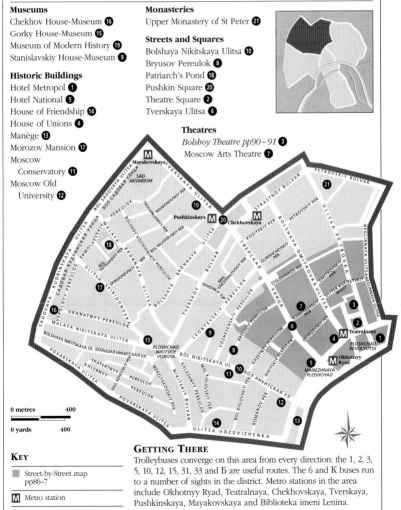

Street-by-Street map pp86–7

M Metro station

GETTING THERE

Trolleybuses converge on this area from every direction: the 1, 2, 3, 5, 10, 12, 15, 31, 33 and Б are useful routes. The 6 and К buses run to a number of sights in the district. Metro stations in the area include Okhotnyy Ryad, Teatralnaya, Chekhovskaya, Tverskaya, Pushkinskaya, Mayakovskaya and Biblioteka imeni Lenina.

◁ **The exquisitely ornate interior of the 19th-century Yeliseev's Food Hall *(see p89)* on Tverskaya ulitsa**

Street-by-Street: Around Theatre Square

MOSCOW'S THEATRELAND is centred, quite appropriately, around Theatre Square. Dominating the square is one of the most famous opera and ballet stages in the world, the Bolshoy Theatre. The Malyy (Small) Theatre is on the east side of the square, while the Russian Academic Youth Theatre is on the west. Further to the west is the city's main shopping street, Tverskaya ulitsa, and two more theatres, the Yermolova Theatre and the Moscow Arts Theatre. There are also several excellent restaurants and bars in this lively neighbourhood.

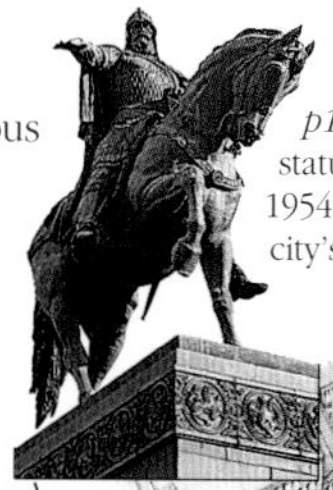

Yuriy Dolgorukiy, Moscow's founder *(see p17)*, is depicted in this statue. It was unveiled in 1954, seven years after the city's 800th anniversary.

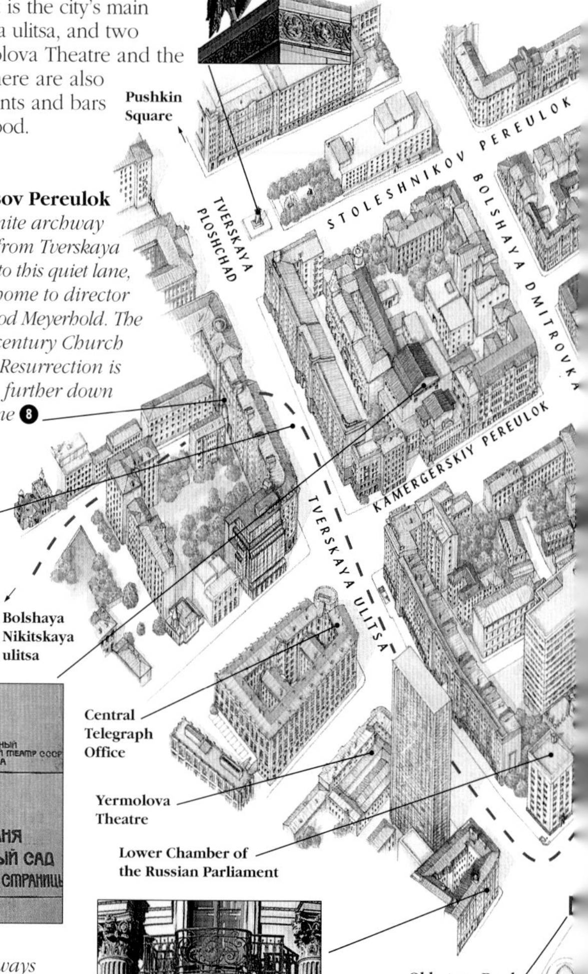

Bryusov Pereulok
A granite archway leads from Tverskaya ulitsa to this quiet lane, once home to director Vsevolod Meyerhold. The 17th-century Church of the Resurrection is visible further down the lane ❽

Tverskaya Ulitsa
Most of the imposing Stalinist blocks on Moscow's main shopping street date from the 1930s, but a few older buildings survive ❻

Moscow Arts Theatre
This famous theatre will always be associated with the dramatist Anton Chekhov (see p92). *Several of his plays, including* The Cherry Orchard, *were premiered here* ❼

Hotel National
Designed by Aleksandr Ivanov, the National (see p169) *is a mix of Style Moderne and Classical style. Now fully restored, its decor is as impressive as it was before the Revolution, when it was Moscow's finest hotel* ❺

STAR SIGHTS

★ **Bolshoy Theatre**

★ **House of Unions**

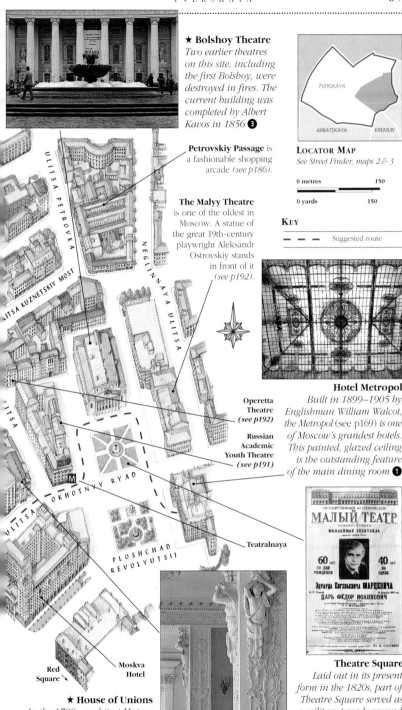

★ Bolshoy Theatre
Two earlier theatres on this site, including the first Bolshoy, were destroyed in fires. The current building was completed by Albert Kavos in 1856 ❸

LOCATOR MAP
See Street Finder, maps 2 & 3

0 metres 150

0 yards 150

KEY

Suggested route

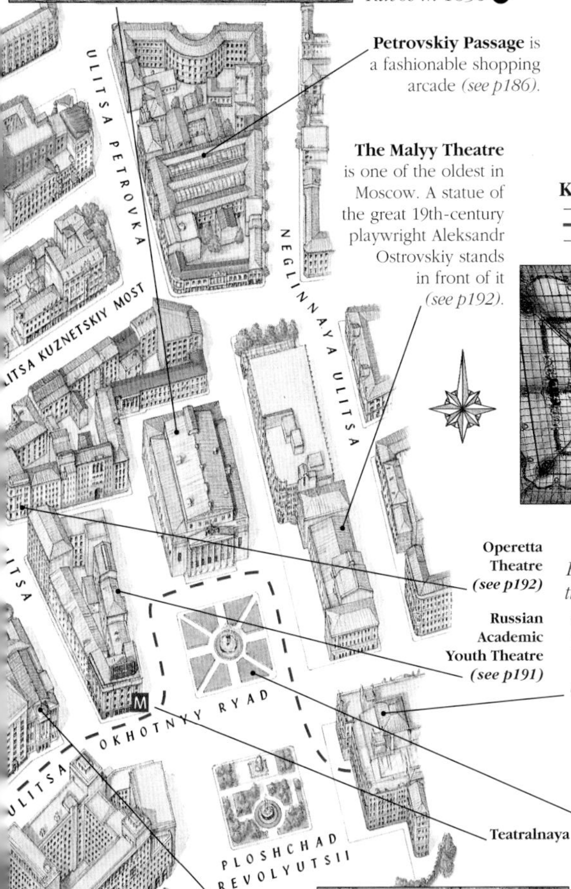

Petrovskiy Passage is a fashionable shopping arcade *(see p186)*.

The Malyy Theatre is one of the oldest in Moscow. A statue of the great 19th-century playwright Aleksandr Ostrovskiy stands in front of it *(see p192)*.

Operetta Theatre *(see p192)*

Russian Academic Youth Theatre *(see p191)*

Teatralnaya

Red Square

Moskva Hotel

Hotel Metropol
Built in 1899–1905 by Englishman William Walcot, the Metropol (see p169) *is one of Moscow's grandest hotels. This painted, glazed ceiling is the outstanding feature of the main dining room* ❶

Theatre Square
Laid out in its present form in the 1820s, part of Theatre Square served as a military parade ground from 1839–1911. Playbills around the city advertise performances in the theatres on the square ❷

★ House of Unions
In the 1780s, architect Matvey Kazakov converted this Neo-Classical mansion into a noblemen's club. The trade unions took it over in the Soviet era ❹

The statue of Aleksandr Ostrovskiy in front of the Malyy Theatre

Hotel Metropol ❶

Гостиница Метрополь
Gostinitsa Metropol

Teatralnyy prospekt 1/4. **Map** 3 A5. 927 6000. Ⓜ *Teatralnaya. See* ***Where to Stay*** *p169.*

The Hotel Metropol, built by William Walcot and Lev Kekushev in 1899–1905, is a fine example of Style-Moderne architecture *(see p45)*. The exterior walls sport a number of ceramic panels, including Mikhail Vrubel's large work at the top of the façade. Called *The Daydreaming Princess*, it is based on scenes from the play *La Princesse Lointaine*, written in 1895 by Edmond Rostand, author of *Cyrano de Bergerac*. The building also has ornate wrought-iron balconies and a superb painted glass roof in its Metropol Zal restaurant.

Over the years the Metropol has welcomed guests as varied and famous as Irish dramatist George Bernard Shaw and American pop star Michael Jackson.

The façade of the Hotel Metropol, designed by William Walcot

Theatre Square ❷

Театральная площадь
Teatralnaya ploshchad

Map 3 A5. Ⓜ *Teatralnaya, Ploshchad Revolyutsii, Okhotnyy Ryad.*

This elegant square is named after the theatres on three of its sides. Originally this area was marshy ground, regularly flooded by the Neglinnaya river. In the 1820s it was paved over and the square was laid out to a design by Osip Bove *(see p45)*. In 1839–1911 a military parade ground occupied part of the square. Today, Theatre Square is dominated by the Bolshoy Theatre.

On the square's east side is a converted private mansion that houses the Malyy (Small) Theatre *(see p192)*. The Malyy is particularly associated with playwright Aleksandr Ostrovskiy (1823–86), whose satirical plays were performed here. A sombre statue of him by Nikolay Andreev was erected in the forecourt in 1929.

The Russian Academic Youth Theatre *(see p191)*, with its elaborate Neo-Classical porch, stands on the square's west side. Originally designed by Osip Bove *(see p45)*, it was almost entirely rebuilt by Boris Freidenberg in 1882. The theatre has occupied this building since 1936.

To the northwest of Theatre Square is the Operetta Theatre *(see p192)*. In the 1890s the private opera company of the wealthy industrialist and arts patron Savva Mamontov (1842–1914) performed here. The careers of opera singer Fyodor Shalyapin *(see p83)*, composer Sergei Rachmaninov and artist Vasiliy Polenov, who designed sets and costumes, all began here with Mamontov's company.

In the centre of the square is a granite statue of Karl Marx. Sculpted in 1961 by Leonid Kerbel, it bears the words "Workers of the world unite!"

Bolshoy Theatre ❸

See pp90–91.

The well-proportioned Hall of Columns in the elegant, 18th-century House of Unions

House of Unions ❹

Дом Союзов
Dom Soyuzov

Bolshaya Dmitrovka ulitsa 1. **Map** 3 A5. *for performances only.* Ⓜ *Teatralnaya, Okhotnyy Ryad.*

This green and white Neo-Classical mansion was originally built in the first half of the 18th century. In the early 1780s, it was bought by a group of Moscow nobles who commissioned architect Matvey Kazakov *(see pp44–5)* to turn it into a noblemen's club. Kazakov added a number of rooms to the existing building including the magnificent ballroom, known as the Hall of Columns. It was here, in 1856, that Tsar Alexander II addressed an audience of the Russian nobility on the need to emancipate the serfs.

After the Revolution, trade unions took over the building, hence its current name. In 1924 the hall was opened to the public for more than a million people to file past Lenin's open coffin. Many of his closest colleagues, members of the guard of honour on that occasion, were later tried here during the show trials of 1936–8 *(see p27)*. Stalin, who was behind these travesties of justice, also lay in state here in 1953.

Nowadays the House of Unions is used for concerts and public meetings.

Hotel National ❺

Гостиница Националь

Gostinitsa Natsional

Mokhovaya ulitsa 15/1. **Map** 2 F5. *258 7000.* *Okhotnyy Ryad.* See **Where to Stay** *p169.*

Designed in 1903 by architect Aleksandr Ivanov, the Hotel National is an eclectic mixture of Style-Moderne and Classical-style architecture *(see pp44–5)*. The façade is decorated with sculpted nymphs and ornate stone tracery, but is topped by a mosaic from the Soviet era. This features factory chimneys belching smoke, oil derricks, electricity pylons, railway engines and tractors.

The National's most famous guest was Lenin, who stayed in room 107 at the hotel for a week, in March 1918, before he moved to the Kremlin.

Tverskaya ulitsa, one of Moscow's most popular shopping streets

The National was completely refurbished in the early 1990s and its Style-Moderne interiors have been faithfully restored to their original splendour.

Tverskaya Ulitsa ❻

Тверская улица

Tverskaya ulitsa

Map 2 F5, F4, E3. *Okhotnyy Ryad, Tverskaya, Pushkinskaya.*

Tverskaya ulitsa was the grandest thoroughfare in Moscow in the 19th century, when it was famous for its restaurants, theatres, hotels and purveyors of French fashions. Stalin's reconstruction of the city in the 1930s resulted in Tverskaya ulitsa being widened by 42 m (138 ft) and its name being changed to ulitsa Gorkovo to commemorate the writer Maxim Gorky. Many buildings were torn down to make way for huge apartment blocks to house party bureaucrats, such as those at Nos. 9–11. Other buildings were rebuilt further back to stand on the new, wider road. Now called Tverskaya ulitsa again, the street carries a huge volume of traffic. However, it is still one of the city's most popular places to eat out and shop.

Lobby of the Hotel National, with Style-Moderne windows and Classical statues

At No.7 is the Central Telegraph Office, a severe grey building with an illuminated globe outside. It was designed by Ilya Rerberg in 1927. Through the arch on the other side of the road is a green-tiled building with floral friezes and tent-roofed turrets. Built in 1905, this was the Moscow mission of the Savvinskiy Monastery. It is now luxury flats and offices.

Further up the street is the soulless Tverskaya square, dominated by an equestrian statue of Moscow's founder, Prince Yuriy Dolgorukiy *(see p86)*. On the west side of the square looms the red and white city hall. Designed in 1782 by Matvey Kazakov *(see pp44–5)*, it was the residence of the governor-general before the Revolution and later became the Moscow City Soviet or town hall. In 1944–6 extra storeys were added, more than doubling its height.

Beyond Tverskaya square, at No. 14, is Moscow's most famous delicatessen. Now known by its pre-Revolutionary name, Yeliseev's Food Hall *(see p186)*, in Soviet times it was called Gastronom No.1. In the 1820s this mansion was the home of Princess Zinaida Volkonskaya, whose soirées were attended by great figures of the day, including Alexander Pushkin *(see p73)*. In 1898 Grigoriy Yeliseev bought the building, and had it lavishly redecorated with stained-glass windows, crystal chandeliers, carved pillars, polished wood counters and large mirrors. It now stocks a wide range of imported and Russian delicacies.

Bolshoy Theatre ❸

Большой театр
Bolshoy teatr

HOME TO ONE OF THE OLDEST, and probably the most famous, ballet companies in the world, the Bolshoy Theatre is also one of Moscow's major landmarks. The first Bolshoy Theatre opened in 1780 and presented masquerades, comedies and comic operas. It burnt down in 1805, but its successor was completed in 1825 to a design by Osip Bove *(see p45)* and Andrey Mikhaylov. This building too was destroyed by fire, in 1853, but the essentials of its highly praised design were retained in Albert Kavos' reconstruction of 1856. Today the theatre still provides a magnificent setting for performances of ballet and opera by the Bolshoy Theatre company.

★ Royal Box
Situated at the centre of the gallery, the royal box, hung with crimson velvet, is one of over 120 boxes. The imperial crown on its pediment was removed in the Soviet era but has now been restored.

Neo-Classical Pediment
The relief on the Neo-Classical pediment was an addition by Albert Kavos during his reconstruction of the theatre. It depicts a pair of angels bearing aloft the lyre of Apollo, the Greek god of music and light.

★ Apollo in the Chariot of the Sun
This eye-catching sculpture by Pyotr Klodt, part of the original 1825 building, was retained by Albert Kavos. It depicts Apollo driving the chariot on which he carried the sun across the sky.

Vestibule
Patrons entering the theatre find themselves in this grand, black and white tiled vestibule. Magnificent staircases, lined with white marble, lead up from either side of the vestibule to the spacious main foyer.

Beethoven Hall
This ornately decorated room was formerly known as the Imperial Foyer. It is now used for occasional chamber concerts and lectures. The stuccoed decoration on the ceiling includes approximately 3,000 rosettes and the walls are adorned with delicately embroidered panels of crimson silk.

Visitors' Checklist

Teatralnaya ploshchad 1. **Map** 3 A4. 927 6982. *Teatralnaya.* *2, 12, 33.* *K.* *Tue – Sun, for performances.* *July – Aug.* *in auditorium.* www.bolshoi.ru

Apollo and the Muses
The ten painted panels decorating the auditorium's ceiling are by Pyotr Titov. They depict Apollo dancing with the nine muses of Greek myth, each of which is connected with a different branch of the arts or sciences.

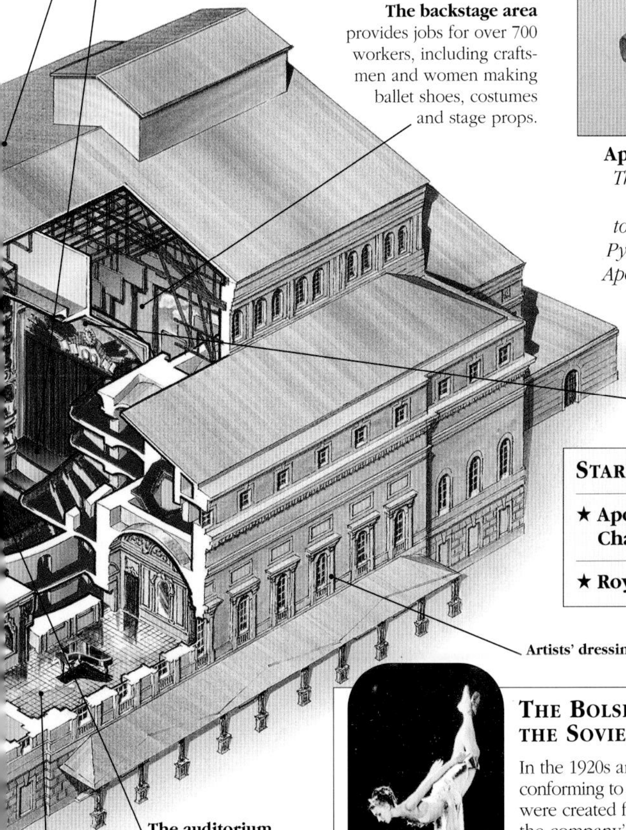

Main stage

The backstage area provides jobs for over 700 workers, including craftsmen and women making ballet shoes, costumes and stage props.

Artists' dressing room

The auditorium has six tiers and a seating capacity of 2,500. When Kavos rebuilt it he modified its shape to improve the accoustics.

The main foyer extends around the whole of the front of the building on the first floor. Its vaulted ceiling is decorated with paintings and elaborate stucco work.

Star Features

- ★ **Apollo in the Chariot of the Sun**
- ★ **Royal Box**

The Bolshoy Ballet in the Soviet Era

In the 1920s and 1930s new ballets conforming to Revolutionary ideals were created for the Bolshoy, but the company's heyday was in the 1950s and 1960s. Ballets such as *Spartacus* were produced and the dancers toured abroad for the first time to widespread acclaim. Yet a number of dancers also defected to the West in this period, in protest at the company's harsh management and a lack of artistic freedom.

A production of *Spartacus* (1954), by Aram Khachaturian, at the Bolshoy

Arch at the entrance to Bryusov pereulok, a street where artists and musicians lived in the 1920s

Moscow Arts Theatre 7

МХАТ имени АП Чехова

MKhAT imeni AP Chekhova

Kamergerskiy pereulok 3. **Map** 2 F5. 229 8760. M *Teatralnaya, Okhotnyy Ryad.* *performances only. See* ***Entertainment*** *p192.*

THE FIRST EVER performance at the Moscow Arts Theatre (MKhAT) took place in 1898. The theatre was founded by a group of young enthusiasts, led by the directors Konstantin Stanislavskiy and Vladimir Nemirovich-Danchenko. The MKhAT company had an early success with their production of Anton Chekhov's play *The Seagull* in the theatre's first year. When the play had been performed three years earlier in St Petersburg, it had been a disastrous flop but, performed using Stanislavskiy's new Method acting, it was extremely well received.

The Moscow Arts Theatre entrance with *The Wave* bas-relief above

In 1902 architect Fyodor Shekhtel *(see p45)* completely reconstructed the interior of the theatre, adding innovations such as a central lighting box and a revolving stage. The auditorium had very little decoration, so that audiences were forced to concentrate on the performance.

The theatre continued to flourish after the Revolution, but its repertoire was restricted by state censorship. Most of the plays produced were written by Maxim Gorky, whose work was in favour with the government. The frustrations and compromises of the period were brilliantly satirized in the 1930s by Mikhail Bulgakov (who also worked as an assistant director in the theatre) in his novel *Teatralnyy Roman*. These problems continued and in the 1980s part of the company moved to the Gorky Arts Theatre on Tverskoy bulvar.

Today a variety of productions are staged at the Moscow Arts Theatre, including many of Anton Chekhov's plays.

Stylized seagull on the exterior of the Moscow Arts Theatre

Bryusov Pereulok 8

Брюсов переулок

Bryusov pereulok

Map 2 F5. M *Okhotnyy Ryad, Arbatskaya.*

A GRANITE ARCH on Tverskaya ulitsa marks the entrance to this quiet side street. It is named after the Bruces, a Scots family who were involved with the Russian court.

In the 1920s new apartments here were assigned to the staff of the Moscow state theatres. No. 17 was the home of two actors from the Moscow Arts Theatre, Vasiliy Kachalov and Ivan Moskvin.

No. 12 was home to the avant-garde director Vsevolod Meyerhold, who directed premieres of Vladimir Mayakovsky's satires. He lived here from 1928 until his arrest in 1939 at the height of Stalin's Great Purge *(see p27)*.

The Composers' Union was at Nos. 8–10. It was here that composers Sergey Prokofiev and Dmitriy Shostakovich were forced to read an apology for works that deviated from Socialist Realism *(see p135)*.

About halfway along Bryusov pereulok is the 17th-century single-domed Church of the Resurrection. This was one of the few churches to remain open during the Soviet era.

Stanislavskiy and Chekhov

Konstantin Stanislavskiy in the play *Uncle Vanya* by Chekhov

Konstantin Stanislavskiy's successful production of Anton Chekhov's *The Seagull* took the theatre world by storm. Stanislavskiy's secret was his new school of Method acting, in which performers explored their characters' inner motives. Stanislavskiy and Chekhov collaborated on the premieres of other Chekhov plays and the success of the productions was such that their names have been linked ever since.

Stanislavskiy House-Museum ❾

Дом-музей КС Станиславского
Dom-muzey KS Stanislavskovo

Leontevskiy pereulok 6. **Map** 2 E5. *229 2855.* *Arbatskaya, Tverskaya.* *11am–5pm Thu, Sat–Sun, 2pm–7pm Wed, Fri.* *public holidays.*

This 18th-century mansion was the home of the great director and actor Konstantin Stanislavskiy. He lived on the first floor from 1920 until he died in 1938, at the age of 75.

Stanislavskiy found himself disillusioned with the conservative ethos of the old Moscow Theatre School, and created an outlet for his innovative ideas by founding the Moscow Arts Theatre (MKhAT) in 1898. After moving into this flat, he converted his ballroom into a makeshift theatre where he rehearsed his experimental Opera Dramatic Group. Later, when he was too ill to go out, he also held rehearsals here for the MKhAT company.

Stanislavskiy's living room and study, the dining room and the bedroom of his wife, Maria Lilina, are all open. Also on display are an early Edison phonograph and a vase that was a gift from the dancer Isadora Duncan. Downstairs are props and costumes from Stanislavskiy's productions.

Bolshaya Nikitskaya Ulitsa ❿

Большая Никитская улица
Bolshaya Nikitskaya ulitsa

Map 2 F5, E5. *Arbatskaya, Okhotnyy Ryad, Biblioteka imeni Lenina.*

This historic street, once the main road to Novgorod, is named after the Nikitskiy Convent which was founded in the 16th century, but pulled down by Stalin in the 1930s.

Prominent aristocratic families such as the Menshikovs and Orlovs built their palaces here in the 18th century. The finest is the former residence of Prince Sergey Menshikov, which can be reached via Gazetniy pereulok. The pale blue façade was reconstructed following the great fire of 1812 *(see pp24–5)*. The Neo-Classical rear façade, which survived the fire, dates from around 1775.

Just opposite the Moscow Conservatory *(see p94)*, is the attractive white Church of the Little Ascension. Built around the end of the 16th century, it was restored in 1739 following a fire. Behind it is the Gothic tower of St Andrew's Anglican Church. It was built for Moscow's English community in 1882 by British architect Richard Freeman.

Stone relief on Church of the Great Ascension

The heavily ornamented red-brick building at Nos. 19–20 was once called the Paradise Theatre. It was renamed the Mayakovsky Theatre after the poet Vladimir Mayakovsky *(see p111)*. His plays *Bath House* and *The Bed Bug* were premiered here in 1928 and 1929, directed by avant-garde director Vsevolod Meyerhold. One of the greatest innovators of his era, Meyerhold was executed by the State in 1940, largely because his work did not agree with the canons of Socialist Realism *(see p135)*.

About halfway along the road is Nikitskie Vorota ploshchad, named after the medieval gate that used to stand here. On the square is a modern white building with a sign in the shape of a large globe hanging beneath its porch. This is the ITAR-TASS news agency, the mouthpiece of the Communist Party in the Soviet era and now Russia's main news agency.

Opposite is the Church of the Great Ascension. Begun in 1798, it was rebuilt after the 1812 fire. Alexander Pushkin *(see p73)* married Natalya Goncharova here in 1831.

Sign in the shape of a globe hanging outside the ITAR-TASS news agency

The Bolshoy Zal (Great Hall) in the Moscow Conservatory

Moscow Conservatory ⓫

Московская консерватория

Moskovskaya Konservatoriya

Bolshaya Nikitskaya ulitsa 13. **Map** 2 F5. *229 7412.* M *Arbatskaya, Pushkinskaya.* *performances only.*

THE LARGEST MUSIC SCHOOL in Russia, the Moscow Conservatory was founded in 1866 by Nikolay Rubinstein, the brother of composer and pianist Anton Rubinstein.

One of the Conservatory's teachers was the young Pyotr Tchaikovsky, who taught here until 1878. On the forecourt is his statue, wielding a baton despite the fact that Tchaikovsky detested conducting. The work of Vera Mukhina, it dates from 1954. The pattern on the forecourt railings is made up of the opening notes from some of Tchaikovsky's works.

Portraits of famous composers adorn the walls of the light, airy Bolshoy Zal (Great Hall). Used for concerts since 1898, it is also the setting for the prestigious Tchaikovsky International Competition *(see p192)*. The Conservatory has a small museum that is open during perfomances.

The Conservatory has always been an important training ground for young Russian composers and performers. Among its best-known alumni are pianist-composers Sergei Rachmaninov and Aleksandr Skryabin *(see p72)*. Dmitriy Shostakovich, the great Soviet composer, lived nearby, at the Composers' Union on Bryusov pereulok *(see p92)* . He taught at the Conservatory from 1942 until he fell from favour and was sacked six years later for "professional incompetence" during Stalin's Purges *(see p27)*.

Moscow Old University ⓬

Московский университет

Moskovskiy Universitet

Mokhovaya ulitsa 9. **Map** 2 F5. M *Okhotnyy Ryad, Biblioteka imeni Lenina.*

MOSCOW UNIVERSITY was founded by the scholar Mikhail Lomonosov in 1755, and is the oldest university in Russia. It moved into this imposing building (now called the Old University) in 1793. Designed by Matvey Kazakov *(see pp44–5)*, it was extensively rebuilt by Domenico Gilardi after the 1812 fire *(see pp24–5)* and is a fine example of Neo-Classical architecture *(see pp44–5)*. Outside are statues of radical writers Nikolay Ogarev and Aleksandr Herzen.

Statue of Mikhail Lomonosov

In 1836 the university acquired a building on the far side of Bolshaya Nikitskaya ulitsa. In front of the New University is a statue of Mikhail Lomonosov. Nearby is the chapel of St Tatyana, whose feast day is celebrated by the students.

Manège ⓭

Манеж

Manezh

Manezhnaya ploshchad 1. **Map** 6 F1. *202 8976.* M *Biblioteka imeni Lenina, Okhotnyy Ryad.* *exhibitions only.*

THE MANEGE was originally built in 1817 as a military parade ground to a design by General Augustin de Béthencourt. The 45-m- (148-ft-) wide roof had no supporting columns, leaving an uninterrupted floor space large enough for an infantry regiment to practise in. However, in the 1930s the roof started to sag and had to be reinforced with interior pillars.

In 1823–5 Osip Bove *(see p45)* added a colonnade and decorative frieze to the exterior.

The Manège became the Central Exhibition Hall in 1957 and it was at an exhibition here in 1962 that Nikita Khrushchev *(see p30)* famously condemned abstract art. The brunt of the attack was borne by the sculptor Ernst Neizvestniy but, curiously, in his will Khrushchev chose Neizvestniy to design his tombstone *(see p131)*. Today the Manège is still mostly used to house exhibitions.

The Manège, designed by Augustin de Béthencourt in 1817

The extravagant interior of the 19th-century House of Friendship

House of Friendship ⓮

Дом дружбы

Dom Druzhby

Vozdvizhenka ulitsa 16. **Map** 6 E1. ☎ *290 2069.* Ⓜ *Arbatskaya, Biblioteka imeni Lenina.* ◯ *performances only.*

This incredible mansion has towers encrusted with stone shells and topped by lacelike stonework. Vladimir Mazyrin designed it at the end of the 19th century for the playboy Arseny Morozov, a member of the wealthy Morozov family *(see p96)*. The interior is as showy as the façade. Its rooms include a Greek atrium and a hunting hall filled with carved animal heads. The only way to see inside is to attend a concert or lecture held here. In Soviet times the mansion was used by the Union of Friendship Societies, hence its name.

Gorky House-Museum ⓯

Дом-музей АМ Горького

Dom-muzey AM Gorkovo

Malaya Nikitskaya ulitsa 6/2. **Map** 2 E5. ☎ *290 0535.* Ⓜ *Pushkinskaya.* ◯ *10am–4pm Thu, Sat–Sun, 12pm–6pm Wed, Fri.* *English.*

A frieze of irises against a background of blue and purple clouds runs round the top of the yellow glazed-brick walls of this extraordinary mansion. Fyodor Shekhtel designed this masterpiece of Style-Moderne architecture *(see p45)* in 1900. The house belonged to arts patron and millionaire banker Stepan Ryabushinskiy until he left Russia with his family after the Revolution. In 1931 Stalin presented the mansion as a gift to the famous socialist writer Maxim Gorky.

The interior of the house is spectacular, featuring ceilings with elaborate mouldings, stained-glass windows and carved door frames. However, the *pièce de résistance* is the flowing staircase of polished Estonian limestone, which ends in a twisted post with a bronze lamp resembling a jellyfish.

By the time Gorky moved to this house, his career as a novelist and playwright was in decline. While living here, he wrote only one play, *Yegor Bulychev and Others* (1932), and part of a novel, *The Life of Klim Samgin* (unfinished at his death). However his fame and his earlier support for the Bolshevik Party made him a useful propaganda tool for the Soviet government. He served this function by being president of the Union of Writers, which explains why the rooms are full of photos of the author in the company of aspiring dramatists, Young Pioneers and ambitious Communist officials.

On display are Gorky's hat, overcoat and walking stick, his remarkable collection of oriental carvings and many of his letters and books, including some first editions.

Shortly after Gorky died in 1936, Genrikh Yagoda, the former head of the NKVD (secret police), was accused of murdering him. Although the charge was probably fabricated, Yagoda was found guilty in one of the last of the notorious show trials *(see p27)*. Rumours persist that Gorky was killed on Stalin's orders.

The spectacular Style-Moderne staircase in the Gorky House-Museum

Chekhov House-Museum ⓰

Дом-музей АП Чехова

Dom-muzey AP Chekhova

Sadovaya-Kudrinskaya ulitsa 6. **Map** 2 D5. *291 6154.* *Barrikadnaya.* *11am–4pm Tue, Thu, Sat, 2pm–6pm Wed, Fri.* *(book in advance).*

ANTON CHEKHOV (1860–1904) lived in this two-storey house in 1886–90. It was later refurbished in consultation with the author's widow, actress Olga Knipper-Chekhova, and opened as a museum in 1954. However, it is only partially successful in recreating a period feeling and contains few of Chekhov's possessions.

Chekhov was a qualified doctor and was practising medicine when he lived here, as the brass plate by the front door testifies. He shared the house with his parents, his brother, Mikhail, and his sister, Mariya. As the family's main breadwinner, Chekhov could only write in his spare time, but it was here that he created his first major play, *Ivanov*. He also wrote many short stories and several one-act plays here.

Exhibits in the study, which doubled as a consulting room, include Chekhov's doctor's bag, manuscripts and pictures, including some of him with Leo Tolstoy *(see p134)*.

Upstairs are a richly decorated living room and Mariya's room, which, in some ways, is the most attractive in the house. Its furnishings include a sewing machine, ornaments and embroidered tablecloths.

There is also an exhibition about Chekhov's later career as a playwright *(see p93)*, which includes adverts for his plays and first editions of his works.

Picture of Chekhov (on the left) talking with Leo Tolstoy, in the Chekhov House-Museum

The Gothic-style Morozov Mansion, designed by Fyodor Shekhtel

Morozov Mansion ⓱

Дом ЗГ Морозовой

Dom ZG Morozovoy

Ulitsa Spiridonovka 17. **Map** 2 D4. *Mayakovskaya.* *to public.*

FYODOR SHEKHTEL *(see p45)* built this house for his patron, Savva Morozov, in 1893–8. Savva Morozov was a wealthy textiles manufacturer and arts patron, a member of one of the city's richest merchant families.

The mansion was built in the Gothic style to resemble a baronial castle, with turrets, gargoyles and arched windows. Some of the stained-glass windows were designed by the Symbolist artist Mikhail Vrubel.

The building, now owned by the Foreign Ministry, is often host to important negotiations.

Patriarch's Pond ⓲

Патриаршие пруды

Patriarshie prudy

Map 2 D4. *Mayakovskaya.*

JUST A FEW MINUTES' WALK from the busy Garden Ring is a secluded, tree-lined square with the large Patriarch's Pond at its heart. The pond is named after the patriarch, the head of the Russian Orthodox Church *(see p137)*, who formerly owned the land.

Near the children's playground is a bronze statue of the 19th-century playwright and writer of popular fables Ivan Krylov. Sculptures of the creatures from his stories are dotted among the trees.

Patriarch's Pond is probably best known as the setting for the opening scene in Mikhail Bulgakov's novel *The Master and Margarita*, in which the Devil causes havoc in Moscow. In 1921–4 Bulgakov lived near Patriarch's Pond, on Bolshaya Sadovaya ulitsa. He began the novel in 1928, but only finished it just before his death in 1940. It was not published until 1966 for political reasons.

Graffiti at Bulgakov's flat by enthusiasts of his work

MIKHAIL BULGAKOV

Many of the satirical, anti-Bolshevik plays of Mikhail Bulgakov (1891–1940) were banned by the authorities. In 1930 Bulgakov became so frustrated that he wrote to Stalin asking to be exiled. Instead he was given a job at the Moscow Arts Theatre *(see p92)* and, in 1932, Stalin lifted the ban on *The Days of the Turbins*. Most of Bulgakov's work, including *The Master and Margarita*, was only published after his death.

Maxim gun used in the Civil War, in the Museum of Modern History

Museum of Modern History 19

Музей современной истории
Muzey sovremennoy istorii

Tverskaya ulitsa 21. **Map** 2 E4. *299 6724.* *Pushkinskaya, Tverskaya.* *10am–5:30pm Tue– Sat, 10am–6pm Sun.* *English.*

A PAIR OF STONE LIONS guards this elegant red mansion, built in the late 18th century. The wings and Empire-style façade *(see p45)* were added some decades later. In 1831 the mansion became a gentlemen's club, known as the English Club, and until the Revolution, the Muscovite aristocracy drank and gambled here.

Ironically, this building, with all its aristocratic associations, became the Museum of the Revolution. However, since the Soviet Union broke up in 1991, the collections display a more objective view of 20th-century Russian history; the name of the museum has also been changed to reflect this shift.

Laid out chronologically, the exhibits cover 1900–91. They include home-made grenades, a Maxim gun on a converted carriage (used in the Civil War), sweet wrappers depicting Marx and Lenin and former premier Nikita Khrushchev's hat and camera from his 1959 trip to the United States. The collection of so-called propaganda porcelain and a display of gifts presented to Soviet rulers are also interesting.

Pushkin Square 20

Пушкинская площадь
Pushkinskaya ploshchad

Map 2 F4. *Pushkinskaya, Tverskaya, Chekhovskaya.*

THE BRONZE STATUE of poet Alexander Pushkin was unveiled in the presence of two other Russian literary giants, Fyodor Dostoevsky and Ivan Turgenev, in 1880. The statue, located on the south side of Pushkin Square, was sculpted by Alexander Opekushin.

Pushkin has long epitomized the spirit of freedom in Russia and the statue became a rallying point for dissident human rights demonstrations in the 1960s and 1970s. These often ended in violent clashes between the KGB and demonstrators.

Before the Revolution Pushkin Square was called Strastnaya ploshchad (Passion Square) after the 17th-century Convent of the Passion which used to stand here. The convent was demolished in 1935 to make way for the monstrous Rossiya cinema *(see p193)*.

The statue of poet Alexander Pushkin, on Pushkin Square

Just beyond the cinema, on Malaya Dmitrovka ulitsa, is the Church of the Nativity of the Virgin in Putinki. Built in 1649–52, this attractive church has clustered tent roofs, tiered *kokoshniki* gables *(see p44)* and blue onion domes.

On the northeast corner of the square stand the offices of the newspaper *Izvestiya*. Once an official mouthpiece of the Soviet government, *Izvestiya* is now one of Russia's independent daily newspapers.

Upper Monastery of St Peter 21

Высоко-Петровский монастырь
Vysoko-Petrovskiy monastyr

Ulitsa Petrovka 28. **Map** 3 A3. *923 7580.* *Pushkinskaya, Chekhovskaya.* *9:30am–6pm daily.*

THIS MONASTERY was founded in the reign of Ivan I *(see p18)*. It was rebuilt in the late 17th century with sponsorship from the Naryshkin family, relatives of Peter the Great. Its six churches include the Church of the Metropolitan Peter after which the monastery is named. This single-domed church was built in 1514–17 to a design by Aleviz Novyy. The Church of the Icon of the Virgin of Bogolyubovo commemorates three of Peter the Great's uncles killed in the 1682 Streltsy Rebellion *(see p22)*. The Refectory Church of St Sergius has five cupolas and scallop shell decoration. The monastery complex also includes a green-domed bell tower and the monks' cells.

Iconostasis in the Baroque bell tower of the Upper Monastery of St Peter

RED SQUARE AND KITAY GOROD

Moscow's first suburb, Kitay Gorod, was settled as early as the 12th century by tradesmen and artisans employed by the tsar. The word *kitay* is thought to refer to the wattle used to build the ramparts around the suburb. Red Square was created as a market square beside the Kremlin *(see pp52–67)* in the late 15th century. Behind it, trading rows were set up, each line of wooden cabins specializing in a particular item, such as icons, pans or hats. In the 16th century, a number of boyars *(see p20)*, including Russia's future rulers, the Romanovs, built their estates nearby, while the presence of merchants from Novgorod and as far away as England was actively encouraged. Later, in the 19th century, Kitay Gorod became Moscow's financial district, home to the Stock Exchange and major banks.

Icon of St George, Resurrection Gate

SIGHTS AT A GLANCE

Cathedrals, Churches, Convents and Monasteries

Church of the Trinity in Nikitniki 4
Convent of the Nativity of the Virgin 22
Kazan Cathedral 8
Monastery of the Epiphany 6
St Basil's Cathedral pp108–9 13

Streets and Squares

Chistoprudnyy Bulvar 19
Ivanovskaya Hill 14
Lubyanka Square 18
Nikolskaya Ulitsa 7
Red Square 10
Ulitsa Ilinka 5
Ulitsa Varvarka 1

Historic Buildings

GUM 12
Menshikov's Tower 20
Old English Court 2
Perlov Tea House 21
Resurrection Gate 9
Sandunovskiy Baths 23

Museums and Galleries

History of Moscow Museum 16
Lenin Mausoleum 11
Mayakovsky Museum 17
Palace of the Romanov Boyars 3
Polytechnical Museum 15

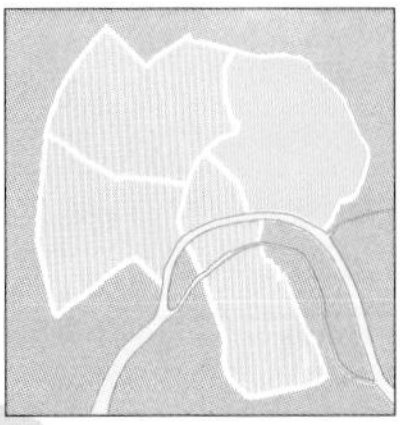

0 metres 400
0 yards 400

KEY

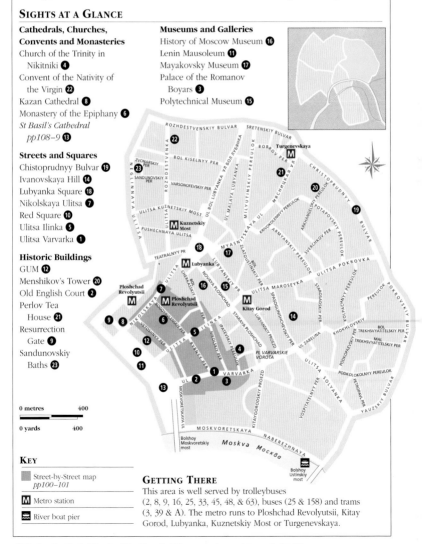

Street-by-Street map *pp100–101*

Metro station

River boat pier

GETTING THERE

This area is well served by trolleybuses (2, 8, 9, 16, 25, 33, 45, 48, & 63), buses (25 & 158) and trams (3, 39 & A). The metro runs to Ploshchad Revolyutsii, Kitay Gorod, Lubyanka, Kuznetskiy Most or Turgenevskaya.

◁ **The Russian-Revival façade of the Historical Museum at the northern end of Red Square**

Street-by-Street: Kitay Gorod

COMMERCE AND RELIGION go hand-in-hand in this ancient part of the city. The heart of Moscow's financial district is Birzhevaya ploshchad, and the surrounding area has been home to traders for centuries. Among the banks and offices are an increasing number of up-market stores, especially lining Nikolskaya ulitsa, and the area now rivals Russia's best-known shopping arcade, GUM *(see p107)*. At one time there were more than 40 churches and monasteries dotted about these narrow streets. Only around a dozen have survived and most of these are now undergoing painstaking restoration.

Monastery of the Epiphany
Founded in 1296, this is the second oldest monastery in Moscow. Its cathedral, built between 1693–6, is a fine example of florid Moscow Baroque ❻

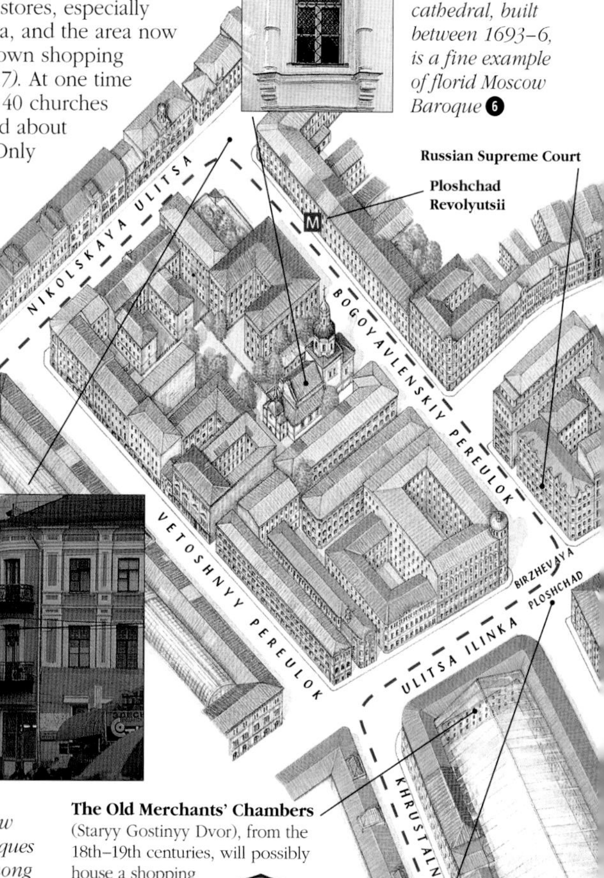

Nikolskaya Ulitsa
Well-heeled shoppers now head to this street's boutiques and jewellery shops. Among its more colourful sights is the Gothic-style Synodal Printing House, which dates from the 19th century ❼

The Old Merchants' Chambers
(Staryy Gostinyy Dvor), from the 18th–19th centuries, will possibly house a shopping arcade.

Ulitsa Ilinka
Halfway along ulitsa Ilinka is Birzhevaya ploshchad, where the former Stock Exchange is located. Constructed in 1873–5 by Aleksandr Kaminskiy, this attractive, pink, Classical-style building is now the home of the Russian Chamber of Industry and Commerce ❺

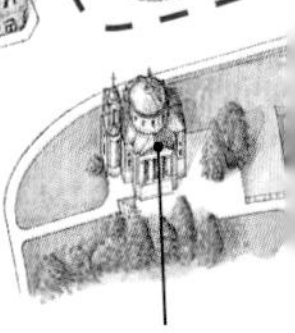

Church of St Barbara

STAR SIGHTS

- ★ **Church of the Trinity in Nikitniki**
- ★ **Palace of the Romanov Boyars**

KEY

– – – Suggested route

Ulitsa Varvarka
Several historic churches line this ancient route out of Moscow. Among them is the Church of St Maxim the Blessed, which was paid for by Novgorod merchants trading in Kitay Gorod and consecrated in 1698 ❶

Locator Map
See Street Finder, maps 3 & 7

★ Church of the Trinity in Nikitniki
Commissioned by the wealthy merchant Grigoriy Nikitnikov and completed in 1635, the Church of the Trinity in Nikitniki is famous both for its exuberant architecture and for the vivid frescoes that decorate its interior ❹

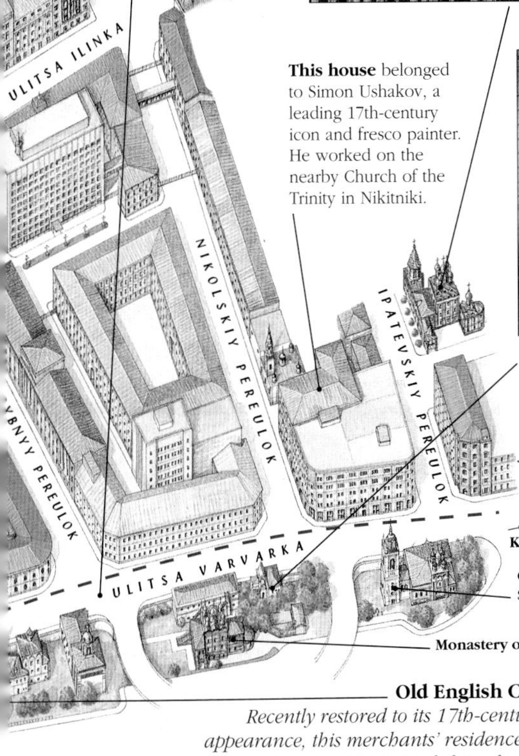

This house belonged to Simon Ushakov, a leading 17th-century icon and fresco painter. He worked on the nearby Church of the Trinity in Nikitniki.

★ Palace of the Romanov Boyars
This palace was originally lived in by powerful Muscovite boyar (see p20) *Nikita Romanov. It is now a fascinating museum which evokes the life of noble families in the 16th and 17th centuries* ❸

Old English Court
Recently restored to its 17th-century appearance, this merchants' residence was given to visiting English traders by Ivan the Terrible in the hope of securing arms and other goods from them ❷

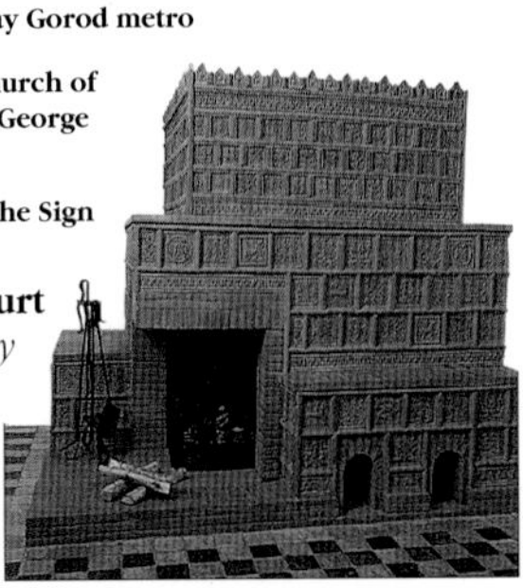

Ulitsa Varvarka ❶

Улица Варварка

Ulitsa Varvarka

Map 7 B1–C1. *Kitay Gorod.*

THE HEART OF the former merchants' quarter of Zaryade, ulitsa Varvarka is one of Moscow's oldest streets. It is named after the original Church of St Barbara (Varvara) the Martyr. This earlier building was demolished in 1796 to make way for a new pink and white Neo-Classical church of the same name, designed by Rodion Kazakov.

A little further along is the single-domed Church of St Maxim the Blessed. Built by traders from Novgorod to house the bones of St Maxim, it was consecrated in 1698. Between the two churches stands the Old English Court.

Across the road are the Old Merchants' Chambers (Staryy gostinyy dvor), which are fronted by a row of Corinthian columns. Italian architect Giacomo Quarenghi drew up plans for this market in 1790, and the work was supervised by Moscow architects Semen Karin and Ivan Selekhov. There are shops here and performances and exhibitions are held in the covered yard. Beyond the Church of St Maxim are the 17th-century Monastery of the Sign and the Palace of the Romanov Boyars.

At the end of ulitsa Varvarka is the Church of St George, built in 1657–8 by merchants from Pskov, a town known for its architects *(see p44)*. To the right, on Kitaygorodskiy proezd, is one of the few sections of the old city walls to survive. At the end of this street, beside the Moskva river, is the mid-16th-century Church of the Conception of St Anna.

The five domes of the Church of St George on ulitsa Varvarka

A view along ulitsa Varkarva, with the Old English Court straight ahead

Old English Court ❷

Старый английский двор

Staryy angliyskiy dvor

Ulitsa Varvarka 4a. **Map** 7 B1. *298 3952.* *10am–6pm Tue, Thu, Sat–Sun, 11am–7pm Wed, Fri.* *Ploshchad Revolyutsii, Kitay Gorod.* *English.*

IN 1553, while searching the northern coast of Russia for a passage to the east, the English merchant adventurer Richard Chancellor *(see p21)* was shipwrecked. He was taken to Moscow and received by Ivan the Terrible, whose desire to trade with England later led him to propose marriage to Queen Elizabeth I. On returning to Russia in 1556, Chancellor and his trading mission were given this large property in Zaryade. It was to serve as a storage and trading house and as accommodation for English merchants.

In the mid-17th century, the estate passed into Russian hands and by the 1900s it had been extensively altered. After the Revolution *(see pp26–9)*, the house was restored. It later reopened as a museum during the official visit of Queen Elizabeth II to Russia in 1994.

Inside, an exhibition highlights the history of the Old English Court and its role in developing Anglo-Russian relations. Winding stone staircases lead down to the cellars and the official chamber used for negotiations and functions. The English merchants fitted the Russian stove in this chamber with an open hearth to remind themselves of home.

Spartan interior of the official chamber in the Old English Court

Palace of the Romanov Boyars ❸

Музей-палаты в Зарядье

Muzey-palaty v Zaryade

Ulitsa Varvarka 10. **Map** 7 B1. *298 3706.* *10am–5pm Sun. Pre-booked groups only: 10am–5pm Thu–Sat, Mon, 11am–6pm Wed.* *Kitay Gorod.* *English.*

ONLY THE UPPER storeys of this palace can be seen from ulitsa Varvarka. This is largely because the palace is built on a steep slope leading away from the street down towards the Moskva river.

The palace was originally built by the boyar *(see p20)* Nikita Romanov in the 16th century. It was home to the Romanovs until 1613 when

Mikhail Romanov *(see p19)* became tsar and the family moved to the Kremlin. The palace has been protected as a museum since 1859.

The main entrance is reached via a courtyard; a double-headed eagle, the Romanov family crest, adorns the archway leading to the courtyard.

The ground and first floors of the palace probably date from the 17th century. In the painted hall, personal effects of the early Romanovs are displayed, including gold dishes, ancient title deeds, ledgers inlaid with precious gems and the robes of Nikita's eldest son, Patriarch Fyodor Filaret. The rooms have been refurbished in the lavish style of the period, with walls covered in gilt-embossed leather or painted in rich reds, greens and golds.

In the 16th and 17th centuries even the richest families had to tolerate rather cramped and dim conditions. The portals in the palace are so low that a man of average height has to stoop, and little light is let in by the windows as they are made of mica, a translucent mineral, rather than glass.

In the mid-19th century the light and airy, wooden upper storey was added to the building. The main hall on this level has a beautifully carved wooden ceiling. An anteroom has a display of embroidery.

The vaulted cellars are the least interesting rooms of the museum and contain an odd mix of baskets, trunks and kitchen equipment.

Ornate dining room in the Palace of the Romanov Boyars

Gilded iconostasis in the Church of the Trinity in Nikitniki

Church of the Trinity in Nikitniki ❹

Церковь Троицы в Никитниках

Tserkov Troitsy v Nikitnikakh

Nikitnikov pereulok 3. **Map** 7 C1.
Ⓜ *Kitay Gorod.* ● *to public.*

LIKE THE CHURCHES on ulitsa Varvarka, this marvellous church is dwarfed by monstrous post-war buildings that were formerly Communist Party offices. When it was founded in 1635 by the wealthy merchant, Grigoriy Nikitnikov, the church would have dominated the local skyline. It is at present closed while it is being restored.

The church has five green domes, a profusion of decoration and painted tiles, and tiers of *kokoshniki* gables *(see p44)*. The equally elaborate tent-roofed bell tower, which is linked to the main building by an enclosed gallery, was added shortly after the church was finished.

Carvings on the porch of the Church of the Trinity in Nikitniki

The Church of the Trinity is famous for its frescoes, which were finished in 1656, shortly after Nikitnikov died from the plague. They portray scenes from the Gospels, such as *The Parable of the Rich Man*, in direct, emotional terms.

Among the artists who made an important contribution to the church's decoration was the great fresco and icon painter Semen Ushakov. He painted a number of the frescoes and several of the panels in the splendid gilded iconostasis. Among his works is the *Annunciation of the Virgin*, which can be seen to the left of the Royal Gate *(see p61)* on the iconostasis.

Members of the Nikitnikov family are commemorated in the frescoes in the corner Chapel of St Nikita the Martyr.

Semen Ushakov was a parishioner and his house is around the corner from the church on Ipatevskiy pereulok. It is an unremarkable 17th-century, red-brick building.

Striking 19th-century commercial buildings lining ulitsa Ilinka

Ulitsa Ilinka 5

Улица Ильинка

Ulitsa Ilinka

Map 7 B1. M *Kitay Gorod.*

IN THE 19TH CENTURY this narrow but majestic street was the commercial heart of Kitay Gorod, and home to numerous banks and trading offices. Their richly decorated façades were intended to impress and are still the chief pleasure of a stroll along the street. Today, ulitsa Ilinka is once more the location of a number of commercial and financial institutions, including the Ministry of Finance.

The name Ilinka refers to the former Ilinskiy Monastery, of which no traces now remain. The monastery once stood where the 17th-century Church of St Elijah can now be seen, at No. 3. Further along, at No. 6, on the corner of Birzhevaya ploshchad, is a peach-coloured building with a Neo-Classical portico, which at present houses the Russian Chamber of Industry and Commerce. Originally these were the premises of Moscow's Stock Exchange, which was re-built by Aleksandr Kamenskiy in 1873–5, having first opened in 1836. At that time many of Moscow's merchants still wore long patriarchal beards and the traditional kaftan, and were used to dealing with one another in the street. They at first refused to enter the new Stock Exchange and, in the end, were coralled into the building by the police.

Across the street from this building is the former Trinity Sergius Hostel, which was the city mission of the Trinity Monastery of St Sergius *(see pp156–9)*. Now part of the Russian Supreme Court, it was built by Pavel Skomoroshenko in 1876 and is a restrained example of the Russian-Revival style *(see p45)*.

A building which formerly served as offices for the Soviet government stands at the corner of ulitsa Ilinka and Bolshoy Cherkasskiy pereulok. Uncompromisingly plain, with glazed tiles and rows of narrowly spaced windows, it was designed by Vladimir Mayat in the 1920s.

Monastery of the Epiphany 6

Богоявленский монастырь

Bogoyavlenskiy monastery

Bogoyavlenskiy pereulok 2, stroenie 4.
Map 3 A5. *298 3771.*
M *Ploshchad Revolyutsii.*
8am–8pm daily.

FOUNDED BY Prince Daniil, father of Grand Prince Ivan I *(see p18)* in 1296, the Monastery of the Epiphany is Moscow's second oldest monastery, after the Danilovskiy Monastery *(see pp136–7)*. It was built at what was at that time the edge of the city, beyond the merchants' quarters.

The oldest building to survive is the cathedral. This is an addition to the original medieval complex and dates from 1693–6. The building is distinguished by its massive but refined tower, a masterpiece of Moscow Baroque *(see p44)*. Among the other surviving features are a bishop's palace, a few 18th-century monastic cells and some trading rows.

Nikolskaya Ulitsa 7

Никольская улица

Nikolskaya ulitsa

Map 3 A5.
M *Lubyanka, Ploshchad Revolyutsii.*

BY THE END of the 12th century, this street, which is named after the Kremlin's Nicholas' Tower *(see p66)*, had been settled by merchants and traders. Trading stalls and shops remained a feature of the street until the Revolution. Following a dowdy period under communism, Nikolskaya ulitsa has recently moved up-market with the arrival of several expensive clothing stores and jewellers.

Through the courtyard at No. 7 is a gateway leading into the Zaikonospasskiy Monastery, which was founded in the 15th century or earlier. The name means Saviour Beyond the Icons and recalls the time when there was a brisk trade in icons here. The monastery church, with its dilapidated red brick tower and spire, dates from the 17th century. It is now open again for worship. From 1687–1814 the monastery also housed Moscow's first institute of higher education, referred

Gothic-style façade of the Synodal Printing House, Nikolskaya ulitsa

Kazan Cathedral, a faithful 1990s reconstruction of the original cathedral

to laboriously as the Slavic Greek Latin Academy. Among its pupils was the famous polymath and future founder of Moscow University, Mikhail Lomonosov *(see p94)*.

At No. 15 are the fanciful Gothic-style spires of the Synodal Printing House. The pale blue building, with a lion and unicorn sculpted over its central window, contrasting with an incongruous hammer and sickle above, dates from 1810–14. The courtyard is enhanced by a colourful chequered roof and walls of blue and white tiles. In the chambers previously on this site Ivan Fyodorov produced Russia's first printed book, *The Acts of the Apostles*, in 1564.

Next door, in the courtyard of No. 17, is the Slavyanskiy Bazaar restaurant, which opened in 1870. Among its former patrons is Anton Chekhov *(see p96)*. This restaurant is also where the theatre directors Konstantin Stanislavskiy and Vladimir Nemirovich-Danchenko began a meeting which concluded with the founding of the Moscow Arts Theatre *(see p92)*. Following a fire in 1994, the restaurant was closed for repair, but there are plans to reopen it when this has been completed.

On the opposite side of the road is a building that used to house the Chizhevskoe Inn, a combined inn and warehouse for traders passing through Kitay Gorod. In the courtyard behind it is the 17th-century Church of the Assumption.

Floodlit Resurrection Gate, inside which is the Chapel of the Iverian Virgin

Kazan Cathedral ❽

Казанский собор

Kazanskiy sobor

Nikolskaya ulitsa 3. **Map** 3 A5. *298 0131.* *Okhotnyy Ryad.*

THIS DIMINUTIVE CATHEDRAL is a replica of an original demolished in 1936. Its predecessor was consecrated in 1637 and housed the Icon of the Kazan Virgin. The icon was revered because it had accompanied Prince Dmitriy Pozharskiy during his victorious campaign against the invading Poles 25 years earlier *(see p108)*.

Detailed plans and photographs, preserved by architect Pyotr Baranovskiy, assisted reconstruction of the cathedral in 1990–93 *(see p44)*. It was reconsecrated by Patriarch Aleksey II in the presence of President Boris Yeltsin and the mayor of Moscow, Yuriy Luzhkov. The Icon of the Kazan Virgin in the cathedral is a copy, the original having been stolen in 1904.

Resurrection Gate ❾

Воскресенские ворота

Voskresenskie vorota

Krasnaya ploshchad. **Map** 3 A5. *Okhotnyy Ryad, Ploshchad Revolyutsii.*

REBUILT IN 1995 *(see p44)*, this gateway, with its twin red towers topped by green tent spires, is an exact copy of the original completed on this site in 1680. The first gateway was demolished in 1931. Note the mosaic icons on the gate, one of which depicts Moscow's patron saint, St George, slaying the dragon.

Within the gateway is the equally colourful Chapel of the Iverian Virgin, originally built in the late 18th century to house an icon. Whenever the tsar came to Moscow, he would visit this shrine before entering the Kremlin *(see pp52–67)*. Visitors should try to see the gate at night, when it is impressively lit up.

The vast expanse of Red Square, with the Historical Museum at the far end

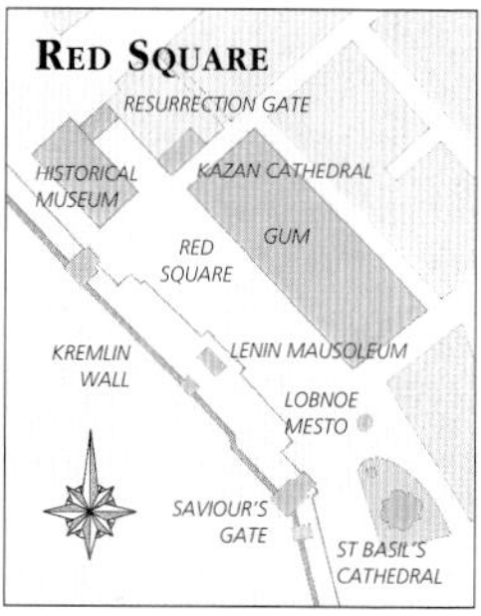

Red Square ⑩

Красная площадь

Krasnaya ploshchad

Map 7 B1. Ⓜ *Ploshchad Revolyutsii, Okhotnyy Ryad.* **Historical Museum** 292 4019. *11am–7pm Wed–Mon*

TOWARDS THE END of the 15th century, Ivan III *(see p18)* gave orders for houses in front of the Kremlin to be cleared to make way for this square. It originally served as a market called the *torg*, but the wooden stalls burned down so often that the area later became popularly known as Fire Square. The current name dates from the 17th century and is derived from the Russian word *krasnyy*, which originally meant "beautiful" but later came to denote "red". The association between the colour red and Communism is purely coincidental.

Red Square, which is approximately 500 m (1,600 ft) in length, was also the setting for public announcements and executions. At its southern end, in front of St Basil's Cathedral *(see pp108–9)*, there is a small circular dais. Called Lobnoe Mesto, this is the platform from which the tsars and patriarchs would address the people. In 1606 the first "False Dmitry" *(see p19)*, an usurper of the throne, was mutilated and killed by a hostile crowd in Red Square. His body was finally left at Lobnoe Mesto.

Six years later, a second pretender to the throne, who like the first "False Dmitry" was backed by Poland, took power. He was expelled from the Kremlin by an army led by the Russian heroes Dmitriy Pozharskiy and Kuzma Minin, who proclaimed Russia's deliverance from Lobnoe Mesto. In 1818, a statue was erected in their honour *(see p108)*. This now stands in front of St Basil's.

Lobnoe Mesto, the platform from which the tsar spoke

Red Square has also long been a stage for pageants and processions. Before the Revolution *(see pp26–9)*, the patriarch would ride an ass through Saviour's Gate *(see p66)* to St Basil's each Palm Sunday to commemorate Christ's entry into Jerusalem.

Religious processions were abolished in the Communist era. Military parades took their place and were staged each year on May Day and on the anniversary of the Revolution. Rows of grim-faced Soviet leaders observed them from outside the Lenin Mausoleum. They, in turn, would be keenly studied by professional kremlinologists in the West trying to work out the current pecking order.

Today the square is used for a variety of cultural events, concerts, firework displays and other public occasions.

The red-brick building facing St Basil's Cathedral was constructed by Vladimir Sherwood in 1883 in the Russian-Revival style *(see p45)*. It houses the Historical Museum. The museum boasts over four million exhibits covering the rise and expansion of the Russian state.

In front of the museum's façade on Manezhnaya ploshchad is a statue by Vyacheslav Klykov of one of the heroes of World War II *(see p27)*, Marshal Georgiy Zhukov. This statue of him was unveiled in 1995 to mark the 50th anniversary of the end of World War II.

Aleksey Shchusev's Lenin Mausoleum, with the Kremlin Wall behind

Lenin Mausoleum ⓫

Мавзолей ВИ Ленина

Mavzoley VI Lenina

Krasnaya ploshchad. **Map** 7 A1. *923 5527.* *Ploshchad Revolyutsii, Okhotnyy Ryad.* *10am–1pm Tue–Thu, Sat–Sun.* *Bags are not allowed.*

FOLLOWING LENIN'S DEATH in 1924, and against his wishes, it was decided to preserve the former Soviet leader's body for posterity. The body was embalmed and placed in a temporary wooden mausoleum in Red Square. Once it became clear that the embalming process had worked, Aleksey Shchusev *(see p45)* designed the current mausoleum of a pyramid of cubes cut from red granite and black labradorite.

Paying one's respects to Lenin's wan and whiskered mummy was once akin to a religious experience, and queues used to trail all over Red Square. In 1993, however, the goose-stepping guard of honour was replaced by a lone militiaman and now the mausoleum attracts mostly tourists. There are rumours that Lenin will soon be moved elsewhere or buried.

Behind the mausoleum at the foot of the Kremlin Wall are the graves of other famous communists. They include Lenin's successors, Joseph Stalin (at one time laid alongside Lenin in the Mausoleum), Leonid Brezhnev and Yuriy Andropov. Lenin's wife and sister are also buried here, as are the first man in space, Yuriy Gagarin, writer Maxim Gorky and American John Reed. The latter was honoured as the author of *Ten Days that Shook the World*, an account of the October Revolution.

The glass-roofed interior of Russia's largest department store, GUM

GUM ⓬

ГУМ

GUM

Krasnaya ploshchad 3. **Map** 7 B1. *921 5763.* *Ploshchad Revolyutsii, Okhotnyy Ryad.* *8am–8pm Mon–Sat, 11am–7pm Sun.*

BEFORE THE REVOLUTION, this building was known as the Upper Trading Rows after the covered market that used to stand on the site. In fact, lines of stalls used to run all the way from here to the Moskva river. GUM has three separate arcades which are still called "lines". The store's name, Gosudarstvennyy universalnyy magazin, dates from its nationalization in 1921.

The building was designed by Aleksandr Pomerantsev in 1889–93 in the then fashionable Russian-Revival style. Its archways, wrought-iron railings and stuccoed galleries inside are especially impressive when sunlight streams through the glass roof.

There were once more than 1,000 shops here, selling goods ranging from furs and silks to humble candles. For a period, however, during the rule of Stalin *(see p27)*, GUM's shops were requisitioned as offices. Nowadays, Western firms like Benetton, Estée Lauder and Christian Dior dominate the prestigious ground floor along with a variety of Western-style cafés and restaurants.

EMBALMING LENIN

"Do not raise monuments to him, or palaces to his name, do not organize pompous ceremonies in his memory." Such were the words of Lenin's widow, Krupskaya. Despite this, Lenin's body was embalmed by two professors and, after a delay to see if the process had worked, put on display. A laboratory is dedicated to preserving the body, which needs regular applications of special fluids. Rumours that parts or all of the body have been replaced with wax substitutes are vigorously denied.

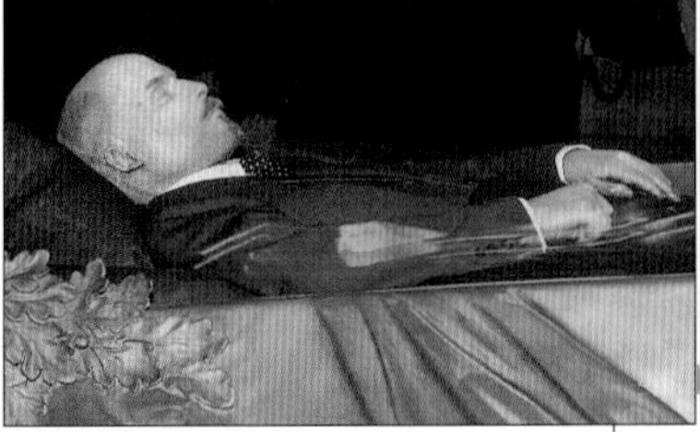

St Basil's Cathedral ⓭

Собор Василия Блаженного

Sobor Vasiliya Blazhennovo

Detail, Chapel of the Entry of Christ into Jerusalem

COMMISSIONED BY Ivan the Terrible *(see p18)* to celebrate the capture of the Mongol stronghold of Kazan in 1552, St Basil's Cathedral was completed in 1561. It is reputed to have been designed by the architect Postnik Yakovlev. According to legend, Ivan was so amazed at the beauty of his work that he had him blinded so that he would never be able to design anything as exquisite again. The church was officially called the Cathedral of the Intercession because the final siege of Kazan began on the Feast of the Intercession of the Virgin. However, it is usually known as St Basil's after the "holy fool" Basil the Blessed whose remains are interred within. The cathedral's design, which was inspired by traditional Russian timber architecture, is a riot of gables, tent roofs and twisting onion domes.

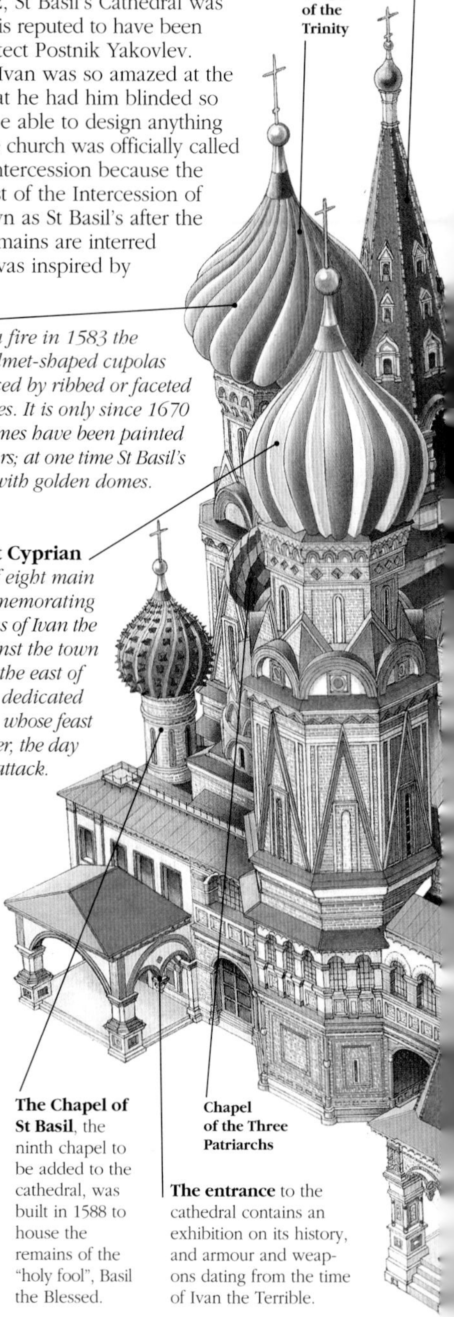

Bell tower

Chapel of the Trinity

★ Domes

Following a fire in 1583 the original helmet-shaped cupolas were replaced by ribbed or faceted onion domes. It is only since 1670 that the domes have been painted many colours; at one time St Basil's was white with golden domes.

Chapel of St Cyprian

This is one of eight main chapels commemorating the campaigns of Ivan the Terrible against the town of Kazan, to the east of Moscow. It is dedicated to St Cyprian, whose feast is on 2 October, the day after the last attack.

The Chapel of St Basil, the ninth chapel to be added to the cathedral, was built in 1588 to house the remains of the "holy fool", Basil the Blessed.

Chapel of the Three Patriarchs

The entrance to the cathedral contains an exhibition on its history, and armour and weapons dating from the time of Ivan the Terrible.

MININ AND POZHARSKIY

A bronze statue by Ivan Martos depicts two heroes from the Time of Troubles *(see p19)*, the butcher Kuzma Minin and Prince Dmitriy Pozharskiy. They raised a volunteer force to fight the invading Poles and, in 1612, led their army to victory when they drove the Poles out of the Kremlin. The statue was erected in 1818, in the triumphal afterglow of the Napoleonic Wars. Originally placed in the centre of Red Square facing the Kremlin, it was moved to its present site in front of St Basil's during the Soviet era.

Monument to Minin and Prince Pozharskiy

Central Chapel of the Intercession
Light floods in through the windows of the tent-roofed central church, which soars to a height of 61 m (200 ft).

★ Main Iconostasis
The Baroque-style iconostasis in the Central Chapel of the Intercession dates from the 19th century. However, some of the icons contained in it were painted much earlier.

VISITORS' CHECKLIST

Krasnaya ploshchad 2. **Map** 7 B1. *298 3304. May–Nov: 10am–5pm Wed–Mon (Dec–Apr: 10am–4pm). Okhotnyy Ryad, Ploschad Revolyutsii. 25. 8. English. religious hols.* www.shm.ru

STAR FEATURES

- ★ **Domes**
- ★ **Gallery**
- ★ **Main Iconostasis**

The Chapel of the Entry of Christ into Jerusalem was used as a ceremonial entrance during the annual Palm Sunday procession. On this day the patriarch rode from the Kremlin to St Basil's Cathedral on a horse dressed up to look like a donkey.

★ Gallery
Running around the outside of the Central Chapel, the gallery connects it to the other eight chapels. It was roofed over at the end of the 17th century and the walls and ceilings were decorated with floral tiles in the late 18th century.

Ivanovskaya Hill ⓮

Ивановская горка

Ivanovskaya gorka

Map 3 C5. Ⓜ *Kitay Gorod.*

THIS HILLY AREA takes its name from the Ivanovskiy Convent on the corner of ulitsa Zabelina and Malyy Ivanovskiy pereulok. The convent's rather neglected remains can be seen behind a twin-towered gateway and high encircling walls.

Yelena Glinska, mother of Ivan the Terrible *(see p18)*, founded the convent in 1533 as a gesture of thanks for the birth of her son. Later, however, it doubled as a prison for many years – its most famous inmate was Avgusta Tarakanova, the illegitimate daughter of Tsarina Elizabeth *(see p22)* and Count Aleksey Razumovskiy. She was educated abroad before being brought to Russia in 1785 and put into the convent under an assumed name. She spent the rest of her life here as a solitary nun, forbidden to receive any visitors except for the mother superior. She died in 1810.

Across the road is the Church of St Vladimir in the Old Gardens. It was built in 1514 by Italian architect Aleviz Novyy, but it was extensively altered at the end of the 17th century. Its name refers to the tsar's orchards, which used to occupy the slopes of the hill.

One of the pleasures of this area is exploring its unusually quiet backstreets. At the end of Malyy Ivanovskiy pereulok, which runs down from the Ivanovskiy Convent, is Podkolokolnyy pereulok (Lane Beneath the Bells). This street is dominated by the Church of St Nicholas the Wonderworker, which dates from the mid-17th century and is recognizable by its outsized red bell tower. Perhaps the most impressive church in the area is SS Peter and Paul on Petropavlovskiy pereulok. It was built in 1700 and contains an icon of the Bogolyubovskaya Virgin, which used to hang in a chapel near the gate to the city at the end of ulitsa Varvarka *(see p102)*.

To the north, at No. 10 Kolpachiy pereulok is the 17th-century mansion that reputedly belonged to the Ukrainian chief Ivan Mazepa. He fled to Turkish-controlled Moldova in 1709, after betraying Peter the Great *(see p22)* to the Swedes and then being defeated by him. Tchaikovsky set the story to music in his opera, *Mazepa*. The name of another street, Kokhlovskiy pereulok, may also have a Ukrainian link; Ukrainians used to be known as *khokhly* because of the tufts of hair they grew at the back of their shaved heads; (*khokhly* means tufted in Russian).

A typically quiet, gently sloping backstreet on Ivanovskaya Hill

The most notable building standing on ulitsa Maroseyka is the blue and white mansion at No. 17. This is now the Belarussian embassy.

Russian space programme exhibit at the Polytechnical Museum

Polytechnical Museum ⓯

Политехнический музей

Politekhnicheskiy muzey

Novaya ploshchad 3/4. **Map** 3 B5. *923 0756.* *10am–5:30pm Tue–Sun.* Ⓜ *Kitay Gorod.* *English (book in advance).*

DESIGNED BY architect Ippolit Monighetti, the central section of this museum was built in 1877 and is a superb example of Russian-Revival architecture *(see p45)*, which was very popular in the late 19th century. The north and south wings were added in 1896 and 1907 respectively.

The items on display were originally assembled for an exhibition staged in the Alexander Gardens *(see p67)* in 1872. This marked the 200th anniversary of the birth of Peter the Great, himself an enthusiastic amateur scientist.

The museum is today a popular outing for parties of Russian schoolchildren. Its original collection has been expanded to trace the development of Russian science and technology during the 19th and 20th centuries. Exhibits range from early clocks and cameras to cars and space capsules. Every two hours there are demonstrations of devices such as robots, working models and sound equipment.

History of Moscow Museum ⓰

Музей истории города Москвы

Muzey istorii goroda Moskvy

Novaya ploshchad 12. **Map** 3 B5. ☎ *924 8490.* ○ *10am–6pm Tue, Thu, Sat–Sun; 11am–7pm Wed, Fri.* **M** *Lubyanka.*

This museum was founded in 1896 and is housed in the 19th-century church of St John the Divine Under the Elm. There has been some speculation about finding larger premises, but this has yet to be decided upon.

Only a fraction of the one million items in the collection can be displayed at any time. These include Iron and Bronze Age artifacts, colossal timbers from a medieval log cabin, unearthed during the building of the State Kremlin Palace *(see p56)* in the Kremlin, and a growing treasure-trove of jewellery, toys and pottery. There are also priceless early maps, rare illuminated books, paintings, glass, ceramics and scale models of the Kremlin and other historic buildings.

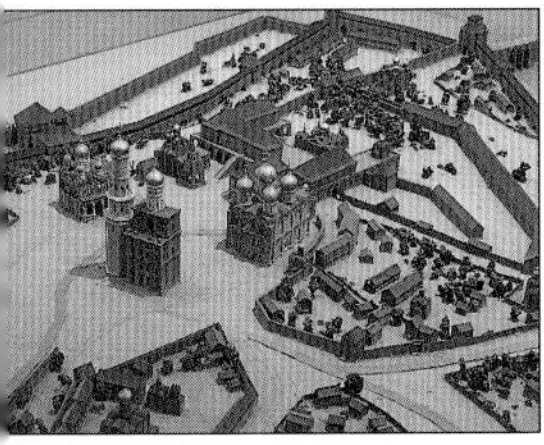

Wooden model of the Kremlin in the History of Moscow Museum

Mayakovsky Museum ⓱

Музей-квартира ВВ Маяковского

Muzey-kvartira VV Mayakovskovo

Lubyanskiy proezd 3/6. **Map** 3 B5. ☎ *921 9387.* ○ *10am–5pm Fri–Tue, 1–8pm Thu.* **M** *Lubyanka.*

Vladimir Mayakovsky, poet, iconoclast, exhibitionist and consummate self-publicist, was above all a revolutionary. In his short but eventful life his poetry, plays, film scripts and poster art gave a strident voice to the Revolution and its vision of modernity. The terse and uncompromising agitprop posters he designed with Aleksandr Rodchenko are a prominent feature of the museum.

The striking Constructivist entrance to the Mayakovsky Museum

By nature, Mayakovsky was both provocative and extraordinary, and this is brilliantly reflected in this apparently anarchic museum. Huge frameworks of metal bars, designed in the Constructivist style influential in the 1920s, lean at fantastic angles and provide a backdrop for the other exhibits. Mayakovsky's artworks and belongings are intermingled: chairs, old boots, typewriters, painted cannon balls, large posters and photomontages, cracked mirrors, sewing machines and manuscripts.

Room designed to symbolize Mayakovsky's poetic origins

Mayakovsky actually lived in this block from 1919 until his death in 1930: a single room on the fourth floor has been furnished to look as it would have done when he moved in. While living in this house, Mayakovsky continued his long-running love affair with Lilya Brik, the wife of his friend Osip Brik. This was also the period in which he wrote his best-known plays, the caustic satires *The Bed Bug* and *Bath House.*

The last part of the exhibition deals with Mayakovsky's suicide at the age of 37. On display are two death masks, one black and one white. After his death, Stalin *(see p27)* praised Mayakovsky as the most talanted of Soviet poets and continued to use his work for propaganda purposes.

Vladimir Mayakovsky

Born in Georgia in 1893, Mayakovsky was brought up in Moscow, where he became involved in the revolutionary movement at the tender age of 14. Earning his revolutionary honours by being arrested three times in the space of two years, he was also drawn to the avant-garde and in 1912 became a founder of the Futurist movement by contributing to its manifesto, *A Slap in the Face for Public Taste.* Mayakovsky wholeheartedly endorsed the Revolution *(see p26–9)*, becoming one of its most effective propagandists, but became increasingly disillusioned with the straitjacketed attitudes of Soviet society in the 1920s; this may have contributed to his suicide in 1930.

Lubyanka Square 18
Лубянская площадь
Lubyanskaya ploshchad

Map 3 B5. **M** *Lubyanka.*

SYNONYMOUS WITH terror and the secret police, the name Lubyanka struck fear into the hearts of generations of Soviet citizens. In 1918, the Cheka (the forerunners of the KGB), led by the hated "Iron" Feliks Dzerzhinskiy, took over what had been the Rossiya Insurance Offices at the northern end of the square.

In the 1930s the building was extended and the enormous, underground Lubyanka Prison added, where the KGB interrogated, tortured, imprisoned and killed hundreds of thousands of people. By 1947 the incredible numbers of those accused in the course of Stalin's rule *(see p27)* led to the building of an additional wing, designed by Aleksey Shchusev *(see p45)*. Despite numerous changes of name (and protestations of changes in ethos), the Russian intelligence services still occupy the building.

Feliks Dzerzhinskiy (1877–1926)

A statue of Dzerzhinskiy used to stand in the centre of Lubyanka square. It was unceremoniously toppled in front of a cheering crowd, following the unsuccessful coup against President Gorbachev in 1991 *(see p31)*. The statue can now be seen in the Graveyard of Fallen Monuments *(see p135)*.

With their customary lack of irony, the Soviet authorities built Russia's largest toy store, Detskiy Mir (Children's World) *(see p185)*, directly opposite the KGB headquarters in 1957.

The infamous former headquarters of the KGB on Lubyanka Square

Chistoprudnyy Bulvar 19
Чистопрудный бульвар
Chistoprudnyy bulvar

Map 3 C4. **M** *Chistye Prudy.*

THIS ROAD is part of the historic Boulevard Ring, which was laid out along the line of the old Belyy Gorod (White City) wall after the great fire of 1812 *(see p24)*. There are several fine houses located along Chistoprudnyy bulvar. At No. 19a is the elegant, Classical-style portico of the Sovremennik Theatre, which was built as a cinema by Roman Klein in 1914. Just beyond is the mansion where Sergey Eisenstein, director of *October* and *Battleship Potemkin*, lived from 1920–34. Chistoprudnyy bulvar is part of the area which used to be known as Myasnitskaya after the butchers *(myasniki)* who worked here in the 17th century. The *myasniki* are still commemorated in the name of Myasnitskaya ulitsa, which runs from Lubyanka Square to Chistoprudnyy bulvar.

Between the carriageways of Chistoprudnyy bulvar is a large pond. It was created as a place for the butchers to dump offal and other waste products but, by 1703, the stench and risk of disease were so bad that the pond was cleared and renamed Chistye prudy (Clean Pond).

The beautiful, pale blue mansion just round the corner, at No. 22 ulitsa Pokrovka, was built between 1766–72. Before the communist coup in October 1917, the building used to be one of the best male secondary schools in Moscow, dating from 1861.

Detail of the fine stone carvings on Menshikov's Tower

Menshikov's Tower 20
Меншикова башня
Menshikova bashnya

Arkhangelskiy pereulok 15.
Map 3 C4. **M** *Turgenevskaya, Chistye Prudy.*

THIS CHURCH was constructed on the orders of Prince Aleksandr Menshikov, Peter the Great's advisor and favourite. With Peter the Great's backing, Menshikov rose from the position of lowly pie-seller to be one of most powerful and wealthy men in Russia. It was typical of the flamboyant Menshikov that, when he commissioned the church from Ivan Zarudnyy in 1701, he instructed the architect to make it just a little taller than the Ivan the Great Bell Tower *(see p57)*, until then the tallest structure in all of Russia.

Specialist stonemasons from Yaroslavl and Kostroma and a variety of Italian sculptors worked on the church, accounting for the beauty of the stone carvings and stuccoed festoons. The wooden spire was capped by a gilded angel and contained an expensive English clock, which chimed on the quarter-hour.

However, pious Muscovites remained unimpressed by the display of wealth and when the tower was destroyed by lightning in 1723 many saw in it the hand of God. The tower was rebuilt without the spire in 1773–80. The church was one of the few to remain open during the Soviet era and much of its interior decoration has survived.

Next to the tower is the small Church of St Fyodor Stratilit, which was heated in winter for the benefit of the parishioners. It was built in 1806, probably by Ivan Yegotov.

Perlov Tea House ㉑

Чай-кофе магазин
Chay-kofe magazin

Myasnitskaya ulitsa 19. **Map** 3 B4. *925 4656.* *8am–1pm, 2pm–8pm Mon–Sat.* *Chistye Prudy, Turgenevskaya.*

THIS BUILDING WAS originally designed by Roman Klein in 1890 for the tea merchant Sergey Perlov. Five years later Perlov heard that the official representative of the Chinese emperor would be visiting Moscow. He hastily commissioned Karl Gippius to redesign the shop in the hope of receiving him. The façade is a fanciful vision of the Orient, including serpents, dragons and pagoda-style details. The oriental theme is followed up inside with lacquered columns and counters painted with golden dragons. In the event the Chinese official mistakenly visited Perlov's nephew, who was also a tea merchant.

Shelves of tea behind the counter of the elegant Perlov Tea House

Convent of the Nativity of the Virgin ㉒

Рождественский монастырь
Rozhdestvenskiy monastyr

Ulitsa Rozhdestvenka 20. **Map** 3 A4. *921 3986.* *8am–7:30pm daily.* *Kuznetskiy Most.*

CONVERTED to provide housing in Soviet times, this small cluster of buildings was neglected until 1991, when it was returned to the Russian Orthodox Church.

Founded in 1386 by Princess Maria Serpukhovskiy, daughter-in-law of Ivan I *(see p18)*, the convent was one of a ring of fortified monasteries constructed around Moscow.

The bell tower of the Convent of the Nativity of the Virgin

The beautifully proportioned cathedral, commissioned between 1501–5 by Tsar Ivan III *(see p18)*, has tiers of *kokoshniki* gables *(see p44)* surmounted by a single cupola.

The small Church of St John of Zlatoust, with five domes, has also survived, along with a short section of the original brick ramparts. The yellow, tiered bell tower was designed by Nikolay Kozlovskiy in 1835.

The waiting area inside the luxurious Sandunovskiy Baths

Sandunovskiy Baths ㉓

Сандуновские бани
Sandunovskie bani

Neglinnaya ulitsa 14, stroenie 4–7. **Map** 3 A4. *925 4631.* *8am–10pm daily (last adm 8pm).* *Kuznetskiy Most.*

THE ORIGINAL Sandunovskiy Baths were built for actor Sila Sandunov in 1808. In 1895 they were replaced by this building designed by Boris Freidenberg and with a decorative Beaux Arts façade.

The main entrance is through an ornate archway, decorated with sculptures of nymphs on horseback, emerging from the sea and using triton shells as trumpets.

However, it is the sumptuous interiors, decorated in a flamboyant mix of Baroque, Gothic and Moorish styles, which make the baths famous. The Alhambra Palace in Spain was one of the sources of inspiration for the ornate decoration. The baths can accommodate up to 2,000 customers a day. The best, most expensive, rooms are located off a series of narrow alleys on the first floor. Here patrons can still buy birch twigs to beat themselves with, an essential part of a Russian steam bath.

ZAMOSKVORECHE

FIRST SETTLED in the 13th century, Zamoskvoreche (literally "beyond the Moscow river") acted as an outpost against the Mongols. Its main road, Bolshaya Ordynka, was the route to the *Orda*, or Golden Horde, the Mongol headquarters on the Volga river. Later, under Ivan the Terrible, the Streltsy (royal guard) was stationed here. Artisans serving the court also moved in, living in areas according to their trades, each of which sponsored a church. These historic churches, now in varying states of repair, and the fact that the area was almost untouched by the replanning of the 1930s, give it a more old-fashioned atmosphere than the centre, which is dominated by massive Soviet architecture. In the 19th century wealthy merchants settled here, many of whom, such as Aleksey Bakhrushin and Pavel Tretyakov, were patrons of the arts. Based on its founder's acquisitions, the Tretyakov Gallery is the nation's most important collection of Russian art.

Icon at the Convent of SS Martha and Mary

SIGHTS AT A GLANCE

Churches and Convents

Church of the Consolation of All Sorrows 3
Church of the Resurrection in Kadashi 2
Church of St Catherine 6
Church of St Clement 4
Church of St Nicholas in Pyzhy 5
Convent of SS Martha and Mary 7

Museums and Galleries

Bakhrushin Theatre Museum 9
Tretyakov Gallery pp118–21 1
Tropinin Museum 8

Streets

Sophia Embankment 10

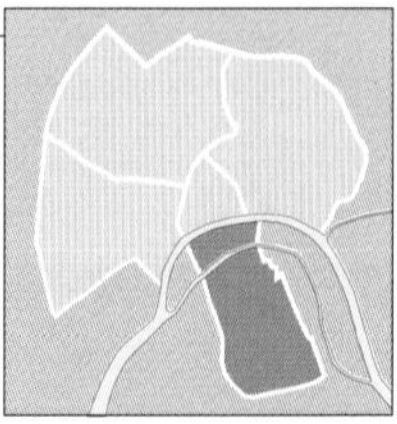

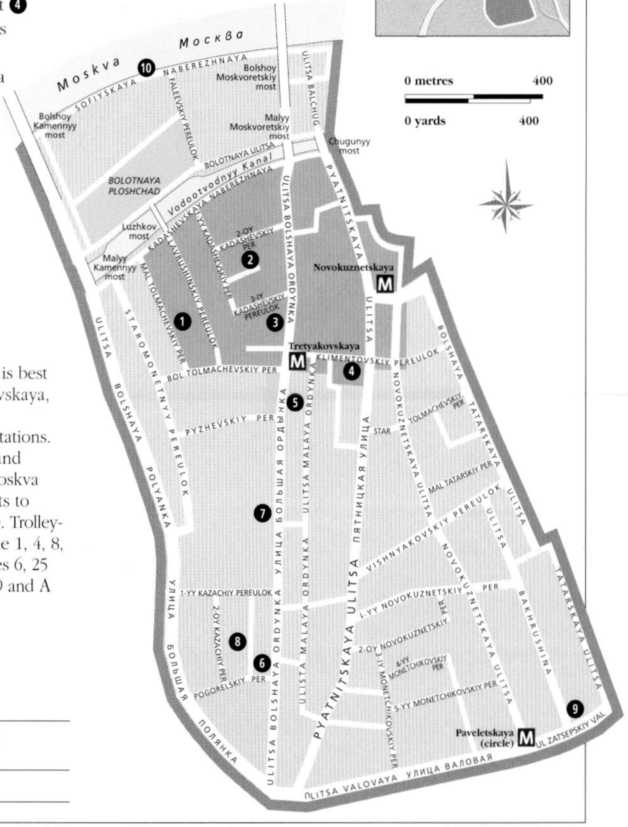

GETTING THERE

If using the metro, it is best to head for Tretyakovskaya, Novokuznetskaya or Paveletskaya metro stations. Trolleybuses, buses and trams all cross the Moskva River at various points to reach Zamoskvoreche. Trolleybus routes include the 1, 4, 8, 33 and 62, while buses 6, 25 and K and trams 3, 39 and A also serve the area.

KEY

Street-by-Street map *pp116–17*

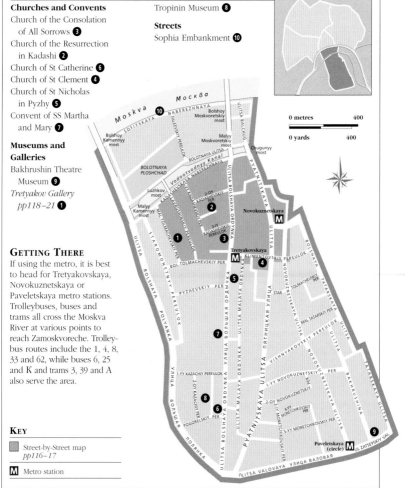

M Metro station

◁ **The Vodootvodnyy canal in Zamoskvoreche, blanketed by snow in Moscow's freezing winter**

Street-by-Street: Around Pyatnitskaya Ulitsa

An old-fashioned atmosphere still prevails in the area around Pyatnitskaya ulitsa. The well-established streets are lined with attractive 19th-century churches and imposing Neo-Classical mansions. The busiest part of the district is the area around Tretyakovskaya metro. The market stalls on the station forecourt spill over onto Klimentovskiy pereulok, and nearby Pyatnitskaya ulitsa is the main shopping street. A short walk to the west is the stunning Tretyakov Gallery. To the north, the area is bordered by the Vodootvodnyy canal, which was built in 1783–6 to prevent the regular spring flooding of the Moskva river.

Vodootvodnyy canal

★ Church of the Resurrection in Kadashi
With its tapering bell tower and lavish limestone ornamentation this magnificent church is a fine example of the style known as Moscow Baroque (see p44) ❷

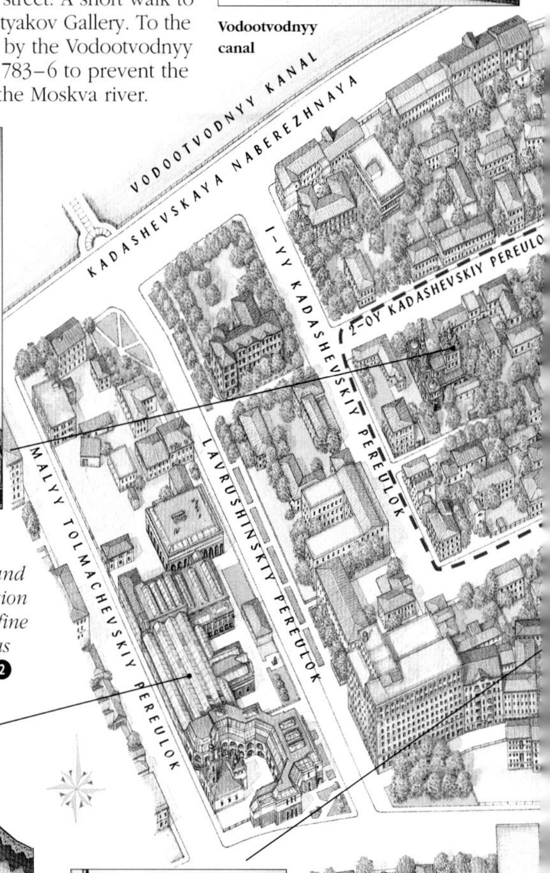

★ Tretyakov Gallery
The world's largest collection of Russian art is housed here. Taken down in the Soviet era, the statue of Pavel Tretyakov (see p120) *has now been restored to its rightful place in front of the gallery* ❶

The Demidov House was built in 1789–91 by a family of well-known industrialists.

Church of the Consolation of All Sorrows
Two of Moscow's best-known architects contributed to this much-loved church. Vasiliy Bazhenov designed the bell tower and Osip Bove (see p45) *the rotunda* ❹

The Church of SS Michael and Fyodor, dating from the late 17th century, is named after two martyrs killed by Mongols when they refused to renounce Christianity.

Church of St John the Baptist has a distinctive green bell-tower and was built in the 18th century.

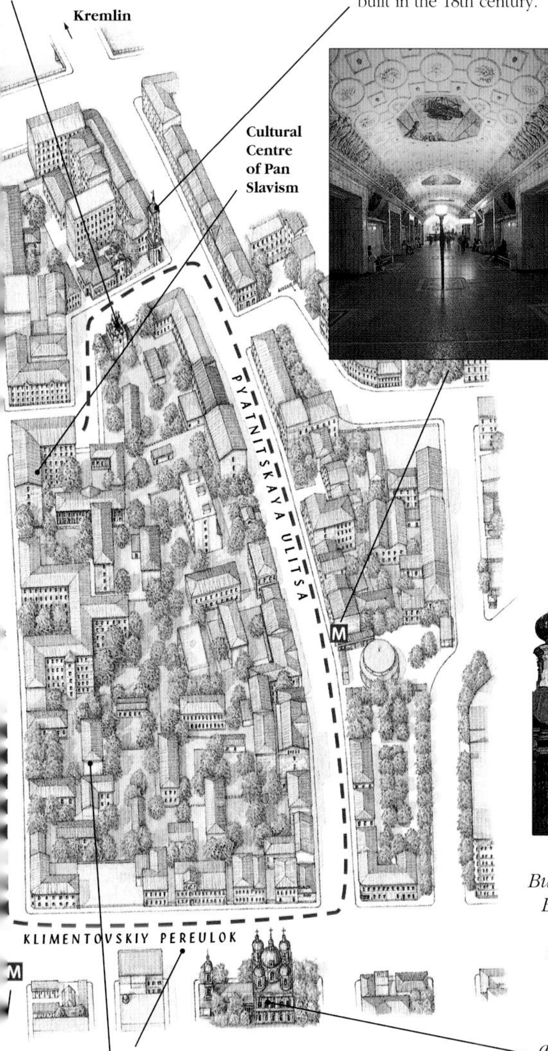

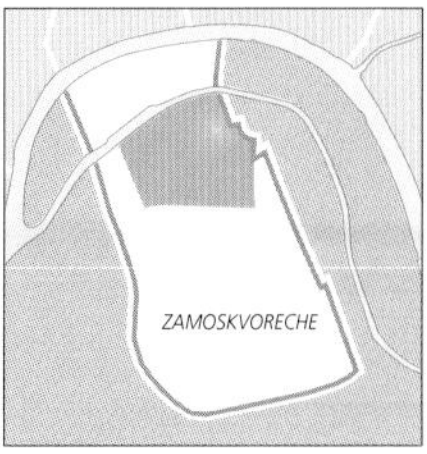

Locator Map
See Street Finder, map 7

Novokuznetskaya Metro Station, designed by Ivan Taranov and Natalia Bykova, was opened in 1943 at the height World War II, and the design of the interior is based on military subjects.

Church of St Clement
Building began on this splendid Baroque church in 1720 and continued in phases over the next few decades: in 1756–8 a rectory and belfry were added. The church has four black, star-spangled domes and a central golden dome ❺

Small shops on Klimentovskiy pereulok sell groceries, magazines, perfumes and other goods.

0 metres 100

0 yards 100

The Dolgov House has an elaborately decorated Neo-Classical exterior. This fine town house was built in the 1770s for a wealthy merchant named Dolgov, possibly by his son-in-law, Vasiliy Bazhenov *(see p44)*.

Star Sights

★ **Tretyakov Gallery**

★ **Church of the Resurrection in Kadashi**

Key

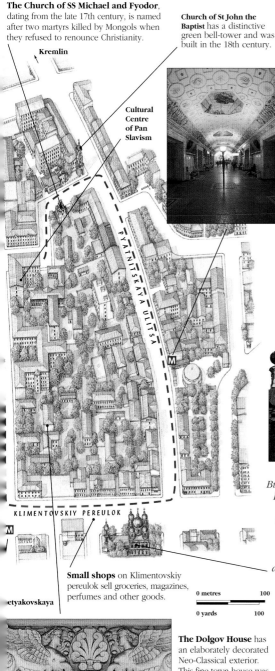

Suggested route

Tretyakov Gallery ❶

Третьяковская галерея
Tretyakovskaya galereya

In 1892 the millionaire merchant and textiles manufacturer Pavel Tretyakov presented his private museum of Russian art to the city of Moscow. His brother Sergey also donated a number of works and the gallery's collection has been expanding ever since. Today the Tretyakov has the largest and finest collection of Russian art in the world. The building has a striking façade, designed by artist Viktor Vasnetsov, with a bas-relief of St George and the dragon at its centre. A new wing was added to the gallery in 1930. Many of the early 20th-century works from the collection have now been housed in the New Tretyakov Gallery *(see p135).*

The Rooks Have Come *(1871)*
This bleak winter scene by Aleksey Savrasov contains a message of hope: rooks are taken by Russians as a sign of the coming spring.

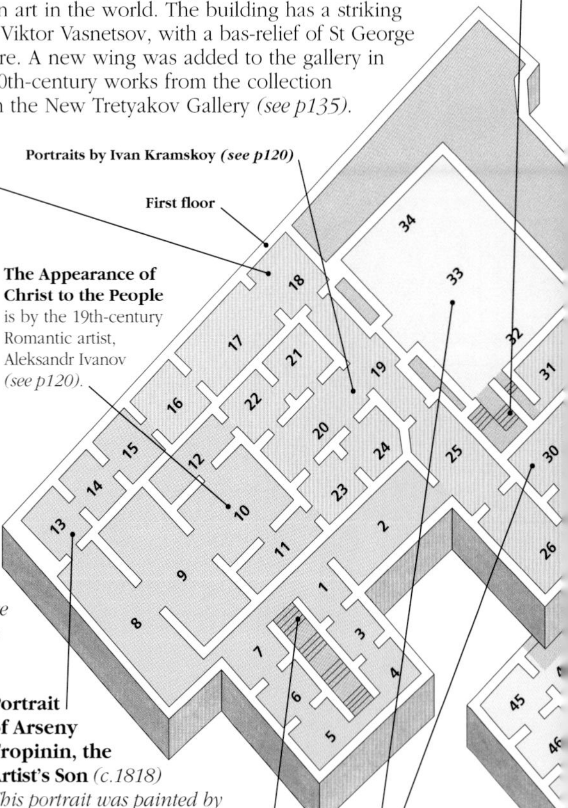

The Appearance of Christ to the People is by the 19th-century Romantic artist, Aleksandr Ivanov *(see p120).*

Portrait of Arseny Tropinin, the Artist's Son *(c.1818)*
This portrait was painted by the renowned artist Vasiliy Tropinin. He was a serf for 47 years before gaining his freedom and finding commercial success.

★ **Demon Seated** *(1890) This is one of several paintings by Mikhail Vrubel, who adopted a new, strikingly modern style. They are inspired by Mikhail Lermontov's Symbolist poem,* The Demon (see p82), *with which Vrubel became obsessed.*

Gallery Guide

The gallery has 62 rooms on two main floors. On entering the museum, visitors first descend to the basement ticket office, then head straight up to the first floor. Paintings are hung in chronological order in rooms 1–54: visitors take some stairs back down to the ground floor after viewing room 34. Russian jewellery is housed on the ground floor in room 55, while rooms 56–62 contain icons and jewellery.

Religious Procession in Kursk Province
(1880–3) Ilya Repin painted this to show the different attitudes of those in the procession to the icon being carried at the head of it.

The Morning of the Execution of the Streltsy is by Vasiliy Surikov, who specialized in using historical subjects to illustrate contemporary social issues.

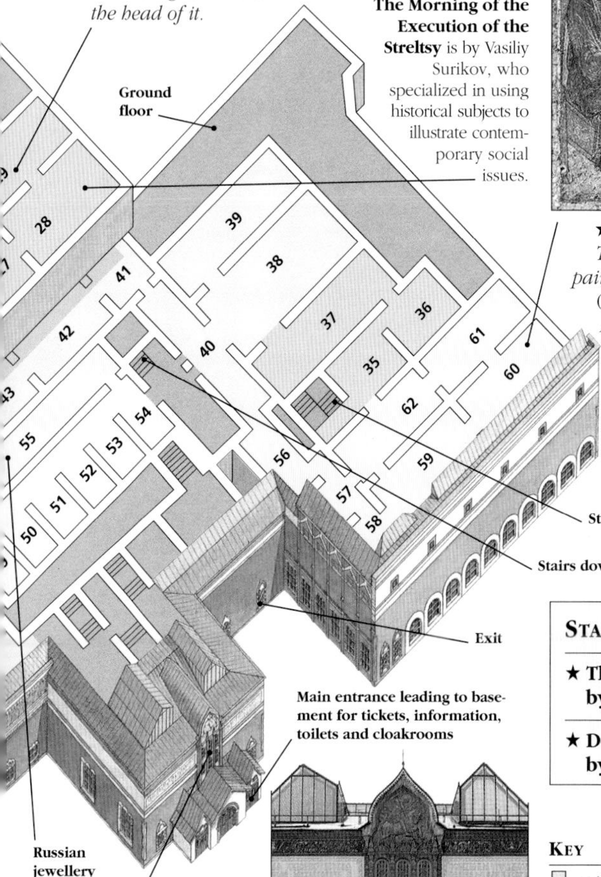

Visitors' Checklist

Lavrushinskiy pereulok 10. **Map** 7 A3. *951 1362.* *Tretyakovskaya.* 6, K, 25. *1, 4, 8, 33, 62.* *10am–6:30pm Tue–Sun.* *Eng.* *Eng.* www.tretyakov.ru

★ The Trinity *(1420s)*
This beautiful icon was painted by Andrey Rublev (see p61) *for the Trinity Monastery of St Sergius* (see pp156–9), *where he had been a novice monk. He dedicated it to the monastery's founder, St Sergius of Radonezh* (see p159).

Star Exhibits

★ The Trinity by Rublev

★ Demon Seated by Vrubel

Main Façade
The gallery's façade was designed in 1902 by Viktor Vasnetsov. An example of the Russian-Revival style (see p45), *it has a frieze inspired by medieval manuscripts.*

Key

- 18th and early 19th centuries
- Second half of the 19th century
- Late 19th and early 20th centuries
- Drawings and watercolours of the 18th–20th centuries
- Icons and jewellery
- Non-exhibition space

Exploring the Tretyakov Gallery

ALTHOUGH THE GALLERY'S COLLECTION began with the paintings donated by Pavel Tretyakov, it continued to expand after the Revolution as numerous private collections were nationalized by the Soviet regime. There are currently more than 100,000 Russian works in the collection. Paintings from after the Revolution – mainly Socialist-Realist works – are now exhibited in the New Tretyakov Gallery *(see p135)*, while the main gallery displays Russian art ranging from the icons of the medieval period to early 20th-century paintings.

***Portrait of Ursula Mnichek* by Dmitriy Levitskiy**

18TH AND EARLY 19TH CENTURIES

PAINTING IN RUSSIA was exclusively religious in character for over 600 years. However, a profound transformation occurred in the 18th century as secular art from Europe began to influence Russian artists. Portrait painting came into its own with technically accomplished canvases by artists such as Vladimir Borovikovskiy (1757–1825), Fyodor Rokotov (c.1736–1808) and Dmitriy Levitskiy (c.1735–1822), whose charming *Portrait of Ursula Mnichek* is among those in the gallery. The Romantic movement is represented in the collection by such pictures as Vasiliy Tropinin's refined but sentimental portrait of his son and Orest Kiprenskiy's famous *Portrait of the Poet Alexander Pushkin* (1827). Several of Aleksandr Ivanov's (1806–58) historical canvases are also displayed here, including his outstanding painting, *The Appearance of Christ to the People*. Begun in 1837, it took 20 years to finish.

SECOND HALF OF THE 19TH CENTURY

THE ART OF THIS PERIOD was dominated by Realism. In 1870 a group of artists founded the Association of Travelling Art Exhibitions. Its members, who became known as the Wanderers *(peredvizhniki)*, began to produce "socially useful art" highlighting injustices and inequalities. One of the leaders of the movement was Vasiliy Perov (1834–82) whose satirical *Tea-drinking in Mytishchi* exposes hypocrisy among the clergy. Another Wanderer was Vasiliy Surikov, whose picture of *The Morning of the Execution of the Streltsy* (1881) instils new realism into a dramatic episode of Russian history. Ivan Kramskoy, the head of the group, aimed to portray the moral character of his subjects in paintings such as *Portrait of an Unknown Lady* and *Portrait of Pavel Tretyakov*.

Landscapes were popular subjects for the Wanderers and the gallery's many examples include Vasiliy Polenov's *A Moscow Courtyard* (1878) and *The Rooks Have Come* (1871) by Aleksey Savrasov.

A number of works by Ilya Repin (1844–1930), the most versatile of the Wanderers, is on display. They include the enormous canvases *Religious Procession in Kursk Province*; *They Did Not Expect Him* and *Ivan the Terrible and his Son Ivan on 16 November 1581*, and striking portraits of Repin's friends and contemporaries.

PAVEL TRETYAKOV

Pavel Tretyakov began collecting Russian art in 1856 and was particularly interested in works by the Wanderers *(peredvizhniki)*. His collection grew and in 1892 he donated it to the city of Moscow. His home was opened as a gallery and, much extended, still houses the collection today. Pavel Tretyakov was director of the gallery for the last six years of his life.

***Portrait of Pavel Tretyakov* (1876) by Ivan Kramskoy**

***Portrait of an Unknown Lady*, painted by Ivan Kramskoy in 1883**

***Bathing the Red Horse*, painted in 1912 by Kuzma Petrov-Vodkin**

Late 19th and Early 20th Centuries

During the 1890s, the social ideals that inspired the Wanderers no longer appealed to a new generation of artists. Instead they rallied behind a call for "art for art's sake".

The innovative artist Mikhail Vrubel (1856–1910) was influenced by the poetry of the Russian Symbolists. Many of his dark, brooding works, such as *Demon Seated*, also reflect his troubled mental state.

French painting had a huge impact on this and subsequent generations of artists. This influence can be seen in the Impressionist work *Paris, Boulevard des Capucines*, painted in 1911 by Konstantin Korovin. The style of Valentin Serov's (1865–1911) early paintings was also close to Impressionism. His *Girl with Peaches (see p47)* is a charming portrait of the daughter of art patron Savva Mamontov.

In the decade leading up to World War I, Moscow was the centre of Russia's avant-garde movement, receptive to developments from abroad, such as Cubism and Futurism, as well as taking ideas from indigenous folk art, which inspired Primitivism. Primitivist works feature bold shapes and bright colours. *Staro Basmannaya – Board No. 1* by Vladimir Tatlin (1885–1953) and *Bathing Horses* by Natalya Goncharova (1881–1962) are among the gallery's works in this style. Kuzma Petrov-Vodkin's (1878–1939) main concern, in paintings such as *Bathing the Red Horse*, was technique.

Freedom of expression was not always possible for artists in Russia and some, such as Marc Chagall (1887–1985) and Vasily Kandinsky (1866–1944), spent most of their lives abroad. However, a number of their paintings are on show here, including *Over the City* (1924) by Chagall.

Some 20th-century works have now been moved to join the Socialist-Realist art in the New Tretyakov Gallery.

***The Transfiguration* (c.1403), painted by a follower of Theophanes the Greek**

Drawings and Watercolours

The gallery owns a substantial collection of sketches, lithographs and watercolours by artists from the 18th–20th centuries but, to avoid exhibits being damaged by exposure to light, only a small proportion are on show at any time.

Among the watercolours are a delightful equestrian portrait by Karl Bryullov (1799–1852) and some preparatory biblical sketches by Aleksandr Ivanov. Landscapes by Isaak Levitan (1861–1900) and Konstantin Korovin contrast with delicate pencil portraits by artists as diverse as Ilya Repin, Valentin Serov and Natalya Goncharova.

Icons and Jewellery

A fine collection of religious icons dating from the 12th–17th centuries is housed in the Tretyakov. Russian icon painting inherited the dark colours and immobile, otherworldly images of the saints from Byzantine art. One of the most revered icons, the 12th-century Virgin of Vladimir *(see p61)*, originated in Byzantium, but was brought to Moscow via Kiev and Vladimir.

However, Russian icon painters lightened their palettes, introducing shades such as yellow ochre, vermilion and white. A typical example is *The Transfiguration* (c.1403), painted by a follower of Theophanes the Greek *(see p61)*. It shows Christ standing over cowering sinners.

Andrey Rublev's stunning icon *The Trinity* dates from around 1420.

Alongside it are icons by other masters of the Moscow school *(see p61)*, including Dionysius (c.1440–c.1508).

Also on the ground floor is a room devoted to Russian jewellery from the 13th–20th centuries.

Church of the Resurrection in Kadashi ❷

Церковь Воскресения в Кадашах
Tserkov Voskreseniya v Kadashakh

2-oy Kadashevskiy pereulok 7. **Map** 7 B3. Ⓜ *Tretyakovskaya.* ● *to public.*

This five-domed church is among the most striking examples of Moscow Baroque *(see p44)* and is thought to have been designed by Sergey Turchaninov, favourite architect of Patriarch Nikon *(see pp56–7)*. The small group of buildings around it also includes a refectory and tiered bell tower. It was paid for by a wealthy guild of weavers who had moved into the street by the 17th century. Before that an earlier church stood here, in what was at that time the district of Kadeshevo, hence the name that survives today.

The church was built around 1687, and the slender, tapering bell tower added in the 1690s. Apart from the five green onion domes, visible from all over the neighbourhood, the most notable features are the tiers of lace-like limestone balustrades just below the drums supporting the domes. The church is now an art restoration workshop.

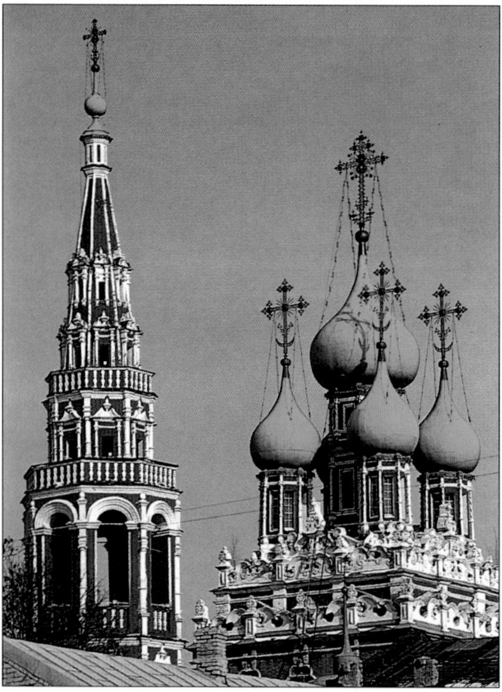

The bell tower and domes of the Church of the Resurrection in Kadashi

Church of the Consolation of All Sorrows ❸

Церковь Богоматери Всех Скорбящих Радость
Tserkov Bogomateri Vsekh Skorbyashchikh Radost

Ulitsa Bolshaya Ordynka 20. **Map** 7 B3. Ⓜ *Tretyakovskaya.*

Both the Church of the Consolation of All Sorrows and the Neo-Classical yellow mansion opposite belonged to the Dolgovs, a wealthy merchant family. After completion of their house in the 1770s, they commissioned the church from Vasiliy Bazhenov *(see p44)*, a relation by marriage. He first built a new belfry and refectory, which are among the few surviving buildings in Moscow by this talented architect, and then replaced the existing medieval church in 1783–91. It was finished by the Kumanins, another merchant family.

The Empire-style Church of the Consolation of All Sorrows

That church, however, was destroyed in the great fire of 1812 *(see p24)*. Another new one was designed by Osip Bove *(see p45)*, who was the architect in charge of Moscow's reconstruction after the fire. His Empire-style rotunda and dome, which still survive today, were finished in 1833.

The interior is unusual in an Orthodox church due to its lavish Empire-style colonnade, theatrical iconostasis and exuberant sculpted angels. On display in the church's left aisle, originally dedicated to the Transfiguration, is the Icon of Our Lady of Consolation of All Sorrows. It is said to have miraculously cured the ailing sister of Patriarch Joachim in the 17th century.

Church of St Clement ❹

Церковь Святого Климента
Tserkov Svyatovo Klimenta

Klimentovskiy pereulok 7. **Map** 7 B3. Ⓜ *Tretyakovskaya.* ● *to public.*

This imposing, red-painted 18th-century church is now in a sadly decayed state. In 1756–8 the present refectory and belfry were built onto a church dating from the 1720s. This was pulled down in the 1760s when a new church was commissioned by the merchant Kuzma Matveev, a wealthy

The remarkably decorated, 17th-century Church of St Nicholas in Pyzhy

parishoner. The result is an outstanding example of late Moscow Baroque. The design is thought to have been conceived by the Italian architect Pietro Antonio Trezzini. The building of the church was completed by 1774.

The red and white façade is crowned by four black domes with golden stars surrounding a fifth, golden, cupola. Unfortunately, the church has been unsafe to enter for some years and it is unlikely that it will reopen in the near future.

Baroque domes of the Church of St Clement, completed in 1774

Church of St Nicholas in Pyzhy ❺

Церковь Николая в Пыжах

Tserkov Nikolaya v Pyzhakh

Ulitsa Bolshaya Ordynka 27a/8. **Map** 7 B3. **M** *Tretyakovskaya.*

SMALL CROWNS, as well as the traditional crosses, decorate the silver domes of this splendid church. It was constructed between 1670–72 in the area of the city once inhabited by the Streltsy, the royal guard, who provided the funds for it. Some of these men were later executed by Peter the Great for their role in the 1682 Streltsy Rebellion *(see p22)*. Funds were, in particular, generously lavished on the exterior decoration, which includes remarkable fretted cornices and finely chiselled window frames. The church's slender, tiered bell tower is one of the finest in the city, whilst the iconostasis contains some original icons as well as copies of more famous ones.

Church of St Catherine ❻

Церковь Екатерины

Tserkov Yekateriny

Ulitsa Bolshaya Ordynka 60/2. **Map** 7 B3. **M** *Tretyakovskaya.*

ORIGINALLY A WOODEN church built by the cosmetic merchants' guild in the 16th century, Catherine the Great commissioned the architect Karl Blank to redesign and rebuild the church in the 1760s. It is dedicated to St Catherine of Alexandria who was beheaded in the 4th century on the orders of the Roman emperor Maximian for refusing to renounce her Christian faith.

The distinct architecture of the Church of St Catherine combines certain elements of Moscow baroque and rococo. Of interest are the ornate metal railings outside, which are superb and unique examples of 18th-century metalwork. Originally, they were located in the Kremlin between the Cathedral of the Archangel Michael and the Patriarchal Palace.

The rotunda of the Church of St Catherine

In 1931 the church was closed, its bell-tower dismantled and almost all the icons (painted by Levitsky and Vasilevsky) were removed. Since the early 1990s, however, it has been undergoing a programme of restoration to return it to its former glory.

The Convent of SS Martha and Mary, founded in 1908 and designed by Aleksey Shchusev

Convent of SS Martha and Mary ❼

Марфо-Мариинская обитель

Marfo-Mariinskaya obitel

Ulitsa Bolshaya Ordynka 34. **Map** 7 B4. ☎ *951 8446.* Ⓜ *Tretyakovskaya, Polyanka.* ◯ *10am–7pm.* ▣

A LOW ARCHWAY leads from the street to this secluded compound, containing what appear at first glance to be medieval buildings. In fact they date from 1908–12 and were designed by Aleksey Shchusev *(see p45)*.

The convent was conceived to house a dispensary, a clinic, a small women's hospital and a school. It was run by the Order of the Sisters of Charity which was founded by the Grand Duchess Yelizaveta Fyodorovna, sister-in-law of Tsar Nicholas II. She had turned to charitable work after her husband, Grand Prince Sergei (Tsar Nicholas II's uncle), was assassinated by a terrorist bomb in the troubled year of 1905 *(see p26)*. Yelizaveta also met a violent death: the day after the shooting of Tsar Nicholas II and his family in 1918, the Bolsheviks pushed her down a mine shaft with further members of the royal family.

When designing the Church of the Intercession, the convent's main building, Shchusev carried out considerable research into Russian religious architecture, particularly that of the Pskov and Novgorod schools *(see p44)*. Shchusev's ingenious design juxtaposed a highly traditional style with Style-Moderne features such as boldly pointed gables, limestone carvings of mythical creatures and Slavonic script on the outer walls.

The artist Mikhail Nesterov, a protegé of industrialist and art patron Savva Mamontov *(see p154)*, was commissioned to design and paint the frescoes in the interior of the church. He also designed the pale grey and white habits of the nuns.

After the Revolution the Order of the Sisters of Charity was suppressed and the church was used as a workshop for restoring icons for a number of years. The nuns have now returned to staff the clinic.

Tropinin Museum ❽

Музей ВА Тропинина

Muzey VA Tropinina

Shchetininskiy pereulok 10. **Map** 7 B4. ☎ *953 9750.* Ⓜ *Dobryninskaya, Polyanka.* ◯ *noon–6pm Mon, Thu, Fri, 10am–4pm Sat–Sun.* ▣ ▣ ▣

A HIGHLY TALENTED portrait artist, Vasiliy Tropinin executed a staggering 3,000 paintings in his life. As well as painting figures in high society, he is noted as one of the first Russian artists to depict working people. Works spanning his career are displayed in this attractive museum set in a blue and white Neo-Classical house. The furnishings and ornaments are from Tropinin's time and are mostly in Empire style.

The museum's collection is based on works gathered by Feliks Vishnevskiy (1902–78). Having been an ardent supporter of the Revolution, he was able to collect during the Soviet period when paintings were relatively cheap. In addition to Tropinin's oil portraits, there are works by

***Girl in Ukrainian Dress* painted by Vasiliy Tropinin**

VASILIY TROPININ (1776–1857)

Though born a serf in Karpovo near Novgorod, Vasiliy Tropinin's prodigious talent was recognized at an early age. He was sent to the St Petersburg Academy of Arts in 1798, but was withdrawn by his master and brought back to work as an interior decorator, pastry-cook and footman on his estates. Tropinin and his wife gained their freedom in 1823 and moved to Moscow, where Tropinin became a professional portrait artist. Unlike many other painters of the time, he did not limit himself to painting members of the aristocracy. Instead, his portraits depicted a cross-section of society, from peasants to nobles.

Some of the Empire-style furnishings in the Tropinin Museum

some of his contemporaries, including Orest Kiprenskiy and Dmitriy Levitskiy. Like Tropinin, they were students at the St Petersburg Academy of Arts. There are also some fine landscapes of 19th-century Moscow. The Tretyakov Gallery *(see pp118–21)* contains further works by these artists.

Bakhrushin Theatre Museum ❾

Театральный музей имени А.А. Бахрушина

Teatralnyy muzey imeni AA Bakhrushina

Ulitsa Bakhrushina 31/12. **Map** 7 C5. *953 4470.* *Paveletskaya.* *noon–6pm Wed–Mon.* *English (book in advance).*

FOUNDED IN 1894 by Aleksey Bakhrushin, a merchant and patron of the arts, this museum contains probably the most important collection of theatre memorabilia in Russia. Spread over two floors, the exhibits range from sets and costumes to theatre tickets, programmes, advertisements and signed photographs.

The basement is filled with items relating to the career of the great opera singer Fyodor Shalyapin *(see p83)*. One of the highlights is a richly brocaded costume he wore for the title role in Modest Mussorgsky's opera *Boris Godunov*.

A display on early Russian theatre includes puppets, models of theatres and sets, and paintings and engravings of theatrical entertainments.

Exhibits on 19th-century theatre include costumes and sets from the Ballets Russes. This famous company, formed by Sergey Diaghilev in 1909, revolutionized ballet. The sets include some designed by Michel Fokine, the company's inspired choreographer. A pair of ballet shoes belonging to Vaslaw Nijinsky, one of the principal dancers, is also on show.

The room on 20th-century avant-garde theatre includes stage models created for outstanding directors Konstantin Stanislavskiy *(see p93)* and Vsevolod Meyerhold *(see p92)*.

Set design by Michel Fokine, on show in the Bakhrushin Theatre Museum

View of the Kremlin from the Sophia Embankment

Sophia Embankment ❿

Софийская набережная

Sofiyskaya naberezhnaya

Map 7 A2. *Kropotkinskaya, Borovitskaya, Novokuznetskaya.*

SITUATED OPPOSITE the Kremlin, on the southern bank of the Moskva river, the Sophia Embankment stretches from the Bolshoy Kamennyy most (Great Stone bridge) to the Bolshoy Moskvoretskiy most (Great Moscow river bridge).

The embankment was built up to its current height at the end of the 18th century and was greatly improved in 1836. It offers spectacular views over the Kremlin and the city.

Novgorodians settled on the river bank in the 14th century and built the original Church of St Sophia. The present church dates from the mid-17th century. Aleksandr Kaminskiy added the bell tower in 1862.

The mansion at No. 14 was designed by Vasiliy Zalesskiy in 1893 for a sugar baron and is now the British ambassador's residence. The interiors are by Fyodor Shekhtel *(see p45)*.

FURTHER AFIELD

MOSCOW'S SUBURBS are generally rather bleak, but they conceal a surprising number of attractions, all accessible by metro. To the south of the centre lies a number of fortified monasteries, built to defend the city against the Mongols and the Poles. The most spectacular of them is Novodevichiy Convent, a serene 16th-century sanctuary with a glorious cathedral, but the Donskoy Monastery is also well worth a visit. The Danilovskiy Monastery, with its handsome cathedral, is the oldest in the city.

Cathedral fresco, Novodevichiy Convent

Visitors to Moscow are often surprised at the beauty and variety of its green spaces. Gorky, Izmaylovo and Victory parks are the perfect places in which to relax, while Sparrow Hills offers fantastic views. The city's best-kept secrets, however, are the grand estates away from the centre in what was formerly countryside. There the Sheremetev family built two elegant Neo-Classical summer residences: Kuskovo and Ostankino. Both have beautifully preserved gardens and palaces full of fine paintings and period furnishings.

SIGHTS AT A GLANCE

Churches, Convents and Monasteries
Church of the Intercession in Fili 1
Church of St John the Warrior 10
Church of St Nicholas of the Weavers 8
Danilovskiy Monastery 12
Donskoy Monastery 11
Krutitskoe Mission 15
Monastery of the Saviour and Andronicus 17
Novodevichiy Convent pp130–31 6

Palaces
Kuskovo pp142–3 16
Ostankino Palace 21

Museums and Galleries
Kolomenskoe pp138–9 13
New Tretyakov Gallery 9
Tolstoy House-Museum 7
Vasnetsov House-Museum 20

Historic buildings
Tsaritsyno 14
White House 2

Parks and Open Spaces
All-Russian Exhibition Centre (VVTs) 22
Gorky Park 5
Izmaylovo Park 18
Komsomolskaya Ploshchad 19
Sparrow Hills 4
Victory Park 3

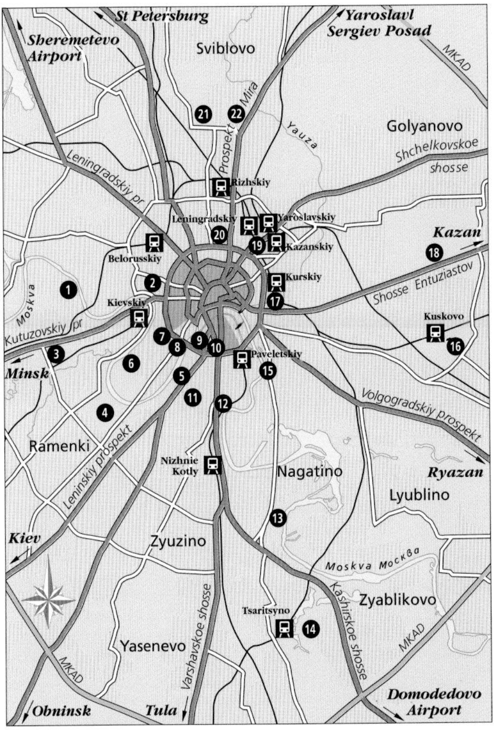

0 kilometres 5

0 miles 5

KEY

Central Moscow
Greater Moscow
Railway station
Motorway
Major road
Minor road
Railway

◁ **Ostankino's magnificent Italian Pavilion, designed by Moscow-based Italian architect Vincenzo Brenna**

Church of the Intercession in Fili ❶

Церковь Покрова в Филях

Tserkov Pokrova v Filyakh

Ulitsa Novozavodskaya 6. *148 4552.* M *Fili.* *11am–6pm Thu–Mon (May–Oct: upper church only).*

THIS STUNNING CHURCH was commissioned by an uncle of Peter the Great, Prince Lev Naryshkin, and is in the style known as Moscow, or Naryshkin, Baroque *(see p44)*. Built by an unknown architect, between 1690 and 1693 it is an extraordinary tiered structure of red brick, with lace-like ornamentation and pilasters of white stone.

Russian churches often comprise two buildings: a grand, unheated one for summer, and a smaller, simpler one that can be heated easily in winter.

Here, the winter church at ground level has changing displays of religious art. In front of it a double staircase rises to a terrace surrounding the upper summer church. This staircase would once have provided the setting for processions. Inside, there is an iconostasis, mainly the work of the 17th-century painter Karp Zolotarev, and a carved gilt pew used by Peter the Great.

The elegant Church of the Intercession in Fili, the city's best example of Moscow Baroque

Gilded crest on the clock tower of the White House

White House ❷

Белый дом

Belyy dom

Krasnopresnenskaya naberezhnaya 2. **Map** 1 B5. M *Krasnopresnenskaya.* *to public.*

A MARBLE-CLAD building with a gilded clock tower, the White House is still a "must-see" for tourists interested in recent political history.

Once the seat of the Russian Federation's parliament, it first claimed the world's attention in August 1991 when it was the focus of resistance to the Communist hardliners' coup against Mikhail Gorbachev, the president of the Soviet Union. The rebels detained Gorbachev at his Black Sea villa, where he was holidaying at the time, so it was Boris Yeltsin, the president of the smaller Russian Federation, who led the opposition to the coup. The world watched as he passed through the lines of tanks surrounding the White House without anyone daring to arrest him. Then he climbed onto a tank to proclaim: "You can build a throne of bayonets, but you cannot sit on it for long".

The coup failed, and the victory of Yeltsin and his supporters was soon followed by the break-up of the Soviet Union and the end of Communist rule.

However, in September 1993, a reversal of roles occurred at the White House when Yeltsin became the besieger. Hundreds of deputies locked themselves into it in protest when Yeltsin summarily suspended parliament over its increasing opposition to his new draft constitution. The siege ended after two weeks when army tanks bombarded the deputies into submission.

The charred building was quickly repaired, but never regained its former significance; today the Russian parliament occupies a building on ulitsa Okhotnyy ryad *(see p86)*, and the presidential offices are in the Kremlin *(see pp52–67)*.

The Triumphal Arch, celebrating Napoleon's defeat in the 1812 war

Victory Park ❸

Парк победы

Park pobedy

Kutuzovskiy prospekt. M *Kutuzovskaya.* **Museum of the Great Patriotic War** *148 5550.* *10am–5pm Tue–Sun.* **Borodino Panorama Museum** *148 1967.* *10am–6pm Sat–Thu.*

COMMEMORATING victory in the Great Patriotic War, the Russian name for World War II *(see p27)*, Victory Park was originally intended to have a vast monument to Mother Russia at its centre. After the end of Communist rule, plans were scaled down and the park was finally completed in 1995, in time for the 50th anniversary of the end of the war.

The park is formally laid out, with straight alleys dividing the sparsely-treed grass. The main, fountain-lined avenue leads

The Stalinist-Gothic skyscraper of the Moscow State University

from Kutuzovskiy prospekt to the central Nike Monument, a towering, 142-m (466-ft) obelisk designed by Zurab Tsereteli to honour the Greek goddess of victory.

Behind the monument is the domed, semi-circular Museum of the Great Patriotic War. The dioramas, models, maps and weapons on show give an informative picture of the war as experienced by the Russians.

Just to the side of the central avenue is the simple Church of St George the Victorious, built in 1995, probably the first to be built in Russia after the Revolution. Next to it is a monument to war victims.

East along Kutuzovskiy prospekt are two large-scale memorials to the war of 1812 *(see pp23–5)*. Moscow's final deliverance from the French is celebrated by the grand Triumphal Arch. It was designed by Osip Bove *(see p45)*, with sculptures of Russian and Classical warriors by Ivan Vitali and Ivan Timofeev. Originally built on Tverskaya ulitsa in 1834, the arch was dismantled in the 1930s during street-widening. The sculptures were preserved and in 1968 the arch was rebuilt at its present site.

Further along the street, at No. 38, is the circular Borodino Panorama Museum, which contains a vast painting, 115-m (377-ft) long and 14-m (46-ft) high. It was created by Franz Roubaud in 1912 to mark the centenary of the battle waged between Russian forces and Napoleon's army at Borodino *(see p152)* outside Moscow.

Sparrow Hills ❹

Воробьёвы горы

Vorobevy gory

Ⓜ *Universitet.*

THE SUMMIT of this wooded ridge offers unsurpassed views across the city. There is an observation point on ulitsa Kosygina and newly-wed couples traditionally come here to have their photograph taken against the panorama. It is also a favourite pitch for a large number of souvenir sellers.

The hills are dominated by the Moscow State University (MGU) building commissioned by Stalin, designed by Lev Rudnev and completed in 1953. At 36 floors high it is the tallest of the seven Stalinist-Gothic "wedding-cakes" *(see p45)*.

Plaque at the entrance to Gorky Park

The small, green-domed Church of the Trinity (1811) can also be seen close by, to the left of the observation platform. There are also a couple of long, but somewhat rickety, ski jumps on the hills.

On prospekt Vernadskovo, on the southeast edge of the hills, is the Palace of Youth and Creative Work, a studio complex built for the Communist youth organization. Also on this street are the silver-roofed New Moscow Circus *(see p190)* built in 1971, and the Nataliya Sats Children's Musical Theatre *(see p191)*.

Gorky Park ❺

Парк культуры и отдыха имени М. Горького

Park Kultury i otdykha imeni M. Gorkovo

Krymskiy val 9. **Map** 6 E4. Ⓜ *Park Kultury, Oktyabrskaya.* ☎ *237 0707.* 🕒 *10am–10pm daily.* ♿

MOSCOW'S MOST FAMOUS park is named in honour of the writer Maxim Gorky and extends for more than 120 ha (297 acres) along the banks of the Moskva river. Opened in 1928 as the Park of Culture and Rest, it incorporates the Golitsyn Gardens, laid out by Matvey Kazakov *(see p44)* in the late 18th century, and a 19th-century pleasure park. Later, during the Soviet era, loudspeakers were set up and used to broadcast speeches by Communist leaders across the park. Today the attractions include fairground rides, woodland walks, boating lakes, a 10,000-seat outdoor theatre and, in the winter months, an ice-skating rink.

The park was immortalized in the opening scenes of Michael Apted's film *Gorky Park*. However, because of the tense political climate of 1983, the film was actually shot in Finland.

Outdoor ice-skating in Gorky Park, a popular activity in the winter months

Novodevichiy Convent ❻

Новодевичий монастырь
Novodevichiy monastyr

PROBABLY THE MOST BEAUTIFUL of the semi-circle of fortified religious institutions to the south of Moscow is Novodevichiy Convent, founded by Basil III in 1524 to commemorate the capture of Smolensk from the Lithuanians. Only the Cathedral of the Virgin of Smolensk was built at this time. Most of the other buildings were added in the late 17th century by Peter the Great's half-sister, the Regent Sophia. After Peter deposed her and reclaimed his throne in 1689 *(see p22)*, he confined her here for the rest of her life. In 1812 Napoleon's troops tried to blow up the convent but, according to a popular story, it was saved by the nuns, who snuffed out the fuses.

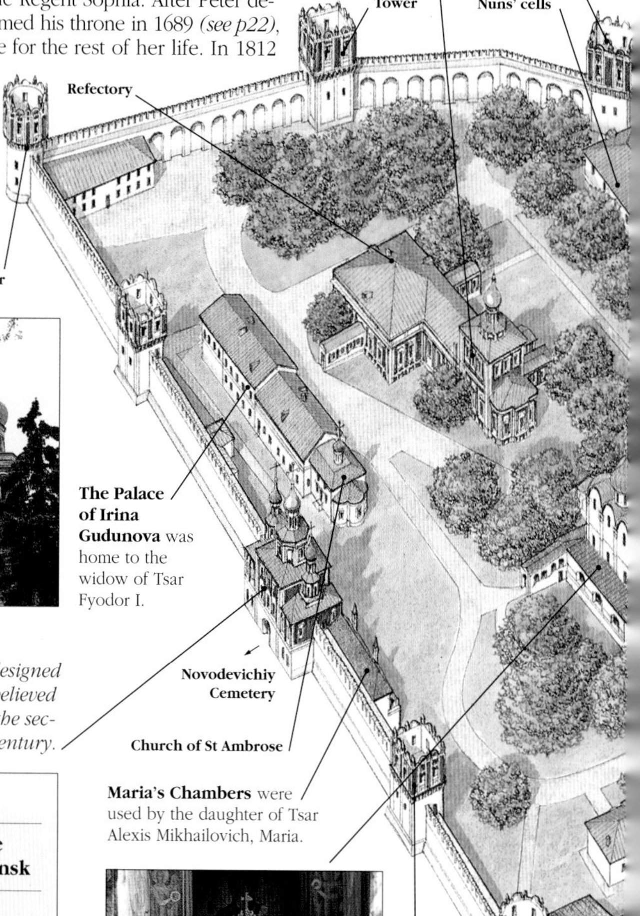
The Church of the Assumption and adjoining refectory were built in the 1680s on the orders of the Regent Sophia.
Saviour's Tower
Faceted Tower
Nuns' cells
Refectory
Setunskaya Tower
The Palace of Irina Gudunova was home to the widow of Tsar Fyodor I.
Novodevichiy Cemetery
Church of St Ambrose
Maria's Chambers were used by the daughter of Tsar Alexis Mikhailovich, Maria.
Vorobeva Tower
Shoemaker's tower
0 metres 25
0 yards 25

Gate Church of the Intercession
It is not known who designed this church, but it is believed to have been built in the second half of the 17th century.

STAR FEATURES

- ★ **Cathedral of the Virgin of Smolensk**
- ★ **Bell Tower**
- ★ **Gate Church of the Transfiguration**

★ Cathedral of the Virgin of Smolensk
The oldest building in the convent is the cathedral, built in 1524. The five-tier iconostasis, the rich frescoes and the onion domes all date from the 17th century.

The tombstone of Nikita Khrushchev

Novodevichiy Cemetery

Many famous Russians are buried in this cemetery. Among the leading cultural figures are playwright Anton Chekhov, writer Nikolai Gogol, composers Sergey Prokofiev, Aleksandr Skryabin *(see p72)* and Dmitriy Shostakovich and opera singer Fyodor Shalyapin *(see p83)*. The cemetery is also the final resting place for numerous military and political dignitaries from the Soviet era, including the former Russian premier Nikita Khrushchev *(see p30)*.

Visitors' Checklist

Novodevichiy proezd 1. *246 8526.* **M** *Sportivnaya. 64, 132 (see p219). 5, 15. 10am–5pm Wed–Mon. some public hols. grounds only. English (book in advance). 8am, 5pm Mon–Sat, 7am & 10am Sun.* **Cemetery** *10am–6pm daily.* www.shm.ru

★ Gate Church of the Transfiguration

A cornice of scallop-shell gables, topped by five gilded domes and crosses, crowns this grand Baroque church. It stands over the main gate to the convent and was completed in 1688.

★ Bell Tower

Completed in 1690, this tower is one of the most exuberant examples of Baroque architecture in Moscow. The Church of St John the Divine occupies the second storey of the six-tiered, octagonal tower, which stands 72 m (236 ft) high.

Lopukhin Palace

This palace was built in 1687–9. After Peter the Great's death in 1725 his first wife, Yevdokiya Lopukhina, moved here from the Suzdal convent where she had been sent after Peter tired of her.

Magnificent towers and domed churches of Novodevichiy, viewed from the north

Tolstoy House-Museum ❼

Музей-усадьба ЛН Толстого
Muzey-usadba LN Tolstovo

Ulitsa Lva Tolstovo 21. **Map** 6 D4.
246 9444. *Park Kultury.*
Apr–Sep: 10am–5pm Tue–Sun; Oct–Mar: 10am–3:30pm Tue–Sun.
English (book in advance).

The presence of one of Russia's greatest novelists can be felt in every corner of this evocative, wooden house. It was here that Leo Tolstoy (1828–1910) spent the winters between 1882 and 1901 with his long-suffering wife, Sofya Andreevna, and the nine surviving of their 13 children. The summers were spent on the Tolstoy ancestral estate at Yasnaya Polyana *(see p161)*, 200 km (124 miles) away.

The Moscow house was turned into a museum in 1921 on Lenin's orders and has been preserved much as it would have been when Tolstoy and his family resided here.

On the ground floor, the large table in the dining room is still laid with crockery. The evening meal in the Tolstoy household always began promptly at 6pm to the summons of the cuckoo clock on the wall. Next door is the "corner room" where, at one time, the elder sons, Sergey, Ilya and Lev, would retire to play Chinese billiards.

Leo Tolstoy

By the time Tolstoy was in his 50s, he was an author of international renown and had written his two great masterpieces *War and Peace* (1865–9) and *Anna Karenina* (1873–7). He continued to write fiction, but later renounced his earlier books and the world they depicted. Instead Tolstoy concentrated on his highly individual brand of Christian Humanism, a doctrine that included non-violence, vegetarianism and total sexual abstinence. It was in this period that he wrote the stories *The Death of Ivan Ilych* and the *Kreutzer Sonata* and his last great novel, *Resurrection*, which strayed so far from Orthodoxy that the Holy Synod excommunicated him in 1901. Tolstoy left Moscow the same year for Yasnaya Polyana, where he devoted himself totally to mysticism and the education of the peasants on the estate.

The dining room with a painting of Tolstoy's favourite daughter Mariya

The house exudes a sense of ordered, comfortable family life, but Tolstoy and his wife frequently quarrelled violently, largely on account of his wish to renounce society and live as simply as possible. The couple were reconciled for a short time when Vanya, their much-loved youngest child died from scarlet fever at the age of seven. His memory is preserved in his small bedroom near the scullery, where his high chair, rocking horse and books can be seen.

The bedroom of Tolstoy's second daughter, Tatyana, is crammed with ornaments and keepsakes. She was a talented artist and her own paintings and sketches are hung on the walls.

The stairs to the first floor open into the salon, a large hall where frequent guests were treated to supper. They included the young Sergei Rachmaninov who accompanied the bass, Fyodor Shalyapin *(see p83)*, on the piano here, the artist Ilya Repin, whose portrait of Tatyana now hangs in the "corner room", the music critic Vladimir Stasov, and the writer Maxim Gorky *(see p95)* with whom Tolstoy would play chess. The drawing room next door was decorated by Sofya Andreevna herself.

The bedroom of Tolstoy's favourite child, Mariya, is rather spartan, testifying to her sympathy for her father's ideals and way of life.

At the far end of the upstairs passage is Tolstoy's study, a spacious room overlooking the garden. Reflecting his passion for austerity, the room is simply furnished in black leather. The plain, solid desk where he wrote his novel *Resurrection* is lit by candles. Rather than admit to being shortsighted, Tolstoy sawed off the ends of his chair legs to bring himself closer to his papers. In the adjoining washroom are dumbbells and a bicycle – evidence of his interest in keeping fit. Also on show are the tools he used for his hobby of shoemaking, with some of the pairs he made. The back stairs close by lead to the garden, which is only accessible to those taking a guided tour.

The simple desk in Tolstoy's study where he wrote his final novel, *Resurrection*

The luxurious interior of the Church of St Nicholas of the Weavers

Church of St Nicholas of the Weavers 8

Церковь Николая в Хамовниках

Tserkov Nikolaya v Khamovnikakh

Ulitsa Lva Tolstovo 2. **Map** 6 D4. *246 2719* *Park Kultury.* *during services*

DEDICATED TO the patron saint of weavers, sailors and farmers, this spectacular church was founded in 1679 by local weavers (*khamovniki*). Their aim was to surpass the Church of the Resurrection in Kadashi *(see p122)*, which was built a few years before by rival weavers across the river.

While staying at their winter home nearby, Tolstoy and his family used to attend services here until his rift with the Church authorities. The church continued to function throughout the Communist era.

The exterior is decorated with vivid orange and green gables and topped with five golden domes, while the walls are decorated with patterned tiles imitating woven motifs.

Inside the church there is an iconostasis featuring a 17th-century Icon of St Nicholas. A separate Icon of the Virgin, Helper of Sinners, is reputed to perform miracles.

The Church of St Nicholas of the Weavers, topped by golden domes

New Tretyakov Gallery 9

Третьяковская галерея

Tretyakovskaya galereya

Krymskiy val 10. **Map** 6 F3. *238 1378.* *Park Kultury, Oktyabrskaya.* *10am–8pm Tue–Sun.* *English.* www.tretyakov.ru

THIS HUGE WHITE BOX of a building is an annexe of the Tretyakov Gallery *(see pp118–21)* in the centre of town. It is devoted to Russian art from the early 1900's to the present. Most of the canvases here belong to the official movement known as Socialist Realism and reflect the cultural straitjacket imposed by Stalin *(see p27)* in the 1930s. It had its roots in the Wanderers movement of the 1860s, which was based on the principle that art has, first and foremost, a social role to play, though lyricism and beauty in paintings were also important *(see p120)*. In contrast, the hard--hitting art of the Communist era served the state's interests, reflecting socialist goals and achievements. A few examples of the titles given to the paintings say it all: *Life is Getting Better; Building New Factories; Unforgettable Meeting* (between Stalin and a spellbound young woman). Technological achievements were also immortalized in pictures such as *The First Russian Airship*.

Many people will find the Modernist paintings at the beginning of the exhibition more aesthetically pleasing. These include pictures by previously outlawed artists, such as the *Black Square* by Kazimir Malevich and works by Constructivists such as Aleksandr Rodchenko and the brothers Georgiy and Vladimir Stenberg.

Outside, on the Moskva river embankment, is the Graveyard of Fallen Monuments, a collection of some of the sculptures removed from around Moscow at the end of the Soviet era. Pride of place belongs to the huge statue of the secret police chief, Feliks Dzerzhinskiy, which was taken down from outside the KGB headquarters in Lubyanka Square *(see p112)* in 1991. A striking addition to the view from the Tretyakov's gardens is a huge statue of Peter the Great by Zurab Tsereteli, completed in 1997.

The vast statue of Peter the Great, erected in 1997, viewed from the Graveyard of Fallen Monuments

The distinctive, colourful Church of St John the Warrior

Church of St John the Warrior ⑩

Церковь Иоанна Воина

Tserkov Ioanna Voina

Ulitsa Bolshaya Yakimanka 46. **Map** 6 F4. *238 2056.* *Oktyabrskaya.*

THE PLANS FOR this famous church, attributed to the architect Ivan Zarudniy, are said to have been personally approved by Peter the Great *(see p22)*. Building work took place from 1709–13 and the result is a notable example of Petrine Baroque, a style which had begun to flourish in St Petersburg, the tsar's new capital. The church's most eye-catching feature is a tiered octagonal tower, with an elegant balustrade and coloured roof tiles forming bold, geometric designs.

St John the Warrior is one of the few churches to have stayed open after the Revolution and a number of historic works of religious art were transferred here for safekeeping. These can still be seen in the church and include the 17th-century Icon of the Saviour, which hung in a chapel near the Saviour's Tower in the Kremlin. Across the road is the extremely striking Igumnov House, which was built in 1893 for a rich merchant by Nikolay Pozdeev. It is a typically flamboyant example of Russian-Revival architecture *(see p45)*, and now houses the French Embassy.

The Old Cathedral, Donskoy Monastery

Donskoy Monastery ⑪

Донской монастырь

Donskoy monastyr

Donskaya ploshchad 1. *952 4901.* *Shabolovskaya.* *7am–7pm daily.* *grounds only.*

THE DONSKOY MONASTERY was founded in 1593 by Boris Godunov to honour the Icon of the Donskoy Virgin, credited with having twice saved Moscow from the Mongols. The first time was in 1380 when Prince Dmitriy Donskoy carried the icon into battle at Kulikovo *(see p155)*. Boris Godunov also used it to rally his troops in 1591 against the army of Khan Kazy Girei, which retreated after minor skirmishes. The crescent moons, below many of the golden crosses on top of the monastery buildings, symbolize the defeat of Islam.

The modest scale of the original monastery is reflected in the beautifully understated Old Cathedral with its bright blue dome and *kokoshniki* gables *(see p44)*. Two orthodox prelates are buried within the Old Cathedral: Archbishop Amvrosiy, killed by a mob during a plague riot in 1771, and Patriarch Tikhon, who was imprisoned by the Bolsheviks after the Revolution.

In the late 17th century the monastery acquired greater prestige under the patronage of the Regent Sophia and her lover Golitsyn. The fortified outer walls and New Cathedral are additions from this period.

Built in 1684–98 in the Moscow-Baroque style *(see p44)*, the New Cathedral is a towering brick building with five domes. Inside are a stunning seven-tiered iconostasis and some exuberant frescoes, painted in 1782–5 by Italian artist Antonio Claudio. The Icon of the Donskoy Virgin is now in the Tretyakov Gallery *(see pp118–21)*, but a copy is on show in the Old Cathedral.

The Donskoy Monastery's imposing 17th-century New Cathedral

Danilovskiy Monastery ⑫

Даниловский монастырь

Danilovskiy monastyr

Danilovskiy val 22. *958 0502.* *Tulskaya.* *7am–8pm daily.* http://sdm.infomos.ru

FOUNDED BY Prince Daniil in 1298–1300, the Danilovskiy Monastery is the city's oldest. It was used as a factory and youth detention centre after the Revolution, but since 1988 it has been the headquarters of

The Russian Orthodox Church

Christianity was adopted as Russia's official religion in AD 988 when Vladimir I *(see p17)* married the sister of the Byzantine Emperor and had himself baptized in the Orthodox faith. In the 13th century monasteries became a focus for resistance against the invading Mongols. Thereafter the Church played a vital role in Russian life until the Revolution, when it was forced underground. As the Soviet Union broke up, the church revived and, in 1992, Boris Yeltsin became the first Russian leader to attend church services since 1917.

Delicate stone tracery on the Figured Gate at Tsaritsyno

the Russian Orthodox Church, which has offices in its more modern, plainer buildings.

The green-domed Church of the Holy Fathers of the Seven Ecumenical Councils is the oldest of the three churches within the fortified walls. It was founded by Ivan the Terrible *(see p18)* in the 16th century. The main church, on the first floor, has a 17th-century iconostasis with contemporary icons.

At the heart of the monastery is the elegant yellow Cathedral of the Trinity, designed by Osip Bove *(see p45)* in 1833 and completed five years later.

The pretty pink bell tower in the northern wall contains the Gate Church of St Simeon the Stylite. It was built in 1730–32, but knocked down in the 1920s. The bells were sold to Harvard University, but have now been restored to the rebuilt gate and bell tower.

Kolomenskoe ⓭

See pp138–9.

Tsaritsyno ⓮

Царицыно

Tsaritsyno

Ulitsa Dolskaya 1. *321 0743.* *Orekhevo, Tsaritsyno.* *11am–6pm Wed–Sun (Oct–Mar: 10am–4pm).*

Catherine the Great *(see p23)* bought this tract of land in 1775 and changed its name from Chyornaya Gryaz (Black Mud) to Tsaritsyno (the Tsarina's Village). In doing so, she commissioned one of her most imaginative architects, Vasiliy Bazhenov *(see p44)*, to design and construct a lavish imperial palace which would rival any found in St Petersburg.

Bazhenov conceived an innovative palace complex combining Gothic, Baroque and even Moorish styles and Catherine approved the plans. She visited the site in 1785 and, although construction was well under way, proclaimed herself dissatisfied. Bazhenov's young colleague Matvey Kazakov *(see pp44–5)* was told to rebuild the palace but, after a further decade of construction, lack of funds left it still incomplete.

Today the grounds boast charming lakes and woodland walks. Some of the ruins have been restored, but the forlorn remainder have a beauty which the completed palace might never have matched. Although the shell of Kazakov's Grand Palace is the most imposing building on the estate, some of Bazhenov's smaller structures are equally impressive. Visitors can see the Figured Gate with its elegant Gothic-style towers and lancet windows, the Figured Bridge and the ornate two-storey Opera House, one of the few buildings Catherine approved. The extraordinary Bread Gate, with its arch of sharply pointed stone "teeth", leads to the kitchens, while the Octahedron was built as the servants' quarters. The attractive Church of Our Lady of the Life-Giving Spirit was added in the 19th-century.

A small museum on the estate displays icons, china, glass and some Fabergé eggs, as well as landscapes and architectural exhibits. However, only a fraction of the items in the cellars below the palace are on show at any one time.

The iconostasis in the Church of the Holy Fathers, Danilovskiy Monastery

Kolomenskoe ⓭

Коломенское
Kolomenskoe

THE EARLIEST KNOWN REFERENCE to Kolomenskoe village is in the will of Ivan I *(see p18)*, dated 1339. By the 16th century Kolomenskoe was a favourite country estate of the tsars. The oldest surviving building is the Church of the Ascension, constructed in 1532. A superb wooden palace was built for Tsar Alexis Mikhailovich *(see p19)* in 1667–71, but it was demolished in the 18th century. After the Revolution the park was designated a museum of architecture, and wooden buildings, such as Peter the Great's cabin from Archangel, were moved here from all over Russia. Also located on the estate is the Front Gate Museum. Its exhibits include a model of Tsar Alexis' palace and Russian craft objects, such as tile paintings and woodcarvings.

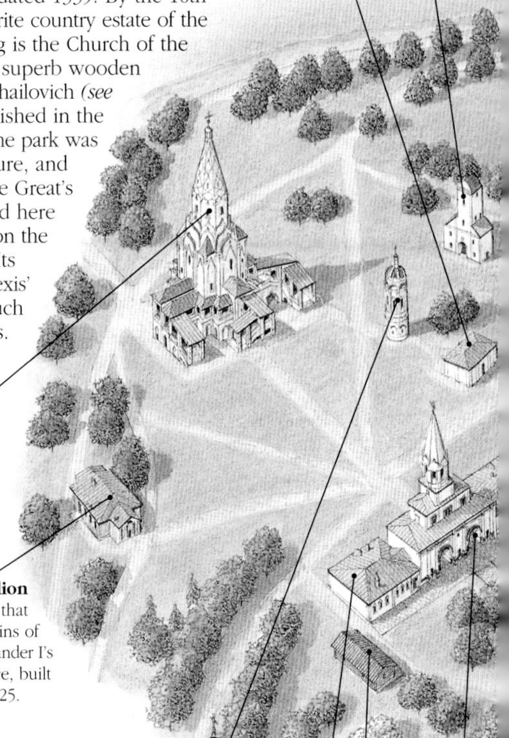

The Falcon Tower was constructed in 1627. It was used as a water tower.

Refectory

The Pavilion is all that remains of Alexander I's palace, built in 1825.

Mead Brewery

Front Gate Museum

The Front Gate was the ceremonial entrance to Tsar Alexis' palace. The chambers on either side of the gate now form the Front Gate Museum.

★ Church of the Ascension
This magnificent church was erected by Basil III in 1532 to celebrate the birth of his son Ivan (later the Terrible). Its most striking feature is its tent-roofed tower, one of the first in Russia to be built from stone.

Church of St George
The 16th-century Church of St George once stood on this site, but today only the church's bell tower still stands.

MODEL OF WOODEN PALACE

Kolomenskoe underwent a major expansion during the reign of Tsar Alexis Mikhailovich, father of Peter the Great. He added a new centrepiece, an astonishing wooden palace with fanciful barrel-shaped roofs, onion domes and carved ornamentation, which visiting diplomats described as the "eighth wonder of the world". It was demolished in 1768 on the orders of Catherine the Great. Fortunately she had a model made, which is now displayed in the Front Gate Museum.

STAR FEATURES

- ★ **Church of the Ascension**
- ★ **Church of Our Lady of Kazan**

Church of St John the Baptist

Located to the south of the main estate, this church was commissioned by Ivan the Terrible to celebrate his accession to the throne in 1547.

VISITORS' CHECKLIST

Prospekt Andropova 39. *114 8298.* *Kolomenskaya (see p219).* **Front Gate Museum & Churches** *10:30am–6pm Tue–Sun.* *Eng. (book in adv).* **Grounds** *24 hours.* www.museum.ru/kolomen

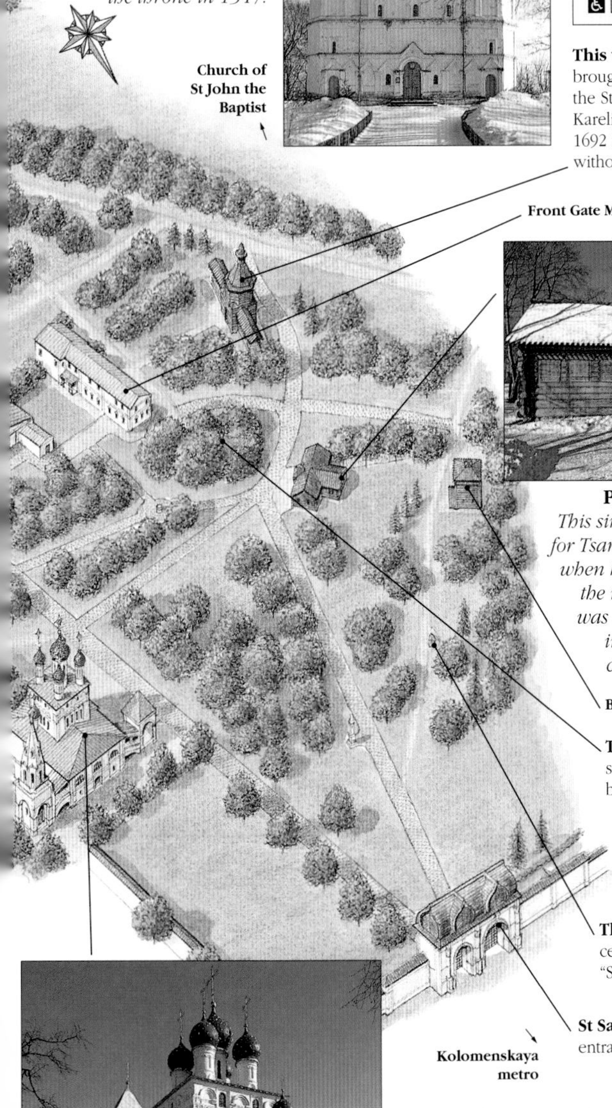

This wooden gate tower was brought to Kolomenskoe from the St Nicholas Monastery at Karelia in 1932. It was built in 1692 from interlocking sections without using a single nail.

Peter the Great's Cabin

This simple log cabin was built for Tsar Peter the Great in 1702 when he visited Archangel (on the north coast of Russia). It was brought to Kolomenskoe in 1934 and its four low-ceilinged rooms restored.

These ancient oaks are said to have been planted by Peter the Great.

The Boris Stone (12th century) bears the inscription, "Strong, brave, holy Boris".

St Saviour's Gate is the main entrance to the complex.

★ Church of Our Lady of Kazan

Completed in 1650 for Tsar Alexis, this stunning church is an early example of Moscow Baroque (see p44). *It is now open again for worship. A replica of the Icon of Our Lady of Kazan, which is believed to have helped Russia drive out Polish invaders in 1612, can be found inside the church.*

Krutitskoe Mission ⓯

Крутицкое подворье
Krutitskoe podvore

Krutitskaya ulitsa 11. **Map** 8 E5. *276 9724.* *Proletarskaya.* **Grounds** *8am–8pm daily.*

THE METROPOLITAN originally resided in the Kremlin, but after the creation of the patriarchate in the 16th century the bishops of Krutitsy became metropolitans *(see p56)*. The Mission's name derives from the Russian *krutoy*, meaning steep, and refers to the nearby bank of the Moskva river.

The Baroque buildings seen today are undergoing restoration and are dominated by the bulky Cathedral of the Assumption, which was built in 1685. The entire edifice, including the onion domes, is built of bricks.

A covered gallery links the cathedral to the Metropolitan's Palace via a double-arched gateway topped by a small pavilion or *teremok*. The gallery and pavilion are by Osip Startsev, who was famous in Russia in the late 17th century as a designer of religious buildings. The northern façade of the *teremok* is decorated with intricately carved window frames and turquoise tiles with yellow floral motifs.

The Metropolitan's Palace is a handsome, though plainer, red brick building with pyramidal chimneys and an impressive staircase at the rear.

Since falling into disrepair early in the 19th century, the Mission has served as a barracks, a prison and, after the Revolution, a workers' hostel: their wooden living quarters still survive. Now, the youth movement of the Orthodox Church is based here.

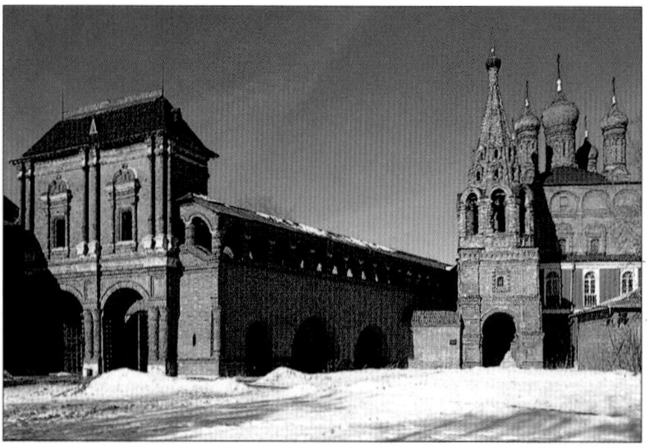

Gateway at Krutitskoe, linking the cathedral to the Metropolitan's Palace

Kuskovo ⓰

See pp142–3.

Monastery of the Saviour and Andronicus ⓱

Спасо-Андрониковский монастырь
Spaso-Andronikovskiy monastyr

Andronevskaya ploshchad 10. **Map** 8 F2. *Ploshchad Ilyicha.* *11am–6pm Thu–Tue.* **Museum** *278 1467.* *(book in advance).*

TRAVELLING BACK from the city of Constantinople in 1360, Metropolitan Aleksey survived a storm at sea. To give thanks he founded the Monastery of the Saviour on the banks of the Yauza river. He then appointed the monk Andronicus to be the first abbot and to oversee the building works.

The best-known monk to have lived here was Andrey Rublev, Russia's most brilliant icon painter *(see p61)*. He is thought to have died and been buried here in about 1430, but the location of his grave is unknown. Rublev is commemorated by the monastery's Andrey Rublev Museum of Old Russian Art. There are no icons by Rublev himself here, but some excellent copies of his works are on show, along with genuine pieces by his contemporaries. Original Rublev icons can be seen in the Tretyakov Gallery *(see pp118–21)*. The museum's collections are on show in two of the monastery buildings. The 16th-century Abbot's House, decorated with tiles and just to the right of the main entrance, displays decorative arts of the 11th–20th centuries. The Baroque Church of the Archangel Michael, built in 1691–94, displays Russian art of the 13th–17th centuries. Highlights include the 17th-century Icon of the Tikhvin Virgin, originally from the Donskoy Monastery *(see p136)*, and paintings depicting the life of St Nicholas of Zaraysk, one of Russia's favourite saints. The 18th-century monks' building, which contained monks' cells, is being renovated and will provide further gallery space.

Icon of St John the Baptist, 15th century

The Cathedral of the Saviour, with characteristic *kokoshniki* gables

The beautiful, single-domed Cathedral of the Saviour was built in either 1390 or 1425–7. If the former date is correct, this would make it the oldest church in Moscow. The interior was painted by Rublev but only traces of his work survive, around the altar windows.

Izmaylovo Park ⓲

Парк Измайлово

Park Izmaylovo

Narodniy prospekt 17. 166 7909. Izmaylovskiy Park, Shosse Entuziastov. 24 hours daily.

One of the largest parks in Europe, Izmaylovo covers nearly 12 sq km (4.7 sq miles). It features attractions such as sports facilities, children's amusements, cafés and woods, as well as an outdoor theatre, a famous flea market *(see p185)*, a cathedral and the picturesque remains of one of the tsars' country estates.

Izmaylovo passed to the Romanov family in the 16th century and became one of their favourite hunting lodges. In 1663, Tsar Alexis *(see p19)* built an enourmous wooden palace here and dedicated the land to experiments in animal and vegetable husbandry and various cottage industries.

Peter the Great later spent an idyllic childhood at Izmaylovo, secluded from palace intrigues. It was here that his lifelong fascination with the sea began, when he learned to sail an old boat on a lake. The boat was later nicknamed the "grandfather of the Russian navy".

The wooden palace has long since disappeared, demolished by Catherine the Great in 1767. However, about 500 m (550 yds) east of Izmaylovskiy Park metro, the remains of other buildings can be seen on an island near the sports stadium. The lake surrounding them was once part of a network of 37 ponds previously created by Tsar Alexis for breeding fish and irrigating experimental crops. He planted exotic species such as mulberry trees and cotton and ordered seeds from his ambassadors in England.

17th-century Cathedral of the Intercession, Izmaylovo Park

The island is reached over a small bridge. The iron archway at its far end was built in 1859 and led to three buildings commissioned by Nicholas I and designed by Konstantin Ton *(see p45)* in the 1840s for retired soldiers. Rising above the trees ahead, behind the remains of the estate's walls, are the five, formidable black domes of the Cathedral of the Intercession, built in 1671–9. The domes are tiled with metallic "scales". The *zakomary* gables *(see p44)* beneath them are beautifully decorated with "peacock's eye" tiles, by Stepan Polubes, a late-17th-century Belorussian ceramicist working in Moscow.

Triple-arched Ceremonial Gate, the surviving entrance to the tsars' former estate, Izmaylovo Park

On the cathedral's right is a tiered red-brick arch with a tent roof. Built in 1671, this is the Bridge Tower, all that remains of a 14-span bridge that once crossed the estate's extensive waterways. Its tower was used for meetings of the boyars' council under Tsar Alexis. The top tier of the bridge gives fine views over the whole estate.

On the opposite side of the cathedral from the Bridge Tower stands the white, triple-arched Ceremonial Gate. It was designed by Terentiy Makarov in 1682 and is one of two gates that originally led to the palace.

The flea market, just to the northwest of the lake, trails down the hill from the concrete tower blocks of the Izmaylovo Hotel, offering an amazingly eclectic variety of goods. Muscovites come here in large numbers to buy items such as second-hand household goods and vehicle parts. Tourists are likely to be greeted by a storm of shouts in English from people selling their wares.

Kuskovo ⓰

Кусково
Kuskovo

Statue of Minerva

For over 200 years before the Revolution, Kuskovo was the country seat of one of Russia's wealthiest aristocratic families, the Sheremetevs. The present buildings were commissioned by Count Pyotr Sheremetev after his marriage to the heiress Varvara Cherkasskaya in 1743. Among their 200,000 serfs were the architects Fyodor Argunov and Aleksey Mironov who played a major role in Kuskovo's construction, probably under the supervision of professional architect Karl Blank. Apart from the elaborate gardens, the main attraction is the two-storey wooden palace, completed in 1777. A ceramics museum, with a renowned collection of porcelain, occupies the Orangery.

★ Formal Gardens
The gardens were laid out in the French, geometrical style, which led to Kuskovo gaining a reputation as the Russian Versailles.

The Hermitage has distinctive rounded walls and is topped by a dome.

Obelisk

Church of the Archangel Michael
Constructed in 1737–8, the church is the oldest building on the estate. The statue on its dome is of the Archangel Michael. The wooden bell tower and golden spire were added in 1792.

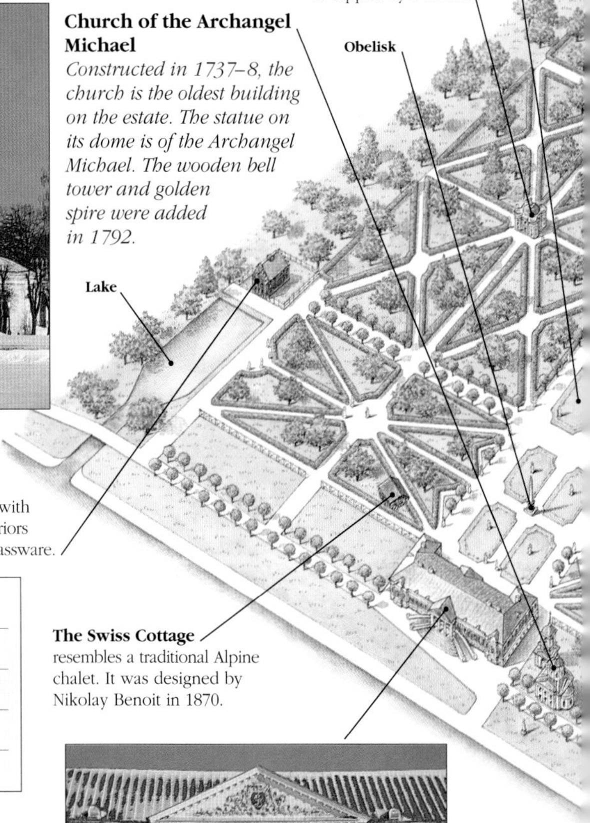

Lake

The Dutch Cottage was built in 1749 in the homely style of 17th-century Dutch architecture, in red brick and with stepped gables. The tiled interiors house Russian ceramics and glassware.

The Swiss Cottage resembles a traditional Alpine chalet. It was designed by Nikolay Benoit in 1870.

Star Features

- ★ **Wooden Palace**
- ★ **Grotto**
- ★ **Orangery**
- ★ **Formal Gardens**

★ Wooden Palace
Surprisingly, this Neo-Classical palace is made entirely of wood, plastered and painted to resemble stone. Carriage ramps sweep up to the main portico, which is emblazoned with the crest of the Sheremetev family.

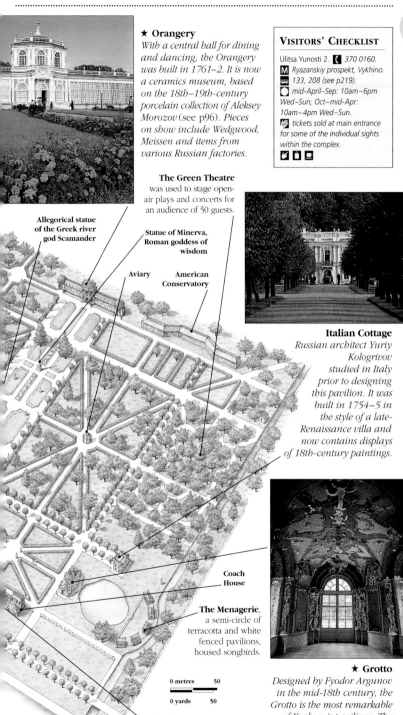

★ Orangery
With a central hall for dining and dancing, the Orangery was built in 1761–2. It is now a ceramics museum, based on the 18th–19th-century porcelain collection of Aleksey Morozov (see p96). *Pieces on show include Wedgwood, Meissen and items from various Russian factories.*

VISITORS' CHECKLIST

Ulitsa Yunosti 2. *370 0160.* *Ryazanskiy prospekt, Vykhino.* *133, 208 (see p219).* *mid-April–Sep: 10am–6pm Wed–Sun; Oct–mid-Apr: 10am–4pm Wed–Sun.* *tickets sold at main entrance for some of the individual sights within the complex.*

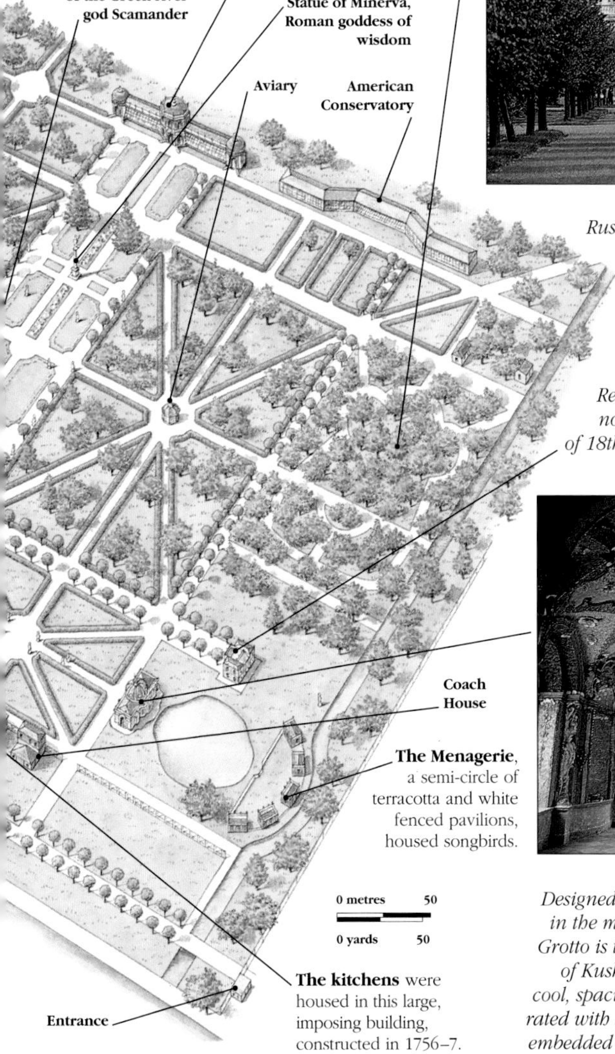

The Green Theatre was used to stage open-air plays and concerts for an audience of 50 guests.

The Menagerie, a semi-circle of terracotta and white fenced pavilions, housed songbirds.

The kitchens were housed in this large, imposing building, constructed in 1756–7.

Italian Cottage
Russian architect Yuriy Kologrivov studied in Italy prior to designing this pavilion. It was built in 1754–5 in the style of a late-Renaissance villa and now contains displays of 18th-century paintings.

★ Grotto
Designed by Fyodor Argunov in the mid-18th century, the Grotto is the most remarkable of Kuskovo's pavilions. The cool, spacious interior is decorated with shells and porcelain embedded in sand and stucco.

Main entrance of the Style-Moderne Yaroslavskiy station on Komsomolskaya ploshchad

Komsomolskaya Ploshchad ⓳

Комсомолская площадь

Komsomolskaya ploshchad

Map 4 D2. *Komsomolskaya.*

THE THREE railway stations on this large square are long-standing rivals for the affection of Muscovites. The oldest, Leningradskiy station (formerly Nikolaevskiy station), opened in 1851, serving as the terminus of the line from St Petersburg to Moscow. The building was designed according to the tenets of historicism by Konstantin Ton *(see p45)*, architect of the Great Kremlin Palace *(see p63)*.

In complete contrast is the turreted Yaroslavskiy station, rebuilt in 1902 by architect Fyodor Shekhtel *(see p45)*. The station is a colourful Style-Moderne building with a tiled frieze and an unusual, steeply pitched roof. The Trans-Siberian Railway starts here.

Shekhtel's radical design for his station goaded his rival, Aleksey Shchusev *(see p45)*, into adopting an equally bold approach when designing the third station, Kazanskiy, on the opposite side of the square. Begun in 1912, the station has a tiered central tower modelled on the citadel in the Mongol capital Kazan. The terminal was completed in 1926 and serves the Urals.

The porticoed pavilion of Komsomolskaya metro station *(see pp39–41)* is also a striking feature of the square. It is named after the Komsomol (Communist Youth volunteers) who helped to build it. It has a luxurious interior, lit by glittering chandeliers.

Komsomolskaya ploshchad itself is a seething mass of beggars, families with apparently everything they own in tow, street hawkers, drunks, drug dealers and, in the evenings, prostitutes. Over recent years it has assumed an unnerving atmosphere to say the least, so it is advisable not to linger here long, especially at night.

Vasnetsov House-Museum ⓴

Дом-музей ВМ Васнецова

Dom-muzey VM Vasnetsova

Pereulok Vasnetsova 13. **Map** 3 A2. *281 1329.* *Sukharevskaya, Prospekt Mira.* *10am–5pm Wed–Sun.*

A GRAPHIC ARTIST, sculptor, painter, theatre designer and architect, Viktor Vasnetsov (1848–1926) was a member of the artists' colony set up by arts patron Savva Mamontov at Abramtsevo *(see p154)*. He is probably best known for the highly original façade of the Tretyakov Gallery *(see pp118–21)*, where many of his paintings are also housed.

Ornate roof of the wooden house designed by Viktor Vasnetsov

Vasnetsov designed this unusual house for himself and his family in 1893–4 and lived here until he died in 1926, at the age of 78. As an enthusiastic advocate of traditional Russian folk art and architecture, he employed peasant carpenters from Vladimir *(see pp160–61)* to build his remarkable, log-cabin-like, timber house with green roofs.

The ground-floor rooms display highly individual pieces of furniture, many designed by Vasnetsov and his similarly talented younger brother, Apollinariy (1856–1933). The stoves are decorated with colourful tiles made by fellow artists from Abramtsevo.

A spiral staircase hung with 17th-century chain mail and weaponry leads up to the artist's studio, which resembles a vaulted medieval hall. This is the perfect backdrop for Vasnetsov's arresting canvases, many of which take figures from Russian legends as their subjects. For example, *Baba Yaga* portrays Russia's forest witch indulging in her favourite occupation, stealing children. The enormous painting of *The Sleeping Princess*, painted in the last year of Vasnetsov's life, shows a scene from the classic fairy story of Sleeping Beauty.

Ostankino Palace ㉑

Московский музей-усадьба Останкино

Moskovskiy muzey-usadba Ostankino

1-ya Ostankinskaya ulitsa 5a. *286 6288.* *VDNKh.* *10am–5pm Wed–Sun.* *Oct–April.* *gardens only.* *English.*

LIKE THE ESTATE at Kuskovo *(see pp142–3)*, Ostankino was built by the serf architects Pavel Argunov and Aleksey Mironov for the Sheremetevs, one of Russia's richest families. Count Nikolay Sheremetev was a prominent patron of the arts and built his palace around a theatre, where a company of 200 serf actors and actresses performed plays of his choosing. In 1800 the Count married Praskovia Zhemchugova-Kovaleva, one of the actresses. Secluded at their palace, they

Main façade of the imposing, Neo-Classical Ostankino Palace

were able to shelter themselves from the disapproval of polite society, but sadly Praskovia died three years later. The count never recovered from the loss and left the palace, which fell into disuse.

Ostankino is a handsome palace, with a shallow green dome and impressive classical 18th century interiors. The main building has an admirably restrained Neo-Classical façade. It was built in wood in 1792–8 and skilfully plastered over to look like brick and stone. It demonstrates the remarkable workmanship of Sheremetev's serf craftsmen. The halls are a wonder of *trompe l'oeil* decor. Carved wooden mouldings are painted to resemble bronze, gold and marble, parquet floors are patterned in birchwood and mahogany, while a huge crystal chandelier hangs from the frescoed ceiling of the main hall. The pavilion also serves as a sculpture gallery and among the sculptures is a Roman marble head of Aphrodite from the 1st century AD.

The *pièce de résistance* of the palace is the theatre, a breathtaking, elliptical hall with a superb painted ceiling supported by rows of Corinthian columns. In 1796 the building was partly reconstructed to allow the installation of an ingenious mechanical device which raised the auditorium floor so that the theatre could also be used as a ballroom. In the summer, concerts of classical music are still held here.

On the road leading from the estate is the ornate Church of the Trinity with a cluster of green domes. It was built in 1678–83 for the Cherkasskiy family, who owned Ostankino estate before the Sheremetevs.

Theatre auditorium, Ostankino Palace, once home to Count Sheremetev's serf actors

All-Russian Exhibition Centre ㉒

Всероссийский Выставочный Центр (ВВЦ)

Vserossiyskiy Vystavochniy Tsentr (VVTs)

Prospekt Mira. ☎ *181 9504.* Ⓜ *VDNKh.* **Pavilions** ◯ *May–Oct: 10am–6pm Mon–Fri, 10am–7pm Sat–Sun, hols; Nov–Apr: 10am–5pm Mon–Fri, 10am–6pm Sat–Sun, hols.* ♿ **Space Museum** ☎ *283 7914.* ◯ *10am–6pm daily.* ♿ *English.*

ONCE ONE OF the city's main tourist attractions, the former Exhibition of Economic Achievements of the USSR (VDNKh) has now become the All-Russian Exhibition Centre (VVTs). The site began life in 1939 as a major agricultural exhibition, but 20 years later it was transformed by Soviet leader Nikita Khrushchev into a vast park extolling the nation's achievements in economics, science and technology. After the disintegration of the Soviet Union in 1991, the pavilions were taken over by the private sector. Although more than 70 of them now function as retail showrooms for products such as electronic goods, computers and cars, the whole complex is a shadow of its former self.

A stroll round the grounds will take you past some of the sculptures for which the former VDNKh was famous. The main entrance to the park is a triumphal arch, topped by the figures of a tractor driver and woman collective farmer, holding up a sheaf of corn.

On one side of the main gates, on prospekt Mira, is the emblematic statue *Worker and Woman Collective Farm Worker*. The two figures stride forwards together into the future, holding aloft a hammer and sickle. Sculpted by Vera Mukhina, the statues won her international recognition at the Paris Exhibition in 1937.

On the other side of the gates is the Space Obelisk by Andrey Faydysh-Krandievskiy. Over 100 m (328 ft) high, it represents a rocket lifting off on a plume of flame, and was erected in 1964, three years after Yuriy Gagarin became the first man in space. Nearby is the Space Museum, which houses *Vostok 1*, in which Gagarin orbited the Earth.

VDNKh was also intended as a recreational area, and families still flock here at weekends. The main attraction is the fairground, but there are also cinemas and cafés.

Statue of tractor driver and woman atop the main entrance of the VVTs

Beyond Moscow

BEYOND MOSCOW

THE MAGNIFICENCE OF SOME *of the palaces and churches outside Moscow and the historic interest of some of the towns make excursions there justly rewarding. Although parts of the landscape are unappealingly industrial, the large areas of true countryside are green, forested and dotted with villages of small wooden* dachas.

Visitors may find it a good idea to take an organized tour *(see p198)* to out-of-town sights as public transport can be erratic, though perfectly feasible for those who prefer mixing with local daily life *(see p219)*. There are several places of historic and cultural importance within easy reach of the city. To the west is Borodino *(see p152)*, site of the great battle between Napoleon's army and Russian forces under the command of Field Marshal Mikhail Kutuzov. To the north is the magnificent Trinity Monastery of St Sergius *(see pp156–9)* and to the northeast the towns of the Golden Ring *(see p155)*. The political heyday of these towns was in the 12th and 13th centuries, before the rise of Moscow, and their churches and wooden buildings make them well worth exploring.

Field Marshal Mikhail Kutuzov

Also outside Moscow are houses lived in by two of Russia's most famous sons, Pyotr Tchaikovsky *(see p153)* and Leo Tolstoy *(see p134)*.

On Friday nights the trains and roads into the countryside are packed with families travelling to their *dacha*, a migration that leaves the capital rather deserted. Each *dacha* has a small plot of land that is used for growing fruit and vegetables. For some Muscovites this was, and often still is today, an essential source of food. In the last few years, brick houses have started to spring up where farmers used to grow crops, built for New Russians who have adopted Western commuter habits. However, many have been abandoned half-built as construction firms have gone out of business in the fast-changing economic climate.

***The Sacred Supper*, painted in 1685, displayed in the Treasury at the Trinity Monastery of St Sergius**

◁ **The Church of the Prophet Elijah, one of many picturesque churches in the Golden Ring town of Suzdal**

Exploring the Moscow Region

DESPITE THE NUMEROUS attractions of Moscow, it is well worth spending time in the surrounding region. Several country estates lie within easy reach of the city and make for delightful one- or two-day trips. Among them are Yasnaya Polyana, where Leo Tolstoy *(see p134)* lived for many years, the house in Klin rented by Pyotr Tchaikovsky *(see p153)* and Abramtsevo Estate-Museum, a former artists' colony. However, the star attraction of the region is the Trinity Monastery of St Sergius. Once a place of pilgrimage for the tsars, this huge complex has several superb cathedrals.

Moscow is also an ideal base for visiting the Golden Ring towns, which include Pereslavl-Zalesskiy, Suzdal and Vladimir. Founded by Russians seeking shelter from invading tribes, these attractive settlements still have many historic buildings.

Tiles by artist Mikhail Vrubel on a bench at Abramtsevo

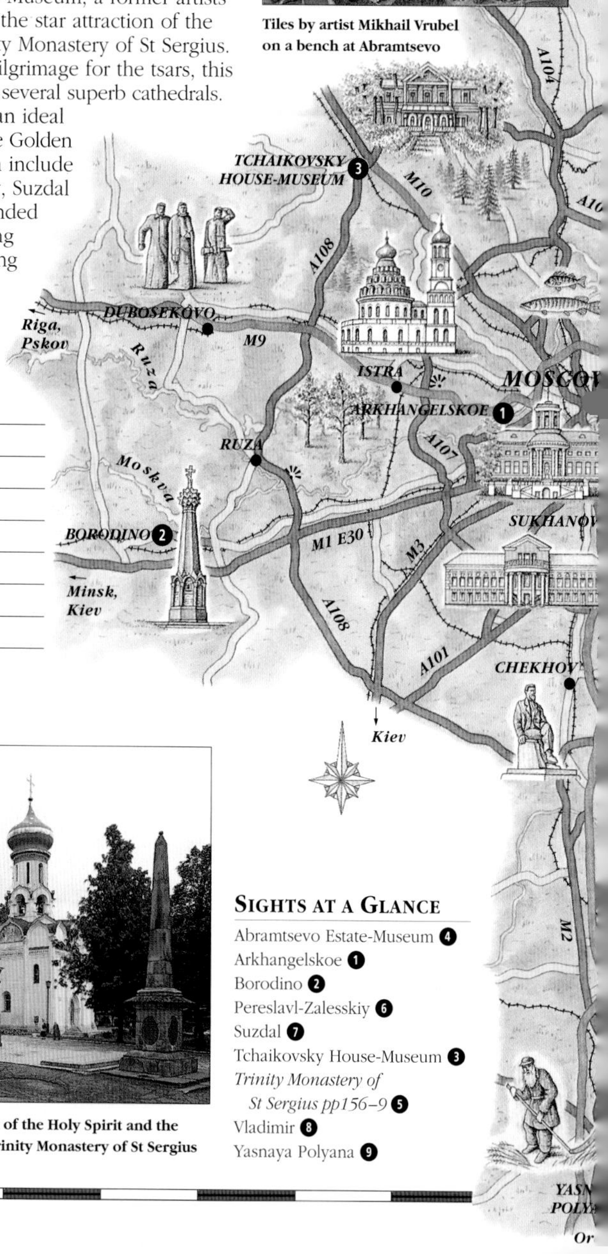

KEY

- Motorway
- Major road
- Minor road
- Scenic route
- Railway
- River
- Viewpoint

The blue-domed Church of the Holy Spirit and the Chapel Over the Well, Trinity Monastery of St Sergius

SIGHTS AT A GLANCE

Abramtsevo Estate-Museum 4
Arkhangelskoe 1
Borodino 2
Pereslavl-Zalesskiy 6
Suzdal 7
Tchaikovsky House-Museum 3
Trinity Monastery of St Sergius pp156–9 5
Vladimir 8
Yasnaya Polyana 9

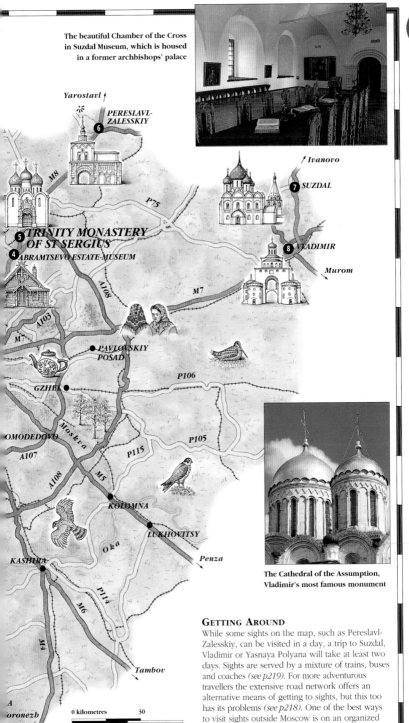

The beautiful Chamber of the Cross in Suzdal Museum, which is housed in a former archbishops' palace

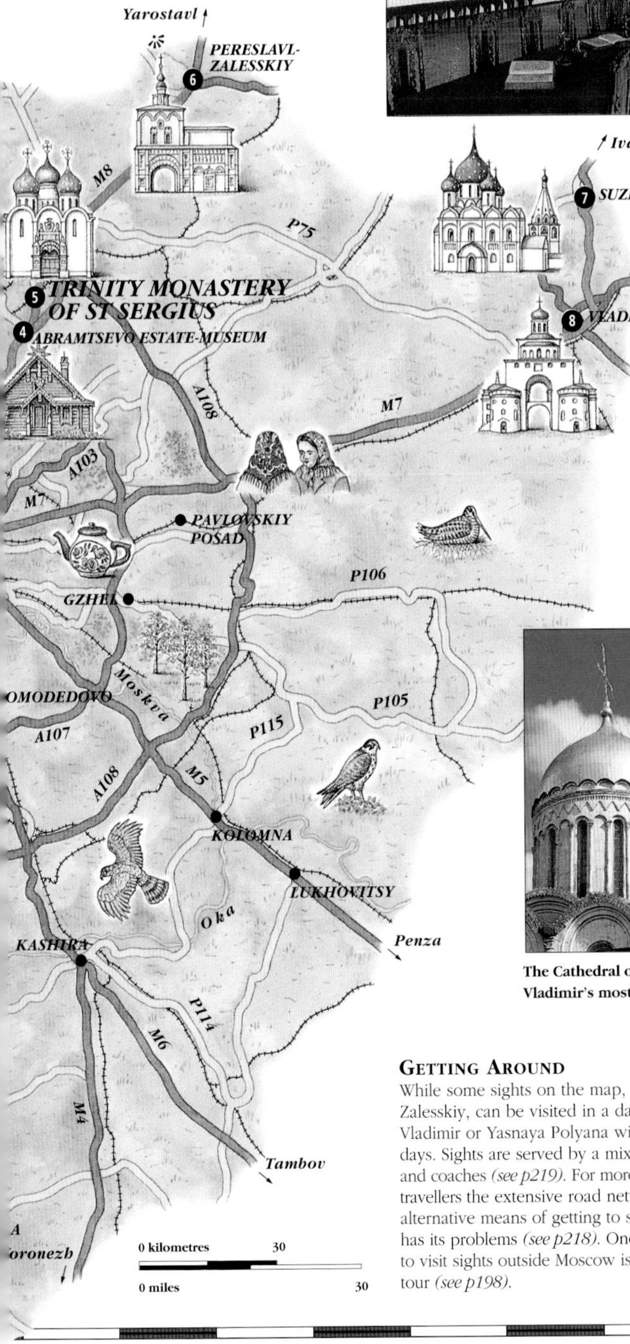

The Cathedral of the Assumption, Vladimir's most famous monument

Getting Around

While some sights on the map, such as Pereslavl-Zalesskiy, can be visited in a day, a trip to Suzdal, Vladimir or Yasnaya Polyana will take at least two days. Sights are served by a mixture of trains, buses and coaches *(see p219)*. For more adventurous travellers the extensive road network offers an alternative means of getting to sights, but this too has its problems *(see p218)*. One of the best ways to visit sights outside Moscow is on an organized tour *(see p198)*.

The southern, garden façade of the Neo-Classical, stucco-covered, wooden palace at Arkhangelskoe

Arkhangelskoe ❶

Архангельское

Arkhangelskoe

20 km (12 miles) W of Moscow. ☎ *363 1375.* ◯ *10am–4pm Wed–Sun.* **M** *Tushinskaya, then bus (see p219).* ♿ *pavilions and grounds only.*

Most of the buildings on this country estate date from the 18th and 19th centuries. The only one to predate them is the charming Church of the Archangel Michael, completed in 1667, from which the name of the estate is derived.

The Golitsyn family acquired the estate in 1703. In the 1780s Prince Nikolay Golitsyn began a wholesale rebuilding, including a new palace which was built to a design by the French architect Charles de Guerne. Constructed from wood, it was covered with stucco to give the effect of stone. When Golitsyn died in 1809, the estate was purchased by Prince Nikolay Yusupov, who continued to add Neo-Classical buildings. Recently restored, the palace's sumptuous rooms are filled with fine furniture, fabrics and antiques. There is also an excellent art collection.

The formal gardens were laid out in the 18th century. Within them stand pavilions such as the diminutive Caprice Palace, built in 1819 for soirees. In 1910–16 a lavish mausoleum was erected for the Yusupov family, but it was never used because of the Revolution.

The gorgeously painted dome of the Yusupov mausoleum, built in 1910–16, at Arkhangelskoe

Borodino ❷

Бородино

Borodino

130 km (80 miles) SW of Moscow. ☎ *8238 51057.* ◯ *9am–6pm Tue–Sun.* 🚆 *Mozhaisk or Borodino, then bus (see p219).* ♿

One of the fiercest military confrontations of the 19th century took place at Borodino on 7 September 1812. For over 15 hours Napoleon Bonaparte's Grande Armée and the Russian army, led by Field Marshal Mikhail Kutuzov, fought each other to a bloody impasse. It is estimated that 40,000 Russian and 30,000 French soldiers were killed. Napoleon called it the "most terrible" of all his battles, but claimed victory on the grounds that the Russians were forced to continue their retreat to Moscow. Posterity, however, awarded the laurels to the Russians. The French followed the Russians, but arrived to find the city and the Kremlin deserted. The Muscovites then started a great fire *(see pp24–5)* in the city, and faced with a Russian winter in the open, the French were finally forced to retreat.

The battlefield covers over 100 sq km (40 sq miles), but the main places of interest are reasonably accessible. A museum, 1 km (½ mile) south of Borodino village, recounts the story of the battle with the aid of models and an illuminated map. More than 30 monuments are strewn around the area. Russia's most distinguished general to fall in battle, Prince Pyotr Bagration, was buried at the base of a column dedicated to the fallen just east of the museum. Nearby is the inn, now a museum, where Leo Tolstoy stayed to research the background for his epic novel *War and Peace.*

Monument to the fallen of Borod[ino]

The small Empire-style Spasskiy Church of 1822 was the first monument to be constructed on the battlefield. A re-enactment of the battle takes place every 7 September.

Tchaikovsky House-Museum ❸

Дом-музей ПИ Чайковского
Dom-muzey PI Chaykovskovo

90 km (55 miles) NW of Moscow. Ulitsa Tchaikovskaya 48, Klin. ☎ *539 8196.* ◯ *10am–5pm Fri–Tue.* 🚉 *Klin (see p219).*

The reception area in the house at Klin, containing Tchaikovsky's piano

IN A LETTER to his brother Anatoly in May 1892 Pyotr Tchaikovsky wrote, "I have rented a house in Klin. What a blessing it is to know that no-one will come, either to interrupt my work, or my reading or walking". Previous stays in the village of Frolovskoe near Klin had inspired some of his best music, including the ballets *The Sleeping Beauty* and *The Nutcracker*, and the opera *The Queen of Spades* based on Pushkin's novel *(see p73)*. Tchaikovsky enjoyed Klin for only a few months, as he died in 1893. In 1894 his younger brother, Modest, opened the estate to visitors. The ground floor of the clapboard house, once occupied by Tchaikovsky's servant, Aleksey Safronov, is closed to the public, but on entering the composer's rooms on the first floor visitors find themselves in a bright, spacious reception area. The walls are covered with photos of his family, his classmates at law school and fellow musicians. The grand piano in the centre of the room was a gift from the Russian firm Becker. Though an excellent pianist, Tchaikovsky never performed in public. The winner of the Tchaikovsky International Competition *(see p192)* gives a recital here on the composer's birthday, 7 May.

Tchaikovsky's wooden house in Klin, in the quiet of the Russian countryside he loved so much

Tchaikovsky was a great collector of souvenirs. On a shelf behind the piano is a Statue of Liberty inkpot, which he brought back from his triumphant conducting tour of the United States in 1891.

The bedroom is separated from the reception area by a curtain. Warm and intimate, it contains Tchaikovsky's diminutive slippers and a beautiful coverlet made by his niece. Tchaikovsky finished his *Sixth Symphony*, the *Pathétique*, at the table by the window.

Also open to visitors are the handsome wood-panelled library and the study where Modest Tchaikovsky worked as the Klin archivist until his death in 1916. A memorial room to the composer holds some of his personal possessions, including his top hat, gloves and evening clothes.

Tchaikovsky habitually took a stroll in the garden before breakfast and after lunch. His favourite flowers, lilies of the valley, are still planted here. Concerts are held year round in a hall built in the grounds.

PYOTR TCHAIKOVSKY

Probably Russia's most famous composer, Tchaikovsky was born in 1840. After graduating initially in law, he studied music at the St Petersburg Conservatory. One of his teachers helped the young composer to get a job teaching music at the Moscow Conservatory *(see p94)* in 1866 where he then taught for the next 12 years. It was during this period that Tchaikovsky composed his first four symphonies and the ballet *Swan Lake* (1876). In 1877 he married a student from the Conservatory in an effort to suppress his homosexuality.

Statue of Pyotr Tchaikovsky at the Moscow Conservatory

However, the marriage was unhappy and short-lived. Tchaikovsky composed prolifically in the 1880s, completing such works as the ballet *The Sleeping Beauty* (1889) and the overture *The Year 1812* (1880). In 1892 he moved to Klin, outside Moscow. He died of cholera in November 1893, while overseeing the premiere of his final work, the *Sixth Symphony*, in St Petersburg. It is rumoured that he knowingly drank infected water as a dignified form of suicide after the exposure of his homosexual involvement with a young aristocrat.

Iconostasis in the Church of the Saviour, Abramtsevo Estate-Museum

Abramtsevo Estate-Museum ❹

Музей-усадьба Абрамцево

Muzey-usadba Abramtsevo

60 km (35 miles) NE of Moscow. *Khotkova or Sergiev Posad, then bus (see p219).* 8254 32470. 10am–5pm Wed–Sun. *English (book in advance).*

IN THE SECOND half of the 19th century this delightful rural retreat became a hive of cultural activity. Until his death in 1859, the house was owned by the writer Sergey Aksakov, whose sons were leading Slavophile thinkers. The estate's creative legacy was continued in 1870 when it was acquired by Savva Mamontov, an industrialist and art patron. Mamontov's generosity and zeal led to the establishment of an artists' colony here, and to a re-evaluation of traditional Russian folk art and craftwork. The work of local peasant craftsmen, whose children were educated in the estate's school, was a source of inspiration for many of the artists.

Dotted around the estate are a number of remarkable buildings. The artists' studio, with a spectacular carved roof, was designed in 1872 by Viktor Gartman. Displayed here are ceramics by the two distinguished artists Valentin Serov and Mikhail Vrubel. The *teremok*, meanwhile, is a free improvization on the typical peasant hut *(izba)*, and was originally built as a bathhouse by Ivan Ropet in 1873. It was later used as a guesthouse. Inside are the original wooden furnishings and ornaments, such as carved statuettes, kitchen utensils and a tiled stove designed by Mikhail Vrubel.

The House on Chicken Legs stands on stilts. Designed by Viktor Vasnetsov, it is now a popular children's attraction, recalling the witch of Russian folklore, Baba Yaga, whose house in the forest is built on giant chicken legs.

A woodland path leads to the most remarkable building on the estate. The Church of the Saviour Not Made by Human Hand is modelled on the medieval churches of Novgorod, but was brought up to date by the addition of bands of painted majolica tiles to its walls of white-washed brick. The church was built in 1881–2, to a design by Viktor Vasnetsov; the mosaic floor is also his work, while the icons were painted by Vasnetsov, Ilya Repin and his wife Vera, Vasiliy Polenov and Nikolay Nevrev. A small oratory holds Savva Mamontov's remains and those of his son Andrey, who died, aged 19, in 1891.

The manor house still contains Aksakov's original Empire-style furnishings, left by Mamontov out of respect for his predecessor. Aksakov knew the novelists Nikolai Gogol and Ivan Turgenev, and, here, in the red sitting-room, Gogol would read aloud from his masterpiece, *Dead Souls.* The dining room features a beautiful, tiled corner fireplace and a profusion of paintings. The gaze, however, is drawn to a copy of Valentin Serov's arresting portrait of Vera, Savva Mamontov's daughter, seated at the dining table. Entitled *Girl with Peaches* (1887), the original can be found in the Tretyakov Gallery *(see p121).*

Trinity Monastery of St Sergius ❺

See pp156–9.

Pereslavl-Zalesskiy ❻

Переславль-Залесский

Pereslavl-Zalesskiy

135 km (85 miles) NE of Moscow. 43,400. *Sergiev Posad, then bus (see p219).*

FOUNDED as a fortress in 1152 by Yuriy Dolgorukiy, and overlooking Lake Pleshcheevo, Pereslavl-Zalesskiy was an independent princedom until 1302, when it came under the control of Moscow. Peter the Great *(see p22)* developed plans for the Russian navy here. Sights of interest include the 12th-century **Cathedral of the Transfiguration** and the **Goritskiy Monastery of the Assumption**, founded in the 14th century but dating mainly from the 17th–18th centuries.

Cathedral of the Goritskiy Monastery of the Assumption, Pereslavl-Zalesskiy

The History of the Golden Ring

THE FIRST IMPORTANT cities in Russia were Novgorod in the north and Kiev in the south, which were situated on trade routes connecting the Baltic and the Black Sea. From the 11th century, as hostile tribes invaded Kievan Rus *(see p17)* and many Russians were forced northward, new settlements were founded such as Rostov, Yaroslavl, Vladimir and Suzdal. Like Novgorod and Kiev, these towns flourished on trade from Western Europe, Byzantium and Central Asia, while Sergiev Posad, location of the Trinity Monastery of St Sergius *(see pp156–9)*, became an important centre for the Orthodox Church. Moscow was also founded during this era *(see p17)* and, by the 16th century, had become Russia's capital. By this time the cluster of towns northeast of Moscow had paled into insignificance, although in the 1960s their historic importance brought them the title the Golden Ring.

16th-century icon from the Golden Ring

THE GOLDEN RING

Prince Vladimir Monomakh (see p59) *founded a small trading settlement in the late 11th century. It was named Vladimir in 1108. Monomakh's son, Yuriy Dolgorukiy* (see p17), *expanded the town and it was later the capital of Northern Rus.*

Andrey Bogolyubskiy*, the son of Yuriy Dolgorukiy, moved his court to Vladimir in 1157, where his craftsmen were to recreate the splendour of Kiev. His boyars later murdered him for being a dictator.*

A campaign *by Suzdal against Novgorod in 1169 is the subject of this icon. Created by the 15th-century Novgorod School* (see p61), *it recalls Sudzal's strength before Moscow became pre-eminent.*

Angels denote that the campaign against the Mongols was blessed.

Dmitriy Donskoy

The Battle of Kulikovo (see p18), *in 1380, was a turning point in the history of the Golden Ring. The Mongols made many inroads into the area, sacking Suzdal in 1238 and demanding tribute from the Russians. Dmitriy Donskoy* (see p18) *won a decisive victory against them at Kulikovo, with a blessing, it is said, from monk Sergius of Radonezh* (see p159).

Many churches *were built in the towns of the Golden Ring, a sign of their comparative wealth. Some wooden churches are preserved in a museum at Suzdal* (see p160).

Trinity Monastery of St Sergius ❺

Троице-Сергиева Лавра
Troitse-Sergieva Lavra

FOUNDED AROUND 1345 by Sergius of Radonezh *(see p159)*, the Trinity Monastery of St Sergius in the town of Sergiev-Possad is one of Russia's most important religious centres and places of pilgrimage. In 1608–10, during the Time of Troubles *(see p19)*, the monks survived a siege by the Polish army and in the 1680s the young Peter the Great found refuge here during the Streltsy Rebellion *(see p22)*. The monastery was closed down by the Communists in 1919, but was allowed to open again in 1946, when it became headquarters of the Russian Orthodox Church. The headquarters transferred to new premises at the Danilovskiy Monastery *(see pp136–7)* in 1988.

Chapel Over the Well
This delightful, Moscow-Baroque (see p44) *chapel was built in the late 17th century to mark the site of a holy spring.*

★ Trinity Cathedral
Built in 1422–3 over the grave of St Sergius, this splendid church contains an iconostasis painted by a team of artists led by Andrey Rublev (see p61).

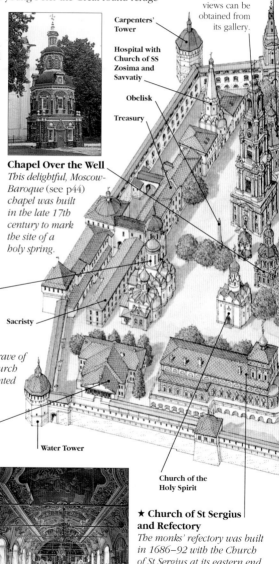

The Church of the Virgin of Smolensk was built in 1745 to house the Icon of the Smolensk Virgin.

The bell tower was begun in 1741 and completed 28 years later. Spectacular views can be obtained from its gallery.

Palace of the Metropolitans
This grand palace was completed in 1778. It was the residence of the metropolitans and patriarchs in 1946–88.

★ Church of St Sergius and Refectory
The monks' refectory was built in 1686–92 with the Church of St Sergius at its eastern end. The colourful façade features pillars with vine leaf decoration and chequered walls. The interior is equally lavish.

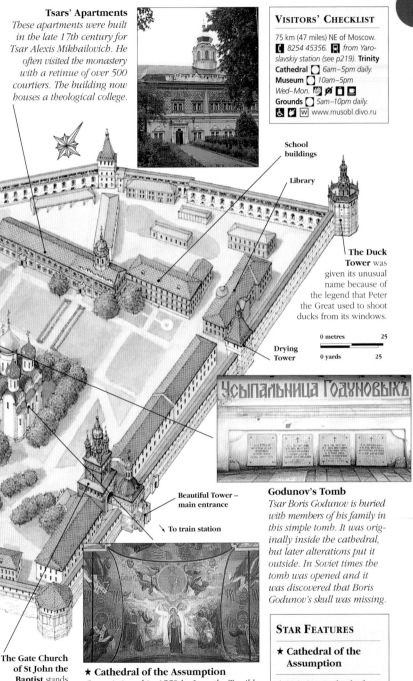

Tsars' Apartments
These apartments were built in the late 17th century for Tsar Alexis Mikhailovich. He often visited the monastery with a retinue of over 500 courtiers. The building now houses a theological college.

VISITORS' CHECKLIST

75 km (47 miles) NE of Moscow. *8254 45356.* *from Yaroslavskiy station (see p219).* **Trinity Cathedral** *6am–5pm daily.* **Museum** *10am–5pm Wed–Mon.* **Grounds** *5am–10pm daily.* www.musobl.divo.ru

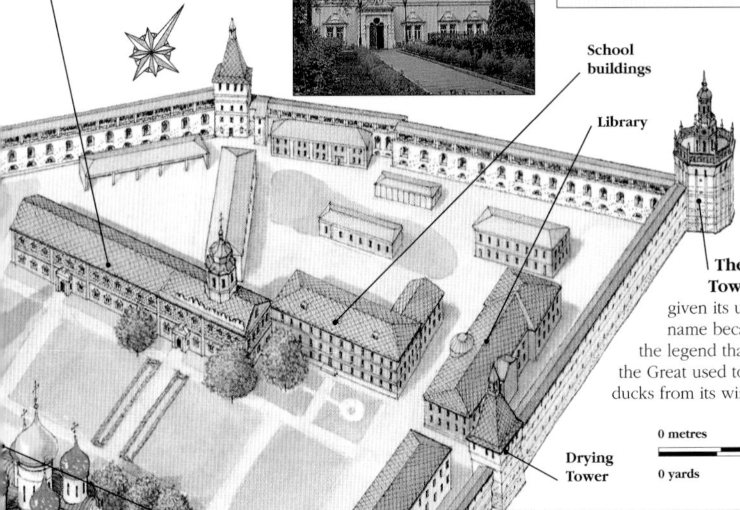

The Duck Tower was given its unusual name because of the legend that Peter the Great used to shoot ducks from its windows.

Godunov's Tomb
Tsar Boris Godunov is buried with members of his family in this simple tomb. It was originally inside the cathedral, but later alterations put it outside. In Soviet times the tomb was opened and it was discovered that Boris Godunov's skull was missing.

★ Cathedral of the Assumption
Commissioned in 1559 by Ivan the Terrible to commemorate the capture of Kazan, this is the monastery's main cathedral. Its sumptuous interior was decorated by artists from Yaroslavl over a century later.

The Gate Church of St John the Baptist stands over the main entrance. It was built in 1692–99 by the wealthy Stroganov family.

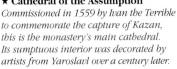

STAR FEATURES

- ★ **Cathedral of the Assumption**
- ★ **Trinity Cathedral**
- ★ **Church of St Sergius and Refectory**

Exploring the Trinity Monastery of St Sergius

IN THE 14TH CENTURY, Sergius of Radonezh built a small wooden church in the forests to the north of Moscow and consecrated it to the Holy Trinity. Many pilgrims were attracted to the site by reports of Sergius' piety. He organized them into a community and the Trinity Monastery was born. The monastery expanded as it gained wealth and influence and today the huge complex is enclosed by white walls around 1.6 km (1 mile) long. Its stunning churches, grouped around the spectacular Cathedral of the Assumption, are among the most beautiful in Russia.

The fortified Trinity Monastery of St Sergius seen from the southeast

The superb 17th-century iconostasis in the Cathedral of the Assumption

Church of St Sergius and Refectory

The monks' refectory was built in 1686–92 using money donated by Peter the Great and his half-brother, Ivan V, in gratitude for the refuge given them by the monastery during the Streltsy Rebellion *(see p22)*.

The exterior walls are divided into a series of panels, topped by carved scallop shells and separated by pillars decorated with sculpted vines. Each panel is painted so that it looks as though it has three-dimensional facets similar to those of the Faceted Palace *(see p62)* in the Kremlin. The refectory's main façade features a covered terrace with a wealth of ornamentation. At the eastern end of the refectory is the Church of St Sergius. Its iconostasis was brought here from Moscow's Church of St Nicholas on Ilinka in 1688. Delicate fretwork on the iconostasis seems to be metal, but is actually made of wood.

Baroque pillars on the Church of St Sergius and the Refectory

Cathedral of the Assumption

This magnificent cathedral, with its central golden cupola surrounded by four blue, star-spangled domes, is located at the heart of the monastery. Ivan the Terrible commissioned the cathedral in 1559 to celebrate his defeat of the Mongols at Kazan *(see p19)*. It was completed 26 years later to a design inspired by Aristotele Fioravanti's Cathedral of the Assumption *(see pp58–9)* in the Kremlin. Painters from the acclaimed Yaroslavl school of artists, led by Dmitriy Grigorev, took just 100 days to decorate the lofty interior in 1684. Their names are inscribed beneath a fresco of the Last Judgement on the west wall. The sumptuous five-tiered iconostasis dates from the same period but incorporates a number of icons from the 16th century.

Trinity Cathedral

This exquisite white cathedral is decorated with *kokoshniki* gables *(see p44)* above a triple-banded frieze and is the oldest stone building in the monastery. It was built over the tomb of St Sergius in 1422, the year of his canonization. St Sergius' remains are now

***Christ in Majesty* (1425–7) in the Trinity Cathedral's iconostasis**

encased in a silver shrine inside the cathedral and are still a focus for visiting pilgrims.

The original decoration of the interior was the work of master artists Andrey Rublev and Daniil Chernyy. Most of their frescoes have since been painted over. Their iconostasis has survived, but Rublev's icon *The Trinity* (1420s) is a copy. The original is in the Tretyakov Gallery *(see pp118–21)*. Also in the iconostasis are two icons by renowned painter Simon Ushakov: *The Holy Face* (1674) and *Christ Enthroned* (1684).

Open rotunda over the holy spring, next to the Chapel Over the Well

Other Churches

There are five smaller churches within the monastery walls. The oldest is the Church of the Holy Spirit, built in 1476 by craftsmen from Pskov *(see p44)*, a town to the northwest of Moscow. The infirmary and its adjoining tent-roofed Church of SS Zosima and Savvatiy were constructed in 1635–8.

The Chapel Over the Well was built at the end of the 17th century over a holy spring. The open rotunda next to it was added in the 19th century. Pilgrims still come to fill bottles with holy water from the spring beneath the rotunda.

Just in front of the Church of St Sergius stands the small Church of St Micah. This single-domed church is named after one of St Sergius' pupils, who is buried beneath it.

The Baroque Church of the Virgin of Smolensk, a small, blue and white rotunda, was built in 1745. The last of the monastery's churches to be constructed, it houses the Icon of the Smolensk Virgin.

The Holiest Monk

Sergius of Radonezh (c.1319–92) was born into a noble family but, with his brother, withdrew from the world and founded the Trinity Monastery. Sergius was instrumental in encouraging Russia's princes to unite against the Mongol invaders and, in 1380, Prince Dmitriy Donskoy, commander of the Russian army, asked for his blessing before attacking the Mongols at Kulikovo *(see p155)*. The Russian victory, along with the discovery that Sergius' body was miraculously unharmed in a Mongol attack on the monastery in 1408, led to Sergius' canonization in 1422.

A 16th-century icon of the appearance of the Virgin and Saints Peter and Paul to Sergius of Radonezh

Palaces and Museums

Gifts from the tsars are among the monastic treasures in the former Sacristy and Treasury. Visitors can see jewelled icon covers, exquisite crosses, icons, gospels in gilded covers, vestments and some wonderful tapestries, including the pall from the coffin of St Sergius.

Built in the late 17th century for Tsar Alexis Mikhailovich, the Tsar's Apartments are now used as a theological college. Parts of the slightly shabby exterior are painted to appear faceted. In the southwest corner of the monastery is the 18th-century Palace of the Metropolitans. It was the first of the buildings to come back into religious use when the Soviets allowed the patriarchs and metropolitans to return in 1946.

Towers and Gate Churches

The Trinity Monastery was originally fortified in the reign of Ivan the Terrible *(see p18)*. Its formidable walls are 12 m (39 ft) high and date, in their present form, from the early 17th century. The monastery's main gate is in the Beautiful Tower. The frescoes on its archway depict the life of St Sergius. Behind the Beautiful Tower is the red-brick Gate Church of St John the Baptist.

At the north end of the walls is the Duck Tower, so called because Peter the Great shot ducks from its windows. The spire, with its carved duck, and the upper tiers were added in 1672–86.

The soaring, five-tiered, blue and white bell tower was built between 1741 and 1769.

One of the frescoes depicting scenes from St Sergius' life, on the archway of the Beautiful Tower

Suzdal ❼

Суздаль

Suzdal

200 km (124 miles) NE of Moscow. *12,100.* *Vladimir, then bus.* *(see p219).* *Sun*

NESTLING ON the banks of the Kamenka river, Suzdal is the best preserved of the Golden Ring *(see p155)* towns. Its clusters of 17th- and 18th-century whitewashed churches, built by local merchants, and its streets of low, wooden houses with traditional carved eaves and windows mean that it is also one of the most attractive towns in the area.

The first records of Suzdal date from 1024. Shortly afterwards the founder of Moscow, Prince Yuriy Dolgorukiy *(see p17)*, built the town's kremlin on a grassy rampart above the river. Its dominant building is the **Cathedral of the Nativity** with its blue, star-spangled domes. Although it was built in the 13th century, most of the current building dates from the 16th century. The south and west doors are of gilded copper, etched with biblical scenes. Frescoes dating from the 13th to the 17th centuries cover the interior walls.

The Cathedral of the Nativity, in the grounds of Suzdal's kremlin

Next to it stands the former archbishop's palace, now the **Suzdal Museum**. Its collection of icons and ancient art is housed in the main room, the magnificent Chamber of the Cross, one of the largest unsupported vaults in Russia. To the northeast, on Suzdal's main street, a long, arcaded building dating from 1806–11 was the former merchants' quarters.

Suzdal also contains five important religious foundations, including the **Monastery of St Euthymius**. Once the richest in the area, with more than 10,000 serfs at its disposal, the monastery has a commanding position in the north of Suzdal, overlooking the town. Its fortified walls are almost 6 m (20 ft) thick. The monks' cells now house the **Museum of Arts and Crafts**, which has an impressive collection, including religious paintings and jewellery.

Icon of St Nicholas, dating from the 15th century, in the Suzdal Museum

To the south of the monastery is the **Aleksandrovskiy Convent**. It was originally founded in 1240, but it burned down and was rebuilt in the 17th century. Its Cathedral of the Ascension was built at this time by Nataliya Naryshkina, mother of Peter the Great.

Rising from the meadows directly across the river here is the **Convent of the Intercession**. Founded in the 14th century, it was completed in the reign of Basil III in 1510–14. Its retreat houses offer overnight lodgings.

On the southwest edge of town is the **Suzdal Museum of Wooden Architecture** an open-air exhibition of wooden buildings brought from all over Russia. Particularly impressive is the Church of the Transfiguration, built in 1756. With domes made with overlapping shingles, it was built without using any metal nails.

Suzdal Museum
Ul Kremlyovskaya. *809231 20444.* *Wed–Mon.* *English (book in advance).*

Museum of Arts and Crafts
Ul Lenina. *809231 20444.* *Tue–Sun.* *English (book in advance).*

Suzdal Museum of Wooden Architecture
Ul Kremlyovskaya. *809231 20444.* *Wed–Mon.* *English (book in advance).*

The Golden Gate, the entrance to Vladimir from the Moscow road

Vladimir ❽

Владимир

Vladimir

170 km (106 miles) NE of Moscow. *360,000.* *(see p219).* *Daily* www.museum.vladimir.ru

FOUNDED ON the Klyazma river by Prince Vladimir Monomakh *(see p155)* in the late 11th century, Vladimir really began to flourish during the rule of his son, Prince Yuriy Dolgorukiy *(see p17)*. In 1157 Dolgorukiy's heir, Prince Andrey Bogolyubskiy, brought his court here and made it the capital of the new principality of Vladimir-Suzdal. The town's heyday was in the 12th and

The 12th-century Cathedral of the Assumption in Vladimir

early 13th centuries and most of the architectural monuments worth seeing date from this period. Like Suzdal, Vladimir was later eclipsed by Moscow in political importance, but it remained a significant trading centre. Today, Vladimir looks like any industrial city of the Soviet era, although, fortunately, the chemical plants and tyre factories are situated at some distance from the picturesque old part of the town, with its fine views.

When approaching Vladimir by the Moscow road, the visitor will still enter the city through the splendid **Golden Gate**. This was constructed in 1164, and combines the functions of both triumphal arch and defensive bastion. The icons above the archway were whitewashed by the Communists and have only recently been restored. The gate now contains a small exhibition on military history.

A short stroll down the main street takes the visitor past the 19th-century trading arcades and shops to the **Cathedral of the Assumption**, Vladimir's most famous monument. Built in 1158–60, high above the banks of the Klyazma, it was originally decorated with prodigious quantities of gold and silver, precious gems, majolica tiles and white stone carvings. Craftsmen came from all over Russia, Poland and the Holy Roman Empire to contribute to what was then the tallest building in Russia. The coronation of many of Russia's princes, including Dmitriy Donskoy *(see p18)* and Aleksandr Nevskiy *(see p17)*, took place here.

A detail of the carved bas-reliefs on the Cathedral of St Dmitriy

The cathedral was damaged by fire in 1185, and when it was repaired, four domes were added. When, in the 15th century, Ivan III wanted to build the Cathedral of the Assumption in Moscow *(see pp58–9)*, he instructed his Italian architect, Aristotele Fioravanti, to use the cathedral of the same name in Vladimir as his model.

The famous Icon of the Virgin of Vladimir *(see p61)* used to hang in the cathedral, but it is now in the Tretyakov Gallery *(see p121)*. However, some superb frescoes by medieval masters Andrey Rublev and Daniil Chernyy are still visible under the choir's gallery on the west wall.

A short distance away is the **Cathedral of St Dmitriy**, built in 1194–7 by Prince Vsevolod III. A single-domed church of white limestone, its exterior is covered with more than a thousand bas-reliefs featuring griffons, centaurs, prancing lions and fantastic birds and plants, as well as a portrait of Vsevolod and his family. Over the window on the south wall is a carving of Alexander the Great ascending to heaven, a symbol of princely authority.

Yasnaya Polyana ❾

Ясная Поляна

Yasnaya Polyana

180 km (112 miles) S of Moscow.
0872 339118. *10am–5:30pm Wed–Sun.* *Tula, then bus.* *(see p219).*

THE BELOVED country estate of Leo Tolstoy *(see p134)*, Yasnaya Polyana is located in a peaceful valley surrounded by forests. Tolstoy was born on the estate in 1828. From the mid-1850s he spent the summers here with his wife and children, and the family moved here permanently in 1901. The house and its contents are much as they were in Tolstoy's day. The rooms on show include the study, where Tolstoy wrote *War and Peace* and *Anna Karenina*. Other buildings on the estate include the Dom Volkonskovo, where the serfs lived, and a pavilion for the guests. A small literary museum is housed in the former peasants' school that Tolstoy established.

Leo Tolstoy's house on his beloved family estate, Yasnaya Polyana

Travellers' Needs

WHERE TO STAY

THE HOTEL SITUATION in Moscow has improved considerably since Russia became an independent state in 1992. New hotels have been built and grand old residences renovated. These works are likely to continue as Yuriy Luzhkov, the city's dynamic mayor, has made new accommodation a priority. Despite the improvements, there is still a great shortage of hotels of all types in the city. Worse still, as with much in modern Russian life, expansion tends to have taken place at the top end of the market and there is precious little available in the mid-price range. The selection of hotels on pages 168–71 is divided into central or further afield locations and arranged in price order. Prices are liable to rapid change so should always be checked. There are no accommodation agencies in Moscow, but it is possible to make a reservation at most hotels directly by phone or fax. The best alternative is to book through a travel agent in advance.

A mosaic by Aleksandr Golovin on the Metropol's façade *(see p88)*

TYPES OF HOTEL

IN THEORY there are more than 200 hotels in Moscow. Many of these, however, are little more than hostels for professional delegations, with names such as The Oncological Research Centre Hotel. With occasional exceptions, therefore, the foreign visitor is in effect confined to hotels that fall into two broad categories: luxury hotels, and cheaper, plainer "ex-Soviet" hotels.

Luxury hotels are often foreign-owned or run as joint Russian-Western ventures. Many occupy historic buildings (some pre- and some post-Revolution), and have rooms combining period furniture with modern facilities. Service is similar to that in the best hotels in the West, but a double room rarely costs less than the equivalent of $200 a night. Hotels of this type are often referred to as Western-style.

The spacious lobby at the luxurious Baltschug Kempinski *(see p169)*

The more modest, so-called "ex-Soviet" hotels that were formerly run by the state often appear tired. The service can seem to take little account of what guests actually want, but rooms are usually clean and of a good size. These hotels can offer a fascinating insight into how the elite in the Soviet era used to live.

A spacious, elegantly appointed room in the National *(see p89)*

LOCATION OF HOTELS

MOST OF THE luxury hotels are within 15 minutes' drive or metro ride of the centre. Ex-Soviet hotels tend to be a little further out, but there are some options in the centre of the city, too.

For both types of hotel, the price is unlikely to be affected very much by location. However, when choosing a hotel, visitors should think about how they want to get around the city and take into consideration whether or not they will have a car, whether they want to get to the main sights on foot, or if their ability to read Cyrillic script is adequate to allow them to use buses and the metro with confidence.

MAKING A RESERVATION

DURING THE Soviet era all accommodation had to be arranged before going to Russia. It is still impossible to obtain a tourist visa without pre-booking but, once there, it is now theoretically possible to walk into any hotel and book a room on the spot. In practice, though, it is best to make arrangements before arriving, which can be done through most travel agents dealing with trips to Russia. Many of the more expensive hotels get booked up quite a while in advance, particularly for weekdays. In ex-Soviet hotels, attitudes left over from the days of restricted travel can make them wary of guests

Guest sitting room adjoining a bedroom at the Danilovskaya *(see p170)*

walking in off the street wanting a room. Almost all the hotels listed here will accept reservations by fax or phone. All the luxury hotels have staff who speak good English, but it is advisable to book rooms at ex-Soviet hotels by fax, asking for written confirmation. Luxury hotels will usually ask for a credit card number as a deposit.

FACILITIES

ALL LUXURY HOTELS provide the facilities that would be found in an expensive hotel in the West. These include television (often satellite), business facilities, such as a message-taking service and meeting room, mini-bars, a laundry service and 24-hour room service. All rooms have a bathroom with a bath or shower, or both. Fitness facilities or a swimming pool are available in only a handful of hotels. Not even all of the top hotels have air-conditioning, which can be a drawback in the hot summers.

Rooms in an ex-Soviet hotel always contain a television, a fridge and a telephone. International calls from rooms are expensive and may not be easy to make if they have to be booked through the operator. En-suite bathrooms with a bath or shower are also standard. Ex-Soviet hotels, particularly the cheaper places, do not often have sophisticated room service, although laundry can usually be arranged.

Many ex-Soviet hotels still have a *dezhurnaya* sitting at a desk on each floor. As one of their duties, these sometimes rather fearsome ladies look after guests' keys while they are out. Visitors should make sure they do not lose the card given to them when the keys are handed in, as it sometimes has to be shown to get back in through the main entrance. Friendly relations with the *dezhurnaya* will increase the chances of receiving good service or obtaining food and drink at unusual hours.

Opulent dining room at the Savoy *(see p168)*

All hotels have bars and restaurants. The luxury hotels contain some of the city's finest restaurants, but do not expect to find a bargain here. Ex-Soviet hotels tend to be less flexible about mealtimes, and the food is much less exciting. Continental breakfasts are the norm in luxury hotels. In ex-Soviet establishments guests usually help themselves from a large buffet which includes eggs, cold meats and bread. Breakfast is not usually included in the room price.

USING THE LISTINGS

The hotels on pages 168–71 are listed according to location and price category. The symbols summarize the facilities at each hotel.

all rooms have bath and/or shower.
1 single-rate rooms available
rooms for more than two people available, or an extra bed can be put in a double room
24 24-hour room service
TV television in all rooms
mini-bar in all rooms
gym/fitness facilities
business facilities: fax service, message-taking service, desk and telephone in room; meeting room.
wheelchair access
lift
P hotel parking available
bar
restaurant
★ highly recommended
credit and charge cards accepted:
AE American Express
DC Diners Club
MC MasterCard
V Visa
JCB Japanese Credit Bureau

Price categories are based on a standard double room per night in high season, including tax, service and, in some cases, breakfast.
$ under US$100
$$ US$100–175
$$$ US$175–250
$$$$ US$250–325
$$$$$ over US$325

The Sovietskiy's elegant Yar restaurant, where mirrored walls add to the feeling of spaciousness ***(see p170)***

Payment

The general shortage of accommodation in Moscow means that, almost without exception, hotel rooms in the city are over-priced. The rates given in this book are the standard rates quoted by the hotels. However, very few guests actually pay the full rate. Business guests usually have cheaper rates negotiated at the expensive hotels by their companies and most tourists book through an agent, again at more favourable rates. It is worth remembering that it is rarely economical to book any hotel room personally. Travellers interested in a particular hotel should ask their travel agent to enquire about special rates, or should find a travel agent who has already dealt with the hotel. Leisure weekend discounts should be available at many luxury hotels, since most of their clients are business people staying during the week.

The luxury hotels generally quote prices in a foreign currency (usually US dollars). However, it is illegal to pay in any currency other than roubles. The easiest way to pay in these hotels is undoubtedly with a credit card (few take travellers' cheques). This eliminates the necessity of carrying large amounts of cash around or changing money. Ex-Soviet hotels do not normally quote prices in dollars and mostly take only cash (in roubles), though some will take credit cards. They do not accept travellers' cheques.

Luxury hotels frequently quote prices exclusive of VAT and city tax; this can add more than 20 per cent to the bill. Visitors should also bear in mind that tax rates in Russia are liable to change at short notice.

The façade of the Tverskaya, imitating early 20th century Style-Moderne

Breakfast is rarely included in room prices and can be a significant addition to the bill. The cost of making international or even local phone calls from a hotel room can also come as a shock. The local phone network *(see p206)* is cheaper.

Stylish and modern, the bar area of the Palace Hotel

Travelling with Children

Russians idolize their children, but this rarely seems to translate into hotel facilities for families. In most hotels it should be possible to have an extra bed put in a room for an additional fee, and most luxury hotels will provide babysitters. Generally, however, hotels are more interested in business guests or tour groups, so do not expect to find extensive facilities for children or favourable room rates for families.

The Marco Polo Presnya, centrally located in a quiet street ***(see p168)***

Disabled Travellers

Few hotels in Moscow have wheelchair access, and those that do generally have few facilities. Disabled travellers should check in advance with their travel agents or the hotels, making sure to enquire about any specific needs.

Security

While many of the dangers of life in Moscow are exaggerated, hotels (particularly those owned by foreign companies) take security very seriously. Do not be surprised to see men with walkie-talkies patrolling the entrances of even the most refined establishments. Luxury hotels all have safe-deposit boxes and hotel guests generally have few problems with personal safety.

Ex-Soviet hotels also have a very good record on security. Porters keep undesirables out, and the *dezhurnaya (see p165)* on each floor keeps a pretty close eye on her own patch.

However, as in other major cities, tourists are often targets for petty criminals. Take particular care when leaving the hotel, as pickpockets are known to hang around outside tourist hotels.

The Stalinist-Gothic tower of the Ukraine ***(see p169)***

Staying with Families

A few organizations now arrange stays with families in Moscow. While this can be a good option for those who want to improve their Russian or get closer to "real" Russian life, staying with a family can be difficult for visitors who speak no Russian. When booking accommodation with a family, it is important to check where their apartment is – few flats are centrally located, so those choosing this option will need to be confident about travelling from the suburbs into the centre of Moscow to go sightseeing. It is also important to be quite clear about whether items such as meals and laundry are included in the basic cost. Guests are normally given a separate bedroom, but should expect to share the bathroom and other facilities with the host family.

Budget Accommodation

Options for travellers on a tight budget are very limited. Some of the cheaper ex-Soviet hotels have rooms for the equivalent of less than $50. The service may be rather sullen and the rooms a little shabby, but they should be clean. Their restaurants may be uninspiring.

Bed and Breakfast rents out apartments with cleaning included, most of them close to Belorusskaya metro. Flats for one person cost the equivalent of about $50 a night; the rate decreases for more people sharing.

The Ukraine's lobby ***(see p169)***

There are very few hostels in Moscow, but the **Prakash Guest House** and the **Travellers' Guest House** specifically cater for travellers on a budget. They offer dormitory accommodation from the equivalent of $15 and $25 a night respectively. The service is friendly and the dormitories are clean.

Directory

Staying with Families

Moscow Bed and Breakfast
Tel *457 3508.*
FAX *457 3508.*

Interchange (in UK)
Tel *0181 681 3612.*
FAX *0181 760 0031.*

Budget Accommodation

Bed and Breakfast
Tel *147 0021.*

Prakash Guest House
Общежитие Пракаш
Profsoyuznaya ulitsa 83, korpus 1, podezd 2.
Tel *334 2598.*
FAX *334 2598.*

Travellers' Guest House
Bolshaya Pereyaslavskaya ulitsa 50, 10th floor.
Tel *971 4059.*
FAX *280 7686.*

Choosing a Hotel

The hotels in this guide have been selected for their good value, facilities and location. The list of hotels covers a variety of areas and price categories with additional information to help you choose a hotel that best meets your needs. Hotels within the same price category are listed alphabetically. For map references *see pages 230–237*.

City Centre

Hotel	Credit Cards	Number of Rooms	Children Welcome	Swimming Pool	Air Conditioning
Belgrade Белград $ Smolenskaya ulitsa 8. **Map** 5 C1. Tel *248 1643.* Fax *230 2129.* The service in the Belgrade can be rather perfunctory, a reminder of pre-democracy standards, but the restaurant serves good east-European food and the hotel fulfils a useful role as a functional and economical ex-Soviet hotel in the centre of Moscow. ★	AE DC MC V	434			
Leningradskaya Ленинградская $ Ulitsa Kalanchevskaya 21/40. **Map** 4 D2. Tel *975 3032.* Fax *975 1802.* W http://leningradskaya.all-hotels.ru One of the most famous hotels in Moscow. Designed by architect L. Polyakov in 1954, the building has been designated an architectural monument and is protected by the state. Situated near Komsomolskaya Square, and just 15 minutes by metro to Red Square and the Kremlin, it provides wonderful views over Moscow. ★	AE DC MC V	329			
Peking Пекин $ Bolshaya Sadovaya ulitsa 5/1. **Map** 2 D3. Tel *209 2215.* Fax *200 1420.* @ hotel-pekin@ringnet.ru The decor of this hotel is characterized by order and gentle comfort, with high ceilings and marble staircases. Various categories of rooms are available from comfortable, reasonably priced rooms of an international standard to even more luxurious accommodation. The Peking Restaurant is the largest and most beautiful Chinese restaurant in the city and is highly regarded by Chinese visitors. ★	AE DC MC V JCB	120			
Budapesht Будапешт $$ Petrovskie Linii ulitsa 2/18. **Map** 3 A4. Tel *924 8820.* Fax *921 5290.* @ hotel-budpest@mtu-net.ru The Budapesht is located on a quiet street off ulitsa Petrovka close to the Bolshoy Theatre. The hotel was built in 1876 and the communal parts have a slightly shabby air. The rooms are bright and clean, with sparse furnishings and a faint smell of disinfectant. The hotel bar has been decorated as a traditional English pub. The restaurant offers traditional Russian food. ★	AE DC MC V	120			
Arbat Арбат $$$ Plotnikov pereulok 12. **Map** 6 D2. Tel *244 7635.* Fax *244 0093.* W www.hotelarbat.ru For those who want somewhere reasonably quiet and central, the Arbat is a very good option. The rooms are quite large, but the bathrooms and furnishings generally have the slightly tired look of so many of the ex-Soviet hotels. There is a very nice veranda where guests can sit and have a drink outside in summer. ★	AE DC MC V JCB	105			
Katerina Катерина $$$ Shluzovaya Naberezhnaya 6/1. **Map** 8 D5. Tel *933 0401.* Fax *315 7442.* W www.katerina.msk.ru Located on the bank of the Moskva river, this hotel is decorated in a contemporary Swedish style. The hotel offers a range of services to suit those visiting Moscow on business as well as tourists. The restaurant offers European and Russian fare and there are two bars. Rooms are warm and clean with modern furniture.	AE DC MC V JCB	119		●	■
Marco Polo Presnya Марко Поло Пресня $$$$ Spiridonevskiy pereulok 9. **Map** 2 E4. Tel *244 3631.* Fax *926 5402* @ marco_polo_presnja_hotel@co.ru W www.presnja.ru/eng/ Although some way from public transport, visitors heading out from the hotel will pass along some of Moscow's most attractive residential streets. Its smaller size contributes to its quiet atmosphere. Despite the faint air of neglect and the slightly sullen service, the hotel offers a low-key alternative to the city's grander establishments. ★	AE DC MC V JCB	68	■		

Price categories are for a standard double room per night in high season, inclusive of tax, service and, in some cases, breakfast:
- $ under US$100
- $$ US$100–US$175
- $$$ US$175–US$250
- $$$$ US$250–US$325
- $$$$$ over US$325.

CREDIT CARDS
Indicates which credit cards are accepted: AE American Express; DC Diners Club; MC Master Card/Access; V Visa; JCB Japanese Credit Bureau.

CHILDREN WELCOME
Child cots and a baby-sitting service available. Some hotel restaurants have children's portions and high chairs.

SWIMMING POOL
The hotel has an indoor or outdoor swimming pool.

AIR CONDITIONING
All rooms are air conditioned.

SAVOY Савой $$$$
Rozhdestvenka ulitsa 3. **Map** 3 A4. *929 8500.* FAX *230 2186.* W www.savoy.ru
Tucked away on a quiet side street, the Savoy's unassuming exterior belies its luxurious interior. The rich fittings and subdued lighting give it an atmosphere akin to a gentleman's club from a past era. The corridors double as an art gallery. The bedrooms are small, with high ceilings, reproduction furniture and modern facilities. ★

BALTSCHUG KEMPINSKI Балчуг Кемпинский $$$$$
Ulitsa Balchug 1. **Map** 7 B2. *230 6500.* FAX *230 6502.*
@ reservation.mos@kempinski.com W www.kempinski-moscow.com
Hidden within a handsome late-19th century building is a luxurious, modern interior. The bedrooms are smart, though uninspiringly decorated. Rooms on the river side offer magnificent views of the Kremlin and St Basil's Cathedral. The hotel's restaurant offers an excellent Sunday brunch. ★

MARRIOTT GRAND HOTEL Марриотт Гранд отель $$$$$
Tverskaya ulitsa 26. **Map** 2 E3. *935 8500.* FAX *937 0001.* W www.marriott.com
This luxury establishment was completed in 1997 and offers every modern amenity, including computer ports in every room. The conference hall and meeting rooms attract business travellers. There are three restaurants: the smartest serves both Russian and Western cuisine; the buffet restaurant; and an informal Russian taverna. ★

METROPOL Метрополь $$$$$
Teatralnyy proezd 1/4. **Map** 3 A5. *927 6000.* FAX *927 6010.*
W www.all-hotels.ru/moscow/metropol/
The Metropol is a wonderful example of Style Moderne *(see p45)* from the turn of the 20th century. Its spectacular interior is adorned with mosaics, golden chandeliers and stained glass. Set beneath an impressive vaulted glass ceiling, the Metropol Restaurant is lit by great rings of lamps on long gilded stalks. Many of the bedrooms are similarly lavish, combining antique furniture with modern facilities. ★

NATIONAL Националь $$$$$
Mokhovaya ulitsa 15/1. **Map** 2 F5. *258 7000.* FAX *258 7100.* W www.national.ru
Renovated in the early 1990s the National has firmly re-established itself as one of Moscow's top luxury hotels. The bedrooms have high ceilings and wooden floors and the more expensive ones contain antique furniture and rugs. The rooms tend to get smaller and less impressive the higher up they are, and views of the Kremlin come at a premium. The service is impeccable, but the food is expensive. ★

FURTHER AFIELD

KOSMOS Космос $$
Prospekt Mira 150. *234 1000.* FAX *215 8880.* @ hcosmos@dol.ru W www.hotelcosmos.ru
Opened in 1980 in time for the Moscow Olympics, the Kosmos looks out over the All-Russian Exhibition Centre *(see p145)*. The cavernous lobby is dated but the rooms are a good size and get plenty of light, and those on the top floors have splendid views. The lower ground floor contains a late-night bar and a bowling alley. ★

UKRAINE Украина $$
Kutuzovskiy prospekt 2/1. **Map** 5 B1. *933 6801.* FAX *933 6839.*
@ ukraina@calnat.msk.ie
Occupying one of the seven Stalinist-Gothic *(see p45)* tower blocks and set on the west bank of the Moskva river, the Ukraine looks across to the White House *(see p128)* on the other side. Bedrooms have parquet floors and contain period furniture, but the place is a little dated and shabby. Nevertheless, a stay here is a rare chance to see inside a building constructed when the Soviet Union was at its most powerful. ★

Hotel	Credit Cards	Number of Rooms	Children Welcome	Swimming Pool	Air Conditioning
Savoy	AE DC MC V JCB	90	■		■
Baltschug Kempinski	AE DC MC V JCB	234	■	●	■
Marriott Grand Hotel	AE DC MC V JCB	392	■	●	■
Metropol	AE DC MC V JCB	373	■	●	■
National	AE DC MC V JCB	231	■	●	■
Kosmos	AE DC MC V JCB	1,776			
Ukraine	AE DC V	1,600	■		

For key to symbols *see p165*

Price categories are for a standard double room per night in high season, inclusive of tax, service and, in some cases, breakfast:
$ under US$100
$$ US$100–US$175
$$$ US$175–US$250
$$$$ US$250–US$325
$$$$$ over US$325.

CREDIT CARDS
Indicates which credit cards are accepted: AE American Express; DC Diners Club; MC Master Card/Access; V Visa; JCB Japanese Credit Bureau.

CHILDREN WELCOME
Child cots and a baby-sitting service available. Some hotel restaurants have children's portions and high chairs.

SWIMMING POOL
The hotel has an indoor or outdoor swimming pool.

AIR CONDITIONING
All rooms are air conditioned.

DANILOVSKAYA Даниловская $$$
Bolshoy Starodanilovskiy pereulok 5. *954 0503.* FAX *954 0750.*
www.hotel-danilovskaya.da.ru
A five-storey block in the grounds of the fortified Danilovskiy Monastery *(see pp136–7)*. It is run by the Russian Orthodox Church, and portraits of Moscow's patriarchs hang in the corridors and religious icons decorate the rooms. Clean, quiet rooms and up-to-date facilities. It is not within walking distance of the main sights. ★

Credit Cards	Number of Rooms	Children Welcome	Swimming Pool	Air Conditioning
AE DC MC V JCB	116			■

HOTEL SOVETSKIY Отель Советский $$$
Leningradskiy prospekt 32/2. **Map** 1 B1. *960 2000.* FAX *250 8003.* @ hotelsov@cnt.ru
Built in Stalinist style, the Sovetskiy is wonderfully grandiose. The bedrooms are large, with high, moulded ceilings, wooden floors and period furniture but with slightly shabby bathrooms. The hotel's restaurant is a spectacular mirrored hall, lit by a stunning chandelier. Located 15–20 minutes' drive from the city centre by car. Dinamo, the nearest metro station is about 1 km (1,000 yds) away. ★

Credit Cards	Number of Rooms	Children Welcome	Swimming Pool	Air Conditioning
AE DC MC V	100			

NOVOTEL Новотель $$$
Sheremetevo 2 Airport. *926 5900, 502 220 6611.* FAX *926 5904, 502 220 6604.*
@ novotel.reservations@co.ru www.novotel-moscow.ru
As you would expect from an airport hotel, the Novotel is clean, bright and efficient. The rooms are decently sized and well equipped. Its restaurants and bars are good, although short on character. For visitors stuck at the airport for any length of time, the facilities at the Novotel are infinitely superior to anything in the airport itself. ★

Credit Cards	Number of Rooms	Children Welcome	Swimming Pool	Air Conditioning
AE DC MC V JCB	488		●	■

PRESIDENT HOTEL Президент отель $$$
Ulitsa Bolshaya Yakimanka 24. **Map** 7 A4. *239 3800.* FAX *230 2318*
@ president_hotel_@sovintel.ru www.president-hotel.ru
Opened in 1983, the President Hotel was favoured by top Communist Party officials and the official atmosphere still lingers. Security at the President is extremely tight, making this a popular choice for visiting foreign statesmen. Inside, the hotel has all the hallmarks of late Soviet architecture at its most monumental. The rooms are quite large and furnished functionally. Primarily a business hotel. ★

Credit Cards	Number of Rooms	Children Welcome	Swimming Pool	Air Conditioning
AE DC MC V JCB	209	■	●	■

ART HOTEL Арт отель $$$$
3-ya Peschanaya ulitsa 2. *955 2300.* FAX *955 2310.* @ arthotel@glasnet.ru
Art hotel is clean and well maintained resembling an up-market American motel. Rooms are a decent size containing modern, functional furniture. The beer garden provides a pleasant place to sit outside, weather permiting. About 20 minutes by car from the centre of Moscow, but not very conveniently located for public transport. ★

Credit Cards	Number of Rooms	Children Welcome	Swimming Pool	Air Conditioning
AE DC MC V	86	■		

MEZHDUNARODNAYA Международная $$$$
Krasnopresnenskaya nab 12. **Map** 5 A1. *258 2122.* FAX *253 2051.*
@ hotels@ineurope.org
Known by all as the "Mezh" this is a sprawling complex of hotel rooms, offices, shops and restaurants. It is popular with the business community, although its relatively inaccessible location makes it less attractive for visitors keen on sightseeing. Various bars and restaurants, lead off the foyer. ★

Credit Cards	Number of Rooms	Children Welcome	Swimming Pool	Air Conditioning
AE DC MC V JCB	547	■	●	■

PALACE HOTEL Палас отель $$$$
1-ya Tverskaya-Yamskaya ulitsa 19. **Map** 2 D2. *931 9700, 502 256 3000.*
FAX *931 9704, 502 256 3008.* @ palacehotel.admin@ns.co.ru www.sheraton.com/moscow
Occupying a modern building with a simple façade of granite and mirrored glass. Luxurious surroundings, modern facilities and efficient, friendly staff. Short on the glamour of Moscow's older hotels, for luxury and the range of facilities it is unbeatable. Its entrance leads out onto an extension of Tverskaya ulitsa, one of central Moscow's busiest streets but the hotel itself is fully sound-proofed. ★

Credit Cards	Number of Rooms	Children Welcome	Swimming Pool	Air Conditioning
AE DC MC V JCB	218	■		■

RADISSON-SLAVYANSKAYA Рэдиссон-Славянская $$$$

Berezhkovskaya nab 2. **Map** 5 B2. *941 8021.* FAX *941 8000.*

@ DMorris@radisson.com

The Radisson-Slavyanskaya is next to Kievskiy station, out of walking range of the city centre, but with good public transport connections. Most guests stay here for its business facilities and visitors on holiday may find the working atmosphere and standardized rooms a little unexciting. However, it does possess one of Moscow's English-language cinemas – the American House of Cinema *(see p193).*

AE DC MC V JCB | 410 | ■ | ● | ■

TVERSKAYA Тверская $$$$

1-ya Tverskaya-Yamskaya ulitsa 34. **Map** 2 D2. *258 3000.* FAX *258 3099.*

@ hotels@in-europe.org W www.marriott.com

From an unremarkable lobby in the Tverskaya, glass lifts take guests up into a magnificent atrium stretching up eight floors to the hotel's glass roof. The bedrooms are very comfortably furnished with modern facilities. Style-Moderne features, including extravagantly curved wooden handrails, coloured glass windows and brass fittings.

AE DC MC V JCB | 162 | ■ | | ■

AEROSTAR Аэростар $$$$$

Leningradskiy prospekt 37, korpus 9. *213 9000.* FAX *213 9001.*

@ booking@aerostar.ru W www.aerostar.ru

An uninspiring, white, concrete block, but the bedrooms inside are furnished in a comfortable modern style with windows stretching from floor to ceiling giving them a light and airy feel. Easy access to Sheremetevo airport *(see p208)* makes the Aerostar a popular choice for business travellers. For other visitors, the 20-minute car journey into the city centre may prove a drawback.

AE DC MC V JCB | 413 | ■ | | ■

RENAISSANCE MOSCOW Ренессанс Москва $$$$$

Olimpiyskiy prospekt 18/1. **Map** 3 A1. *931 9000.* FAX *931 9076.*

@ moscow_ren_sales@co.ru W www.renaissancehotels.com

The Renaissance Moscow is a luxury hotel of the modern variety. A little short on character, it makes up for it with excellent facilities. Rooms are small and fitted with functional furniture. Bars, restaurants, shops and an English-language cinema *(see p193)* are situated on the lower ground floor.

AE DC MC V JCB | 475 | ■ | ● | ■

SOFITEL-IRIS Софитель-Ирис $$$$$

Korovinskoye shosse 10. *488 8000.* FAX *937 8700.*

@ sofitel@iris.moscow@co.ru W www.sofitel.com

The open-plan effect, with bedrooms set back on balconies running round the atrium, gives the Stofite-Iris a pleasant, airy feel. The rooms are modern and well equipped. The restaurant offers excellent, if expensive, French food. The hotel is a long way from the centre of town. However a free shuttle service runs from the hotel into the city and back every half an hour from 7.30am until 11.00pm.

AE DC MC V JCB | 195 | ■ | ● | ■

BEYOND MOSCOW

TOUR-CENTRE Тур-Центр $

Korovnikiy ulitsa, Suzdal. *09231 20908.* FAX *09231 20766.*

The best way to consider the Tour-Centre is as a living slice of the conditions prevalent in recent Soviet history. Its bleak lobby, limited facilities and rather unenthusiastic staff, make it a good example of an ex-Soviet hotel. However, the rooms are clean and well equipped. The hotel is 15 minutes' walk from the religious buildings at the centre of the town.

271 | | ● |

MOSCOW Москва $$

Moscow Railway Station Square, Tula. *0872 208952.* FAX *0872 208936.*

The Moscow is probably not the sort of place visitors would choose to book into for a long stay unless on a tight budget. The rooms are clean, but faded and not that large. As members of staff do not usually speak foreign languages, guests should come prepared with sightseeing information. The restaurant will satisfy only the truly hungry.

357

LE MERIDIEN COUNTRY CLUB Ле Меридиен Кантри Клаб $$$$

Nakhabino, Kransnogorsky District. *926 5911.* FAX *926 5921.*

W www.lemeridien-mcc.com

Just 45 minutes by car from the city centre, this hotel offers a luxurious retreat from the urban sprawl. It primarily caters to golfing aficionados, boasting Russia's only 18-hole championship course. Other activities and services are of a high standard.

AE DC MC V | 131 | ■ | ● | ■

For key to symbols *see p165*

Restaurants, Cafés and Bars

The pastime of dining out is a relatively new concept in Russia, and nowhere has it been embraced more strongly than in the capital. In the restrictive Soviet era, the number of good restaurants in Moscow could be counted on one hand. Today, however, the city boasts an array of places to eat which, if not approaching the scope of New York or London, at least provides visitors with numerous desirable options, from Russian and European to Caucasian, Indian and Chinese. Most decent restaurants are moderately expensive – Moscow is still a long way from acquiring a casual café culture – but the frequency with which new places are opening bodes well for the hungry tourist. The following pages will help you locate the best-quality food and most exciting cuisine in all price categories. A detailed review of the selected restaurants is provided on pages 180–81, and ideas for light meals on pages 182–3.

Logo of Russkoe Bistro chain

McDonald's restaurant, now a familiar sight all over Moscow

Where to Eat

Most of Moscow's better known restaurants are to be found in central Moscow; almost all, therefore, are easily accessible by metro. Ulitsa Arbat *(see pp70–71)* has the highest concentration and variety of restaurants, from Russian and Georgian to Italian and Japanese, as well as a now ubiquitous McDonald's *(see p182)*. There is also plenty of choice along Tverskaya ulitsa *(see p89)*, and at Triumfalnaya ploshchad. Russkoe Bistro *(see p183)* is a popular new chain offering fast food Russian style.

Reading the Menu

In restaurants specializing in international cuisine, the menu is almost always in Russian, English, and sometimes a third language. Waiting staff speak English in most restaurants geared towards foreigners. In smaller, local eateries, a knowledge of the Cyrillic alphabet will help with deciphering the menu.

Types of Cuisine

There are surprisingly few good, exclusively Russian restaurants in Moscow. Russians have never made a habit of dining out, nor has Russian cuisine ever enjoyed the prominence of, say, French or Italian. Georgian or Armenian cooking, both of which are delicious and relatively inexpensive, are a better option. Mediterranean and other Western European restaurants, especially Italian ones, are now increasingly popular in Moscow. Chinese and Japanese food is generally overpriced and of variable quality, but there are a few excellent Indian restaurants.

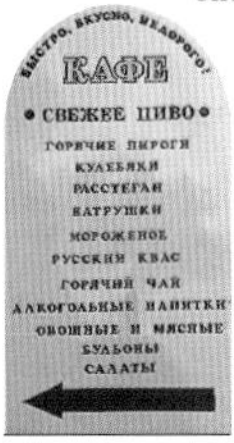

Café sign, listing a selection of Russian dishes

What to Drink

Vodka is the alcoholic drink most often associated with Russia. However, in the years since perestroika beer has become more widely available as an accompaniment to meals. Some restaurants now offer imported and local beer on tap, along with a variety of bottled beers. The better European restaurants have commendable wine lists, though good imported wine tends to be quite expensive. It is a shame to visit Moscow without sampling a bottle of Georgian wine *(see p179)* in one of its many Georgian eateries. This tends to be sweet, and is an excellent accompaniment to the food.

The Central House of Writers *(see p180)*, one of Moscow's most exclusive restaurants

Payment and Tipping

One of the drawbacks of eating out in Moscow is that many restaurants, especially the less touristy ones, only take cash. This situation is gradually changing, but it is still a consideration when deciding where to eat. Generally restaurants that serve Western or Asian cuisine will accept credit cards, but it is a good idea to call ahead and check. Prices vary enormously, from the cheapest local cafeteria *(stolovaya)*,

Outdoor café in Tverskaya, a good place to watch the world go by

where a basic Russian meal might cost the equivalent of around US$5, to the exclusive Central House of Writers, where dinner will come to over US$75. Most international restaurants fall in the moderate to expensive range; it can be difficult to eat cheaply in Moscow without sticking rigidly to the Russian staples of bread, cheese and salami-style sausage *(kolbasa)*.

Tipping is not as ingrained in Russia as elsewhere. A good rule of thumb is to keep to international standards – about 15 per cent – in foreign or prestigious restaurants, but to leave just small change, or nothing at all, in Russian-style restaurants or cafés. Service is rarely included in the bill.

Opening Times

Dinner is the main meal of the day, but many restaurants in Moscow have now adopted the concept of the business lunch. These often take the form of a fixed price menu and can be good value. They are usually served from noon to 4pm. Most restaurants start serving dinner at around 6pm and stop taking orders at 10:30pm; some family-run Georgian establishments close their kitchens as early as 8:30 or 9pm. As Moscow's nightlife picks up speed, however, an increasing number of restaurants are staying open until the early hours of the morning. Several places, both Russian and foreign, also now remain open 24 hours a day.

Cosy interior of Cafe Margarita *(see p178)*, a traditional café

Making a Reservation

Most international and tourist-oriented restaurants take reservations and some of the most popular require them. Generally, it is best to book ahead whenever possible. However, some of the most popular Georgian and Caucasian restaurants do not take reservations and clients may find themselves waiting for up to an hour to be seated, especially at weekends.

Etiquette

Casual or semi-formal dress is acceptable in almost every Moscow restaurant. It is worth bearing in mind, though, that Russians tend to overdress rather than underdress, so it is probably safer to err on the formal side. Children are a rare sight at expensive restaurants and most menus do not have special dishes for them. However, Moscow does have a few family-style restaurants.

Vegetarians

Much of Russian cuisine consists of meat dishes. Even salads often contain meat, so the best option for vegetarians is often a beetroot or tomato platter. Georgian cuisine, featuring numerous excellent bean and aubergine dishes, is usually a much better bet. Only a few restaurants list vegetarian dishes separately on the menu – some Indian ones are the exception. European, Chinese and Japanese restaurants usually have some items suitable for vegetarians, as well as fish dishes.

Smoking

There are generally no areas for non-smokers, and smoking during meals is considered acceptable.

Disabled Persons

Few restaurants in Moscow have facilities for disabled visitors. Some restaurants are located in basements and would therefore pose a problem. It is always best to phone in advance to check if there is full disabled access.

Using the Listings

Key to symbols in the restaurant listings on pp178–81.

- V vegetarian dishes
- suitable for children
- wheelchair access
- formal dress
- outdoor eating
- recommended wine list
- credit cards accepted:
  - *AE* American Express
  - *DC* Diners Club
  - *MC* MasterCard
  - *V* Visa
  - *JCB* Japanese Credit Bureau

Price categories for a three-course meal with a glass of wine, but not including service or tax:

- $ under US$15
- $$ US$15–30
- $$$ US$30–50
- $$$$ US$50–75
- $$$$$ over US$75

What to Eat in Moscow

A sprig of dill

RUSSIA'S VAST RANGE of climates and cultures has given rise to an incredibly diverse cuisine, which has been further influenced by European and Arabic food. Traditionally each region had its own cuisine, but today certain regional specialities, such as the Georgian dish *shashlyk*, are popular all over Russia. Staple ingredients of the Russian diet include potatoes, cabbage, beetroot, onions, pickles, *kasha*, sour cream *(smetana)*, curd cheese *(tvorog)* and herbs such as dill.

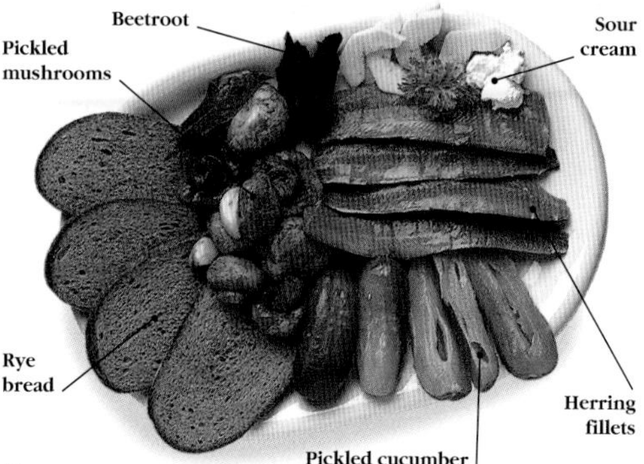

Zakuski

The name given for a variety of hors d'oeuvres, *zakuski* are often served as starters for lunch or dinner. The robust spicy and salty flavours stimulate the appetite. Caviar, smoked sausage *(kolbasa)* and cheese are also typical.

Khachapuri
These cheese-filled breads come in various shapes and sizes. Originally from Georgia, their traditional filling is suluguni *cheese, made from sheep's milk.*

Rassolnik
There are many versions of this classic soup, including recipes using chicken, fish or kidneys. Pickled cucumbers are a vital ingredient in all of them.

Solyanka
Made from either meat or fish, this soup has a distinctive rich, spicy taste. The meat version has a strong tomato flavour.

Borshch
This classic soup gets its colour from beetroot and tastes sweet and sour. It is served hot in winter and chilled in summer.

Shashlyk
This version of a kebab is made from marinated mutton or lamb. The pieces of meat may be interspersed with vegetables such as onions or peppers.

Caviar & Blini

There are two types of Russian caviar (*ikra*). Black caviar is sturgeon roe. It is produced by three species of sturgeon, all found in the Caspian Sea. Beluga is the rarest and has a distinctive nutty taste. Osetrova has a creamy flavour, while sevruga tastes of sea salt. Red caviar is salmon roe. Both types are often served with *blini* (Russian buck-wheat pancakes) and sour cream.

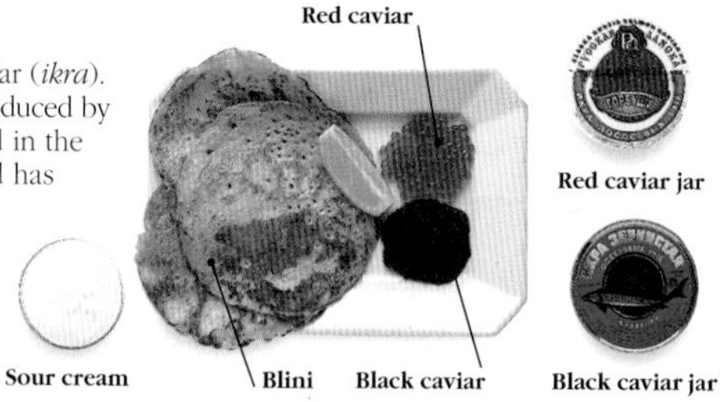

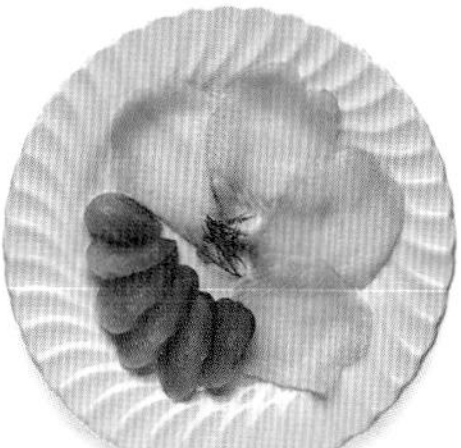

Osetrina
The sturgeon is renowned for its roe (caviar), but the fish itself is also eaten in a variety of ways, such as salted or smoked.

Savoury Pirozhki
These small parcels can be stuffed with a variety of fillings. Favourites include meat and cabbage or curd cheese.

Kotlety po Kievski
Chicken breasts are filled with garlic butter, coated in breadcrumbs and deep fried. This is called Chicken Kiev in the West.

Pelmeni
Originally a Siberian dish, these meat or fish dumplings are typically served in soups or with sour cream, butter or vinegar.

Kulebyaka
Puff or yeast pastry encloses a filling of salmon, rice, hard-boiled eggs and mushrooms. This long pie is served in slices.

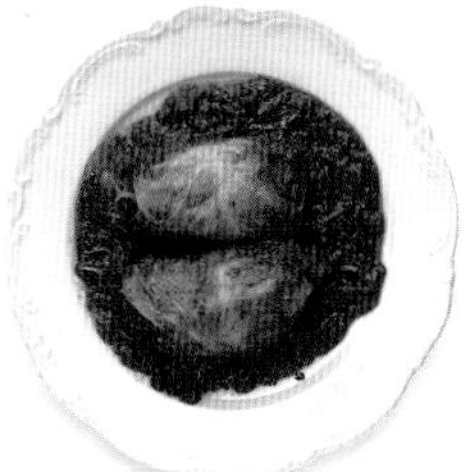

Golubtsy
Minced meat and rice rolled in cabbage leaves, golubtsy *are boiled or baked and are often served with a tomato sauce.*

Bev Stroganov and Kasha
Sautéed strips of beef in a sour cream, onion and mushroom sauce, this dish is often served with boiled buckwheat (kasha).

DESSERTS

An important part of any Russian meal, most desserts are uncompromisingly rich. Russian cuisine has a wide variety of cakes, pies, tarts, pastries and ice cream.

Vatrushki are sweet cheese-filled tartlets.
Vareniki are boiled sweet dumplings with various fruit fillings.
Khvorost are flat, deep-fried biscuits.

Sweet Pirozhki
Made with yeast dough, sweet pirozhki *can have a variety of fillings, including fruit or jam, and may be served with cream.*

Sharlotka
This sponge cake, filled with custard and fruit purée, was devised for Tsar Alexander I by French chef Anton Carême.

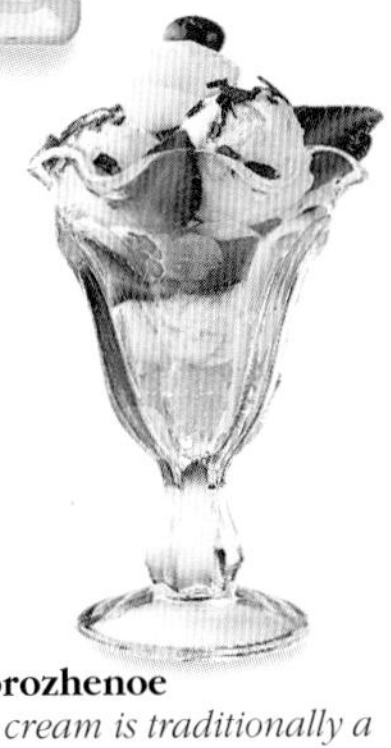

Morozhenoe
Ice cream is traditionally a favourite dessert in Russia. It is often served with fresh fruit.

What to Drink in Moscow

A glass of flavoured vodka

RUSSIA IS RENOWNED for vodka, which has been manufactured there since the 14th or 15th century and was possibly originally invented by Muscovite monks. Vodka produced in Moscow has always been considered to be the finest. Peter the Great *(see p22)* was particularly fond of pepper and anise vodkas and devised modifications to the distillation process which greatly improved the quality of the finished drink.

Tea is Russia's other national drink. Traditionally made using a samovar and served black, tea has been popular in Russia since the end of the 18th century when it began to be imported from China.

A 19th-century Russian peasant family drinking vodka and tea at their *izba*

Stolichnaya

Moskovskaya

Stolichnaya Cristall

CLEAR VODKA

RUSSIAN VODKA IS PRODUCED from grain, usually wheat, although some rye is also used. Stolichnaya is made from wheat and rye and is slighly sweetened. Probably the best known of the Russian vodkas, its name means "from the capital city". Moskovskaya is a high-quality, slightly fizzy vodka, while Kubanskaya, originally produced by the Cossacks, is slightly bitter. The Cristall distillery in Moscow has been hailed as the finest in Russia and produces super-premium versions of several vodkas, including Stolichnaya and Moskovskaya, as well as its own vodka, Cristall. Vodka is almost always served with food in Russia, often with a traditional range of accompaniments called *zakuski (see p176)*. These specialities are usually spicy or salty and their strong flavours complement vodka perfectly.

Kubanskaya

FLAVOURED VODKA

THE PRACTICE of flavouring vodka has entirely practical origins. When vodka was first produced commercially in the Middle Ages, the techniques and equipment were so primitive that it was impossible to remove all the impurities. This left unpleasant aromas and flavours, which were disguised by adding honey together with aromatic oils and spices. As distillation techniques improved, flavoured vodkas became a speciality in their own right. Limonnaya, its taste deriving from lemon zest, is one of the most traditional, as is Pertsovka, flavoured with red chilli pepper pods. Okhotnichya (hunter's vodka) has a wider range of flavourings including juniper, ginger and cloves. Starka (old vodka) is a mixture of vodka, brandy, port and an infusion of apple and pear leaves, aged in oak barrels.

Pertsovka

Limonnaya

Okhotnichya

Starka

Major Wine Regions

- Vine-growing region
- Moldova
- Ukraine
- Russia
- Georgia
- Armenia
- Azerbaijan
- International boundaries

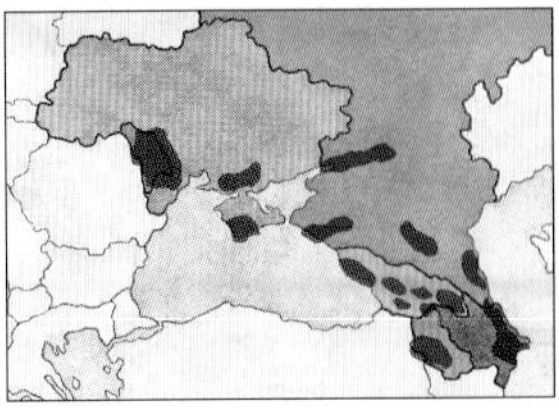

Georgian wines

Shampanskoe

Wine

The former Soviet Union was one of the world's largest producers of wine *(vino)*. Many of its major wine regions, however, are now within independent republics, but their vintages are still popular in Moscow. A wide range of indigenous grape varieties is cultivated in the different regions, along with many types found in other parts of the vine-growing world. Georgia and Crimea (in southeastern Ukraine) have traditionally produced the best wines. Georgian wines include those made from the *rkatsiteli* grape, characterized by a floral aroma and subtle, fruity flavour. Moldova produces white, sparkling wines in the south and central regions, and the south is also known for its red wines. Since 1799 Moldova has also produced vast amounts of a sweet, sparkling wine called *shampanskoe*.

Baltika beer

Armenian brandy

Other Alcoholic Drinks

Originally a by-product of wine-making, brandy *(konyak)* only began to be made commercially in Russia in the 19th century. Among the ex-Soviet republics, Georgia and Armenia both produce brandy. Armenian is considered the finer, with a vanilla fragrance resulting from ageing it in barrels made of 70–100-year-old oak. Although beer *(pivo)* is becoming more popular, it is still served in relatively few restaurants and cafés. Good Russian beers include Zhigulevskoe, Baltika, Kolos and Moskovskoe. Various imported beers are also available.

Mineral water

Kvas

Mors

Other Drinks

Made from barley and rye, *kvas* is a sweet, mildly alco holic drink consumed by adults and children alike. Russia has a huge range of mineral waters *(mineralnaya voda)*, including many with unusually high mineral contents. Those from the Caucasus, Siberia and Georgia are especially prized. Also available are fruit juices *(sok)* sweetened drinks made by boiling fruit with sugar and water (*kompot*). The cranberry equivalent is called *mors*.

Tea

Russian tea is served black with a slice of lemon and is traditionally drunk from a tall glass, called a *stakan*, or a cup. The tea *(chay)* is often sweetened with jam *(varenye)* instead of sugar. The boiling water for making tea traditionally comes from a samovar. The water is used to brew a pot of strong tea, from which a little is poured into the glasses. This is then diluted with more boiling water.

A glass of tea, with jam *(varenye)* to sweeten it

The Samovar

Traditionally made from brass or copper, samovars were once used to provide boiling water for a variety of domestic purposes. Nowadays they are often made of stainless steel and are used for boiling water to make tea. Occasionally eggs are put in the top of the samovar to cook in the boiling water. The word samovar comes from *samo* meaning "itself" and *varit* meaning "to boil".

Choosing a Restaurant

THE RESTAURANTS in this guide have been selected across a wide price range for their exceptional food, good value, and their convenient and/or interesting locations. The chart below lists the restaurants by area, and the entries are alphabetical within each price category. For the map references, *see pages 230–7.*

Restaurant	Price	Credit Cards	CIS Cuisine	Fixed-Price Lunch Menu	Live Entertainment
ARBATSKAYA					
MOO-MOO Му-му Ulitsa Arbat 45/24. **Map** 6 D1. *241 1364.* Busy, self-service restaurant serving Russian and European dishes. A popular place for lunch with people working in the area as well as with tourists. Three other Moo-Moos can be found throughout the city. V	$		●		
5 SPICES 5 специй Sivtsev Vrazhek pereulok 3/18. **Map** 6 E2. *203 1283.* Tasty Indian and Chinese dishes prepared by native chefs are served in a somewhat kitsch interior. Overpriced drinks can significantly puff up the bill. V	$$	*AE DC MC V*		■	
GENATSVALE Генацвале Ulitsa Ostozhenka 12/1, entry from the yard. **Map** 6 E3. *202 0445.* A Georgian restaurant, offering delicious *hachapuri* (cheese-filled bread), *lobio* (beans with walnuts and spices), and other Georgian musts. Loud synthesizer entertainment in the evening. More expensive Genatsvale VIP nearby (Ostozhenka 14/2; 203 1242) offers almost the same menu, with a smarter interior. V	$$	*MC V*	●		●
KISHMISH Кишмиш Ulitsa Novyy Arbat 28. **Map** 5 C1. *290 0703.* Furnished with carpets, pillows, pots and pans, Kishmish offers a large and tasty Uzbek menu. Pilaf, *lagman* (thick noodle soup with lamb and vegetables) *samsa* (lamb pie), *shashlyk*, and Uzbek green tea are highly recommended. V	$$		●		
PATIO PIZZA Патио Пицца Ulitsa Volkhonka 13a. **Map** 6 F2. *298 2530.* Conveniently located just across the street from the Pushkin Fine Arts Museum, this spacious Italian restaurant offers a large variety of tasty pizzas, pastas and an all you can eat salad bar. Several other branches including one at Prospekt Mira, 33. V	$$	*AE DC MC V*		■	
VOSTOCHNYY KVARTAL Восточный квартал Ulitsa Arbat 45/24. **Map** 6 D1 *241 3803.* A casual Uzbek place conveniently located just off the Old Arbat. Peek into the kitchen and watch your food being prepared by real Uzbek chefs. V	$$		●		
MEKHANA BANSKO Механа Банско Smolenskaya ploshchad 9/1. **Map** 5 C1. *244 7387.* A family Bulgarian restaurant. Diverse meat dishes are ordered along with vegetables and *brynza* – soft salty sheep or cow's cheese. *Banitsa* (puff pies with spinach, meat, cheese, pumpkin and walnuts) are highly recommended. Traditional Bulgarian entertainment in the evenings. V	$$$	*AE DC MC V*		■	●
TVERSKAYA					
CAFÉ MARGARITA Кафе Маргарита Malaya Bronnaya ulitsa 28. **Map** 2 E4. *299 6534.* Named after the heroine of Mikhail Bulgakov's *The Master and Margarita* and situated on the corner of the Patriarch's Ponds (*see p96*), this is a small café with a lot of atmosphere. Margarita offers an international menu, including Russian soups, *blini* and *pelmeni* and piano and violin concerts in the evening. V	$$		●	■	●
CITY-GRILL Сити-гриль Sadovaya-Triumfalnaya ulitsa 2/30. **Map** 2 E3. *299 0953.* Tasty European cuisine served in a casual urban interior. Grilled meats and vegetables, seafood, pizzas and a wide choice of desserts. V	$$	*MC V*		■	
DYADYA VANYA Дядя Ваня Ulitsa Bolshaya Dmitrovka 17. **Map** 2 F4. *232 1448.* Traditional Russian dishes and drinks offered in a pleasant wooden interior. The jazz band in the evenings adds to the ambience. Try the herring, *borshch* and homemade cranberry juice. V	$$	*AE MC V*	●	■	●

Price categories for a three-course meal with a glass of wine, but not including service or tax:
- $ under US$15
- $$ US$15–30
- $$$ US$30–50
- $$$$ US$50–75
- $$$$$ Over US$75.

CREDIT CARDS
Indicates which credit cards are accepted: AE American Express; DC Diners Club; MC Master Card/Access; V Visa; JCB Japanese Credit Bureau.

CIS CUISINE
Traditional cuisine from the former Soviet republics which now make up the Commonwealth of Independent States.

FIXED-PRICE LUNCH MENU
A good value lunch menu is offered.

LIVE ENTERTAINMENT
Live music and/or dancing on occasions.

Restaurant	Credit Cards	CIS Cuisine	Fixed-Price Lunch Menu	Live Entertainment
STARLIGHT DINER Свет звезд $$ Bolshaya Sadovaya ulitsa 16. **Map** 2 E3. *290 9638.* Nestled within an old courtyard, this neon-and-chrome diner is an island of 1950s Americana, popular with American businesspeople and Russian fans of hearty burger plates and thick milkshakes. V	AE MC V			
TANDOOR Тандур $$ Tverskaya ulitsa 30/2. **Map** 2 E3. *299 4593.* Tandoor serves Indian and Chinese food prepared by native Indian and Chinese chefs. The Indian menu is highly recommended. Relax in a wicker chair and order tomato soup, excellent tandoori dishes, *naan* bread and much more. Pleasant interior and attentive service. V	AE DC MC V JCB		■	
TESORO Тезоро $$ Romanov pereulok 4. **Map** 2 F5. *937 7730.* Located in a quiet side-street, Tesoro is a pleasant combination of an Italian restaurant and pizzeria. Dinner with wine in the restaurant is can be quite expensive, but the cheaper pizzeria serves excellent minestrone soup, generous pasta servings, rich pizzas and delicious desserts at very modest prices. V	AE DC MC V JCB			
TIBET KITCHEN Тибетская кухня $$ Kamergerskiy per 5/6. **Map** 2 F5. *923 2422.* Tibetan cuisine in a somewhat Buddhist interior, decorated with an altar and Tibetan dolls. Try the spicy soups, chicken, meat and seafood dishes in a variety of delicious sauces and venture to taste salty Tibetan tea. V	AE DC MC V		■	
YAKITORIA Якитория $$ Ulitsa Petrovka 16. **Map** 3 A4. 924 0699. Japanese restaurant serving *sushi* and a large variety of other Japanese dishes prepared by Russian chefs. Very popular with Muscovites and almost always full. A dozen other Yakitorias can be found throughout Moscow. V	MC V JCB		■	
YOLKI-PALKI Ёлки-палки $$ Ulitsa Bolshaya Dmitrovka 23/8. **Map** 2 F4 *200 0965.* One of the coziest of the 20 Yolki-Palki restaurants spread throughout Moscow. Serve yourself pickles, herring, salads, buckwheat and much more arranged on a wooden cart as a lavish buffet – a filling meal in itself. V		●	■	
CAFÉ DES ARTISTES Кафе дез Артист $$$ Kamergerskiy pereulok 5/6. **Map** 2 F5. *292 4042.* This Swiss-run restaurant serves European cuisine with a French accent. Excellent vegetable cream soups, gourmet meat dishes, delicious desserts and a large choice of wines from all over the world. V	AE DC MC V JCB			
IL POMODORO ITALIANO Итальянский помидор $$$ Strastnoy bulvar 16. **Map** 2 F3. *200 13 92.* Genuine Italian cuisine served in a pleasant environment. Excellent *carpaccio* (thinly sliced raw beef), pastas and delicious *tiramisu* dessert. V	AE DC MC V			
SCANDINAVIA Скандинавия $$$$ Malyy Palashevskiy per 7. **Map** 2 E4. *200 4986.* This spacious Swedish-run restaurant is especially popular in the summer, when you can dine under chestnut trees in its pretty courtyard. Quality European cuisine with some Swedish specialties. Excellent steaks and desserts.	AE DC MC V JCB		■	
PUSHKIN Пушкинъ $$$$$ Tverskoy bulvar 26a. **Map** 2 E4. *229 5590.* Equally popular with Russian "cream of the society" and tourists, Pushkin offers a unique Russian dining experience in the elegant antique interior. The first floor is furnished as an 18th-century pharmacy, which it used to house, and serves Russian dishes. The second floor, set as an old library, offers pricier and even more exquisite Russian and French cuisine. In the summer, enjoy the view of Tverskaya Street from the rooftop open-air terrace. V	AE DC MC V	●	■	

For key to symbols *see p173*

Price categories for a three-course meal with a glass of wine, but not including service or tax:
- $ under US$15
- $$ US$15–30
- $$$ US$30–50
- $$$$ US$50–75
- $$$$$ Over US$75.

CREDIT CARDS
Indicates which credit cards are accepted: AE American Express; DC Diners Club; MC Master Card/Access; V Visa; JCB Japanese Credit Bureau.

CIS CUISINE
Traditional cuisine from the former Soviet republics which now make up the Commonwealth of Independent States.

FIXED-PRICE LUNCH MENU
A good value lunch menu is offered.

LIVE ENTERTAINMENT
Live music and/or dancing on occasions.

CENTRAL HOUSE OF WRITERS Центральный дом литераторов $$$$$
Povarskaya ulitsa 50. **Map** 2 D5. *291 1515.*
This former exclusive Soviet writers restaurant, features elegantly carved-oak wood décor, three fireplaces, piano entertainment and a medley of delicious Russian and European dishes prepared by Russian and Italian chefs.

RED SQUARE AND KITAI GOROD

PROPAGANDA Пропаганда $
Bolshoy Zlatoustinskiy pereulok 7. **Map** 3 B5. *924 5732.*
A popular hang-out of young Muscovites and expats, Propaganda serves tasty European cuisine. Pastas, salads and milkshakes are especially recommended. After 11pm the tables are taken away and the place turns into a disco.

ART GARBAGE Запасник $$
Starosadskiy per 5/6. **Map** 3 C5. *928 8745.*
The tasty and varied Russian and European dishes here carry names of paintings. Good and inexpensive cuisine. Thursday to Saturday are concert days – there is an entry charge from 7pm and actual concerts start around 10–11pm.

JAGANNAT Джаганнат $$
Ulitsa Kuznetskiy most 11. **Map** 3 A4. *928 3580.*
Jagannat offers vegetarian cuisine and no alcohol – a rare thing in Moscow. An international, but mainly Indian menu with a salad bar. While not all dishes are great, the collection of teas from all over the world and desserts is excellent.

HOLA MEXICO! Привет Мексика! $$$
Pushechnaya ulitsa 7/5. **Map** 3 A4. *925 8251.*
Delicious Mexican favourites served in three spacious, brightly decorated halls adorned with sombrero hats and Aztec paintings. Live Latino music in the evenings Thursday through Saturday.

MAHARAJA Махараджа $$$
Ulitsa Pokrovka 2/1. **Map** 3 C5. *921 9844.*
Though more expensive than its competitors, Maharaja is a safe bet for delicious Indian food. The restaurant offers tasteful decor and a quiet, low-key atmosphere. Portions are small, but the service is attentive.

NOEV KOVCHEG Ноев ковчег $$$
Maly Ivanovskiy pereulok 9. **Map** 7 C1. *917-0717.*
Extensive, authentic Armenian menu, with a detailed explanation of each dish in English. Often full in the evenings, when you can sip the acclaimed Armenian cognac to the unobstrusive sounds of national music.

1, RED SQUARE Красная площадь, дом 1 $$$$
Red Square 1/2, in the Historical Museum. **Map** 7 A1. *925-3600.*
The food here is cooked according to old Russian recipes found in the Historical Museum archives. Try the mushrooms pickled in barrels at the bottom of a lake, *kedrach* (cedar nut vodka) and other rarities. *evenings.*

KHODZHA NASREDDIN V KHIVE Ходжа Насреддин в Хиве $$$$
Ulitsa Pokrovka 10. **Map** 3 C5. *917 0444.*
Delicious Uzbek cuisine served amidst a stunning blue, turquoise and white décor devoted to the ancient Uzbek city of Khiva. On the second floor you can dine in Eastern fashion – half-lying down on the pillows at the low tables. Clown entertainment and fairy tales for children on weekend afternoons.

GODUNOV Годуновъ $$$$
Teatralnaya ploshchad 5. **Map** 3 A5. *298 5609.*
Godunov serves excellent *borshch* with garlic *pampushki* and other rich Russian soups, delicious *pirozhki*, excellent game, a good choice of vegetarian main dishes and much more. Traditional Russian drinks as well as wines from all over the world are offered. Russian and Gypsy entertainment in the evenings.

Restaurant	Credit Cards	CIS Cuisine	Fixed-Prcie Lunch Menu	Live Entertainment
Central House of Writers	AE DC MC V	●		●
Propaganda			■	
Art Garbage	AE MC V	●	■	●
Jagannat			■	●
Hola Mexico!	AE DC MC V JCB		■	●
Maharaja	AE DC MC V JCB			
Noev Kovcheg	AE DC MC V	●	■	●
1, Red Square	AE DC MC V JCB	●	■	●
Khodzha Nasreddin v Khive	AE DC MC V JCB	●		●
Godunov	AE MC V	●		●

"NOSTALGIE" ART CLUB Арт Клуб "Ностальжи" $$$$$ — AE DC MC V
Chistoprudnyy bulvar 12a. **Map** 3 C4. *925 7625.*
High ceilings, carved wooden interior, candles and antiques – Empire style decor and very pleasant, intimate atmosphere. Excellent view of the pretty Chistye ponds. Nostalgie serves original French and Italian cuisine (a children's menu is available) and has great jazz concerts in the evenings. V

ZAMOSKVORECHE

KORCHMA TARAS BULBA Корчма Тарас Бульба $$ — MC V
Pyatnitskaya ulitsa 14. **Map** 7 B3. *951 3760.*
Hearty Ukrainian cuisine served by waiters in national costumes in a decorative interior. A large menu in all possible European and Asian languages. Excellent salads, good herring starters and a wide choice of varied main dishes. V

PICASSO Пикассо $$ — AE DC MC V
Novokuznetskaya ulitsa 6. **Map** 7 B3. *951 9892.*
European and Russian cuisine is served in a painted theatre-like interior. Extensive adult and children's menu and generous portions. Live music in the evenings for adults and parties for children on weekend afternoons. V

SHESH-BESH Шеш-Беш $$ — AE V
Pyatnitskaya ulitsa 24/1. **Map** 7 B3. *959 5862.*
Shesh-Besh serves mainly Azeri cuisine, heavy on meats, vegetables and greens, in a casual atmosphere. The good value buffet has an excellent selection of hot dishes, salads and vegetables and is a filling meal in itself. V

SULIKO Сулико $$$ — AE DC MC V
Ulitsa Bolshaya Polyanka 42/2. **Map** 7 A4. *238 2586.*
Suliko has a large and tasty Georgian menu and a typical Moscow Georgian restaurant interior – with mini-fountains, fake plants and figurines. If you prefer to skip the loud evening entertainment by a Georgian choir, avoid the main hall and ask to be seated in one of the smaller ones. The Fireplace Hall is one of the coziest, while the Green Hall has all you can eat buffet lunches from midday until 4pm every day for US$30, wine included. V

OBLOMOV Обломов $$$$ — AE DC MC V
1 Monetchikovskiy pereulok 5. **Map** 7 B4. *953 6828.*
The first floor of Oblomov is occupied by a cheaper café "Pizhon" with an art deco interior, serving European cuisine. The second and third floors are the actual restaurant, serving French and Russian cuisine. The Eastern Room on the third floor has water-pipes and even belly-dancing. The restaurant's dovecote adds flavor to the old mansion atmosphere. V

FURTHER AFIELD

AMERICAN BAR & GRILL Американский Бар и Гриль $$ — AE DC MC V JCB
Ul Zemlyanoy Val 59. **Map** 8 E2. *912 3615.*
Decorated cowboy-style, American Bar & Grill serves hearty plates of burgers, steaks, Caesar salad, chicken wings and more. Ambience is pleasant, especially in the summer evenings when tables and a brazier are put in the restaurant's courtyard. Children's menu and weekend entertainment for kids.

U PIROSMANI У Пиросмани $$$ — MC V
Novoidevichiy proezd, 4. **Map** 5 A5. *247 1926.*
Enjoy a gourmet Georgian meal in a restaurant with paintings on the walls and a picturesque view on the Novodevichiy Convent. Meats are cooked in a variety of ways: *chanahi* (lamb with aubergine (egg-plant) served in a clay dish), *abhazuri* (meats mixed with pomegranate) and other specialities. Delicious vegetable starters, salads and Georgian cheese-breads. V

KAVKAZSKAYA PLENNITSA Кавказская пленница $$$$ — AE DC MC V JCB
Prospekt Mira 36. **Map** 3 B1. *280 5111.*
Brightly decorated Georgian restaurant devoted to the Russian's favorite 1970s comedy show set in the Caucasus. In summer you can dine on the open-air terrace facing the restaurant's lovely garden. Clown entertainment for children at weekends. V

TRAKTIR KHLESTAKOV Трактиръ Хлестаковъ $$$$ — AE DC MC V JCB
3-ya Frunzenskaya ulitsa 9/1. **Map** 5 C5. *257 2692.*
This theatre-like restaurant, is named after a play by the Russian Nikolai Gogol, and features 19th-century decor, waiters attired in traditional costumes, a parrot and canaries. The menu, arranged as a 5-act play, offers authentic Russian cuisine.

For key to symbols *see p173*

Light Meals and Snacks

MOSCOW DOES NOT HAVE a café culture in the tradition of many Western European cities but, as the up-market restaurant boom continues, a more casual dining culture is growing steadily alongside it. Visitors to the Russian capital should be aware, however, that the word café does not necessarily promise coffee, nor tables. Many small establishments based on the traditional Soviet cafeteria *(stolovaya)* serve tea and sandwiches that you eat standing at a counter. But Moscow's cafés are gradually catching on to the appeal of a cosy environment in which to take a light meal, a giant step towards comfort for tourists in the city. Several American and European bars sprang up after the end of the Soviet era. They are now joined by a growing number of Russian bars, where you can sample tasty local snacks such as blini *(see p176)* along with your drink.

Where to Eat

THE CITY CENTRE has the highest concentration of cafés and bars, although they are now springing up even in Moscow's more remote areas. Most central, top-class hotels *(see pp168–173)* have their own Western-style cafés and bars. For visitors who are looking for something cheaper and with more local colour the best bet is probably just to wander around the city centre and see what they come across.

Since new cafés and bars are opening with such regularity it is a good idea to pick up a copy of Friday's edition of *The Moscow Times* or *The Moscow Tribune (see p207)*. Both of these list a selection of good venues. Another useful source of up-to-date information is *The Exile*, a biweekly English-language publication which focuses on eating out and nightlife. These papers are available at most hotels and at many restaurants and bars.

Cafés

A CHEAP, CASUAL meal out in Moscow usually means Russian food. The menu in a Russian café tends to consist of soups – borshch *(see p176)* is, of course, a favourite – salads, *buterbrod* (an open sandwich, usually topped with salami, smoked fish, cheese or pâté) and sweet pastries or tortes. Visitors will find excellent examples of such offerings at **Cafe Margarita** *(see p180)*. Some of Moscow's most appealing cafés are tucked away in shopping centres or arts venues. One stylish and popular option is **Art Club Nostalgie** *(see p181)* located inside a children's cinema complex. In a similar vein is **Café Cinema**, adjacent to the Cinema Centre *(see p193)*. This is a wonderful spot for a cup of coffee and a dish of ice cream after a film. Alternatively, **Elki-Palki**, situated in an up-market shopping arcade, offers plenty of opportunity for people-watching.

At up-market cafés, such as those usually found in expensive hotels, the menu often has a European flavour, focusing on light sandwiches and desserts and offering different varieties of coffee and tea. But even a cup of tea can be extortionately expensive. The **Amadeus Café** located in the Radisson-Slavyanskaya Hotel *(see p171)* and the **Vienna Café** in the Renaissance Moscow Hotel *(see p171)* are prime examples.

Bars

FOR SEVERAL YEARS the most popular bars in Moscow were the foreign-run ones, such as the **American Bar and Grill** and the **Crazy Milk**. The food at these bars strikes an appropriately American chord, with burgers, french fries and burritos featuring prominently on the menu. The **Hungry Duck** also serves great American bar food, although diners are advised to arrive early, before the notoriously raucous evening party scene begins.

Somewhat surprisingly, the food at the **John Bull Pub** is not English but Chinese; for some reason the combination of tasty Oriental dishes and a pint of English ale has turned out to be a great success.

Mesto vstrechi, which means Meeting Point, is located in a vault, just off Tverskaya ulitsa *(see p89)*. Decorated with paintings and sculptures, it hosts live modern Russian Jazz, and offers good food at reasonable prices.

Moscow's Russian-managed bars cater to students at one end of the spectrum and to wealthy New Russians at the other. They usually offer food such as *stolichnyy salat* (meat and vegetable salad), and blini, as well as alcoholic drinks. Russian food is well suited to a bar setting due to its emphasis on *zakuski (see p176)*. These snacks often have strong flavours and go well with a shot of vodka *(see p178)*. The menus at **Propaganda** and **Krizis Zhanra** *(see p194)*, though short, offer delicious salads and pastries, and the blini and borshch at **Vermel** are not to be missed.

Opening Times

FEW PLACES in Moscow are open 24 hours a day, but most of the more popular bars stay open until at least 2am, and some do not close until 5am. Visitors may have trouble getting food after about midnight, though.

The standby choice for after-hours dining is the **Starlite Diner** *(see p180)*, which is open around the clock. The **American Bar and Grill** *(see p181)* is also a popular choice for late night dinners and early breakfasts.

Fast Food

FAST-FOOD aficionados in Moscow can take refuge in the familiar at **McDonald's** *(see p174)*. The branch on Bolshaya Bronnaya ulitsa, on the corner of Pushkinskaya ploshchad, is the most famous.

This was the first in the city when it opened in 1990, initially attracting huge queues of Muscovites. There are now nearly a dozen McDonald's franchises around Moscow, including one convenient for shoppers on Tverskaya ulitsa *(see p89)* and another on Gazetnyy pereulok, not far from the Kremlin *(see pp52–67)*. Alternatively, visitors can grab a slice of pizza from one of the branches of **Pizza Sbarro**, or satisfy sweet-tooth cravings at **Deli France**.

Better yet, for a more authentically Russian experience, visit a branch of the **Russkoe Bistro** chain, which has been expanding rapidly thanks to support from the mayor of Moscow. Russkoe Bistro serves salads, excellent *pirozhki* – pastries filled with everything from cabbage and potatoes to liver *(see p177)* – and a refreshing, slightly alcoholic drink called *kvas (see p179)*. Look for the green and gold Russkoe Bistro signs that are now scattered all over the city. Good central branches to try include the four that are located on Tverskaya ulitsa.

Café Etiquette

In small Russian cafés, the menu is usually a handwritten affair, in Russian only and priced in roubles. But in cafés that have a Western flavour, or that have become popular with foreigners, the menu will often be translated into English. Both Russian and expatriate bars usually have menus in Russian and English. Most Russian bars that serve food, and virtually all foreign-run bars, accept credit cards, but Russian cafés rarely do.

Tipping is, by and large, unnecessary in Russian bars and cafés, unless the service has been particularly good. However, in a Western-style venue it is usual to add a tip.

The atmosphere in Moscow's bars and cafés is notoriously smoky. Smoking is not only acceptable everywhere, but seems almost *de rigeur*. Those sensitive to smoky air may well run into difficulties.

Directory

Cafés

Amadeus Café
Амадэус кафе
Radisson-Slavyanskaya Hotel, Berezhkovskaya naberezhnaya 2.
Map 5 B2.
941 8020 ext 3298.

Art Club Nostalgie
Арт клуб ностальжи
Chistoprudnyy bulvar 12a.
Map 3 C4.
916 9478.

Café Cinema
Кафе Синема
Druzhinnikovskaya ulitsa 15.
Map 1 C5.
255 9116.

Deli France
Дели Франс
Tverskaya ulitsa 31.
Map 2 E3.
299 4284.

Donna Klara
Донна Клара
Ulitsa Malaya Bronnaya 21/13. **Map** 2 E4.
290 3848.

Elki-Palki
Елки-палки
Ulitsa Novyy Arbat 11, 2nd floor. **Map** 6 E1.
291 6888

Vienna Café
Венское кафе
Venskoe Kafe
Renaissance Moscow Hotel, Olimpiyskiy prospekt 18/1.
Map 3 A1.
931 9000 ext 2422.

Bars

American Bar and Grill
Американский бар и гриль
Amerikanskiy bar i gril
1-ya Tverskaya-Yamskaya ulitsa 2/1.
Map 2 E3.
251 9671.

Angara
Ангара
Ulitsa Novyy Arbat 19.
Map 6 D1.
203 6936.

Crazy Milk
Крэзи Милк
Ulitsa Bolshaya Polyanka 54. **Map** 7 B5.
230 7333.

Hungry Duck
Хангри дак
Pushechnaya ulitsa 9/6.
Map 3 A4.
923 6158.

John Bull Pub
Smolenskaya ploshchad 2/9.
Map 5 C1.
241 0644.

Mesto Vstrechi
Место встречи
Tverskaya 17. **Map** 2 F4.
229 2373.

Na Semi Kholmakh
На семи холмах
Soimonovskiy proezd 7.
Map 6 E2.
202 6617.

Propaganda
Пропаганда
Bolshaya Zlatoustinskiy pereulok 7. **Map** 3 B5.
924 5732.

Rosie O'Grady's
Ul Znamenka 9/12.
Map 6 F1.
203 9087.

Sally O'Brien's
Салли о'брайнс
Ul Bolshaya Polyanka 1/3.
Map 7 A3.
959 0182.

Sports Bar
Спорт бар
Ulitsa Novyy Arbat 10.
Map 6 E1.
290 4311.

U Yara
У Яра
Hotel Sovetskiy *(see p170)*, Leningradskiy prospekt 33.
Map 1 B1.
945 3168.

Vermel
Вермель
Raushskaya naberezhnaya 4/5.
Map 7 B2.
959 3303.

The Zoo
Зоопарк
Zoopark
Kudrinskaya ploshchad 1.
Map 2 D5.
255 4144.

Fast-Food Restaurants

McDonald's
МакДоналдс
Bolshaya Bronnaya ulitsa 29.
Map 2 E4.
200 5896.
Ulitsa Arbat 50/52.
Map 6 D2.
241 3681.
Gazetnyy pereulok 17/9.
Map 2 F5.
956 9817.

Pizza NA Kutuzovskom
Пицца НА Кутузовском
Kutuzovskiy prospekt 17.
Map 5 A2.
243 1727.

Pizza Sbarro
Пицца Сбарро
Tverskaya ulitsa 10.
Map 2 F4.
229 2013.

Russkoe Bistro
Русское бистро
Tverskaya ulitsa 19a.
Map 2 E4.
299 3800.

Shops and Markets

RUSSIA'S APPETITE for Western goods means that Moscow now offers most of the shopping facilities of a large, modern Western city. There are supermarkets, department stores stocking imported goods and exclusive boutiques with French and Italian designer clothes and shoes for the new rich.

Moscow's most interesting shopping districts are located within the Garden Ring. The main department stores are clustered around the city centre near Red Square, while the best souvenir and antique shops can be found along ulitsa Arbat *(see pp 70–71)*, a charming old pedestrian street. For the more adventurous a trip to the weekend flea market at Izmaylovo Park is a must. Here it is possible to buy everything from Russian dolls and Soviet memorabilia to handmade rugs from Central Asia and antique jewellery.

Russian doll

A display counter in the sumptuously decorated Yeliseev's Food Hall *(see p186)*

Opening Hours

MOSCOW'S SHOPS and businesses rarely open before 10am and often not until 11am. Most stay open until around 7pm. Many shops, especially old, state-run stores, close for an hour at lunchtime, either from 1pm to 2pm, or from 2pm to 3pm. Shops are usually open all day on Saturdays, and nowadays many are also open on Sundays, although often for shorter hours.

Markets generally operate from 10am to 4pm but it is necessary to go in the morning to get the best choice of goods.

How to Pay

UNTIL RECENTLY MANY food shops, department stores and state-run souvenir *(berezhka)* shops used the *kassa* system of payment. This involved visiting several cashier's desks and could be confusing for the uninitiated. Nowadays, the *kassa* system is pretty rare in Moscow and there are hundreds of Western-type shops of all sizes. Throughout the city there are several chain stores, for example, Sedmoi Kontinent, Kopeika, Perekrestok and Ramstor. The latter offers a huge range of products from food to clothes. There are also a few hypermarkets.

The only legal currency in Russia is the rouble and most shops will not accept other currencies. Vendors at the tourist markets may quote prices in US dollars. However, this will not guarantee a discount and visitors should bear in mind that it is illegal. Now that the rampant inflation of the early 1990s is under control there should rarely be pressure to pay in hard currency.

Western-style supermarkets and shops, as well as some up-market Russian boutiques, accept the main credit cards.

A new Western boutique in Moscow's largest department store, GUM

Some shops still display prices in US dollars or, very occasionally, in units that have a fixed rate of exchange with roubles. If so the price will be converted into roubles, at a higher than average exchange rate, before payment is made. Paying by credit card avoids this as credit card slips are nearly always made out in US dollars.

Prices for most goods include 15 per cent VAT. Only staples such as locally produced milk and bread are exempt.

There are a few duty-free shops in the centre of Moscow and at Sheremetevo 2 airport.

Department Stores

THE MOST FAMOUS department store in Russia is the State Department Store, known by its acronym, **GUM** *(see p107)*. Its beautiful edifice houses three arcades of shops under a glass roof. It was built at the end of the 19th century, just before the Revolution put an end to such luxurious capitalism. During Soviet times GUM stocked the same goods as other department stores in the city and was very dingy and run-down. It has recently been renovated and now houses several top Western chains, as well as speciality shops and boutiques. Items such as cosmetics, medicines, cameras and electronic goods are all available along with clothes and household goods.

Moscow's other large department store is **TsUM**, the Central Department Store. Formerly cheaper and a little shabbier than GUM, it has now been

Replica icons on sale at the Trinity Monastery of St Sergius ***(see pp156–9)***

thoroughly renovated and is too expensive for most ordinary Muscovites.

Detskiy Mir (Children's World) is the largest children's store in Russia. It stocks toys made in Russia, model kits and sporting equipment as well as a wide range of imported toys. In the Soviet era the cavernous halls were often almost empty. Now the colourful displays of toys reflect the new affluence of Muscovites and there is even a luxury car showroom for the grown-ups.

Souvenirs on sale at the flea market in Izmaylovo Park

Bazaars and Markets

Many Muscovites buy their cheese, meat, and fresh fruit and vegetables at one of a number of big produce markets dotted around the city. One of the biggest and most picturesque food markets is the **Danilovskiy Market**, which takes its name from the nearby Danilovskiy Monastery *(see pp136–7)*. Also well worth a visit is the colourful **Basmannyy Market** in the heart of the former Nemtskaya Sloboda (German Settlement).

Izmaylovo Market is a flea market held every weekend at Izmaylovo Park *(see p141)*. It is a treasure trove of old and new. All the usual souvenirs are on sale, including Soviet memorabilia and painted Russian *matryoshka* dolls *(see p188)*, as well as antique silver and jewellery, icons, samovars, china and glassware, fur hats, amber and some of the best Central Asian rugs in Russia. In recent years many local artists and craftspeople have set up their stalls here, and a huge range of strange and beautiful toys and decorations makes it easy to browse happily for hours.

Museum Shops

There is a small, but excellent, souvenir shop at the **Museum of Modern History**. Its stock includes old Soviet posters, stamps and badges, amber and lacquer boxes. Both the **Pushkin Museum of Fine Art** *(see pp78–81)* and the **Tretyakov Gallery** *(see pp118–121)* sell a good selection of art books with English commentaries.

Bargaining Etiquette

Visitors who speak a little Russian can have fun negotiating prices for their fruit and vegetables at produce markets. Many vendors come from long-established trading families and expect buyers to bargain for every purchase. However, visitors should not expect to get the better of these enthusiastic salesmen. Most vendors are from the Caucasus and southern Russia, where the best fresh produce is grown.

Many vendors at souvenir markets speak enough English to bargain, but it is not always possible to negotiate a discount as salespeople have a good idea of what they can get for an item and will not want to undercut each other.

The Central Asian salesmen at the carpet market at Izmaylovo Park are persuasive, but as a rule of thumb the first price they name is about twice what they can afford to accept. The customer should open bargaining by halving the first price and expect to agree on a price somewhere in between. Only those who are fairly certain they want to buy should begin bargaining. Once a price is agreed it can be hard to walk away without causing offence.

A stall selling fresh vegetables and herbs at the Danilovskiy Market

Buying Antiques

It is very difficult to take any items made before 1945 out of Russia *(see p200)*. All outgoing luggage is x-rayed by customs officials to check for precious metals, works of art, rugs and icons, and complete documentation for all these objects is required before they can be exported. Permission to export antiques and art can only be obtained from the **Ministry of Culture**. This process takes at least two weeks and an export tax of 50 per cent of the ministry's assessment of the antiques' value will have to be paid.

It is safest to restrict purchases to items less than 50 years old. However, customs inspectors at the airport may still want to see receipts and documentation that proves the age of the objects.

Samovars and other items for sale in one of the many antiques shops along ulitsa Arbat

Where to Shop in Moscow

The increasing number of Western-style shops means that buying food, toiletries and holiday supplies such as photographic film and batteries is much easier than it used to be. Shopping no longer involves queuing for as long as in Soviet times, or visiting hard-currency stores open only to foreigners and the privileged. However, high import duties, transportation costs and the relative lack of competition make consumer goods considerably more expensive than in the West. Far more exciting buys are the colourful Russian arts and crafts available at many locations throughout the city. Exotic goods from the ex-Soviet Republics of Central Asia and memorabilia from the Soviet era also make interesting purchases.

Vodka and Caviar

When buying vodka and caviar there are a few points to remember. It is advisable to buy tins of caviar rather than jars, but even tins should be kept refrigerated at all times. It is best to avoid buying from street stalls or kiosks. Caviar is available from most supermarkets but, for a real Russian shopping experience, go to the slightly run-down **Yeliseev's Food Hall** *(see p89)*. This pre-Revolutionary delicatessen, known as Gastronom No. 1 in Soviet times, boasts chandeliers and stained-glass windows.

There is a great deal of bootleg vodka about, which can be highly poisonous. It is essential to ensure that there is a pink tax label stuck over the top of any bottle of vodka and none should ever be bought on the street. Popular vodkas such as Stolichnaya and Moskovskaya *(see p178)* are available from most supermarkets, including **Sedmoi Kontinent** and **Ramstor**, two of the best Western-style ones. Vodka is also sold in small grocery stores. There are no restrictions on when alcohol can be sold.

Vodka and caviar are also available at the duty-free shops at the airports *(see p208)*, but are much cheaper in town.

Arts and Crafts

Low labour costs mean that handmade goods are generally cheaper here than in the West and they make exotic and interesting souvenirs to take home. The best places to buy are the markets, such as the **Izmaylovo Market** *(see p185)*, and souvenir shops on ulitsa Arbat *(see pp70–71)*. Lacquer trays and bowls, painted china and *matryoshka* dolls can be bought at **Arbatskaya Lavitsa**. Handmade lace and embroidery are on sale in **Russkaya Vyshivka**, while for Russian jewellery and amber visitors should try **Samotsvety**.

A good range of arts and crafts is also available at shops elsewhere in the city, such as **Russkiy Uzory**. **Russkaya Galereia** has an exhibition of paintings for sale, as well as jewellery and lacquer boxes. For more unusual souvenirs, try **Dom Farfora**, which sells hand-painted tea sets and Russian crystal, and the **Salon of the Moscow Cultural Fund**, which has samovars, old lamps and some whimsical sculptures and mobiles.

Antiques

The new Russian rich are hungry for antiques and dealers know the value of goods, so the bargains of a few years ago are no longer available. It is also worth noting that exporting objects made before 1945 from Russia involves a lot of expense and effort *(see p185)*. However, it is still well worth exploring the many wonderful shops full of treasures.

Ulitsa Arbat has many of the best antique shops in Moscow. **Kupina Antiques** offers a good selection of icons, silver, jewellery and china, while **Elisey** has a variety of interesting Soviet porcelain. For larger pieces and furniture visitors should go to **Tradition and Personality**, and **Rokoko** which sells goods for people for a commission. **The Foreign Book Store**, which is principally a bookshop, also sells furniture and a lot of china, lamps and bric-a-brac.

Fashion and Accessories

There are many boutiques in the centre of town around **GUM** *(see p107)* and **TsUM** *(see p184)* and along Tverskaya ulitsa *(see p89)*. The centre also has two arcades. **Petrovskiy Passage** has clothes and shoes as well as furniture and electrical goods. **Gallery Aktyor**, a modern, three-storey arcade, contains Western and designer stores selling clothes, French perfumes and jewellery from Tiffany and Cartier. Clothes by Russian designers are gradually appearing in Moscow's shops.

A little further out from the centre is **Sadko Arcade**, a large shopping and restaurant complex with two supermarkets as well as speciality shops and boutiques. At these more up-market arcades most of the shops accept credit cards.

Authentic Russian fur hats are sold in Petrovskiy Passage and on the second floor of GUM, and there's always a wide range available in winter at Izmaylovo Market.

Books and Music

For English-language books **Anglia British Bookshop**, **Shakespeare & Co** and **Dom Inostrannoi Knigi** are probably the best shops to visit. The enormous **Moscow House of Books** sells some English-language books, and also CDs, records, old icons and Soviet propaganda posters. **Biblio Globus** is a another bookshop well worth having a browse in, while the **Moskva Trade House** deals in Russian and foreign books, as well as selling stamps, art books, small antiques and paintings. **Melodiya** sells a wide range of CDs, records and cassettes of Russian orchestras and performers.

Directory

Department Stores

Detskiy Mir
Детский мир
Teatralnyy proezd 5.
Map 3 A5.
☎ *972 2007.*

GUM
ГУМ
Krasnaya ploshchad 3.
Map 3 A5.
☎ *921 5763.*

TsUM
ЦУМ
Ulitsa Petrovka 2.
Map 3 A4.
☎ *292 1157.*

Bazaars and Markets

Basmannyy Market
Басманный рынок
Baumanskaya ulitsa 47/1.
Map 4 F2.

Danilovskiy Market
Даниловский рынок
Danilovskiy rynok
Mytnaya ulitsa 74.

Izmaylovo Market
Рынок Измайлово
Rynok Izmaylovo
Izmaylovskoe shosse.

Museum Shops

Museum of Modern History
Музей современной истории
Muzey sovremennoy istorii
Tverskaya ulitsa 21.
Map 2 E4.
☎ *299 5217.*

Pushkin Museum of Fine Art
Музей изобразительных искусств имени АС Пушкина
Muzey izobrazitelnykh iskusstv imeni AS Pushkina
Ulitsa Volkhonka 12.
Map 6 F2.
☎ *203 7998.*

Tretyakov Gallery
Третьяковская галерея
Tretyakovskaya galereya
Lavrushinskiy pereulok 12.
Map 7 A3.
☎ *951 1362.*

Vodka and Caviar

Sedmoi Kontinent
Седьмой Континент
Bolshaya Gruzinskaya ul 63.
Map 2 D2.
☎ *251 8835.*

Ulitsa Bolshaya Lubyanka 12.
Map 3 B4.
☎ *928 9527.*

Yeliseev's Food Hall
Елисеевский гастроном
Yeliseevskiy gastronom
Tverskaya ulitsa 14.
Map 2 F4.
☎ *209 0760.*

Arts and Crafts

Arbatskaya Lavitsa
Арбатская Лавица
Ulitsa Arbat 27.
Map 6 E1.
☎ *290 5689.*

Dom Farfora
Дом фарфора
Leninskiy prospekt 36.
☎ *137 6023.*

Russkaya Galereia
Ulitsa Vozdvizhenka 5.
Map 6 E1. ☎ *203 1306.*

Russkiy Uzory
Русские узоры
Ulitsa Petrovka 16.
Map 3 A4.
☎ *923 1883.*

Russkaya Vyshivka
Русская вышивка
Ulitsa Arbat 31.
Map 6 D1.
☎ *241 2841.*

Salon of the Moscow Cultural Fund
Салон Московского фонда культуры
Salon Moskovskovo fonda kultury
Pyatnitskaya ulitsa 16.
Map 7 B3.
☎ *951 3302.*

Samotsvety
Самоцветы
Ulitsa Arbat 35.
Map 6 D1.
☎ *241 0765.*

Antiques

Antikvaz-Metropol
Антиквар-Метрополь
Teatralniy proezd 1/4.
Map 3 A5.
☎ *927 6979.*

Elisey
Елисей
Ulitsa Arbat 4.
Map 6 E1. ☎ *291 7444.*

Kupina Antiques
Антиквариат Купина
Ulitsa Arbat 18.
Map 6 D1.
☎ *202 4462.*

Rokoko
Рококо
Frunzenskaya nab 54.
☎ *242 3664.*

Tradition and Personality
Традиция и личность
Traditsiya i lichnost
Ulitsa Arbat 2, 2nd floor.
Map 6 E1.
☎ *290 6294.*

Fashion and Accessories

Gallery Aktyor
Галерея Актер
Tverskaya ulitsa 16/2.
Map 2 F4. ☎ *290 9832.*

Petrovskiy Passage
Петровский Пассаж
Ulitsa Petrovka 10.
Map 3 A4.
☎ *928 5012.*

Sadko Arcade
Садко Аркада
Krasnopresnenskaya naberezhnaya 14 .
☎ *253 9592.*

Books and Music

Anglia British Bookshop
Англия британские книги
Angliya britanskie knigi
Khlebnyy pereulok 2.
Map 2 E5.
☎ *203 5802.*

Biblio Globus
Библио Глобус
Miasnitskaya ul. 6.
Map 3 B5.
☎ *928 3567.*

Dom Inostrannoi Knigi
Доминостраннои книги
Ulitsa Kuznetskiy most 18.
Map 3 A4.
☎ *928 2021.*

The Foreign Book Store
Иностранная книга
Inostrannaya kniga
Malaya Nikitskaya ul 16/5.
Map 2 D5.
☎ *290 4082.*

Moskva Trade House
Торговый дом Москва
Torgovyy dom Moskva
Tverskaya ulitsa 8.
Map 2 F4.
☎ *229 6483.*

Moscow House of Books
Московский Дом книги
Moskovskiy Dom knigi
Ulitsa Novyy Arbat 8.
Map 6 D1 ☎ *290 3580.*

Rapsodia
Рапсодия
Miasnitskaya ulitsa 17.
Map 3 B4.
☎ *921 7058.*

Shakespeare & Co
Щекспир и компания
Novokuznetskiy pereulok 5/7.
Map 7 C4.
☎ *951 936.*

What to Buy in Moscow

Intricate wooden box

It is easy to find interesting and beautiful souvenirs in Moscow. Traditional crafts were encouraged by the State in the old Soviet Union, so many age-old skills were kept alive. Artisans today continue to produce items ranging from small, low-cost, enamelled badges through to more expensive hand-painted Palekh boxes, samovars and worked semi-precious stones. Other popular items are lacquered trays and bowls, chess sets, wooden toys and *matryoshka* dolls. Memorabilia from the Soviet era also make good souvenirs and Russia is definitely the best place to buy the national specialities, vodka and caviar.

Samovar

Used to boil water to make tea, samovars (see p179) *come in many sizes. A permit is needed to export a pre-1945 samovar.*

Vodka and Caviar

An enormous variety of both clear and flavoured vodkas (such as lemon and pepper) is available (see p178). *They make excellent accompaniments to black caviar* (ikra) *and red caviar* (keta), *which are often served with* blini (see p176).

Flavoured vodka

Clear vodka

Red caviar

Black caviar

Malachite egg

Amber ring

Semi-precious Stones

Malachite, amber, jasper and a variety of marbles from the Ural mountains are used to make a wide range of items – everything from jewellery to chess sets and inlaid table tops.

Wooden Toys

These crudely carved wooden toys often have moving parts. They are known as bogorodskie *toys and make charming gifts.*

Matryoshka Dolls

These dolls fit one inside the other and come in a huge variety of styles. The traditional dolls are the prettiest, but the models painted to represent Soviet political leaders are also very popular.

Chess Sets

Chess is an extremely popular pastime in Russia. Chess sets made from all kinds of materials, including malachite, are available. This beautiful wooden set is painted in the same folkloric style as the traditional matryoshka *dolls.*

Lacquered Artifacts

Painted wooden or papier-mâché artifacts make popular souvenirs and are sold all over the city. The exquisite hand-painted, lacquered Palekh boxes can be very costly, but the eggs decorated with icons and the typical red, black and gold bowls are more affordable.

Palekh Box
The art of miniature painting on papier-mâché items originated in the late 18th century. Artists in the four villages of Palekh, Fedoskino, Mstera and Kholuy still produce these hand-painted marvels. The images are based on Russian fairytales and legends.

Painted wooden egg

Bowl with Spoon
The brightly painted bowls and spoons usually known as "Khokhloma" have a lacquer coating, forming a surface which is durable, but not resistant to boiling liquids.

Russian hand-painted tray

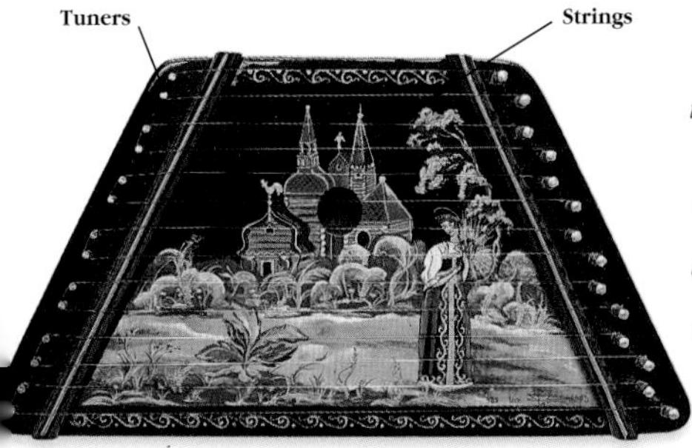

Traditional Musical Instruments
Russian folk music uses a wide range of musical instruments. This gusli *is similar to the Western psaltery, and is played by plucking the strings with both hands. Also available are the balalaika and the* garmon, *which resembles a concertina.*

Russian Shawl
These brilliantly coloured, traditional woollen shawls are good for keeping out the cold of a Russian winter. Mass-produced polyester versions are also available, mostly in big department stores, but they will not be as warm.

Gzhel Vase
Ceramics with a distinctive blue and white pattern are produced in Gzhel, a town near Moscow. Ranging from figurines to household crockery, they are popular with Russians and visitors alike.

Soviet Memorabilia
A wide array of memorabilia from Soviet times can be bought. Old banknotes, coins, pocket watches and all sorts of Red Army kit, including belt buckles and badges, can be found, together with more recent watches with cartoons of KGB agents on their faces.

Pocket watch

Badge with Soviet symbols

Red Army leather belt

Entertainment in Moscow

Moscow offers many forms of entertainment, from great theatre productions, operas and ballets to a wide choice of lively nightlife venues.

Attending a performance at the historic Bolshoy Theatre *(see pp90–91)* remains a must for opera and ballet buffs. Other theatres put on an enormous range of productions, including musicals and special shows for children.

A neon sign advertising one of Moscow's casinos *(see p195)*

Moscow has several cinemas screening foreign-language films. They usually show the latest Western releases only a few weeks after they are premiered in the West. The city also has around 300 nightclubs and many late-night bars and cafés, some of which have live bands. In addition, there is always plenty of free entertainment from street performers, especially on ulitsa Arbat *(see pp70–71)*.

A performance of the opera *Boris Godunov* at the Bolshoy Theatre

Practical Information

Moscow does not have any conventional tourist information offices. However, listings for events such as films, plays, concerts and exhibitions, together with extensive lists of restaurants, bars and nightclubs can be found in the Friday editions of the English-language newspapers *The Moscow Times* and *The Moscow Tribune*. Restaurants and nightclubs are also listed in the English-language *The Exile*. These are available free at large hotels and Western-run restaurants and bars.

Visitors to Moscow should note that the safest way to get back from late-night events is in an official taxi booked in advance *(see p212)*.

Booking Tickets

By far the easiest way to book tickets for a concert, a ballet, an opera or the theatre is through one of the main international hotels, even for visitors not staying there. Both Western-style and Russian-run hotels will usually offer this service. However, tickets bought in this way are often more expensive than those available elsewhere. Hotel ticket-booking desks accept payment by major credit cards, but many will charge a fee for doing so.

Visitors who speak Russian will be able to buy cheaper tickets from a theatre ticket kiosk *(teatralnaya kassa)*. These kiosks are scattered all round the city and in metro stations.

Another alternative is to book tickets at the venues. Although these tickets are usually the cheapest, it can require a lot of patience to obtain them since ticket offices open at unpredictable hours and do not usually sell tickets more than three days in advance.

There are ticket touts outside most

Posters for theatre performances

The Moscow State Circus

Russians have always loved the circus. In the 18th and 19th centuries it was the most popular theatrical entertainment. Troupes travelled round the country performing mostly satirical shows. Today the renowned Moscow State Circus has its permanent home in Moscow. It is famous for its clowns, for the breathtaking stunts of its acrobats and trapeze artists and for its performing animals. The latter often include tigers jumping through burning hoops and bears riding bicycles, and animal-lovers should be aware that they may find some acts distressing.

The original venue, now known as the **Old Circus**, was built in 1880 by Albert Salamonskiy for his private troupe. Salamonskiy's Circus became the Moscow State Circus in 1919. The **New Circus** was built in 1973. Both venues are now in use.

The big top of the New Circus, second venue of the Moscow State Circus

The Arts Cinema *(see p193)*, one of the oldest cinemas in Moscow

events, especially those at the Bolshoy Theatre. However, there is a risk that their tickets are counterfeit and they will almost certainly be overpriced.

Children's Entertainment

Traditional Russian entertainments for children have always included the puppet theatre, the zoo and the circus. Moscow has two puppet theatres: the **Obraztsov Puppet Theatre** *(see p192)*, which puts on matinee performances for children, and the **Moscow Puppet Theatre**. The **Nataliya Sats Children's Musical Theatre** performs excellent shows, great for children of all ages.

The **Russian Academic Youth Theatre** *(see p88)* puts on performances suitable for children from the age of seven.

Moscow Zoo is a great favourite but, unfortunately, the animals often look underfed and cramped in their cages.

The **Durov Animal Theatre** puts on shows that feature trained tigers, elephants and seals, and mice operating a toy railway. In the intervals children are allowed to play with some of the animals and have their photos taken with them. Performances at the **Kuklachev Cat Theatre** include cats pushing toy prams and jumping through hoops. Visitors to both theatres may find some acts upsetting.

At **Arlecchino Children's Club** children can play with toys and computer games or be entertained by clowns.

Miracle City at Gorky Park is an outdoor, Western-style amusement complex

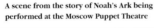

A scene from the story of Noah's Ark being performed at the Moscow Puppet Theatre

Paddle boats, one of the many attractions on offer in Gorky Park

which opens from late spring until late October. Children under 1.2 m (4 ft) tall are given free entry to all the children's rides, which include merry-go-rounds, trains and mini racing cars. There are also adult rides, such as a roller coaster, some of which allow children if accompanied by a grown-up.

Also in Gorky Park is the **Buran Shuttle**. This space shuttle is unusual – its single test flight was unmanned. It has now been converted into a simulator and provides a great chance to experience space flight. Visitors can also sample the tubes of foods such as soups and pâtés that Russian cosmonauts typically eat.

Directory

Arlecchino Children's Club
Детский клуб Арлекино
Detskiy klub Arlekino
Verkhnyaya Radishchevskaya ul 19/3, stroenie 1.
Map 8 E3.
915 1106/07.

Buran Shuttle
Космический корабль Буран
Kosmicheskiy korabl Buran
Gorky Park, ulitsa Krymskiy val 9. **Map** 6 F4.
237 0832.

Durov Animal Theatre
Театр зверей имени Дурова
Teatr zverey imeni Durova
Ulitsa Durova 4. **Map** 3 A1.
971 3047.

Kuklachev Cat Theatre
Театр кошек Куклачёва
Teatr koshek Kuklacheva
Kutuzovskiy prospekt 25.
249 2907.

Miracle City
Чудоград
Chudograd
Gorky Park, ulitsa Krymskiy val 9. **Map** 6 F4.
236 3112.

Moscow Puppet Theatre
Московский кукольный театр
Moskovskiy kukolnyy teatr
Spartakovskaya ulitsa 26.
Map 4 F2.
261 2197.

Moscow Zoo
Зоопарк
Zoopark
Bolshaya Gruzinskaya ul 1.
Map 1 C4.
252 3580.
www.zoo.ru

Nataliya Sats Children's Musical Theatre
Детский музыкальный театр имени Наталии Сац
Detskiy muzykalnyy teatr imeni Natalii Sats
Vernadskovo prospekt 5.
Near Sparrow Hills *(see p129)*. *930 7021.*

New Circus
Новый цирк
Novyy tsirk
Vernadskovo prospekt 7.
Near Sparrow Hills *(see p129)*. *930 0272.*

Obraztsov Puppet Theatre
Кукольный театр имени Образцова
Kukolnyy teatr imeni Obraztsova
Ulitsa Sadovaya-Samotechnaya 3.
Map 3 A2.
299 5373.

Old Circus
Старый цирк
Staryy tsirk
Tsvetnoy bulvar 13.
Map 3 A3.
200 0668.
www.circusnikulin.ru

Russian Academic Youth Theatre
Российский академический молодёжный театр
Rossiyskiy akademicheskiy molodezhnyy teatr
Teatralnaya ploshchad 2.
Map 3 A5.
292 0069.

The Arts in Moscow

FROM JUNE UNTIL LATE SEPTEMBER most of Moscow's concert halls and theatres close and the city's orchestras, theatre and ballet companies perform elsewhere in Russia and abroad. However, for the rest of the year the city has a rich and varied cultural scene. The Bolshoy Theatre *(see pp90–91)*, Moscow's oldest and most famous opera and ballet house, offers an impressive repertoire. Numerous drama theatres put on a variety of plays in Russian, ranging from the conventional to the avant-garde. For non-Russian speakers there is a wide choice of events, ranging from folk dance and gypsy music to classical concerts by top international musicians. Evening performances at most venues begin at 7pm or 7:30pm, while matinées generally start around midday.

BALLET AND OPERA

THERE ARE NUMEROUS venues in Moscow where visitors can see high-quality ballet and opera. Undoubtedly the most famous is the **Bolshoy Theatre**, originally built in 1780. Despite two major fires the theatre has existed on its present site ever since. Today the Bolshoy is still the best venue in Moscow in which to see opera and ballet. Its magnificent main auditorium accommodates some 2,500 people. The world-famous ballets danced there by the company include *Giselle* by Adolphe Adam and *Swan Lake* and *The Nutcracker* by Pyotr Tchaikovsky. The theatre's operatic repertoire includes a number of works by Russian composers. Among them are *Boris Godunov* by Modest Mussorgsky, *The Queen of Spades* and *Eugene Onegin* by Pyotr Tchaikovsky, and *Sadko* by Nikolai Rimsky-Korsakov.

Another much younger company, the Kremlin Ballet Company, can be seen at the **State Kremlin Palace** *(see p56)* in the Kremlin. This gigantic steel and glass building, originally constructed in 1961 as a convention hall for the Communist Party, has a 6,000-seat auditorium. It is a prime venue for those wishing to see visiting Western opera singers, as well as for ballet.

Less grandiose, but nevertheless high-quality, operas and ballets are performed at the **Helicon Opera**, the **Novaya Opera** and the **Stanislavskiy and Nemirovich-Danchenko Musical Theatre**. As its name implies, the **Operetta Theatre** performs operettas, while the **Gnesin Music Academy Opera Studio** stages more experimental productions.

CLASSICAL MUSIC

MOSCOW HAS a strong tradition of classical music and has long been home to several top international music events. One of Moscow's most famous classical music venues is the **Tchaikovsky Concert Hall**. The main feature of this large circular auditorium is a giant pipe organ, which has 7,800 pipes and weighs approximately 20 tonnes. It was made in Czechoslovakia and was installed in 1959.

The **Moscow Conservatory** *(see p94)* is both an educational establishment and a venue for concerts of classical music. It was founded in 1866 and Pyotr Tchaikovsky *(see p153)*, then a young composer at the beginning of his brilliant career, taught here for 12 years. Nowadays the conservatory has more than 1,000 music students at any one time.

The Bolshoy Zal (Great Hall) is used for orchestral concerts, both by the resident orchestra at the conservatory and by visiting orchestras. The Malyy Zal (Small Hall) is used for recitals by smaller ensembles. Over the years many prominent musicians have performed here and every four years the conservatory plays host to the prestigious Tchaikovsky International Competition *(see p33)*. Moscow's most prestigious classical music gathering is the annual Svyatoslav Richter December Nights festival *(see p35)*. Held in the Pushkin Museum of Fine Arts *(see pp78–81)*, the concerts attract a star-studded array of Russian and foreign musicians. In the intervals, the audience is invited to stroll around some of the museum's galleries.

In summer both indoor and outdoor concerts are held outside Moscow at Kuskovo *(see pp142–3)* on Tuesday and Thursday evenings.

THEATRE

MOSCOW HAS more than 60 theatres. Unlike those in many other countries most are repertory theatres. This means that a different production is staged every night. It is therefore crucial that those wishing to see a particular production check when it is on. Listings can be found in the Friday editions of *The Moscow Times* or *The Moscow Tribune*, or in *The Exile (see p207)*.

The **Moscow Arts Theatre** *(see p92)* stages a wide repertoire, but it is particularly famous for its productions of Anton Chekhov's plays, such as *The Seagull*. In constrast, the **Lenkom Theatre** produces musicals and plays by contemporary Russian playwrights.

The **Malyy Theatre**, which is situated across the street from the Bolshoy, is worth visiting since it was Russia's first drama theatre and played a major role in the development of Russian theatre.

The **Obraztsov Puppet Theatre** *(see p191)* is as entertaining for adults as it is for children. It was founded in 1931 and is named after its first director, Sergey Obraztsov. The theatre's repertoire is outstanding and most of the plays can be enjoyed without a knowledge of the Russian language. Evening performances may only be open to those over the age of 18.

Performances at the **Gypsy Theatre** consist of traditional gypsy dancing and singing. Performances of Russian folk dancing are held at various venues throughout Moscow.

Film

The Russian film industry flourished under the Soviet regime and Lenin *(see p28)* himself recognized the value of films for conveying messages. Specially commissioned films shown throughout Russia on modified trains, for example, informed much of the rural population that there had been a revolution in the capital.

Until the Soviet Union's collapse in 1991, the film industry was run by the state. Films were subsidized and their subject matter closely monitored. Russian film-makers now have artistic freedom, but suffer from a shortage of funding. Most cinemas show American blockbusters, but audiences are often relatively small. Recent Russian releases are hard to find in cinemas but can be obtained on video.

Many cinemas have out-of-date equipment, muffled sound and uncomfortable seats, but two central Russian-language cinemas, the **Rossiya** and the **Udarnik**, offer digital sound and good facilities. The **Arts Cinema** is one of the oldest in Moscow. Its sound system is not as good as those at the Rossiya and the Udarnik, but it remains one of the city's most popular cinemas. It shows the latest Russian releases and Western films in Russian. It is also a venue for film festivals.

Kodak Cinema World shows the latest US releases, both in English and in Russian. Moscow also has two English-language cinemas, the **Dome Cinema** at the Renaissance Moscow Hotel *(see p171)* and the **American House of Cinema** within the Radisson-Slavyanskaya Hotel *(see p171)*.

Films from Europe and India can be seen in their original languages at the **Illuzion** and the **Cinema Centre**. The latter is also the venue where the Moscow International Film Festival *(see p33)* is held.

The listings will inform visitors what is on and in what language. Tickets for films can only be bought at the cinemas themselves. At most payment is in cash, but the American House of Cinema, the Dome and Kodak Cinema World accept all major credit cards.

Directory

Ballet and Opera

Bolshoy Theatre
Большой театр
Teatralnaya ploshchad 1.
Map 3 A4. 250 7317.
www.bolshoi.ru

Gnesin Music Academy Opera Studio
Оперная студия академии музыки имени Гнесиных
Opernaya studiya akademii muzyki imeni Gnesinykh
Povarskaya ulitsa 30/36.
Map 2 D5.
290 2422.

Helicon Opera
Геликон опера
Gelikon opera
Bolshaya Nikitskaya ulitsa 19. **Map** 2 E5.
290 0971.

Novaya Opera
Новая опера
Ulitsa Karetnyy ryad 3.
Map 2 F3.
200 0868.

Operetta Theatre
Театр оперетты
Teatr operetty
Ulitsa Bolshaya Dmitrovka 6.
Map 3 A4.
292 1237.

State Kremlin Palace
Государственный Кремлёвский дворец
Gosudarstvennyy Kremlevskiy Dvorets
Kremlin.
Map 7 A1.
917 2336.

Stanislavskiy and Nemirovich-Danchenko Musical Theatre
Музыкальный театр имени Станиславского и Немировича-Данченко
Muzykalnyy teatr imeni Stanislavskovo i Nemirovicha-Danchenko
Ulitsa Bolshaya Dmitrovka 17. **Map** 2 F4.
229 2835.

Classical Music

Moscow Conservatory
Московская консерватория
Moskovskaya konservatoriya
Bolshaya Nikitskaya ulitsa 1.
Map 2 F5. 229 0042.
www.mosconsv.ru

Tchaikovsky Concert Hall
Концертный зал имени ПИ Чайковского
Kontsertnyy zal imeni PI Chaykovskovo
Triumfalnaya ploshchad 4/31.
Map 2 E3.
299 3681.

Theatre

Gypsy Theatre
Театр ромэн
Teatr romen
Leningradskiy prospekt 32/2.
Map 1 B1.
251 8522.

Lenkom Theatre
Театр Ленком
Ulitsa Malaya Dmitrovka 6.
Map 2 F3.
299 0708.

Malyy Theatre
Малый театр
Teatralnaya ploshchad 1/6.
Map 3 A5.
923 2621.

Moscow Arts Theatre
МХАТ имени АП Чехова
MKhAT imeni AP Chekhova
Kamergerskiy pereulok 3.
Map 2 F5.
229 8760.

Film

American House of Cinema
Berezhkovskaya naberezhnaya 2.
Map 5 B2.
941 8747.

Arts Cinema
Художественный кино
Khudozhestvennyy kino
Arbatskaya ploshchad 14.
Map 6 E1.
291 5598.

Cinema Centre
Киноцентр
Kinotsentr
Druzhinnikovskaya ulitsa 15.
Map 1 C5.
205 7306.

Dome Cinema
Olympiyskiy prospekt 18/1.
Map 3 A1.
931 9873.

Illuzion
Иллюзион
Illyuzion
Kotelnicheskaya naberezhnaya 1/15.
Map 8 D2.
915 4339.

Kodak Cinema World
Кодак киномир
Kodak kinomir
Nastasinskiy pereulok 2.
Map 2 E3.
209 3563.

Rossiya
Россия
Pushkinskaya ploshchad 2.
Map 2 F4.
229 2111.

Udarnik
Ударник
Ulitsa Serafimovicha 2.
Map 7 A3.
959 0856.

Music and Nightlife

Under the communist regime Moscow's nightlife was practically non-existent. In the 1930s the bars where people used to relax with a drink and enjoy live music were establishments only for the elite. With the advent of perestroika a host of new bars and clubs began to appear, and bands, previously forced underground, were able to perform publicly. These days Moscow has a flourishing nightlife with hundreds of clubs catering to all musical tastes. Casinos are another great hit and are especially popular with the so-called New Russians, who like to let off steam by trying their luck at Moscow's numerous gambling venues. Cigarettes are still extremely popular in Russia and many venues have rather smoky atmospheres.

Rock Venues

Well-known Russian bands tend to perform at larger nightclubs such as **Manhattan Express**, **Utopia** or **Metelitsa**. These clubs, which often have high entrance fees, are packed with young people, including a good sprinkling of New Russians and the numerous expatriates living in the city. Smaller bars, such as **Krizis Zhanra** *(see p182)* and **Tabula Rasa**, often have bands who are just as talented, but less famous, and the drinks are much cheaper. These venues are always crowded. **Armadillo**, an American-style bar, is another alternative. It offers good live music and reasonably priced drinks and snacks, and has a young professional clientele.

The **Gorbunov House of Culture** is a popular venue for major rock concerts, which are also sometimes staged at large sports stadiums.

Jazz, Blues and Latin Venues

Most of the numerous jazz clubs in Moscow also play host to blues bands. The most famous are the **Bunker**, **B.B. King** and the **R-Club**. Concerts do not take place every night, so it is worth checking listings in the English press for details *(see p207)*. On concert nights the venues tend to be packed and many charge an entrance fee. Otherwise they are often fairly empty and offer moderately priced drinks and snacks. Another great jazz venue is **Woodstock- MKhAT**. Live jazz is performed several times a week, the entrance fee is negligible and the decor is made up of 1960s paraphernalia. The **Brasserie du Soleil** *(see p181)* offers jazz concerts at weekends, a bar and good French cuisine, and is often frequented by a large crowd of expatriates.

Alternatively try **Cabana**, a Brazilian-style bar and restaurant with live music, including Latin American bands.

Nightclubs and Discos

Moscow's nightclubs have never been trend-setters, but they are gradually catching up with the clubs of the other major European capitals. There are hundreds of nightclubs in Moscow, with new ones appearing every month. Most of them are open throughout the evening, but rarely get going before 1am. Admission is usually free before 10pm and can be quite expensive after that. Some clubs offer free entry to unaccompanied women.

The city's nightclubs mostly fall into two categories: those with a floor show of some kind, often featuring strippers or erotic dancers, and those that contain various dance floors and bars.

Among the latter is **Titanic**, a rave venue for the city's rich kids. **Mirazh**, **Hippopotamus** and **Manhattan Express** are more straightforward rock and pop discos. Mirazh has a good-size dance floor, but the dance floors at Hippopotamus and Manhattan Express are so popular that they often fail to accommodate the crowds that pack them out at weekends. The **A-Club** has a large dance floor but is only open two nights a week. Friday brings a young crowd and a cool techno vibe, while Saturday attracts a mixed crowd of Euro expats, New Russians. and groups of partygoers. **Night Flight** is another well-known club, although it has a reputation as a favourite haunt of gangsters and prostitutes.

For a taste of Moscow's more traditional nightlife, **Rasputin** offers a non-stop striptease show from 5pm to 6am, as well as sauna and jacuzzi. Along the same lines, **Tsunami** is a nightclub and restaurant with striptease taking place not only on stage, but also, as part of a special mermaid show, in the swimming pool. Also on offer is a cocktail bar and oriental-style smoking lounge. Another nightclub with a popular striptease show is **Karousel**. It also has a dance floor where the music played ranges from disco to techno.

One of the most lavish of Moscow's nightclubs is **Luxor**, part of the elegant Metropol Hotel *(see p173)*. Russian, French, Japanese and Arabic food is served against a

Spectator Sports

Traditionally, the most popular sports in Russia are football and hockey. Important matches and championships are held at the **Dynamo Central House of Sports**, the **Krylatskoye Sports Complex**, the **Olympic Sports Complex** and the **Luzhniki Central Stadium**. Krylatskoye also has a racecourse and a canal where rowing races take place.

The Olympic Sports Complex is the main venue in Moscow for tennis tournaments.

The recently renovated **Hippodrome** has a large racecourse, and a riding school where horses and riding equipment are available for a fee.

faintly incongruous Ancient Egyptian backdrop. Among the more unusual stage shows on offer here are "Romantic Saxaphone" and "Luxor".

Casinos

Moscow has dozens of casinos, which range from extravagant venues to tiny, seedy joints that are not worth a visit. Gambling is a favourite pastime of New Russians and entrance fees and chip prices are quite high. Some casinos offer a free ride home to clients who either win or lose a large sum. In others, the entrance fee includes drinks and snacks. Most top hotels also have their own casinos which are less grandiose than the purpose-built ones.

Moscow's most famous casinos are the **Aleksandr Blok**, situated on a riverboat, the **Golden Palace**, which has a Las Vegas-style interior with heavily armed guards and fish swimming under a glass floor, and the Cherry Casino at the **Metelitsa** nightclub, favoured by mafia types. The **Beverly Hills** casino waives its entrance charge for foreigners who produce their passports. The **Club Royale** is located at the Hippodrome racecourse, so visitors can follow a flutter on the horses with some serious gambling in the casino. For music lovers, the **Shangri-La** offers excellent live jazz as well as 30 gaming tables.

Directory

Rock, Jazz, Blues and Latin Venues

Armadillo
Армадилло
Khrustalnyy pereulok 1.
Map 7 B1.
293 7835.

B.B. King
Ulitsa Sadovaya-Samotechnaya 4.
Map 2 F2.
299 8206.

Bunker
Бункер
Tverskaya ulitsa 12.
Map 2 F4.
200 1506.

Cabana
Кабана
Raushskaya nab 4.
Map 7 B2.
238 5006.

Forpost
Форпост
Khamovnitcheskiy val 28.
242 1654 ext. 11.

Gorbunov House of Culture
Дом культуры Горбунова
Dom kultury Gorbunova
Novozavodskaya ulitsa 27.
145 8974.

Krizis Zhanra
Кризис жанра
Prechistenskiy per 22/4.
Map 6 D2.
241 1928.

Metelitsa
Метелица
Ulitsa Novyy Arbat 21.
Map 6 D1.
291 1130.

R-Club
4 Roshchinskiy proezd 19.
952 7402.

Tabula Rasa
Табула раса
Berezhkovskaya naberezhnaya 28.
240 9289.

Woodstock-MKhAT
Вудсток-МХАТ
Kamergerskiy pereulok 3.
Map 2 F5.
292 0934.

Nightclubs and Discos

A-Club
А клуб
Sadova-Karetnaya ulitsa 1
Map 2 F2.
972 1132.

Hippopotamus
Гиппопотам
Gippopotam
Mantulinskaya ulitsa 5/1, stroenie 6.
Map 1 A5.
256 2346.

Karousel
Карсель
1-ya Tverskaya-Yamskaya ulitsa 11.
Map 2 D3.
251 6444.

Luxor
Metropol Hotel, Teatralnyy Proezd 1/4.
Map 3 A5.
927 6091.

Manhattan Express
Ulitsa Varvarka 6.
Map 7 B1.
298 5354.

Mirazh
Мираж
Novyy Arbat 21.
Map 6 D1.
291 1423.

Night Flight
Tverskaya ulitsa 17.
Map 2 F4.
229 4165.

Rasputin
Распутин
Zuboskiy bulvar 25.
Map 6 D3.
246 8592.

Titanic
Титаник
Young Pioneers' Stadium, Begovaya ulitsa 21/31.
Map 1 B1.
213 4581.

Tsunami
Цунами
Petrovka ulitsa 24/1.
200 5566.

Casinos

Aleksandr Blok
Александр Блок
Krasnopresnenskaya naberezhnaya 12a.
Map 1 A5.
255 9281.

Beverly Hills
Kudrinskaya ploshchad 1.
Map 2 D5.
255 4228.

Club Royale
Клуб Роял
Begovaya ulitsa 22/1.
Map 1 A1.
945 1410.

Golden Palace
3-ya ulitsa Yamskovo Polya 15.
Map 1 C1.
212 3909.

Shangri-La
Pushkinskaya ploshchad 2.
Map 2 F4.
229 0003.

Sports Venues

Dynamo Central House of Sports
Динамо – Центральный дворец спорта
Dinamo – Tsentralnyy dvorets sporta
Lavochkina ulitsa 32.
453 6501.

Hippodrome
Ипподром
Begovaya ulitsa 22, korpus 1.
Map 1 A2.
945 0437.

Krylatskoye Sports Complex
Спортивный комплекс Крылатское
Sportivnyy kompleks Krylatskoe
Krylatskaya ulitsa 2.
141 2224.

Luzhniki Central Stadium
Центральный стадион Лужники
Tsentralnyy stadion Luzhniki
Luzhniki ulitsa 24.
201 1164.

Olympic Sports Complex
Спортивный олимпийский комплекс
Sportivnyy olimpiyskiy kompleks
Olimpiyskiy prospekt 16.
Map 3 A1.
288 1533.

SURVIVAL GUIDE

Practical Information

Moscow is not as difficult for visitors to find their way around as it may seem at first. Certainly, the city is vast, street names and signs are in Cyrillic, and the traffic can be formidably heavy, especially in the centre. On the other hand, there is an excellent metro system, and passers-by and people working in hotels, restaurants and shops will usually help foreigners. However, it is a good idea for visitors to familiarize themselves with the Cyrillic alphabet in order to decipher signs.

Sign for the Intourist agency

With tourism still a fledgling industry in Moscow, some tourist facilities, such as information services, are fairly basic. The first port of call for visitors wanting information about events and practicalities should be their hotel. Surprisingly, Moscow can be one of the most expensive cities in the world to visit. While public transport is cheap, hotels, restaurants and theatre tickets can cost more than their Western equivalents. It is always worth enquiring about the price before booking something.

Information desk run by concierge in the Baltschug Kempinski Hotel

Tourist Information

There are no conventional tourist information offices in Moscow, so hotels are the main source of guidance for visitors. Concierges in Western-style hotels, such as the Radisson-Slavyanskaya, National, Baltschug Kempinski and Metropol *(see pp168–71)*, will provide assistance. All the large hotels, both Western-style and Russian-run, will book theatre tickets for visitors, but will add commission to the face value. Most also have a flight-booking service, accepting payment by credit card, or will put visitors in touch with a travel agency. The advice of Russian-run hotels on sights and restaurants is often indifferent, but the English-language press *(see p207)*, particularly *The Moscow Times*, *The Moscow Tribune* and *The Exile*, has details of exhibitions, events and opening hours.

Guided Tours and Excursions

Hotels can book places on group guided tours and day trips in several languages. The **Intourist** agency offers a wide range of tours, mainly to the most well-known sights. **Patriarshiy Dom Tours** offers a range of tours in English, including trips around the KGB Museum, the Kremlin and State Armoury, as well as hiking expeditions. The listings of forthcoming trips are published in the Friday edition of *The Moscow Tribune*. Tours should generally be booked at least 48 hours in advance.

Tour bus operated by the Intourist agency

Admission Charges

Many museums and theatres charge foreigners considerably higher admission fees than Russians, although still well within European and North American norms. Those that do include the Tretyakov Gallery *(see pp118–21)*, the State Armoury *(see pp64–5)*, the Pushkin Museum of Fine Arts *(see pp78–81)* and the Bolshoy Theatre *(see pp90–91)*. Schoolchildren and students *(see p200)* are entitled to discounts. Credit cards are never accepted at sights.

The ticket office, recognizable by the касса *(kassa)* sign, is often some distance away from the entrance to the sight; staff at the entrance will point you in its direction.

Tour operator in Red Square signing up visitors for excursions

A woman leaving church after a service, appropriately dressed in a headscarf

Opening Hours

Most museums have standard opening hours, from 10 or 10:30am to 6pm, but ticket offices may close earlier than the museums. The majority of museums close one day a week and one day a month for cleaning. All museums open on Sundays. Some cathedrals and churches are always open, but others only open for services.

Sign for open *(otkryto)*

Sign for closed *(zakryto)*

Visiting Churches

Attending an Orthodox church service is a fascinating experience. The most important services take place on Saturday evenings and Sunday mornings, and on religious holidays. In general, services run for several hours. Russian churches do not have any chairs, and the congregation is expected to stand. It is acceptable for visitors to drop in on a service for a while, but certain dress rules must be observed. Shorts are not acceptable. Men must remove their hats, while women should cover their chest and shoulders and preferably wear a headscarf or hat. Although acceptable in town churches, women wearing trousers are likely to be refused entry to monasteries.

Language

Cyrillic is the alphabet of the Russian language. It is named after Cyril *(see p17)*, the monk who in 860–70 invented the alphabet from which it developed. Various systems for transliterating Cyrillic into Roman characters *(see p252)* exist, but they do not differ enough to cause confusion.

Many Russians who regularly come into contact with visitors can speak some English. However, a knowledge of even one or two words of Russian *(see pp252–6)* on the part of visitors will be taken as a sign of respect and much appreciated.

Etiquette

Russian manners and attitudes are becoming more Westernized, but the linguistic distinction between the formal "you" *(vy)* and informal "you" *(ty)* remains strictly in force. On public transport, young men are expected to give up their seats to the elderly or families with young children.

Smoking and drinking are popular pastimes. Frequent toasts are required to justify the draining of glasses. When invited to someone's home, the toast *za khozyayku* (to the hostess) or *za khozyaina* (to the host) should always be offered by the visitor.

Many Russians are superstitious. Most prefer not to shake hands across the threshold of a doorway and, if someone accidentally steps on a friend's toes, the injured party pretends to step back on the perpetrator's toes.

Paying and Tipping

Roubles are the only valid currency in Russia *(see p205)*. Some large shops and hotels may display prices in US dollars or Deutschmarks, but all cash payments must be in roubles only. Credit cards are accepted in some restaurants and most hotels, but rarely in shops, except for those selling imported goods at much higher prices than abroad.

Tipping is a matter of choice, but baggage handlers at the airport and train stations may ask exorbitant sums. Visitors should simply pay what they consider to be appropriate.

Addresses

Russian addresses are given in the following order: post code, city, street name, house *(dom)* number and, finally, apartment *(kvartira)* number. If a flat is part of a complex, a *korpus (k)* number will also be given to indicate which block it is in. When visiting a flat, it is useful to know which entrance *(podezd)* to the block to use.

After the Revolution of 1917, many streets were renamed to avoid imperial connotations or to commemorate new Soviet heroes. Since perestroika most streets in the centre have officially reverted to their pre-1917 names. This can cause confusion as people often use the Soviet names, forgetting that street signs show the original ones. However, most people happily use both and no offence is caused by using one in preference to the other.

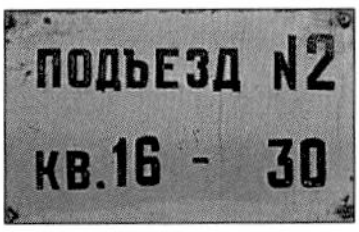

Sign on a block of flats giving a *podezd* number

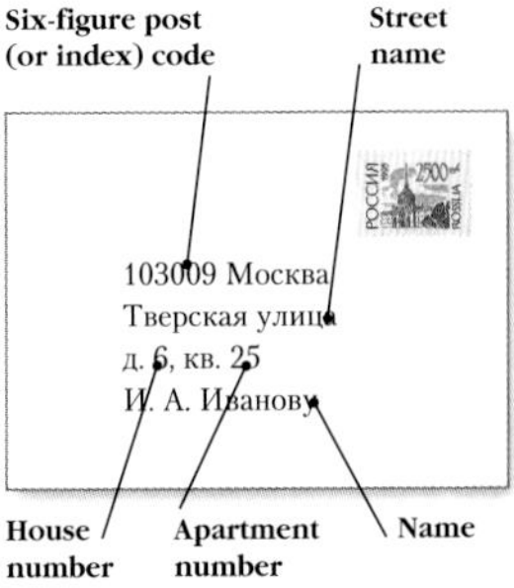

VISAS

VISITORS FROM almost all countries will need a visa. Only those from CIS member states (excluding the Baltic states) are exempt. All visitors travelling to Moscow should check their requirements before departing. Visa formalities are confusing. In the UK there are three types: business (for visitors who have been invited by an organization), private (for those who have been invited to stay at a private address) and tourist (for those intending to stay at a hotel or hotels).

For those on package tours tourist visas will be arranged by the tour companies. For independent travellers, the easiest way to obtain a visa is to pay a modest fee and get a specialist agent, such as **Scott's Tours** in London or **Panorama Travel Ltd** in New York, to arrange it. Moscow-based **Andrew's Consulting** can also arrange visas for visitors of any nationality.

Alternatively, apply to the Russian embassy. Independent tourist visa applications must be supported with appropriate documentation (be sure to find out exactly what this is) as well as proof of pre-booked hotel accommodation. Holders of a private visa have to show an invitation endorsed by **OVIR**, the Visa and Registration Department, at their host's local police station.

Visas normally take around ten days to process but, if speed is important, both Scott's Tours and Andrew's Consulting offer an express service for an extra fee. The cost of a visa depends on the length of its validity as well as how soon it is required. Britons pay from about £30 for a short-term, single-entry visa issued well in advance, to about £100 for a multiple-entry business visa.

While tourist visas cannot be extended, private and business visa extensions can be sought by the individual or organization that issued the invitation. Overstaying, however, can lead to a hefty fine or having to remain until an extension is obtained.

Igumnov House, built in 1893, now the home of the French Embassy

IMMIGRATION AND CUSTOMS

PASSPORTS and visas are thoroughly checked at immigration desks. All visitors have to fill out a customs declaration form on arrival which is available in various languages (some airlines hand them out on the plane). This should be kept for the duration of the stay and handed back together with another declaration form at departure.

It is illegal to take roubles out of Russia (nor, by extension, are they allowed in). There are no limits on how much foreign hard currency may be brought in, but visitors will be expected to have less when they leave (to prove that they have been buying rather than selling things). Valuables such as jewellery and computers should be declared on the customs form on entry, otherwise an import duty may be levied on them on leaving. The departure customs in Russia are generally stricter than in many other countries, particularly with regard to art and antiques *(see p185)*.

REGISTRATION

OFFICIALLY, all foreigners are supposed to register with **OVIR**, the Visa and Registration Department, within three days of their arrival. Hotels can do this for guests. Non-registration is rarely a problem, but sometimes people are fined or ordered to get their paperwork in order, if the authorities become suspicious of them.

EMBASSIES AND CONSULATES

EVERY COUNTRY that has diplomatic relations with Russia has an embassy or consulate in Moscow. Anyone intending to reside in Russia for longer than three months is advised to register with their own one. Should a visitor be robbed, hospitalized, imprisoned or otherwise rendered helpless, the embassy or consular officials will then be able to help, for instance with interpretation, or at least to give advice. They can re-issue passports and, in some cases, provide emergency money.

DISABLED TRAVELLERS

MOSCOW HAS FEW facilities for the disabled. Public transport is difficult to access; steps and narrow doors are everywhere and lifts are rare. It is adviseable to phone in advance to check if a tourist sight has full disabled access.

International Student Identity Card

STUDENT TRAVELLERS

AS WELL AS BEING accepted for discounts in museums, international student cards can also be used to obtain discounts on rail and air travel booked through **STAR Travel**.

Travelling with Children

Russians adore children, and those accompanying visitors to Moscow are likely to attract plenty of compliments. On the other hand, it is not unknown for Russian grannies *(babushki)* to be overly inquisitive and even to offer critical, though well-meaning, remarks on the way they are dressed.

Children under six travel free on public transport, but older ones pay the full price. Museums are free for toddlers and babies, and offer concessions to schoolchildren.

Children playing on a cannon at the Armoury in the Kremlin

Toilet (*tualet*) sign

Men's toilets

Women's toilets

Public Toilets

Few cafés and bars have facilities, and public toilets on the street are not pleasant. It is often best to find the nearest foreign hotel or a pay toilet in, say, a department store. These are usually very cheap. Though the lady who takes the money also hands out rations of toilet paper here, it is always a good idea to carry your own.

Electrical Appliances

The electrical current in Russia is 220 V. Two-pin plugs are needed, but some of the old Soviet two-pin sockets do not take modern European plugs, which have thicker pins. Hotels all have modern sockets. Adaptors are best bought before travelling, but those for old-style plugs are found only in Russia. US appliances need a 220:110 current adaptor.

Photography

There are no longer any serious restrictions on what visitors are allowed to photograph (unless you want to take aerial pictures). Expect to have to pay for the right to take photos or use a video camera in museums.

Time Difference

Moscow time is three hours ahead of Greenwich Mean Time (GMT). Russia has recently come into line with the rest of Europe, putting its clocks forward by an hour at the end of March, and back again in October.

Conversion Table

Imperial to Metric
1 inch = 2.54 centimetres
1 foot = 30 centimetres
1 mile = 1.6 kilometres
1 ounce = 28 grams
1 pound = 454 grams
1 pint = 0.6 litres
1 gallon = 4.6 litres

Metric to Imperial
1 centimetre = 0.4 inches
1 metre = 3 feet, 3 inches
1 kilometre = 0.6 miles
1 gram = 0.04 ounces
1 kilogram = 2.2 pounds
1 litre = 1.8 pints

Directory

Tourist Information and Guided Tours

Intourist
Интурист
Tverskaya ul 3/5, 1st floor.
Map 2 F2.
☎ *292 2190.*
FAX *292 2547.*

Patriarshiy Dom Tours
Патриарший дом турс
Vspolniy per 6. **Map** 2 D4.
☎ *795 0927.*
FAX *795 0927.*

Visa Formalities

Panorama Travel Ltd
156 Fifth Ave, Suite 1019, New York, NY 10010.
☎ *212 741 0033.*
FAX *212 645 6276.*

Scott's Tours
159 Whitfield Street, London W1P 5RY, UK.
☎ *0171 383 5353.*
FAX *0171 383 3709.*

Andrew's Consulting
ulista Volkhonka 18.
Map 6 E2.
☎ *916 9898.*
W www.andrews-consulting.ru

OVIR
ОВИР
Gorodskoye otdel viz i registratsii
Pokrovka ul 42.
Map 4 D4.
☎ *200 8427.*
● *Wed, Sat, Sun.*

Embassies and Consulates

Australia
Kropotkinskiy per 13.
Map 6 D3.
☎ *956 6070.* W www.australianembassy.ru

Canada
Starokonyushenny per 23.
Map 6 E2.
☎ *956 6666.*
W www.canadaeuropa.gc.ca/russia

Ireland
Grokholskiy per 5.
Map 3 C2.
☎ *742 0907*

New Zealand
Ul Povarskaya 44.
Map 2 D5.
☎ *956 3579.*
W www.nzembassy.msk.ru

South Africa
Bolshoy Strochenovskiy per 22/25. **Map** 7 C5.
☎ *230 6869.*
W www.saembassy.ru

UK
Sofiyskaya nab 14.
Map 7 A2.
☎ *956 7200.*
W www.britemb.msk.ru

US
Novinskiy bulvar 19/23 & Bolshoi Devyatinskiy per 8.
Map 2 D5.
☎ *252 2451/59.*
W www.usembassy.state.gov/moscow

Student Travel

STAR Travel
Vorontsovskaya ul 18/20, stroenie 6. **Map** 8 E4.
☎ *935 8336.*

Personal Security and Health

DESPITE LURID WORLDWIDE reporting on the mafia, crime in Moscow is no worse than in any big city. Petty crime should be the visitor's only concern, but even this can usually be avoided if sensible precautions are taken. For language reasons, it is a good idea to have a card with your Russian address written on it for use in taxis and emergencies. Medical insurance is essential. Although many medicines are readily available, local healthcare compares poorly with Western care and English-speaking services and medical evacuation are very expensive.

Protecting your Property

EVERY VISITOR should take out travel insurance. Once in Moscow, visitors can avoid pickpockets by not carrying money in open pockets or displaying large sums of money in public; bags should be kept closed and roubles kept apart from foreign currency and credit cards. It is advisable to carry a small sum of money for purchases, and to keep the rest separately or at the hotel.

It is best not to stop for gypsies who sometimes frequent Tverskaya ulitsa and the central metro stations, apparently begging. Hold tight to valuables and walk determinedly on without aggression.

Travellers' cheques have the advantage that they are insured against loss or theft. However, if they are stolen this should be reported immediately to the issuing company as they can easily be "laundered" in Russia.

It is absolutely essential to report thefts to the police in order to obtain certificates for insurance claims. It is best to report first to hotel security staff who can usually provide interpreters or deal with the whole matter. Embassies will deal with serious situations.

GAI policeman checking documents

Personal Safety

THE GREATEST danger for visitors comes from thieves who might become violent if they encounter resistance. As in any country, it is advisable to hand over belongings if they are demanded with menace.

The mafia, though widespread, has scant contact with foreigners, particularly tourists, who are generally much poorer than Russian businessmen.

Women on their own may be approached by kerb-crawlers, who are best ignored, and may be propositioned if alone in bars and restaurants. At night, it is safer to use taxis booked in advance rather than those hailed on the street. The metro is also safe.

Other threats come from local drivers, who see pedestrians as a nuisance, and from manhole covers, which have a tendency to rock wildly or collapse when stepped on.

Police

SEVERAL KINDS of police operate on Moscow's streets. They change uniforms according to the weather, wearing fur hats and big coats in winter. The normal police or *militsiya*, who always carry guns, are the most frequently seen.

The riot police or OMON *(otryad militsii osobgo naznacheniya)* are rarely seen on the streets and dress in camouflage.

Totally separate are the traffic police, or GIBDD *(gosudarstvennaya inspekcia bezopasnosti dorozhnovo dvizhenia)*. Recognizable by their striped truncheons, they may stop any vehicle to check the driver's documents.

Both the *militsiya* and GIBDD supplement their incomes by picking people up on minor offences, such as jay-walking. It is usually best to pay the "fine", which is about the equivalent of five or ten dollars.

Militsiya

Fire engine with distinctive white stripe

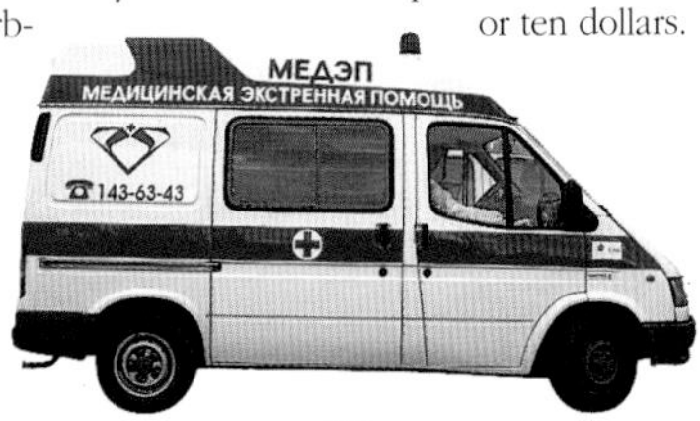

Ambulance

Police car

Pharmacy, identified by the word *apteka*

PHARMACIES

PHARMACIES IN RUSSIA are all signed by the word Аптека *(apteka)* and usually have a green cross hanging outside. The best ones are on ulitsa Novyy Arbat, Tverskaya ulitsa and Kutuzovskiy prospekt. These sell many imported medications, some with the instructions still in the original language. Prescriptions are not necessary for any purchase, and antibiotics and other strong medications can be purchased over the counter. All the assistants are trained pharmacists and can suggest a Russian alternative to visitors who name the drug they are seeking. However, visitors with specific requirements, particularly insulin, should bring enough with them for their whole stay. Moscow has a number of all-night pharmacies *(see directory)*.

Sign for a pharmacy

MEDICAL TREATMENT

MOST HOTELS have their own doctor and this should be the first port of call for anyone who falls ill. There are several companies, notably the **European Medical Centre** and the **American Medical Center**, that specialize in dealing with foreigners. They can provide everything that travellers are likely to need, from basic treatment where they are staying to dental care, x-rays, ultra-sound scans and even medical evacuation home. Their charges are very high, but they are all used to dealing with foreign insurance policies.

Slightly cheaper is **Assist-24**, which has English-speaking Russian doctors who are well able to deal with minor medical emergencies. **US Dental Care** provides a full range of dental treatment.

For those in need of immediate attention, without the time to contact any of the above, the casualty department of the **Botkin Hospital** is the safest bet. The staff can give injections and stitches and carry out general first aid, but no English is spoken.

Anyone waking up in a local hospital should contact their embassy or one of the above medical centres. They can arrange a move or oversee care.

HEALTH PRECAUTIONS

VISITORS SHOULD not drink the tap water in Moscow, but stick to bottled water and avoid fruit and raw vegetables that may have been washed in tap water. Food in a foreign country often unsettles the stomach and eating the meat and sausage pies *(pirozhki)* sold on the streets is a sure route to a stomach upset.

In past years diphtheria has increased among the local population. It is advisable to be inoculated against this before going to Russia.

MOSQUITOES

MOSQUITOES *(komari)* are the bane of everyone's life between June and late September. Plug-in chemical mosquito coils are available and are particularly good at night. Alternatives are sprays, or oil repellants used in vaporizers or burnt in candle form.

In the woods or countryside, some sort of repellent is also necessary and not all of those available locally are effective. It is best to bring repellents and anti-histamine cream, for treating bites, from home.

DIRECTORY

EMERGENCY SERVICES

Fire *(pozhar)*
☎ *01.*
Police *(militsiya)*
☎ *02.*
Ambulance *(skoraya pomoshch)*
☎ *03.*

MEDICAL SERVICES

American Medical Center
Американский медицинский центр
Amerikanskiy meditsinskiy tsentr
Grokholskiy pereulok 1.
Map 3 B2. ☎ *933 7700.*
W www.emc.mos.ru/about-e.cfm

Assist-24
Ассист-*24*
Mira prospekt 69.
Map 3 B2.
☎ *937 6450.*

Botkin Hospital
Боткинская больница
Botkinskaya bolnitsa
2-oy Botkinskiy proezd 5.
Map 1 A1.
☎ *945 0033.*

European Medical Centre
Европейский медицинский центр
Yevropeyskiy meditsinskiy tsentr
Spiridonievskiy pereulok 5.
Map 2 D4.
☎ *933 6655.*

US Dental Care
Американский стоматологический центр
Amerikanskiy stomatologicheskiy tsentr
Shabolovka ul 8, stroenie 3.
Map 6 F5.
☎ *931 9909.*

ALL-NIGHT PHARMACIES

Kutuzovskiy pr 14.
Map 5 A2.
☎ *243 1601.*

Ulitsa Zemlyanoy val 1/4.
Map 4 E4.
☎ *917 1640.*

Nikolskaya ul 19/21.
Map 3 A5.
☎ *921 4942.*

Banking and Local Currency

MOSCOW IS SLOWLY MOVING into the credit card age and major Western cards can now be used to pay in hotels, top restaurants and some shops. Everywhere else, however, cash is the norm, and roubles are the only legal currency. The city is well provided with exchange points where visitors can turn their currency (US dollars still being the most popular), travellers' cheques or credit cards into roubles. Rates of commission vary. Since bank exchange rates are so good, money should never be changed on the street. Apparently "better" offers from private individuals will lead to visitors being cheated.

Changing Money

ROUBLES CANNOT be obtained outside Russia, but there are numerous exchange offices all over Moscow, including at the airports. Some offices are open 24 hours a day.

A passport has to be shown when changing money. Any defect on foreign bank notes, especially vertical tears or ink or water stains, makes them invalid in Russia and they will be refused at the exchange. Make sure that all notes brought into Russia are in good condition and that any US dollars were issued after 1990.

On completing a currency transaction, an exchange slip is issued. All slips should be kept as they must be attached to the customs declaration filled in on arrival in Russia *(see p200)* and presented at customs on leaving the country.

A sign for a currency exchange office *(obmen valyuty)*

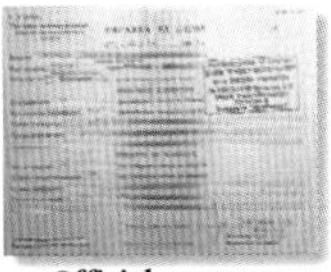

Official currency exchange slip

Automatic cash dispenser

Using Banks

THERE ARE ONLY a few foreign banks in Russia and they mostly do not offer over-the-counter services. Most Russian banks, however, do have on-the-spot exchange services. They take a variety of currencies, credit cards for cash advances, and some take travellers' cheques. **Alfa-Bank** and **Sberbank** offer the best rates. For anyone wishing to have money sent to a bank in Russia, the most reliable are **Alfa-Bank** and **Sberbank**. It is always advisable to check other banks' reliability.

Western Union will transfer money to Russia for you through **Alfa-Bank**, **Guta Bank, Bank Moskvy** and **American Express**, but they are expensive and primarily of use to businesspeople.

Many independent exchange offices in Russia accept only US dollars and euros.

Credit Cards

IT IS NOW POSSIBLE to obtain cash, both roubles and US dollars, with a credit card through the larger banks and from automatic cash dispensers at some banks and in major hotels. The local commission is between 2 and 5 per cent, plus whatever the card company charges. The most commonly accepted card is VISA, with Diners, MasterCard, Eurocard and American Express much less widely recognized. The cash dispensers at **Alfa-Bank** take MasterCard, Eurocard and VISA and charge no local commission, making them a popular option with visitors.

Lost or stolen credit cards should be reported immediately to the credit card company in the home country. No local security service is offered.

Directory

Banks

American Express
Usacheva ul 33, building 1.
Map 5 B5.
☎ *933 8400.*

Sberbank
Сбербанк
Ulitsa Bolshaya Yakimanka 18.
Map 7 A4.
☎ *238 4920.*

Alfa-Bank
Альфа-Банк
Mashi Poryvaevoi ulitsa 9.
Map 4 D2.
☎ *974 2515.*

Vneshtorgbank
Внешторгбанк
Kuznetskiy most 16.
Map 3 A4.
☎ *101 1887.*

Cash Dispensers

American Express
Sadovaya-Kudrinskaya ul 21a.
Map 2 D4.
(Accepts American Express only)

Alfa-Bank
Альфа-Банк
Pokrovka 3/7.
Map 3 C5.
(Accepts VISA, MasterCard, Eurocard)

Radisson-Slavyanskaya Hotel
Гостиница Рэдиссон-Славянская
Gostinitsa Redisson-Slavyanskaya
Berezhkovskaya nab 2.
Map 5 B2.
(Accepts VISA, MasterCard, American Express)

Travellers' Cheques

Banks charge at least 3 per cent to cash travellers' cheques. Only large banks, such as **Alfa-Bank** and **Sberbank**, offer this service. The cheapest alternative is American Express cheques, with a 2 per cent commission if cashed at the **American Express** office. Travellers' cheques can only be used as payment for goods or services in a few large hotels, and are acceptable only in US dollars and euros, or sometimes British pounds. In most cases euro cheques are usually preferred.

Local Currency

The Russian currency is the rouble (or ruble), written рубль or abbreviated to р or руб. The higher denominations of roubles are currently available in banknotes, which all bear images of well-known Russian cities, the lower denominations in coins. The kopek, of which there are 100 in a rouble, is issued in coins.

In 1998 the rouble was revalued owing to its stronger value and lower inflation rate. Values were divided by 1,000 (with 1,000 roubles becoming 1 rouble).

Banknotes

There are five denominations of banknote, with face values of 10, 50, 100, 500 and 1,000 roubles, and they have the same designs as their pre-revaluation equivalents. When changing money check that the notes correspond to those shown here.

10 roubles

50 roubles

100 roubles

500 roubles

1,000 roubles

Coins

The revaluation of the Russian rouble in 1998 led to the revival of the long-redundant but much-loved kopek. Traditionally, the rouble had always consisted of 100 kopeks. In addition to coins for 1, 2 and 5 roubles, there are now coins valued at 1, 5, 10 and 50 kopeks. Any coins issued before 1997, prior to revaluation, are essentially valueless. Visitors should therefore always examine change they receive and refuse to accept any of these old coins.

1 rouble

2 roubles

5 roubles

1 kopek

5 kopeks

10 kopeks

50 kopeks

Communications

MUCH OF MOSCOW'S ANTIQUATED phone system has been brought up to date in the last few years and there is now a good city-wide service. Many hotel and public phones have direct dialling all over the world, but phones in private homes may not have this facility. The same period has seen an explosive increase in the number of magazines, newspapers and television channels. Sadly, Russia's postal system has not improved at the same rate.

A sign outside a post office (*pochta*) that has public telephones (*telefon*)

TELEPHONE SERVICES

COMSTAR SATELLITE phone boxes, which are blue, are installed at airports, in business centres, in most hotel foyers and in some restaurants. They accept credit cards or phonecards on sale in major hotels, restaurants and clubs, but calls are expensive. Moscow's local system is much cheaper. It is possible to call abroad on a direct line from one of the Moscow State Telephone Network (МГТС) blue and white cardphones, located on streets and in some metro stations. Cards for the phones come in 25, 50, 100, 120, 200, 400 and 1,000 units, and are available from kiosks, metro stations and post offices. To make an international call, at least 100 units are needed. International and inter-city calls are cheaper between 10pm and 8am and at all hours at weekends.

Token for a local phone

Old-style, non-card МГТС phones are grey and can only be used for local calls. They take plastic *zhetony* (tokens), which can be bought in the same places as phonecards. Local calls from private phones are free, as they are covered by the cost of the line rental.

МГТС phone box

The **Central Telegraph Office** has rows of local and international phones and calls are paid for at the counter.

Instructions on how to use an МГТС cardphone are given below. Comstar phones work in the same way if used with a phonecard. The instructions automatically come up first in English. If using a credit card with a Comstar phone, insert it into the top left-hand slot and remove it again in one action. Wait 15 seconds for card verification before dialling. For non-card local phones, lift the receiver and dial the number. When someone answers, drop the token into the slot.

REACHING THE RIGHT NUMBER

- Local directory enquiries (Moscow only): dial 09.
- Inter-city call booking via operator: dial 07.
- There is as yet no international directory enquiries service.
- International call booking: dial 8 (tone) 194.
- Direct international dialling:
  UK: dial 8 (tone) 1044, then area code omitting first 0, then number.
  USA: dial 8 (tone) 101 followed by the area code and number.
  Australia: dial 8 (tone) 1061, then area code omitting first 0, then number.
  New Zealand: dial 8 (tone) 1064, then area code omitting first 0, then number.
  Irish Republic: dial 8 (tone) 10353, then area code omitting first 0, then number.
- AT&T Calling Card number: dial 755 5042.

USING AN МГТС PHONECARD OPERATED PHONE

1 Lift the receiver and check that you have a dialling tone.

2 МГТС phones offer instructions in Russian, English, French and German. They always appear in Russian first. Press this button to switch between languages. Instructions are given both on the display and through the earpiece.

3 When instructed, push your phonecard into the slot in the direction of the arrow marked on the card. Wait for card verification.

4 Dial the number. The ringing tone consists of long tones; the engaged signal of shorter tones.

5 Press this button at any time to increase the volume.

6 When someone answers, press this button to speak.

7 To end a call, replace the receiver and pull out the card.

Russian phonecards

Postal Services

Post offices such as the **Main Post Office** and those in hotels sell ordinary and commemorative Russian stamps, postcards, envelopes and phonecards. The smaller post offices are marked почта (*pochta*), and are most plentiful in the centre of the city. They generally have big glass windows and have blue post boxes outside.

International post is often slow and is probably best avoided except for postcards. **Post International**, which also offers poste restante, provides the same service as courier companies. **American Express** runs its usual poste restante service for card holders.

Postbox

Use a courier service for important documents, such as **DHL Worldwide Express**, **Federal Express** and **TNT Express Worldwide**. Anything other than paper, especially computer discs, is checked by customs, which can delay dispatch by an extra day or so.

Fax, Telex, Telegram, and E-mail Services

Many hotels and the **Main Post Office** offer fax, telex and telegram services. Telegrams in foreign languages can also be sent from the **Central Telegraph Office**. In addition to postal services, **Independent Postal Service** offers fax and e-mail services, while internet cafés such as **InternetTsentr** and **RGGU** allow you to browse the internet and send e-mails.

Television and Radio

Hotels have long offered Eurosport, CNN, BBC World Service TV and NBC channels. Russian-language television is dominated by imported soap operas, which are generally dubbed into Russian rather than subtitled The best national news in Russian is on NTV, and the best local news on TV-Tsentr. For English-language radio

Romanesque-inspired façade of Moscow's grand Main Post Office

broadcasts the best are still the BBC World Service and the Voice of America, which are broadcast on medium and shortwave. Ekho Moskvy provides an excellent news service in Russian.

Good pop stations include Radio Maximum (103.7 FM) and Local Europe Plus (106.2 FM) both of which play Western music, and Russkoe Radio (105.7 FM) which plays Russian music. Orfey (72.14 FM) plays classical music without adverts.

Newspapers and Magazines

Moscow has two major English-language newspapers, which are published daily except Sundays and Mondays, *The Moscow Times* and *The Moscow Tribune*. Both cover domestic and foreign news and have extensive listings of exhibitions and events in their Friday editions. The Saturday editions have television programmes listed for the week, including satellite channels. *The Exile*, also in English, carries restaurant and entertainment listings. The

English- and Russian-language newspapers

Russian-language *Kapital* is published every Wednesday and has listings of events. All four are available free in restaurants, hotels, and in some supermarkets and fast-food chains. Current foreign newspapers can be picked up at highly inflated prices from kiosks in the biggest hotels.

Directory

Telephone Services

Central Telegraph Office
Центральный телеграф
Tsentralnyy telegraf
Tverskaya ul 7.
Map 2 F5. *924 4758.* *8am–9pm.* www.ctel.msk.ru

Postal Services

American Express
Ulitsa Usacheva 33.
Map 5 B5. *933 8400.*

Main Post Office
Главный почтамт
Glavnyy pochtamt
Malaya Dmitrovka 29.
Map 3 C4. *733 9073.* *8am–8pm Mon–Fri, 8am–7pm Sat, 9am–7pm Sun, noon–6pm public hols.*

Independent Postal Service
2-ia Brestskaya ul 43.
Map 2 E3. *733 9073.*
9am–8pm Mon–Fri, 10am–5pm Sat, noon–5pm Sun.

Courier Services

DHL Worldwide Express
3-iy Samotechnyy per 11/2.
Map 3 A2. *956 1000.*
www.dhl.ru

Federal Express
125167 Aviatsionnyy per 8/17.
234 3400.
www.FEDEX.com/ru

TNT Express Worldwide
Novy Arbat 2.
Map 6 E1. *202 4796.*
www.tnt.ru/english

Internet Cafés

InternetTsentr
Bolshaya Ordynka 45. **Map** 7 B4.
953 0175. *9am–11pm.*

RGGU
ulitsa Chaianova 15. **Map** 1 E2.
250 6169. *10am–8pm.*

Getting to Moscow

The quickest and most comfortable way to get to Moscow is by plane. Travelling overland, especially by road, can be difficult and often involves crossing numerous borders and negotiating roadworks and pot-holed roads. However, if cost is the priority, rail or coach are possibilities, especially for visitors arriving from St Petersburg or a neighbouring country, such as Ukraine or Belarus. It is essential that visitors plan their journey before applying for a visa *(see p200)* since the Russian authorities require detailed information about travel arrangements, including which cities visitors will use to enter and leave Russia. Whichever route is chosen, it is worth shopping around to find the best deal as prices fluctuate greatly throughout the year.

A plane owned by the Russian airline Aeroflot

Exterior of Sheremetevo 2, Moscow's main international airport

Arriving by Air

There is a reasonable choice of flights to Moscow from the UK. Three carriers – **British Airways**, **Aeroflot** and **Transaero** – operate direct flights, while several other airlines, including **SAS**, **KLM** and **Austrian Airlines** run a variety of flights via a number of destinations. **Transaero**, which now flies direct from London, is the only reliable Russian alternative to Aeroflot. Both Transaero and Aeroflot operate long-haul flights from the USA, Australia and Canada. Despite popular belief that Aeroflot's flights are of an inferior quality, its Moscow to London route is a reasonable option, and its first-class service is excellent.

Cheap trips are advertised in the travel sections of many newspapers and magazines. There are also several agencies in London and New York that book trips to Russia. Some, such as **Eastways Travel Service**, sell only flights, while others, such as **Progressive Tours** and **Panorama Travel Ltd**, also book hotel accommodation or offer inclusive package deals. These can be cheaper than booking flights and accommodation separately. Some agencies also arrange visas for travellers *(see p200)*.

Sheremetevo 2 Airport

Sheremetevo 2 is the main international airport serving Moscow and is the most likely point of arrival for visitors. Situated about 28 km (17 miles) northwest of the city centre, it has one terminal, with flights divided between its right and left wings. Central notice boards, in both the departures and arrivals lounges indicate which wing each flight is expected at or leaving from.

Sheremetevo 2 is not modern, or especially convenient, but it does offer facilities such as a currency exchange *(see p204)*, several shops, a restaurant and a number of fast-food outlets. A reasonable selection of duty-free goods can be purchased at the airport, on arrival as well as departure. While some duty-free items, such as alcohol, are very cheap, others, including caviar, cost almost as much as they do abroad.

Passport control in Russia is still extremely tight, and queuing for it can take up to two hours if several flights arrive at the airport at the same time. Visitors are required to fill in one customs declaration on arrival and another one when leaving *(see p200)*.

Airport signs, Sheremetevo 2

Other Airports

Moscow has four other airports. **Sheremetevo 1**, close to Sheremetevo 2, is used mainly for domestic flights, including those from St Petersburg. It also handles all Transaero flights and some Aeroflot charters from abroad. Flights destined for the nearer parts of Russia and other CIS member states often leave from **Vnukovo** airport, which is located in the southwest of Moscow. **Domodedovo**, south of Moscow, serves more distant places in Russia and the CIS including eastern Russia, Siberia and Central Asia. **Bykovo**, to the west, is Moscow's smallest airport and is used only by small, old-fashioned planes as it does not have the modern runways needed by larger aircraft. Bykovo serves the less important routes within Russia and, in summer, also receives some charter flights.

Bus and Metro Links into the City Centre

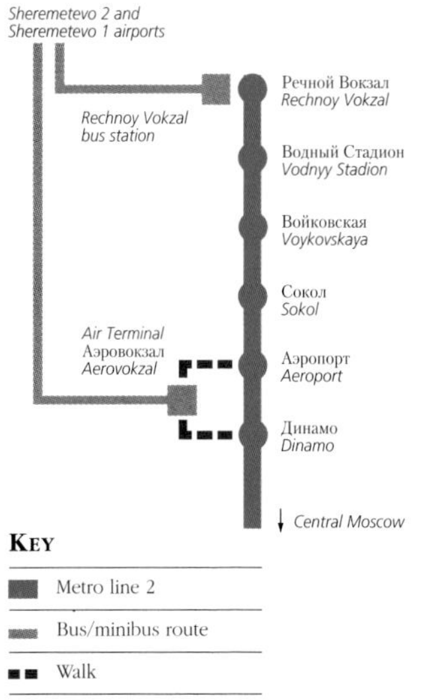

Rechnoy Vokzal metro, at the end of metro line 2

Sign at departure point of express bus to Rechnoy Vokzal bus station

Getting into the City

Although the easiest way of getting into the city from Sheremetevo 2 is by taxi, there are also two bus routes. One runs from the arrivals hall to the air terminal *(aerovokzal)*, around 7 km (4 miles) from the centre of Moscow, and takes 35 minutes. The air terminal is about 15 minutes' walk from either Aeroport or Dinamo metro stations. The other bus route runs to Rechnoy Vokzal bus station, close to Rechnoy Vokzal metro. Both services run from 6:25am to 11:30pm. The trip into the city centre by metro then takes about 15–20 minutes.

Sheremetevo 1 has both bus and minibus services, which also go to Rechnoy Vokzal bus station or the air terminal. Again, both services run from 6:25am until 11:30pm. The minibuses should also run all night, but their schedule is erratic. The destination of each bus is indicated by a sign displayed in its front window.

For those preferring to travel by taxi *(see p212)* there are several things to remember. Firstly, it is much easier for travellers to book a cab prior to arriving, either through a travel agency or through their hotel. Airport taxis are expensive (the equivalent of US$50–60 to the city centre) and not all of them are official. Anyone coming out of customs is met by a wall of taxi drivers offering a lift into town. These unofficial drivers are generally safe, but it is better to walk outside to the rank of official taxis. These yellow cars have black chequered designs on the roof. The taximeters installed in most of them are rarely used so it is vital to negotiate a price for the trip beforehand. Once this has been agreed, no tips are necessary. The journey into the city centre takes about 30–40 minutes if the roads are clear, and up to 90 minutes at busy times.

Novotel, an airport hotel *(see p170)*, is the only hotel to operate a courtesy pick-up bus from Sheremetevo 2. Cars can also be rented at this airport *(see p218)*. Should visitors arrive at one of the smaller airports, they will find a variety of public transport and taxis.

A minibus that takes people from Sheremetevo 1 to Rechnoy Vokzal bus station or the air terminal

Passengers waiting to board a bus from Sheremetevo 2 to Rechnoy Vokzal bus station

Rank of unofficial taxis outside the arrivals hall at Sheremetevo 2, waiting for fares into the city

Arriving by Train

Moscow can be reached by train from Paris, Brussels, Berlin and several other European capitals, but the trip will take at least a day and a night. Travellers should be prepared for a lengthy wait at the Russian border while all of the train's wheels are changed to fit the wider Russian tracks.

Three of Moscow's main railway stations are situated on Komsomolskaya ploshchad *(see p144)*, also known as ploshchad Trekh Vokzalov (Square of the Three Railway Stations). **Yaroslavskiy** and **Kazanskiy** serve domestic routes only. **Leningradskiy** is the terminus for trains from St Petersburg and Finland. Of the other stations, **Rizhskiy** serves the Baltic and **Kievskiy** serves Eastern Europe, while **Belorusskiy** handles trains from Western Europe and Poland. **Paveletskiy** and **Kurskiy** stations are the points of arrival for trains from southern Russia and parts of the Ukraine.

РЕСТОРАН
017
65676
Restaurant car of the Budapest train arriving at Kievskiy station

The imposing main entrance to Belorusskiy station

Tickets for all trains have to be booked in advance. Owing to the long distances covered on many routes, the majority of trains are overnight sleepers, but there are some standard trains operating on the shorter routes. Trains fall into four categories: express *(ekspressy)* trains, which travel the direct route between Moscow and St Petersburg only; fast *(skorye)* trains, which operate on long journeys and stop at only a few stations; passenger *(passazhirskie)* trains, which also operate on long routes, but stop at most or all stations; and suburban *(prigorodnye)* trains *(see p219)*.

Soviet crest on the exterior of Kievskiy railway station

Arriving by Coach

It is possible to get to Moscow by coach, but it is only usually worth it if visitors are travelling from a neighbouring country or are on a tight budget. There are coach routes to Moscow from the Czech Republic, Poland, Hungary and Slovakia. Some run via the Ukraine, while others enter Russia via Belarus. Sometimes a change of coach is necessary and the onward journey from either country takes 12–16 hours as the roads to Moscow from Belarus and the Ukraine are not well maintained.

Moscow's Major Railway Stations

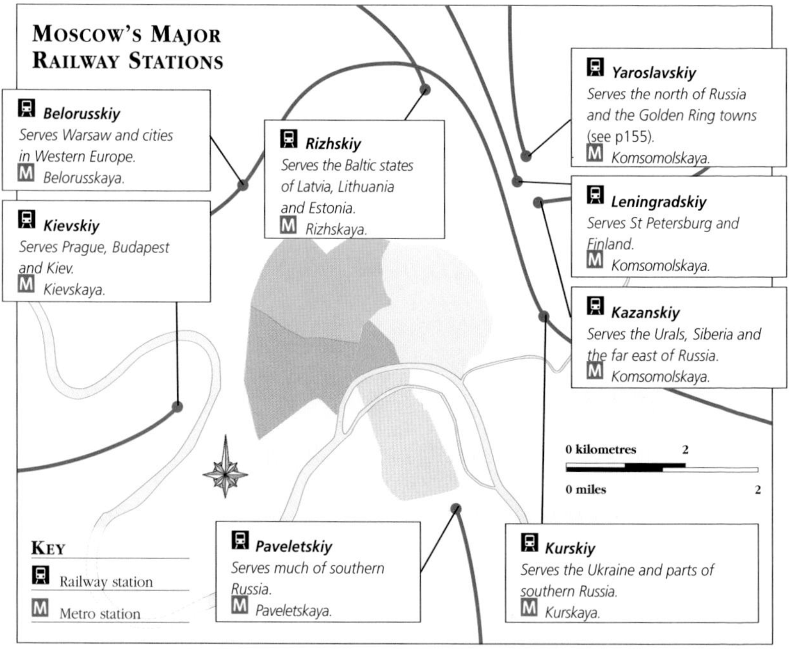
Belorusskiy
Serves Warsaw and cities in Western Europe.
Belorusskaya.
Kievskiy
Serves Prague, Budapest and Kiev.
Kievskaya.
Rizhskiy
Serves the Baltic states of Latvia, Lithuania and Estonia.
Rizhskaya.
Yaroslavskiy
Serves the north of Russia and the Golden Ring towns (see p155).
Komsomolskaya.
Leningradskiy
Serves St Petersburg and Finland.
Komsomolskaya.
Kazanskiy
Serves the Urals, Siberia and the far east of Russia.
Komsomolskaya.
0 kilometres 2
0 miles 2
Paveletskiy
Serves much of southern Russia.
Paveletskaya.
Kurskiy
Serves the Ukraine and parts of southern Russia.
Kurskaya.
Key
Railway station
Metro station

Travelling to Moscow from St Petersburg

The easiest way of getting to Moscow from St Petersburg is by train. Express trains run from Moskovskiy station in St Petersburg to Leningradskiy station in Moscow. It is easiest to organize a ticket through a hotel or travel agent.

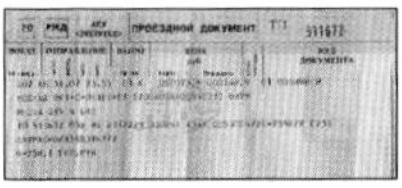

A ticket from a Moscow–St Petersburg express

The best night-time trains are Nos. 1 (called the *Red Arrow*) and 3 from St Petersburg to Moscow, and Nos. 2 and 4, from Moscow to St Petersburg.

Sign indicating the *Aurora* train from St Petersburg to Moscow

All these services leave at midnight and arrive at 8:30 the next morning and are usually on time. Other trains, including Nos. 47 and 159 (the *Aurora*) are almost as good, especially for those who prefer to make the trip in the day. On all these trains travellers should be wary of thieves. Most compartments have locks, which should be used at night.

Ticket prices start at the equivalent of US$10 for a basic seat and rise to US$35 per person for a two-person compartment. Prices are usually higher for foreigners than for Russians. There is a choice between *sidyashchyy* (sitting) tickets and a variety of more expensive sleeper options. Bedlinen costs extra. Food may be available, but visitors are advised to bring their own.

Compartment on the *Red Arrow* St Petersburg–Moscow express

The alternative to taking the train is flying. The flight only takes 50 minutes, but allow plenty of time to get to and from the airports, especially in Moscow *(see p209)*. Planes depart from Pulkovo 1 airport in St Petersburg and arrive at Sheremetevo 1 *(see p208)*. The air fare is considerably more expensive than the train.

Directory

UK and US Travel Agencies

Eastways Travel Service
6 Brick Lane,
London E1 6RS.
020 7247 3823/ 5668.

Interchange
27 Stafford Road,
Croydon CR0 4NE.
020 8681 3612.

Progressive Tours
12 Porchester Place,
London W2 2BS.
020 7262 1676.

Panorama Travel Ltd
156 Fifth Ave, Suite 1019,
New York, NY 10010.
212 741 0033.

Airlines

Aeroflot
Аэрофлот
Leningradskyy prospekt 37.
Map 3 A4. *155 0922.*
020 7355 2233 in UK.
W www.aeroflot.ru

Austrian Airlines
Smolenskaya ulitsa 5,
Map 5 C2.
995 0995.
020 7434 7300 in UK.
W www.austrianairlines.ru

British Airways
1 Tverskaya-Yamskaya ulitsa 23. **Map** 2 D2.
363 2325.
0345 222 111 in UK.
W www.britishairways.ru

KLM
Ulitsa Usacheva 33, Floor 1. **Map** 5 A5.
258 3600.
0990 750 900 in UK.

SAS
1 Tverskaya-Yamskaya ulitsa 5. **Map** 2 D3.
775 4747.
020 7734 4020 in UK.

Transaero
Трансаэро
Ulitsa Okhotnyy ryad 2.
Map 3 A5. *241 7676.*
020 7636 2545 in UK.
W www.transaero.ru

Moscow Airports

Sheremetevo 1 & 2
Шереметьево 1 & 2
578 2372/ 956 4666.

Bykovo
Быково
558 4738.

Domodedovo
Домодедово
323 8160.

Vnukovo
Внуково
436 2813.

Train Stations

Belorusskiy
Белорусский
Ploshchad Tverskoy Zastavy 7. **Map** 1 C2.
973 8191.

Kazanskiy
Казанский
Komsomolskaya ploshchad 2. **Map** 4 D2.
264 6556.

Kievskiy
Киевский
Ploshchad Kievskovo vokzala. **Map** 5 B2.
240 1115.

Kurskiy
Курский
Ulitsa Zemlyanoy val 29.
Map 4 E5.
917 3152.

Leningradskiy
Ленинградский
Komsomolskaya ploshchad 3.
Map 4 D2.
262 9143.

Paveletskiy
Павелецкий
Paveletskaya ploshchad 1.
Map 7 C5.
235 0522.

Rizhskiy
Рижский
Ploshchad Rizhskovo vokzala.
971 1588.

Savelouskiy
Савеловскии
Ploshchad Savelovskovo Vokzala.
285 9005.

Yaroslavskiy
Ярославский
Komsomolskaya ploschad 5. **Map** 4 D2.
921 5914.

General Enquiries
266 9333.

Ticket Bookings
266 8333.

Bus Stations

Moscow Bus Station
Московский автовокзал
Moskovskiy avtovokzal
Nr Shchelkovskaya metro, Uralskaya ulitsa 2.
468 0400.

Getting Around Moscow

Moscow's vast metro network, which has stops close to all the major sights, is the most reliable way of travelling around the city. However, it can get extremely crowded. Moscow is also served by buses, trolleybuses and trams. Services are relatively frequent, although delays are now more common than they were in the Soviet era. A knowledge of the Cyrillic alphabet will help with reading signs on these services.

Indicates a pedestrian area

Suburban buses are particularly useful for travelling around Moscow's outlying districts, beyond the reach of the metro network, and bus routes often start at a major metro station. Trams run as far as the outskirts of the city, but services are gradually being reduced. Trolleybuses are a good means of transport in the city centre, covering the popular routes. Taxis are the most flexible, but most expensive, way of getting around.

The Kremlin, at the heart of Moscow *(see pp52–67)*, must be explored on foot

Walking

Moscow's centre is very spread out and so not easily negotiable on foot. However, the area within the Boulevard Ring, where many sights are located, offers a few good opportunities for walking. At the heart of the city are Red Square *(see p106)* and the Kremlin, which are only accessible on foot. Visitors should allow three hours to cover this area including all the cathedrals in the Kremlin. Across the river from here, beautiful Zamoskvoreche *(see pp114–25)* is another district which pedestrians will enjoy.

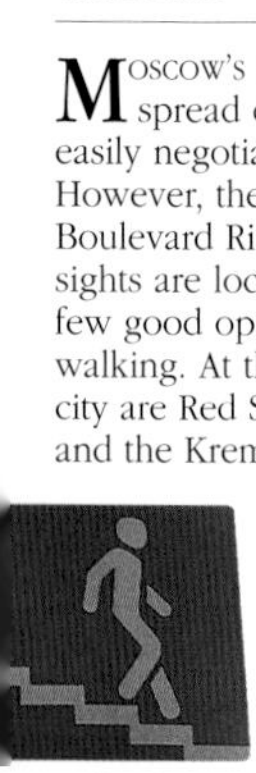

Pedestrian subway sign

Muscovites themselves are not great walkers but, in the evenings or at weekends, they can often be seen taking a stroll around the Old Arbat *(see pp70–71)*, a district of the city frequented by artists, musicians and street performers. Other places to take a walk are Tverskaya ulitsa *(see p89)*, numerous parks – in particular Gorky Park *(see p129)*, Izmaylovo Park *(see p141)* and Sokolniki Park – and by the Moskva river.

When embarking on a walk around the city, it is a good idea to wear sturdy shoes, and preferably old ones as Moscow can be dirty. Traffic is heavy and major roads can often be crossed via subways (although, as in other cities, it is wise to be vigilant when doing so alone). Alternatively use a zebra crossing if a green light shows: drivers in Moscow do not stop at zebra crossings without lights. It is not advisable for anyone, but especially a woman, to walk around any part of the city alone late at night. The best walking tours in English are organized by Patriarshi Dom Tours *(see p198)*.

Taxis

For safety reasons it is best to travel only by official taxis: yellow cabs with a black chequered design on their roofs. They can be booked through the **Moscow Taxi** company, although operators are unlikely to speak English, or alternatively through a hotel. They usually arrive within half an hour. Taxis to the airport should be booked well in advance. Some hotels have their own taxi ranks, but the taxis that wait there can be very expensive. It is possible to flag down an official taxi on the street. Some switch on a green light, either on

Official yellow Moscow taxi

Hot Air Balloons

Taking a trip in a hot air balloon has recently become a popular pastime among well-off New Russians and visitors to the city, especially in the summer. **Avgur** launches its balloons near the Istra river in Zvenigorod outside Moscow. Rides last for about two hours, taking three passengers, who can include children, in addition to the pilot. Trips are expensive, but offer fantastic views of the city including the "Seven Sisters", Stalinist-Gothic skyscrapers *(see p45)*.

Hailing a private car for a ride, a common practice among Russians

their window or on their roof, to indicate they are for hire. Others do not, but if they are for hire they will stop. All official taxis have meters, but some are out-of-date and the driver may prefer to negotiate the fare. It is crucial either to agree on a fare, or to be sure that the driver turns on the meter, before setting off.

Russians themselves prefer to use private taxis (*chastniki*) to official ones. Any car can be hailed and a fee agreed for a journey. Other cars may therefore stop when an official taxi is hailed. Private taxis are cheap and generally safe. However, it is not advisable for visitors to the city who do not speak Russian to use them.

Moscow River Cruises

River boats are extremely popular in summer. They operate from May to October and cover quite a long stretch of the Moskva river. They stop at 10 or so points along the river and you can hop on and off, but must purchase a new ticket each time. All riverboats have two decks and on sunny days the upper deck is great for combining sunbathing with sightseeing.

River cruises pass several major sites and are a good way to get a feel for the city's layout. The main pick-up point for these cruises is opposite Kievskiy station. Major stops are near Moscow State University at Sparrow Hills *(see p129)*, at Gorky Park and near Red Square (Bolshoy Ustinskiy most). **Moscow River Line** is the main company running these cruises. It also hires boats out and organizes parties on them.

Directory

Moscow Taxi
Московское такси
Moskovskoe taksi
238 1001. www.taxi.car.ru

Moscow River Line
Московское регное Пароходство
Moskovskoe pechnoe parohodstvo
459 7150.

Avgur
Авгур
Ulitsa Stepana Shutova 4.
359 1001/1065.

Double-decker river boat, a good way to view the sights along the river

River Cruise Route

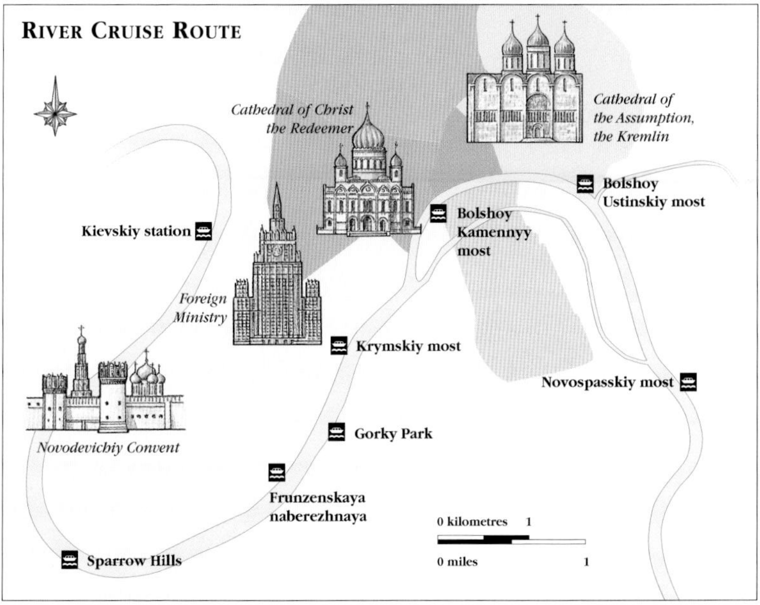

The Metro

Moscow metro symbol

MOSCOW IS A SPRAWLING, hectic city. One of its great assets, however, is its excellent metro network, which extends from the centre right out to many of its suburbs. During the rush hour, in particular, heavy traffic means that it is often faster to travel by metro than by car, let alone any other form of public transport. For years all transport in the Soviet Union was extremely cheap and metro fares are still very good value. At present passengers pay the same fare regardless of the length of their journey. However, the city authorities have announced plans to introduce new variable fares at some point in the future.

The metro system is extremely reliable, with trains running frequently throughout the day. Constructed as part of Stalin's grand plan for rebuilding Moscow, it is also a tourist attraction in its own right *(see pp38–41)*.

The ornate, cavernous interior of Arbatskaya metro

The Network

THE MOSCOW metro network is well planned and extensive, consisting of 10 lines which cover the whole city except its outermost suburbs. One feature worth noting is the circular line connecting all the mainline railway stations *(see p210)*. Changing between the metro and a mainline station is generally easy as both have the same name, but with a slightly different ending. Belorusskiy railway station, for instance, links to Belorusskaya metro, and Kievskiy railway station to Kievskaya metro. However, Komsomolskaya, also on the circle line, is the exception. It links to three mainline railway stations – Leningradskiy, Kazanskiy and Yaroslavskiy.

Emergency intercom to driver

The metro lines are colour-coded and numbered from 1 to 10, and all signs are in Cyrillic only. Trains arrive frequently, generally every 1–2 minutes on weekdays, while services are slightly less frequent at weekends. During the rush hour the interval between trains is usually under a minute.

The Moscow metro is on the whole safe and reliable. All the stations are staffed, although metro attendants are unlikely to speak anything except their mother tongue. Travellers who have a heavy bag or a suitcase will have to pay an added charge.

Main entrance to Tretyakovskaya metro, an interchange station

Changing Lines

FOR THOSE unused to the complexity of Moscow's metro system, journeys can be made even more confusing by the fact that stations where it is possible to change between metro lines often have two or more separate names, one for each line involved. On the metro map *(see p216)* these interchange stations are bracketed together. For instance, near the centre of the city there is an interchange between four lines – 1, 3, 4 and 9 – each of which is served by a different station. Correspondingly, four station names are given on the map: Biblioteka imeni Lenina, Arbatskaya, Aleksandrovskiy Sad and Borovitskaya.

When changing lines at an interchange station it is therefore important to know the name of the station on the other line. It is then easy to reach the right platform by following the переход *(perekhod)* – or "interchange" – signs indicating this name.

Metro train ready to depart from Mayakovskaya metro

Travelling by Tram, Trolleybus and Bus

Moscow has extensive bus, trolleybus and tram routes, and some of the most useful ones are identified on the transport map on the inside back cover of this book. Some routes link in with the metro network *(see pp214–16)*, often starting at one metro station and terminating at another. Main avenues are generally served by both buses and trolleybuses. Trams are less useful but, as a sedate form of transport, they are great for sightseeing. Busy routes can get extremely crowded during the morning and evening rush hours, and traffic is often slow-moving at these times. Moscow's newer, more remote suburbs are well served by these forms of transport. Stops are clearly signed and are at frequent intervals, though tram stops are occasionally further apart.

Queue of people waiting at a bus stop in central Moscow

Trams

Although trams remain Moscow's most traditional means of transport, services are now being cut back and some old tracks have been removed altogether. However, they provide a bumpy, entertaining ride for children and interest and variety for visitors.

The surviving tram services run quite frequently, especially those operating in the suburbs, linking metro stations and apartment blocks. Tram stops are marked by a transparent sign labelled Тр in Cyrillic and usually have a semi-circular shelter with a bench. Trams have one or two carriages, each with three doors. It was customary to get on through the rear door and leave through the front, but this practice is no longer observed.

Tram route A, which starts at Chistye Prudy metro, is useful for visitors to the city as it passes close to quite a few of Moscow's central sights. A special sightseeing tram with an on-board café travels the same route; tickets are sold as you get on.

A yellow and white Moscow tram

A yellow Moscow bus

Trolleybus, powered by an overhead cable and running on a fixed route

Trolleybuses

Trolleybuses are very useful for travelling around the city centre. Even though they are less comfortable and Muscovites prefer travelling by bus, most of the routes are still packed during rush hours. Stops are marked by a plaque with the Cyrillic letter T.

Trolleybuses are blue, red or yellow. Those with two cars have three working doors and those with a single car have two working doors. As with trams, there is no established etiquette as to which door to use when getting on or off.

Trolleybus Б travels around the Garden Ring and is good for getting to know the city.

Trolleybus 15 cuts across the whole city centre, starting at Suvorov ploshchad next to Novoslobodskaya metro and terminating at the Luzhniki Central Stadium *(see pp194–5)*.

Buses

Buses are most useful for travelling in Moscow's suburbs where distances between metro lines are much greater than in the centre. Bus stops are marked by white and yellow plaques showing the cyrillic letter A and are the same distance apart as trolleybus stops. Public buses are yellow, red, or red and white. Bus services in the city centre are limited, and there are none running along Tverskaya ulitsa. However, several bus routes run up Kutuzovskiy prospekt past the Borodino Panorama Museum, the Triumphal Arch and Victory Park *(see pp128–9)*.

Ticket for tram, bus and trolleybus

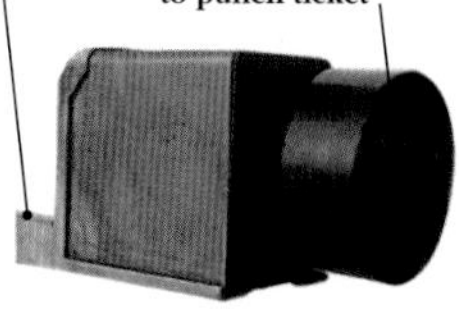

Punching machine for validating tram, trolleybus and bus tickets

Tickets and Travel Cards

One-day travel cards are not available in Moscow, but monthly cards can be bought at metro stations: these cover the metro alone; tram, bus and trolleybus (separately or in any combination); or all four modes of transport. Individual tickets for bus, trolleybus and tram are identical and can be bought in metro stations or at nearby kiosks, or from drivers, but then cost a little more. They must be inserted into the punching machine on any bus, trolleybus or tram to be valid.

Driving in Moscow

DRIVING IN MOSCOW can be quite gruelling for the uninitiated. Most driving regulations, and many principles that would be considered common sense elsewhere, are ignored. For instance, although the majority of drivers will stop at red lights, some carry on regardless. Cars travel in disorderly lanes and veer dangerously to avoid pot holes. Drivers tend to be aggressive and inconsiderate about giving way to one another. Road signs mostly follow international conventions but, as all major roads are sign-posted in Russian only, it is well worth drivers familiarizing themselves with Cyrillic place-names in advance.

Petrol station belonging to one of several chains operating in Moscow

Driving Regulations

DRIVING REGULATIONS in Moscow are complex. GAI, Russia's traffic police *(see p202)*, have the right to stop drivers at any time and ask for documents. They can issue fines on the spot for infringements such as not having a fire extinguisher or first-aid kit and not wearing seat belts. It is compulsory for both drivers and front-seat passengers to wear seat belts, although many people do not. Drivers are not allowed to drink any alcohol at all and fines for drink-driving can be very high. It is illegal to make U-turns on many of Moscow's main streets.

Priority to traffic on the right cancelled

Priority is always given to traffic coming from the right unless a yellow, diamond-shaped sign indicates otherwise.

The buying of driving licences is common in Russia, so visitors should not assume that all road users are qualified and responsible.

Parking and Petrol

PARKING IS EXPENSIVE in most of central Moscow. There are no meters; instead, drivers pay attendants in grey uniforms on either arriving or leaving. Parking time is by half-hour periods, with no time limit. Fines for parking in restricted areas (marked with the international signs) are high. All petrol is leaded. A98 (super-plus) and A95 (super) are suitable for foreign cars; A92 is for Russian-made cars.

Car Hire

THERE ARE SEVERAL well-known companies which operate in Moscow. **Hertz** and **Europcar** have offices both at Sheremetevo 2 airport and in the city centre. Other car-hire companies in Moscow include **National Car Rental** and **Rolf**. Visitors hiring a car need international insurance and must show an international driving licence and their passport and credit card when collecting it. Some of the larger international hotels also arrange car hire.

Multiple lanes of traffic on Teatralniy proezd, one of Moscow's busiest roads

Winter Driving

MOST DRIVERS use studded tyres in winter as roads are often icy and covered with snow. Driving in these conditions can be dangerous and is not advisable unless visitors have had experience in other northern climates.

Driving outside Moscow

THE ROADS leading out of Moscow are in reasonable condition, but Kutuzovskiy prospekt is particularly well-maintained because it is used by government officials and the New Russians who own a *dacha* in this area. It is vital to have a good map because side roads to small villages can easily be missed.

Directory

Car Hire

Avis
Meshchanskaya ulitsa 7/21.
Map 3 B2.
☎ *284 1937.*

Europcar
Leningradskiy prospekt 64.
☎ *155 0170.*
Sheremetevo 2 airport.
☎ *578 3878.*

Hertz
Chernyakhovskovo ulitsa 4.
☎ *937 3274.*
Sheremetevo 2 airport.
☎ *578 5646.*

National Car Rental
Bolshaya Kommunisticheskaya ulitsa 1/5.
☎ *298 6146.*

Rescue Services

Angel
Ангел
Signalnyy proezd 5.
☎ *747 0022.*

Emergency Service Station (24 hours)
Ryazanski pereulok 13.
Map 4 D3.
☎ *267 0113.*

Excursions from Moscow

ARRANGEMENTS TO VISIT SIGHTS outside Moscow *(see pp126–61)* can be made through either a hotel or a travel agency, or the trip can be made independently by train, bus or car. Most of the places mentioned below are not far from Moscow and can be visited on a day trip. A few, such as Suzdal and Vladimir, take two days. Patriarshiy Dom Tours *(see p198)* offers a wide range of excursions to the major sights around Moscow. It is advisable to enquire in good time as reservations with them have to be made 48 hours before departure.

Inside the carriage of one of Moscow's suburban trains

Using Trains and Buses

SUBURBAN TRAINS *(prigorodnye poezda)* to the nearer sights can be caught at the appropriate mainline station *(see p210)*. They usually depart from a station annexe and are cheap as foreigners pay the same fare as Russians. More distant sights are served by passenger trains *(passazhirskie poezda)*.

Suburban buses *(prigorodnye marshruty)* to several closer excursion sights leave from Moscow Bus Station at Shchelkovskaya metro station in the northeast of the city. Towns further from Moscow are served by inter-city buses *(mezhdugorodnye avtobusy)*.

An inter-city bus, which can be used to make long-distance trips

One-Day Trips

BOTH NOVODEVICHIY Convent *(see pp130–1)* and Kolomenskoe *(see pp138–9)* are south of the city centre, the former close to Sportivnaya metro, the latter to Kolomenskaya metro. Kuskovo *(see pp142–3)*, in eastern Moscow, is also best reached by metro, to Ryazanskiy Prospekt or Vykhino. A short bus ride will then take visitors to the estate.

Arkhangelskoe *(see p152)*, 20 km (12 miles) to the west of the city centre, is served by Tushinskaya metro and then a bus. By car it is on a straight route out along Volokolamskoe shosse or Rublevskoe shosse.

It takes around two hours to travel to the village and battlefield of Borodino *(see p152)* by train from Belorusskiy station, by bus from Moscow Bus Station or by car, leaving the city on Mozhayskoe shosse.

The Tchaikovsky House-Museum *(see p153)* is two hours northwest of the city by car on Leningradskoe shosse, by train from Leningradskiy station, or by bus from Moscow Bus Station.

Abramtsevo Estate-Museum *(see p154)* is situated to the northeast of Moscow just off Yaroslavskoe shosse. Trains leave from Yaroslavskiy station and buses from Moscow Bus Station. The journey takes an hour or so.

The Trinity Monastery of St Sergius *(see pp156–9)* is also to the northeast along Yaroslavskoe shosse and the journey also takes just over an hour. It is possible to get there by train or by bus from Yaroslavskiy station, and by bus from Moscow Bus Station.

Pereslavl-Zalesskiy *(see p154)* can be reached by car along Yaroslavskoe shosse, by train from Yaroslavskiy station, or by bus from Moscow Bus Station. The trip takes approximately two hours.

Two-Day Trips

SUZDAL *(see p160)*, 200 km (124 miles) northeast of Moscow, is reached by leaving the city on Gorkovskoe shosse. Buses to Suzdal leave from Moscow Bus Station and take about four hours.

Vladimir *(see pp160–61)* is also situated northeast of the city along Gorkovskoe shosse. The 170-km (106-mile) trip can be made by bus from Moscow Bus Station, by train or by car in about three hours.

Yasnaya Polyana *(see p161)* is 180 km (112 miles) south of Moscow on the Simferopolskoe shosse. Trains run from Kurskiy station and coaches from Moscow Bus Station. Both take almost four hours.

It is worth considering combining a trip to Vladimir and Suzdal; buses run daily between the two. Patriarshiy Dom runs tours to both towns with an overnight stopover, and day trips to Yasnaya Polyana.

Train arriving at Sergiev Posad for the Trinity Monastery of St Sergius

Moscow Street Finder

The key map below shows the areas of Moscow covered by the *Street Finder*. The map references given throughout the guide for sights, restaurants, hotels, shops or entertainment venues refer to the maps in this section. All the major sights have been marked so they are easy to locate. The key below shows other features marked on the maps, such as post offices, metro stations and churches. The *Street Finder* index lists street names in transliteration, followed by Cyrillics (on maps, Cyrillics are only given for major roads). This guide uses the reinstated old Russian street names, not the Soviet versions *(see p199)*. Places of interest are listed by their English names.

A Moscow family out sightseeing

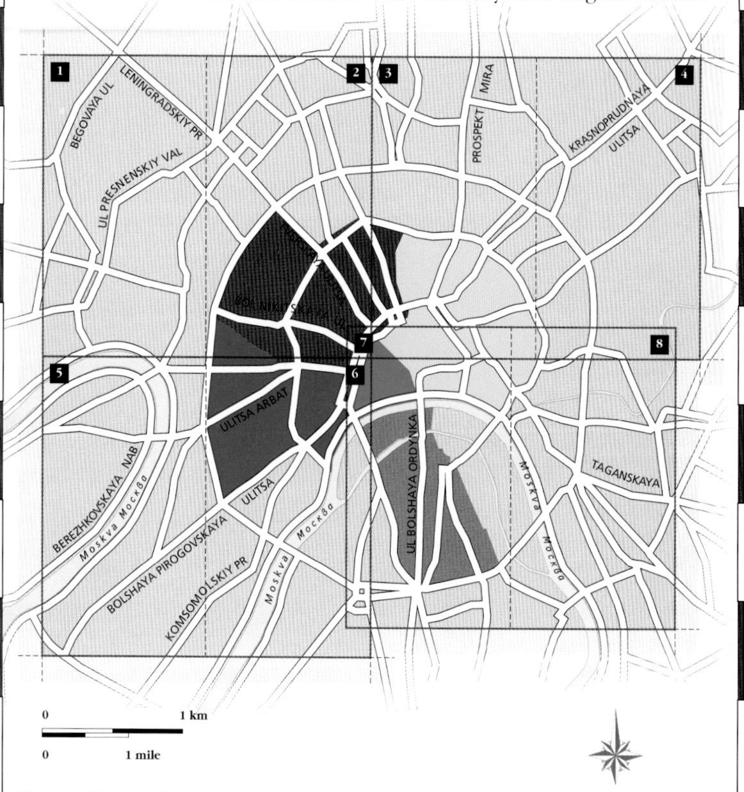

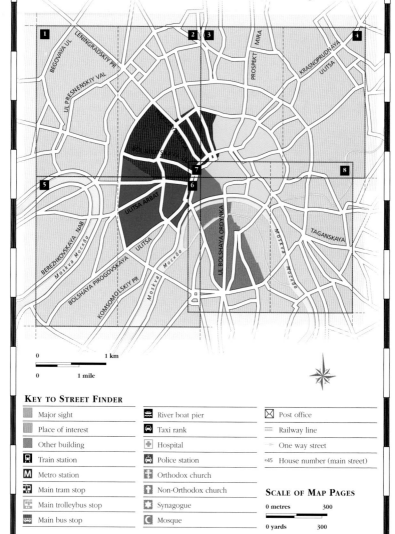

Key to Street Finder

Major sight	River boat pier	Post office
Place of interest	Taxi rank	Railway line
Other building	Hospital	One way street
Train station	Police station	«45 House number (main street)
Metro station	Orthodox church	
Main tram stop	Non-Orthodox church	
Main trolleybus stop	Synagogue	
Main bus stop	Mosque	

Scale of Map Pages

0 metres 300

0 yards 300

Street Finder Index

Abbreviations & Useful Words

ul	**ulitsa**	street
pl	**ploshchad**	square
pr	**prospekt**	avenue
per	**pereulok**	small street/ passage/lane
	most	bridge
	podezd	entrance
	proezd	small street/ passage/lane
	sad	garden
	shosse	road
	stroenie	building
	tupik	cul-de-sac

C

D

E

Kozitskiy pereulok КОЗИЦКИЙ ПЕРЕУЛОК 2F4
Krasina, ulitsa КРАСИНА, УЛИЦА 2D3
Krasnaya ploshchad КРАСНАЯ ПЛОЩАДЬ 3A5, 7B1
Krasnaya Presnya, ulitsa КРАСНАЯ ПРЕСНЯ, УЛИЦА 1B4
Krasnokholmskaya naberezhnaya КРАСНОХОЛМСКАЯ НАБЕРЕЖНАЯ 8D4
Krasnopresnenskaya naberezhnaya КРАСНОПРЕСНЕНСКАЯ НАБЕРЕЖНАЯ 1B5, 5A1
Krasnopresnenskoy Zastavy, ploshchad КРАСНОПРЕСНЕНСКОЙ ЗАСТАВЫ, ПЛОЩАДЬ 1A4
Krasnoproletarskaya ulitsa КРАСНОПРОЛЕТАРСКАЯ УЛИЦА 2F2
Krasnoprudnaya ulitsa КРАСНОПРУДНАЯ УЛИЦА 4E2
Krasnoselskiy, tupik КРАСНОСЕЛЬСКИЙ, ТУПИК 4E1
Kremlevskaya naberezhnaya КРЕМЛЁВСКАЯ НАБЕРЕЖНАЯ 7A2
Krestyanskiy tupik КРЕСТЬЯНСКИЙ ТУПИК 8E4
Krestyanskoy Zastavy, ploshchad КРЕСТЬЯНСКОЙ ЗАСТАВЫ, ПЛОЩАДЬ 8F4
Krivoarbatskiy pereulok КРИВОАРБАТСКИЙ ПЕРЕУЛОК 6D1
Krivokolennyy pereulok КРИВОКОЛЕННЫЙ ПЕРЕУЛОК 3B4
Kropotkinskiy pereulok КРОПОТКИНСКИЙ ПЕРЕУЛОК 6D3
Krutitskaya naberezhnaya КРУТИЦКАЯ НАБЕРЕЖНАЯ 8E5
Krutitskaya ulitsa КРУТИЦКАЯ УЛИЦА 8E5
Krutitskiy val, ulitsa КРУТИЦКИЙ ВАЛ, УЛИЦА 8F5
Krutitskoe Mission 8E5
Krymskaya naberezhnaya КРЫМСКАЯ НАБЕРЕЖНАЯ 6E4
Krymskiy most КРЫМСКИЙ МОСТ 6E4
Krymskiy tupik КРЫМСКИЙ ТУПИК 6F4
Krymskiy val, ulitsa КРЫМСКИЙ ВАЛ, УЛИЦА 6F4
Kseninskiy pereulok КСЕНЬИНСКИЙ ПЕРЕУЛОК 6D4
Kudrinskaya ploshchad КУДРИНСКАЯ ПЛОЩАДЬ 1C5
Kursovoy pereulok КУРСОВОЙ ПЕРЕУЛОК 6F3
Kutuzovskiy prospekt КУТУЗОВСКИЙ ПРОСПЕКТ 5A2
Kuznetskiy most, ulitsa КУЗНЕЦКИЙ МОСТ, УЛИЦА 3A4

L

Lavrov pereulok ЛАВРОВ ПЕРЕУЛОК 8E4
Lavrskiy pereulok ЛАВРСКИЙ ПЕРЕУЛОК 3A2
Lavrushinskiy pereulok ЛАВРУШИНСКИЙ ПЕРЕУЛОК 7A3
Lebyazhiy pereulok ЛЕБЯЖИЙ ПЕРЕУЛОК 6F2
Lenin Mausoleum 7A1
Leningradskiy prospekt ЛЕНИНГРАДСКИЙ ПРОСПЕКТ 1B1
Leninskiy prospect ЛЕНИНСКИЙ ПРОСПЕКТ 6F5
Lenivka, ulitsa ЛЕНИВКА, УЛИЦА 6F2
Leontevskiy pereulok ЛЕОНТЬЕВСКИЙ ПЕРЕУЛОК 2E5
Lermontov House-Museum 2D5, 6D1
Lermontovskaya ploshchad ЛЕРМОНТОВСКАЯ ПЛОЩАДЬ 4D3
Lesnaya ulitsa ЛЕСНАЯ УЛИЦА 2D2
Lesnoryadskaya ulitsa ЛЕСНОРЯДСКАЯ УЛИЦА 4F1
Lesnoryadskiy pereulok ЛЕСНОРЯДСКИЙ ПЕРЕУЛОК 4F1
Letnikovskaya ulitsa ЛЕТНИКОВСКАЯ УЛИЦА 8D5
Likhov pereulok ЛИХОВ ПЕРЕУЛОК 2F3
Lopukhinskiy pereulok ЛОПУХИНСКИЙ ПЕРЕУЛОК 6E2
Lubyanka Square 3B4
Lubyanskaya ploschad ЛУБЯНСКАЯ ПЛОЩАДЬ 3B5
Lubyanskiy proezd ЛУБЯНСКИЙ ПРОЕЗД 3B5, 7C1
Lubyanskiy prospekt ЛУБЯНСКИЙ ПРОСПЕКТ 3B5
Lukov pereulok ЛУКОВ ПЕРЕУЛОК 3B3
Luzhkov most ЛУЖКОВ МОСТ 7A3
Lva Tolstovo, ulitsa ЛЬВА ТОЛСТОГО, УЛИЦА 6D4
Lyalin pereulok ЛЯЛИН ПЕРЕУЛОК 4D4
Lyusinovskaya ulitsa ЛЮСИНОВСКАЯ УЛИЦА 7B5

M

Makarenko, ulitsa МАКАРЕНКО, УЛИЦА 4D4
Malaya Bronnaya ulitsa МАЛАЯ БРОННАЯ УЛИЦА 2D4
Malaya Dmitrovka, ulitsa МАЛАЯ ДМИТРОВКА, УЛИЦА 2E3
Malaya Dorogomilovskaya ulitsa МАЛАЯ ДОРОГОМИЛОВСКАЯ УЛИЦА 5A2
Malaya Gruzinskaya ulitsa МАЛАЯ ГРУЗИНСКАЯ УЛИЦА 1B4
Malaya Kommunisticheskaya ulitsa МАЛАЯ КОММУНИСТИЧЕСКАЯ УЛИЦА 8E3
Malaya Lubyanka, ulitsa МАЛАЯ ЛУБЯНКА, УЛИЦА 3B4
Malaya Nikitskaya ulitsa МАЛАЯ НИКИТСКАЯ УЛИЦА 2D5
Malaya Ordynka, ulitsa МАЛАЯ ОРДЫНКА, УЛИЦА 7B4
Malaya Pionerskaya ulitsa МАЛАЯ ПИОНЕРСКАЯ УЛИЦА 7C5
Malaya Pirogovskaya ulitsa МАЛАЯ ПИРОГОВСКАЯ УЛИЦА 5B5
Malaya Polyanka, ulitsa МАЛАЯ ПОЛЯНКА, УЛИЦА 7A4
Malaya Trubetskaya ulitsa МАЛАЯ ТРУБЕЦКАЯ УЛИЦА 5B4
Malaya Yakimanka, ulitsa МАЛАЯ ЯКИМАНКА, УЛИЦА 7A3
Malye Kamenshchiki, ulitsa МАЛЫЕ КАМЕНЩИКИ, УЛИЦА 8E4
Malyy Demidovskiy pereulok МАЛЫЙ ДЕМИДОВСКИЙ ПЕРЕУЛОК 4E4
Malyy Drovyanoy pereulok МАЛЫЙ ДРОВЯНОЙ ПЕРЕУЛОК 8E2
Malyy Gnezdnikovskiy pereulok МАЛЫЙ ГНЕЗДНИКОВСКИЙ ПЕРЕУЛОК 2F4
Malyy Golovin pereulok МАЛЫЙ ГОЛОВИН ПЕРЕУЛОК 3B3
Malyy Ivanovskiy pereulok МАЛЫЙ ИВАНОВСКИЙ ПЕРЕУЛОК 7C1
Malyy Kamennyy most МАЛЫЙ КАМЕННЫЙ МОСТ 7A3
Malyy Karetnyy pereulok МАЛЫЙ КАРЕТНЫЙ ПЕРЕУЛОК 2F3
Malyy Kazennyy pereulok МАЛЫЙ КАЗЕННЫЙ ПЕРЕУЛОК 4D4
Malyy Kharitonevskiy pereulok МАЛЫЙ ХАРИТОНЬЕВСКИЙ ПЕРЕУЛОК 3C3
Malyy Kislovskiy pereulok МАЛЫЙ КИСЛОВСКИЙ ПЕРЕУЛОК 2E5
Malyy Kozikhinskiy pereulok МАЛЫЙ КОЗИХИНСКИЙ ПЕРЕУЛОК 2E4
Malyy Krasnokholmskiy most МАЛЫЙ КРАСНОХОЛМСКИЙ МОСТ 8D4
Malyy Levshinskiy pereulok МАЛЫЙ ЛЕВШИНСКИЙ ПЕРЕУЛОК 6D2
Malyy Moskvoretskiy most МАЛЫЙ МОСКВОРЕЦКИЙ МОСТ 7B2
Malyy Novopeskovskiy pereulok МАЛЫЙ НОВОПЕСКОВСКИЙ ПЕРЕУЛОК 5C1
Malyy Poluyaroslavskiy pereulok МАЛЫЙ ПОЛУЯРОСЛАВСКИЙ ПЕРЕУЛОК 8E1
Malyy Rzhevskiy pereulok МАЛЫЙ РЖЕВСКИЙ ПЕРЕУЛОК 2D5
Malyy Savvinskiy pereulok МАЛЫЙ САВВИНСКИЙ ПЕРЕУЛОК 5A4
Malyy Sukharevskiy pereulok МАЛЫЙ СУХАРЕВСКИЙ ПЕРЕУЛОК 3A3
Malyy Tatarskiy pereulok МАЛЫЙ ТАТАРСКИЙ ПЕРЕУЛОК 7C4
Malyy Tishinskiy pereulok МАЛЫЙ ТИШИНСКИЙ ПЕРЕУЛОК 1C3
Malyy Tolmachevskiy pereulok МАЛЫЙ ТОЛМАЧЕВСКИЙ ПЕРЕУЛОК 7A3
Malyy Trekhsvyatitelskiy pereulok МАЛЫЙ ТРЕХСВЯТИТЕЛЬСКИЙ ПЕРЕУЛОК 3C5, 8D1

Malyy Vlasevskiy pereulok	МАЛЫЙ ВЛАСЬЕВСКИЙ ПЕРЕУЛОК	**6D2**
Malyy Znamenskiy pereulok	МАЛЫЙ ЗНАМЕНСКИЙ ПЕРЕУЛОК	**6F1**
Mamonovskiy pereulok	МАМОНОВСКИЙ ПЕРЕУЛОК	**2E4**
Mandelshtama, park im	МАНДЕЛЬШТАМА, ПАРК ИМ	**5C5**
Manège		**6F1, 7A1**
Manezhnaya ploshchad	МАНЕЖНАЯ ПЛОЩАДЬ	**7A1**
Manezhnaya ulitsa	МАНЕЖНАЯ УЛИЦА	**6F1, 7A2**
Mansurovskiy pereulok	МАНСУРОВСКИЙ ПЕРЕУЛОК	**6D3**
Mantulinskaya ulitsa	МАНТУЛИНСКАЯ УЛИЦА	**1A5**
Marksistskaya ulitsa	МАРКСИСТСКАЯ УЛИЦА	**8E3**
Marksistskiy pereulok	МАРКСИСТСКИЙ ПЕРЕУЛОК	**8F4**
Maronovskiy pereulok	МАРОНОВСКИЙ ПЕРЕУЛОК	**6F4**
Maroseyka, ulitsa	МАРОСЕЙКА, УЛИЦА	**3B5**
Martynovskiy pereulok	МАРТЫНОВСКИЙ ПЕРЕУЛОК	**8E2**
Mashkova, ulitsa	МАШКОВА, УЛИЦА	**4D4**
Mayakovsky Museum		**3B5**
Mayakovskovo, pereulok	МАЯКОВСКОГО, ПЕРЕУЛОК	**8E3**
Melnikov House		**6D1**
Melnitskiy pereulok	МЕЛЬНИЦКИЙ ПЕРЕУЛОК	**8E1**
Menshikov's Tower		**3C4**
Merzlyakovskiy pereulok	МЕРЗЛЯКОВСКИЙ ПЕРЕУЛОК	**2E5**
Meshchanskaya ulitsa	МЕЩАНСКАЯ УЛИЦА	**3B2**
Milyutinskiy pereulok	МИЛЮТИНСКИЙ ПЕРЕУЛОК	**3B4**
Mira, prospekt	МИРА, ПРОСПЕКТ	**3B2**
Miusskaya ploshchad	МИУССКАЯ ПЛОЩАДЬ	**2D2**
Miusskiy pereulok	МИУССКИЙ ПЕРЕУЛОК	**2D1**
Mokhovaya ulitsa	МОХОВАЯ УЛИЦА	**6F1**
Molochnyy pereulok	МОЛОЧНЫЙ ПЕРЕУЛОК	**6E3**
Monastery of the Epiphany		**3A5, 7B1**
Monastery of the Saviour and Andronicus		**8F2**
Morozov Mansion		**2D4**
Moscow Arts Theatre		**2F4**
Moscow Conservatory		**2E5**
Moscow Old University		**2F5, 7A1**
Moskvoretskaya naberezhnaya	МОСКВОРЕЦКАЯ НАБЕРЕЖНАЯ	**7B2**
Moskvoretskaya ulitsa	МОСКВОРЕЦКАЯ УЛИЦА	**7B1**
Mozhayskiy val, ulitsa	МОЖАЙСКИЙ ВАЛ, УЛИЦА	**5A2**
Museum of Private Collections		**6F2**
Museum of the Revolution		**2E4**
Myasnitskaya ulitsa	МЯСНИЦКАЯ УЛИЦА	**3B4**
Mytnaya, ulitsa	МЫТНАЯ, УЛИЦА	**7A5**

N

Narodnaya ulitsa	НАРОДНАЯ УЛИЦА	**8D4**
Nashchokinskiy pereulok	НАЩОКИНСКИЙ ПЕРЕУЛОК	**6E2**
Nastasinskiy pereulok	НАСТАСЬИНСКИЙ ПЕРЕУЛОК	**2E3**
Nastavnicheskiy pereulok	НАСТАВНИЧЕСКИЙ ПЕРЕУЛОК	**8F1**
Neglinnaya ulitsa	НЕГЛИННАЯ УЛИЦА	**3A4**
Nesvizhskiy pereulok	НЕСВИЖСКИЙ ПЕРЕУЛОК	**5C4**
Nevolnyy pereulok	НЕВОЛЬНЫЙ ПЕРЕУЛОК	**5C2**
New Tretyakov Gallery		**6F3**
Nikitskie vorota, ploshchad	НИКИТСКИЕ ВОРОТА, ПЛОЩАДЬ	**2E5**
Nikitskiy bulvar	НИКИТСКИЙ БУЛЬВАР	**2E5**
Nikitskiy pereulok	НИКИТСКИЙ ПЕРЕУЛОК	**2F5**
Nikolaeva, ulitsa	НИКОЛАЕВА, УЛИЦА	**1B5**
Nikoloyamskaya naberezhnaya	НИКОЛОЯМСКАЯ НАБЕРЕЖНАЯ	**8E2**
Nikoloyamskaya ulitsa	НИКОЛОЯМСКАЯ УЛИЦА	**8D2**
Nikoloyamskiy pereulok	НИКОЛОЯМСКИЙ ПЕРЕУЛОК	**8E2**
Nikolskaya ulitsa	НИКОЛЬСКАЯ УЛИЦА	**3A5**
Nikolskiy pereulok	НИКОЛЬСКИЙ ПЕРЕУЛОК	**3B5, 7B1**
Nikonovskiy pereulok	НИКОНОВСКИЙ ПЕРЕУЛОК	**2F2**
Nizhniy Susalnyy pereulok	НИЖНИЙ СУСАЛЬНЫЙ ПЕРЕУЛОК	**4E4**
Nizhniy Taganskiy tupik	НИЖНИЙ ТАГАНСКИЙ ТУПИК	**8D3**
Nizhnyaya Krasnoselskaya ulitsa	НИЖНЯЯ КРАСНОСЕЛЬСКАЯ УЛИЦА	**4F2**
Nizhnyaya Syromyatnicheskaya ulitsa	НИЖНЯЯ СЫРОМЯТНИЧЕСКАЯ УЛИЦА	**8F1**
Nizhnyaya Taganskaya ploshchad	НИЖНЯЯ ТАГАНСКАЯ ПЛОЩАДЬ	**8D3**
Nizhnyaya ulitsa	НИЖНЯЯ УЛИЦА	**1C2**
Novaya Basmannaya ulitsa	НОВАЯ БАСМАННАЯ УЛИЦА	**4D3**
Novaya ploshchad	НОВАЯ ПЛОЩАДЬ	**3B5**
Novinskiy bulvar	НОВИНСКИЙ БУЛЬВАР	**2D5**
Novoarbatskiy most	НОВОАРБАТСКИЙ МОСТ	**5B1**
Novodevichiy Convent		**5A5**
Novodevichiy proezd	НОВОДЕВИЧИЙ ПРОЕЗД	**5A4**
Novodevichya naberezhnaya	НОВОДЕВИЧЬЯ НАБЕРЕЖНАЯ	**5A5**
Novokhokhlovskaya ulitsa	НОВОХОХЛОВСКАЯ УЛИЦА	**2E1**
Novokonyushennyy pereulok	НОВОКОНЮШЕННЫЙ ПЕРЕУЛОК	**5C3**
Novokrymskiy prospekt	НОВОКРЫМСКИЙ ПРОСПЕКТ	**6E3**
Novokuznetskaya ulitsa	НОВОКУЗНЕЦКАЯ УЛИЦА	**7B3**
Novolesnaya ulitsa	НОВОЛЕСНАЯ УЛИЦА	**2D1**
Novolesnoy pereulok	НОВОЛЕСНОЙ ПЕРЕУЛОК	**2D1**
Novopresnenskiy pereulok	НОВОПРЕСНЕНСКИЙ ПЕРЕУЛОК	**1C4**
Novoryazanskaya ulitsa	НОВОРЯЗАНСКАЯ УЛИЦА	**4E3**
Novoslobodskaya ulitsa	НОВОСЛОБОДСКАЯ УЛИЦА	**2E1**
Novospasskiy most	НОВОСПАССКИЙ МОСТ	**8E5**
Novospasskiy pereulok	НОВОСПАССКИЙ ПЕРЕУЛОК	**8E4**
Novospasskiy proezd	НОВОСПАССКИЙ ПРОЕЗД	**8E4**
Novovagankovskiy pereulok	НОВОВАГАНЬКОВСКИЙ ПЕРЕУЛОК	**1B5**
Novyy Arbat, ulitsa	НОВЫЙ АРБАТ, УЛИЦА	**5C1**

O

Obolenskiy pereulok	ОБОЛЕНСКИЙ ПЕРЕУЛОК	**5C4**
Obukha, pereulok	ОБУХА, ПЕРЕУЛОК	**8E1**
Ogorodnoy Slobody pereulok	ОГОРОДНОЙ СЛОБОДЫ ПЕРЕУЛОК	**3C4**
Okhotnyy ryad, ulitsa	ОХОТНЫЙ РЯД, УЛИЦА	**3A5**
Old English Court		**7B1**
Olimpiyskiy prospekt	ОЛИМПИЙСКИЙ ПРОСПЕКТ	**3A2**
Olkhovskaya ulitsa	ОЛХОВСКАЯ УЛИЦА	**4E2**
Olsufevskiy pereulok	ОЛСУФЬЕВСКИЙ ПЕРЕУЛОК	**5C4**
Orlikov pereulok	ОРЛИКОВ ПЕРЕУЛОК	**4D3**
Orlovo Davydovskiy pereulok	ОРЛОВО ДАВЫДОВСКИЙ ПЕРЕУЛОК	**3B1**
Oruzheynyy pereulok	ОРУЖЕЙНЫЙ ПЕРЕУЛОК	**2E3**

Ostozhenka, ulitsa ОСТОЖЕНКА, УЛИЦА 6E3
Ovchinnikovskaya naberezhnaya ОВЧИННИКОВСКАЯ НАБЕРЕЖНАЯ 7B2
Ozerkovskaya naberezhnaya ОЗЕРКОВСКАЯ НАБЕРЕЖНАЯ 7C3
Ozerkovskiy pereulok ОЗЕРКОВСКИЙ ПЕРЕУЛОК 7C3
Ozerkovskiy tupik ОЗЕРКОВСКИЙ ТУПИК 7C3

P

Palace of Congresses 7A1
Palace of the Romanov Boyars 7B1
Palikha, ulitsa ПАЛИХА, УЛИЦА 2E1
Panfilovskiy pereulok ПАНФИЛОВСКИЙ ПЕРЕУЛОК 5C1
Pankratevskiy pereulok ПАНКРАТЬЕВСКИЙ ПЕРЕУЛОК 3B3
Panteleevskaya ulitsa ПАНТЕЛЕЕВСКАЯ УЛИЦА 3C1
Pashkov House 6F1
Patriarch's Palace 7A1
Patriarch's Pond 2D4
Patriarshiy prudy ПАТРИАРШИЕ ПРУДЫ 2D4
Paveletskaya ploshchad ПАВЕЛЕЦКАЯ ПЛОЩАДЬ 7C5
Pechatnikov pereulok ПЕЧАТНИКОВ ПЕРЕУЛОК 3A3
Perlov Tea House 3B4
Pestovskiy pereulok ПЕСТОВСКИЙ ПЕРЕУЛОК 8E2
Petropavlovskiy pereulok ПЕТРОПАВЛОВСКИЙ ПЕРЕУЛОК 8D1
Petroverigskiy pereulok ПЕТРОВЕРИГСКИЙ ПЕРЕУЛОК 3C5
Petrovka, ulitsa ПЕТРОВКА, УЛИЦА 3A4
Petrovskie linii ulitsa ПЕТРОВСКИЕ ЛИНИИ УЛИЦА 3A4
Petrovskiy bulvar ПЕТРОВСКИЙ БУЛЬВАР 3A3
Petrovskiy pereulok ПЕТРОВСКИЙ ПЕРЕУЛОК 2F4
Platovskaya ulitsa ПЛАТОВСКАЯ УЛИЦА 5A2
Pleteshkovskiy pereulok ПЛЕТЕШКОВСКИЙ ПЕРЕУЛОК 4F3
Plotnikov pereulok ПЛОТНИКОВ ПЕРЕУЛОК 6D2
Plyushchikha, ulitsa ПЛЮЩИХА, УЛИЦА 5C3
Podgorskaya naberezhnaya ПОДГОРСКАЯ НАБЕРЕЖНАЯ 8D2
Podkolokolnyy pereulok ПОДКОЛОКОЛЬНЫЙ ПЕРЕУЛОК 8D1
Podkopaevskiy pereulok ПОДКОПАЕВСКИЙ ПЕРЕУЛОК 3C5, 8D1
Podsosenskiy pereulok ПОДСОСЕНСКИЙ ПЕРЕУЛОК 4D5
Pogodinskaya ulitsa ПОГОДИНСКАЯ УЛИЦА 5B4
Pogorelskiy pereulok ПОГОРЕЛЬСКИЙ ПЕРЕУЛОК 7B4
Pokrovka, ulitsa ПОКРОВКА, УЛИЦА 3C5
Pokrovskiy bulvar ПОКРОВСКИЙ БУЛЬВАР 3C5
Poluyaroslavskaya naberezhnaya ПОЛУЯОСЛАВСКАЯ НАБЕРЕЖНАЯ 8E2
Polytechnical Museum 3B5
Pomerantsev pereulok ПОМЕРАНЦЕВ ПЕРЕУЛОК 6D3
Posledniy pereulok ПОСЛЕДНИЙ ПЕРЕУЛОК 3B3
Potapovskiy pereulok ПОТАПОВСКИЙ ПЕРЕУЛОК 3C4
Povarskaya ulitsa ПОВАРСКАЯ УЛИЦА 2D5
Pozharskiy pereulok ПОЖАРСКИЙ ПЕРЕУЛОК 6E3
Pravdy, ulitsa ПРАВДЫ, УЛИЦА 1C1
Prechistenka, ulitsa ПРЕЧИСТЕНКА, УЛИЦА 6D3
Prechistenskaya naberezhnaya ПРЕЧИСТЕНСКАЯ НАБЕРЕЖНАЯ 6E3
Prechistenskie vorota, ploshchad ПРЕЧИСТЕНСКИЕ ВОРОТА, ПЛОЩАДЬ 6E2
Prechistenskiy pereulok ПРЕЧИСТЕНСКИЙ ПЕРЕУЛОК 6D2
Presidium 7A1
Presnenskiy val, ulitsa ПРЕСНЕНСКИЙ ВАЛ, УЛИЦА 1B3
Priyutskiy pereulok ПРИЮТСКИЙ ПЕРЕУЛОК 2D1
Prosvirin pereulok ПРОСВИРИН ПЕРЕУЛОК 3B3
Protochnyy pereulok ПРОТОЧНЫЙ ПЕРЕУЛОК 5C1
Protopopovskiy pereulok ПРОТОПОПОВСКИЙ ПЕРЕУЛОК 3B1
Pryamoy pereulok ПРЯМОЙ ПЕРЕУЛОК 5C1
Pugovishnikov pereulok ПУГОВИШНИКОВ ПЕРЕУЛОК 6D4
Pushechnaya ulitsa ПУШЕЧНАЯ УЛИЦА 3A4
Pushkarev pereulok ПУШКАРЕВ ПЕРЕУЛОК 3B3
Pushkin House-Museum 6D2
Pushkin Museum of Fine Arts 6F2
Pushkin Square 2F4
Pushkinskaya naberezhnaya ПУШКИНСКАЯ НАБЕРЕЖНАЯ 6E5
Pushkinskaya ploshchad ПУШКИНСКАЯ ПЛОЩАДЬ 2F4
Pyatnitskaya ulitsa ПЯТНИЦКАЯ УЛИЦА 7B2
Pyzhevskiy pereulok ПЫЖЕВСКИЙ ПЕРЕУЛОК 7B3

R

Radio, ulitsa РАДИО, УЛИЦА 4F4
Raevskovo, ulitsa РАЕВСКОГО УЛИЦА 5A2
Rastorguevskiy pereulok РАСТОРГУЕВСКИЙ ПЕРЕУЛОК 1B4
Raushskaya naberezhnaya РАУШСКАЯ НАБЕРЕЖНАЯ 7B2
Red Square 3A5, 7B1
Resurrection Gate 3A5, 7A1
Revolyutsii, ploshchad РЕВОЛЮЦИИ, ПЛОЩАДЬ 3A5
Rochdelskaya ulitsa РОЧДЕЛЬСКАЯ УЛИЦА 1B5
Romanov pereulok РОМАНОВ ПЕРЕУЛОК 2F5
Rossolimo, ulitsa РОССОЛИМО, УЛИЦА 5C4
Rostovskaya naberezhnaya РОСТОВСКАЯ НАБЕРЕЖНАЯ 5B3
Rozhdestvenka, ulitsa РОЖДЕСТВЕНКА, УЛИЦА 3A4
Rozhdestvenskiy bulvar РОЖДЕСТВЕНСКИЙ БУЛЬВАР 3A3
Runovskiy pereulok РУНОВСКИЙ ПЕРЕУЛОК 7C3
Rusakovskaya ulitsa РУСАКОВСКАЯ УЛИЦА 4F1
Ruzheynyy pereulok РУЖЕЙНЫЙ ПЕРЕУЛОК 5C2
Ryazanskiy proezd РЯЗАНСКИЙ ПРОЕЗД 4D2
Rybnikov pereulok РЫБНИКОВ ПЕРЕУЛОК 3B3
Rybnyy pereulok РЫБНЫЙ ПЕРЕУЛОК 3B5, 7B1

S

Sadovaya-Chernogryazskaya ulitsa САДОВАЯ-ЧЕРНОГРЯЗСКАЯ УЛИЦА 4D3
Sadovaya-Karetnaya ulitsa САДОВАЯ-КАРЕТНАЯ УЛИЦА 2F2
Sadovaya-Kudrinskaya ulitsa САДОВАЯ-КУДРИНСКАЯ УЛИЦА 2D4
Sadovaya-Samotechnaya, ulitsa САДОВАЯ-САМОТЕЧНАЯ, УЛИЦА 3A2
Sadovaya-Spasskaya ulitsa САДОВАЯ-СПАССКАЯ УЛИЦА 3C3
Sadovaya-Sukharevskaya ulitsa САДОВАЯ-СУХАРЕВСКАЯ УЛИЦА 3A2
Sadovaya-Triumfalnaya ulitsa САДОВАЯ-ТРИУМФАЛЬНАЯ УЛИЦА 2E3
Sadovnicheskaya naberezhnaya САДОВНИЧЕСКАЯ НАБЕРЕЖНАЯ 7B2
Sadovnicheskaya ulitsa САДОВНИЧЕСКАЯ УЛИЦА 7B2
Sadovnicheskiy proezd САДОВНИЧЕСКИЙ ПРОЕЗД 7C3

T

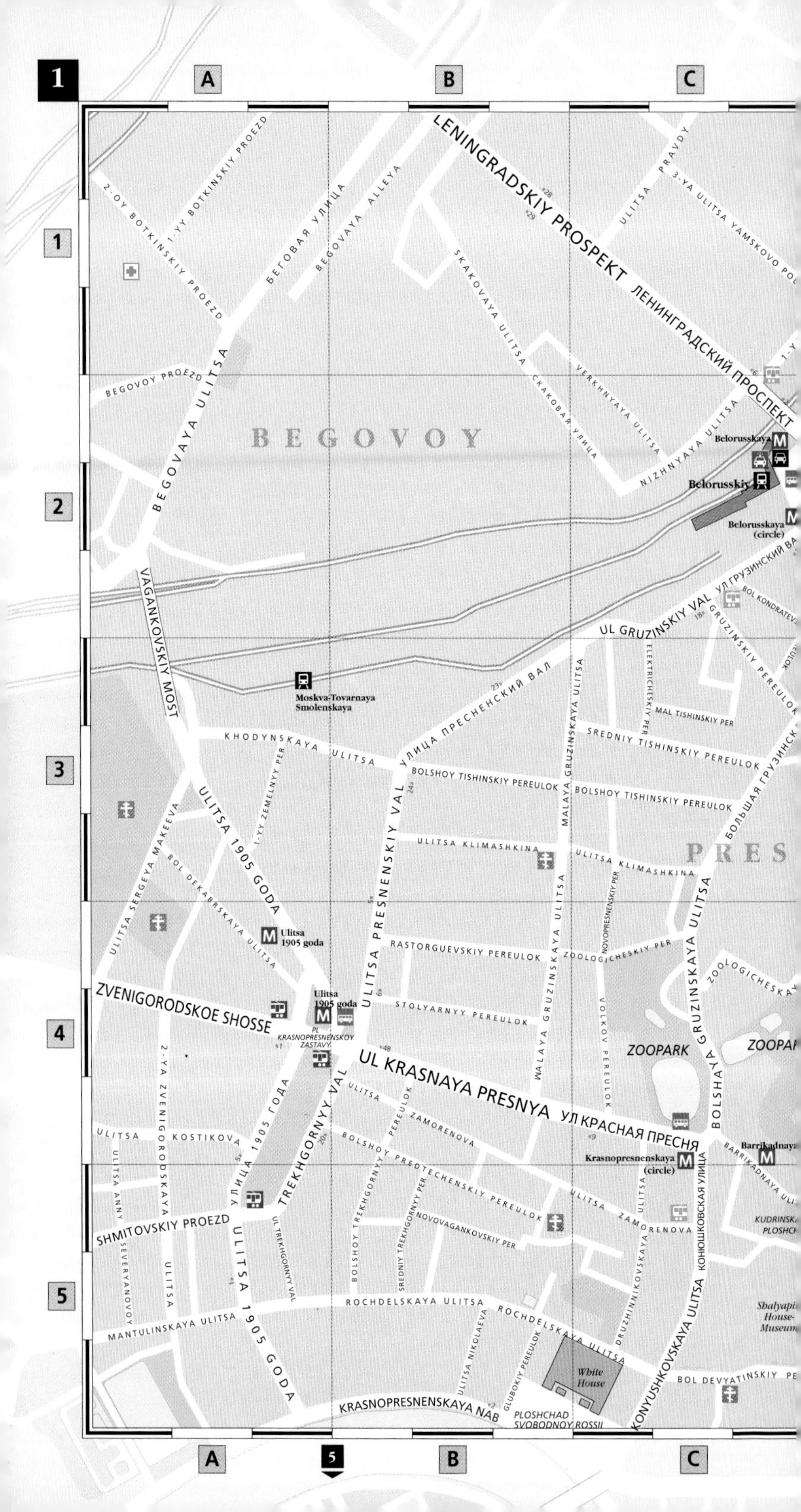
1
A
B
C
1
2
3
4
5
5
2-OY BOTKINSKIY PROEZD
1-YY BOTKINSKIY PROEZD
БЕГОВАЯ УЛИЦА
BEGOVAYA ALLEYA
LENINGRADSKIY PROSPEKT
ЛЕНИНГРАДСКИЙ ПРОСПЕКТ
ULITSA PRAVDY
3-YA ULITSA YAMSKOVO POL
SKAKOVAYA ULITSA
СКАКОВАЯ УЛИЦА
VERKHNYAYA ULITSA
NIZHNYAYA ULITSA
BEGOVOY PROEZD
BEGOVAYA ULITSA
BEGOVOY
Belorusskaya
Belorusskiy
Belorusskaya (circle)
VAGANKOVSKIY MOST
УЛ ГРУЗИНСКИЙ ВАЛ
UL GRUZINSKIY VAL
BOL KONDRATEVS
GRUZINSKIY PEREULOK
ELEKTRICHESKIY PER
MAL TISHINSKIY PER
Moskva-Tovarnaya Smolenskaya
УЛИЦА ПРЕСНЕНСКИЙ ВАЛ
KHODYNSKAYA ULITSA
1-YY ZEMELNYY PER
BOLSHOY TISHINSKIY PEREULOK
MALAYA GRUZINSKAYA ULITSA
SREDNIY TISHINSKIY PEREULOK
БОЛЬШАЯ ГРУЗИНСКАЯ
ULITSA PRESNENSKIY VAL
ULITSA 1905 GODA
ULITSA SERGEYA MAKEEVA
BOL DEKABRSKAYA ULITSA
ULITSA KLIMASHKINA
PRES
NOVOPRESNENSKIY PER
Ulitsa 1905 goda
RASTORGUEVSKIY PEREULOK
ZOOLOGICHESKIY PER
ZOOLOGICHESKAYA
BOLSHAYA GRUZINSKAYA ULITSA
ZVENIGORODSKOE SHOSSE
STOLYARNYY PEREULOK
PL KRASNOPRESNENSKOY ZASTAVY
ZOOPARK
VOLKOV PEREULOK
UL KRASNAYA PRESNYA
УЛ КРАСНАЯ ПРЕСНЯ
2-YA ZVENIGORODSKAYA
ULITSA ZAMORENOVA
ULITSA KOSTIKOVA
УЛИЦА 1905 ГОДА
TREKHGORNYY VAL
BOLSHOY PREDTECHENSKIY PEREULOK
Krasnopresnenskaya (circle)
Barrikadnaya
BARRIKADNAYA ULITSA
ULITSA ANY
SHMITOVSKIY PROEZD
UL TREKHGORNYY VAL
BOLSHOY TREKHGORNYY PER
SREDNIY TREKHGORNYY PER
NOVOVAGANKOVSKIY PER
DRUZHINNIKOVSKAYA ULITSA
КОНЮШКОВСКАЯ УЛИЦА
KUDRINSKA PLOSHCH
SEVERYANOVOY ULITSA
ROCHDELSKAYA ULITSA
Shalyapin House-Museum
MANTULINSKAYA ULITSA
ULITSA NIKOLAEVA
GLUBOKIY PEREULOK
White House
KONYUSHKOVSKAYA ULITSA
BOL DEVYATINSKIY PER
KRASNOPRESNENSKAYA NAB
PLOSHCHAD SVOBODNOY ROSSII

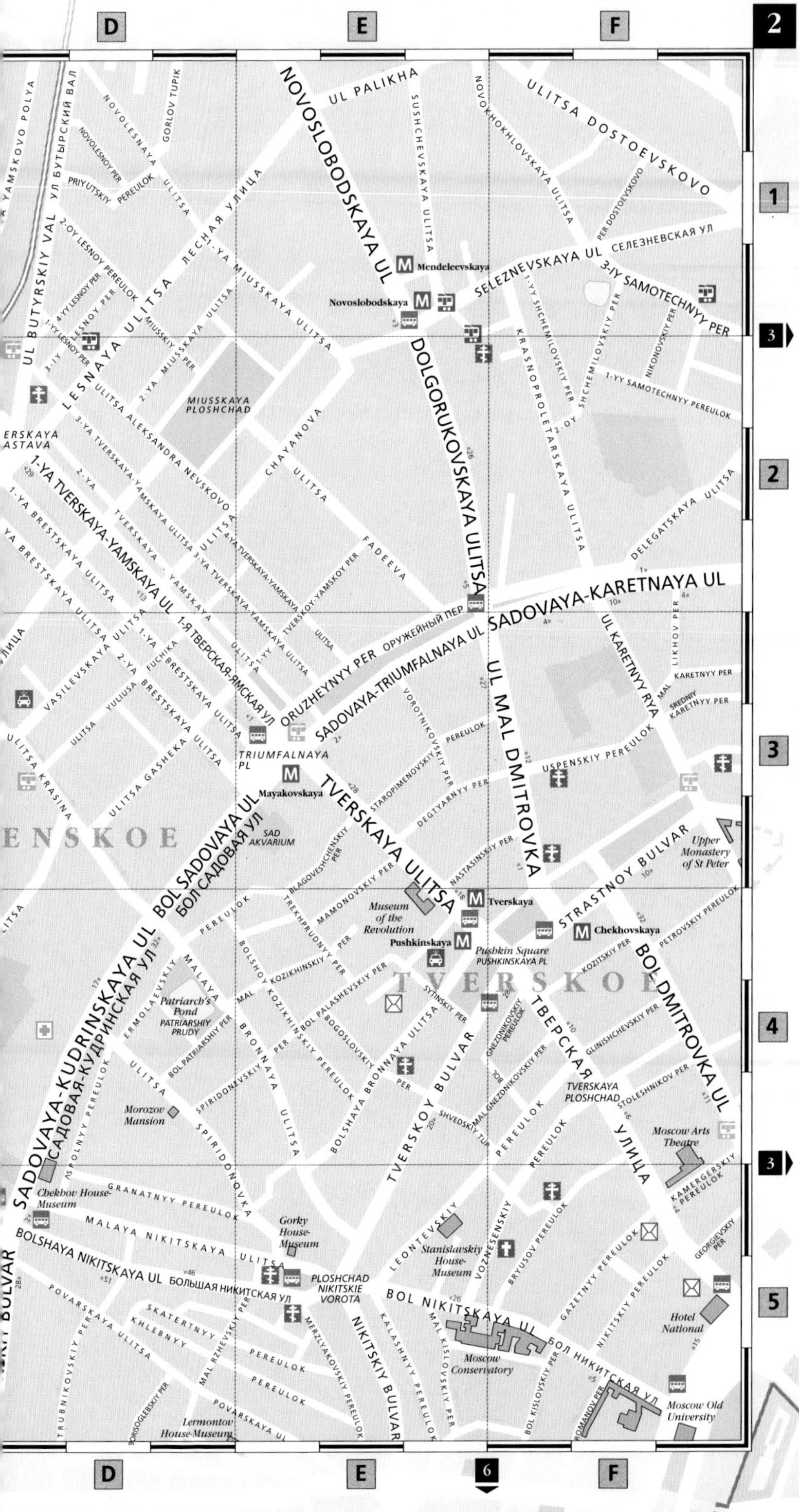

2
D
E
F
1
2
3
4
5
6
NOVOSLOBODSKAYA UL
UL PALIKHA
SUSHCHEVSKAYA ULITSA
NOVOKHOKHLOVSKAYA ULITSA
ULITSA DOSTOEVSKOVO
PER DOSTOEVSKOVO
SELEZNEVSKAYA UL
СЕЛЕЗНЕВСКАЯ УЛ
3-IY SAMOTECHNYY PER
1-YY SAMOTECHNYY PEREULOK
NIKONOVSKIY PER
KRASNOPROLETARSKAYA ULITSA
DELEGATSKAYA ULITSA
Mendeleevskaya
Novoslobodskaya
DOLGORUKOVSKAYA ULITSA
SADOVAYA-KARETNAYA UL
SADOVAYA-TRIUMFALNAYA UL
UL KARETNYY RYA
LIKHOV PER
KARETNYY PER
SREDNIY KARETNYY PER
UL MAL DMITROVKA
USPENSKIY PEREULOK
Upper Monastery of St Peter
STRASTNOY BULVAR
PETROVSKIY PEREULOK
Chekhovskaya
BOLDMITROVKA UL
GLINISHCHEVSKIY PER
STOLESHNIKOV PER
KOZITSKIY PER
TVERSKAYA PLOSHCHAD
ТВЕРСКАЯ УЛИЦА
Moscow Arts Theatre
KAMERGERSKIY PEREULOK
GEORGIEVSKIY PER
Hotel National
Moscow Old University
BOL NIKITSKAYA UL
БОЛ НИКИТСКАЯ УЛ
Moscow Conservatory
BOL KISLOVSKIY PER
ROMANOV PER
GAZETNYY PEREULOK
NIKITSKIY PEREULOK
BRYUSOV PEREULOK
VOZNESENSKIY
Stanislavskiy House-Museum
LEONTEVSKIY
TVERSKOY BULVAR
TVERSKOE
Pushkin Square
PUSHKINSKAYA PL
Pushkinskaya
Tverskaya
Museum of the Revolution
TVERSKAYA ULITSA
Mayakovskaya
TRIUMFALNAYA PL
SAD AKVARIUM
ORUZHEYNYY PER
ОРУЖЕЙНЫЙ ПЕР
VOROTNIKOVSKIY PER
STAROPIMENOVSKIY PER
DEGTYARNYY PER
NASTASINSKIY PER
MAMONOVSKIY PER
BLAGOVESHCHENSKIY PER
TREKHPRUDNYY PER
BOLSHOY KOZIKHINSKIY PER
MAL KOZIKHINSKIY PER
BOL PALASHEVSKIY PER
BOGOSLOVSKIY PER
SYTINSKIY PER
GNEZDNIKOVSKIY PEREULOK
MAL GNEZDNIKOVSKIY PER
SHVEDSKIY TUP
BOLSHAYA BRONNAYA ULITSA
MALAYA BRONNAYA ULITSA
SPIRIDONEVSKIY PER
ULITSA SPIRIDONOVKA
ERMOLAEVSKIY PER
Patriarch's Pond
PATRIARSHIY PRUDY
BOL PATRIARSHIY PER
Morozov Mansion
BOL SADOVAYA UL
БОЛ САДОВАЯ УЛ
SADOVAYA-KUDRINSKAYA UL
САДОВАЯ-КУДРИНСКАЯ УЛ
VSPOLNYY PEREULOK
Chekhov House-Museum
GRANATNYY PEREULOK
MALAYA NIKITSKAYA ULITSA
Gorky House-Museum
BOLSHAYA NIKITSKAYA UL
БОЛЬШАЯ НИКИТСКАЯ УЛ
PLOSHCHAD NIKITSKIE VOROTA
NIKITSKIY BULVAR
KALASHNYY PEREULOK
MAL KISLOVSKIY PER
MERZLYAKOVSKIY PEREULOK
MAL RZHEVSKIY PER
SKATERTNYY PEREULOK
KHLEBNYY PEREULOK
POVARSKAYA ULITSA
BORISOGLEBSKIY PER
TRUBNIKOVSKIY PER
Lermontov House-Museum
CHAYANOVA ULITSA
FADEEVA ULITSA
TVERSKOY-YAMSKOY PER
MIUSSKAYA PLOSHCHAD
1-YA MIUSSKAYA ULITSA
2-YA MIUSSKAYA ULITSA
MIUSSKIY PER
LESNAYA ULITSA
ЛЕСНАЯ УЛИЦА
UL BUTYRSKIY VAL
УЛ БУТЫРСКИЙ ВАЛ
NOVOLESNAYA ULITSA
NOVOLESNOY PER
GORLOV TUPIK
PRIYUTSKIY PEREULOK
2-OY LESNOY PEREULOK
4-YY LESNOY PER
3-IY LESNOY PER
1-YY LESNOY PER
YAMSKOVO POLYA
ULITSA ALEKSANDRA NEVSKOVO
TVERSKAYA ZASTAVA
1-YA TVERSKAYA-YAMSKAYA UL
1-Я ТВЕРСКАЯ-ЯМСКАЯ УЛ
2-YA TVERSKAYA-YAMSKAYA ULITSA
3-YA TVERSKAYA-YAMSKAYA ULITSA
4-YA TVERSKAYA-YAMSKAYA ULITSA
1-YA BRESTSKAYA ULITSA
2-YA BRESTSKAYA ULITSA
VASILEVSKAYA ULITSA
ULITSA YULIUSA FUCHIKA
ULITSA GASHEKA
ULITSA KRASINA
ENSKOE
BULVAR

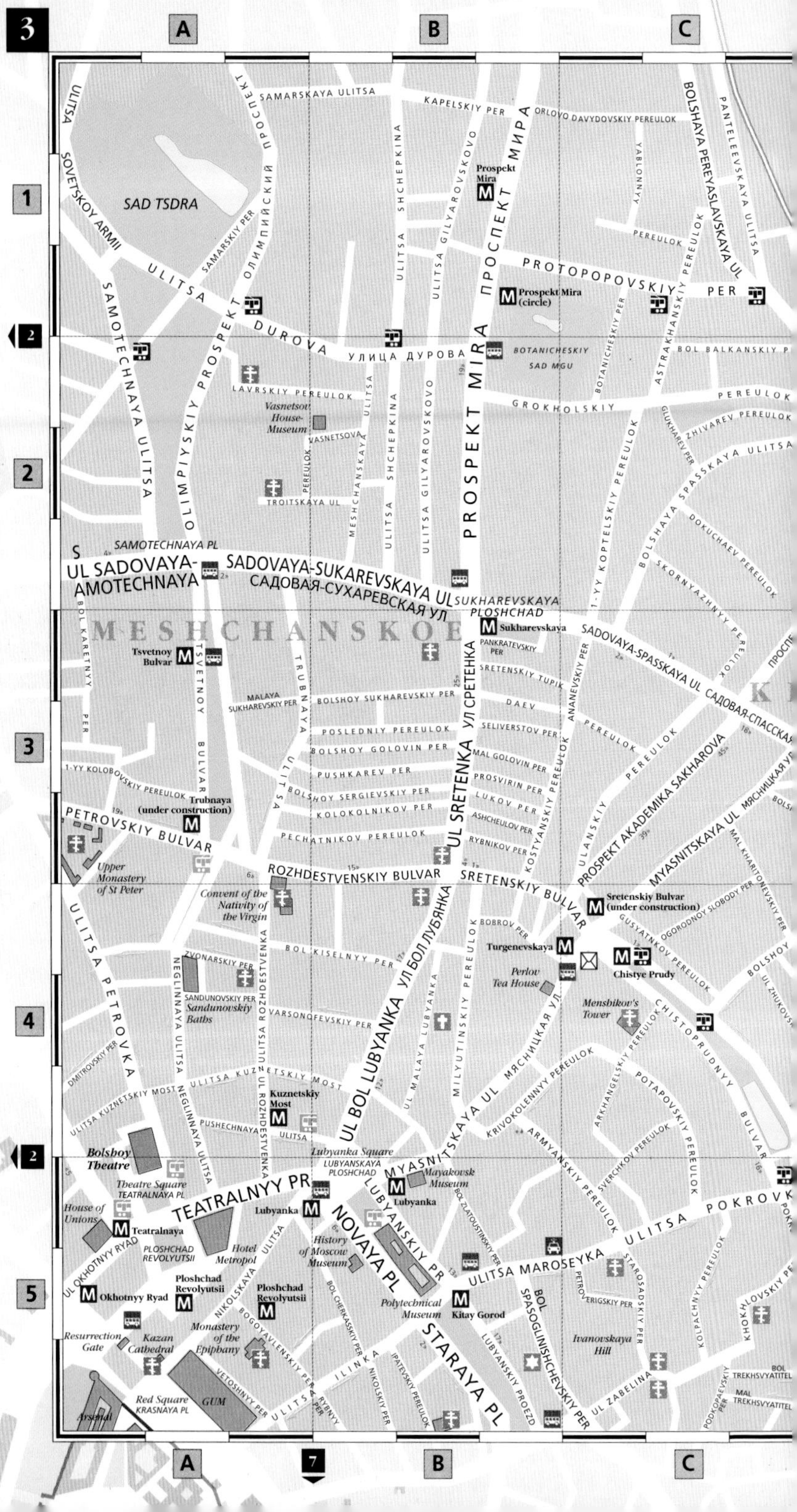
3
A
B
C
1
2
3
4
5
7
SAD TSDRA
ULITSA SOVETSKOY ARMII
SAMARSKAYA ULITSA
KAPELSKIY PER
ORLOVO DAVYDOVSKIY PEREULOK
SAMARSKIY PER
ОЛИМПИЙСКИЙ ПРОСПЕКТ
ULITSA SHCHEPKINA
ULITSA GILYAROVSKOVO
Prospekt Mira
ПРОСПЕКТ МИРА
YABLONNYY PEREULOK
BOLSHAYA PEREYASLAVSKAYA UL
PANTELEEVSKAYA ULITSA
PROTOPOPOVSKIY PER
Prospekt Mira (circle)
ULITSA DUROVA
УЛИЦА ДУРОВА
SAMOTECHNAYA ULITSA
OLIMPIYSKIY PROSPEKT
BOTANICHESKIY SAD MGU
BOTANICHESKIY PER
ASTRAKHANSKIY PEREULOK
BOL BALKANSKIY PER
LAVRSKIY PEREULOK
GROKHOLSKIY PEREULOK
Vasnetsov House-Museum
VASNETSOVA PEREULOK
MESHCHANSKAYA ULITSA
PROSPEKT MIRA
GLUKHAREV PER
ZHIVAREV PEREULOK
BOLSHAYA SPASSKAYA ULITSA
1-YY KOPTELSKIY PEREULOK
TROITSKAYA UL
DOKUCHAEV PEREULOK
SAMOTECHNAYA PL
UL SADOVAYA-SAMOTECHNAYA
SADOVAYA-SUKAREVSKAYA UL
САДОВАЯ-СУХАРЕВСКАЯ УЛ
SUKHAREVSKAYA PLOSHCHAD
SKORNYAZHNYY PEREULOK
MESHCHANSKOE
Tsvetnoy Bulvar
Sukharevskaya
PANKRATEVSKIY PER
SADOVAYA-SPASSKAYA UL
САДОВАЯ-СПАССКАЯ
BOL KARETNYY PER
TSVETNOY BULVAR
TRUBNAYA ULITSA
MALAYA SUKHAREVSKIY PER
BOLSHOY SUKHAREVSKIY PER
SRETENSKIY TUPIK
DAEV PEREULOK
ANANEVSKIY PER
POSLEDNIY PEREULOK
SELIVERSTOV PER
BOLSHOY GOLOVIN PER
MAL GOLOVIN PER
PUSHKAREV PER
PROSVIRIN PER
UL SRETENKA
УЛ СРЕТЕНКА
1-YY KOLOBOVSKIY PEREULOK
BOLSHOY SERGIEVSKIY PER
LUKOV PER
KOLOKOLNIKOV PER
ASHCHEULOV PER
PROSPEKT AKADEMIKA SAKHAROVA
МЯСНИЦКАЯ УЛ
Trubnaya (under construction)
PETROVSKIY BULVAR
PECHATNIKOV PEREULOK
RYBNIKOV PER
KOSTYANSKIY PEREULOK
ULANSKIY PER
MYASNITSKAYA UL
MAL KHARITONEVSKIY PER
Upper Monastery of St Peter
ROZHDESTVENSKIY BULVAR
SRETENSKIY BULVAR
Convent of the Nativity of the Virgin
Sretenskiy Bulvar (under construction)
OGORODNOY SLOBODY PER
ULITSA PETROVKA
BOBROV PER
GUSYATNIKOV PEREULOK
BOL KISELNYY PER
Turgenevskaya
Chistye Prudy
ZVONARSKIY PER
UL BOL LUBYANKA
УЛ БОЛ ЛУБЯНКА
Perlov Tea House
BOLSHOY ZLATOUSTINSKIY PER
NEGLINNAYA ULITSA
SANDUNOVSKIY PER
Sandunovskiy Baths
ULITSA ROZHDESTVENKA
UL MALAYA LUBYANKA
MILYUTINSKIY PEREULOK
МЯСНИЦКАЯ УЛ
Menshikov's Tower
CHISTOPRUDNYY BULVAR
UL ZHUKOVSKOGO
VARSONOFEVSKIY PER
DMITROVSKIY PER
ARKHANGELSKIY PEREULOK
ULITSA KUZNETSKIY MOST
POTAPOVSKIY PEREULOK
Kuznetskiy Most
MYASNITSKAYA UL
KRIVOKOLENNYY PEREULOK
PUSHECHNAYA ULITSA
ARMYANSKIY PEREULOK
SVERCHKOV PEREULOK
Bolshoy Theatre
Lubyanka Square
LUBYANSKAYA PLOSHCHAD
Mayakovsk Museum
Theatre Square
TEATRALNAYA PL
TEATRALNYY PR
Lubyanka
LUBYANSKIY PR
NOVAYA PL
BOL ZLATOUSTINSKIY PER
ULITSA POKROVKA
House of Unions
Teatralnaya
PLOSHCHAD REVOLYUTSII
Hotel Metropol
NIKOLSKAYA ULITSA
History of Moscow Museum
ULITSA MAROSEYKA
UL OKHOTNYY RYAD
Okhotnyy Ryad
Ploshchad Revolyutsii
BOL CHERKASSKIY PER
Polytechnical Museum
Kitay Gorod
BOL SPASOGLINISHCHEVSKIY PER
PETROVERIGSKIY PER
STAROSADSKIY PER
KOLPACHNYY PEREULOK
KOKHLOVSKIY PER
Resurrection Gate
Kazan Cathedral
Monastery of the Epiphany
BOGOYAVLENSKIY PER
STARAYA PL
LUBYANSKIY PROEZD
Ivanovskaya Hill
BOL TREKHSVYATITEL
MAL TREKHSVYATITEL
ILINKA
NIKOLSKIY PER
IPATEVSKIY PEREULOK
UL ZABELINA
PODKOPAEVSKIY PER
Red Square
KRASNAYA PL
GUM
VETOSHNYY PER
ULITSA ILINKA
RYBNYY PER
Arsenal